Writing Histories of Rhetoric

Writing Histories of Rhetoric

Edited by

Victor J. Vitanza

Southern Illinois University Press

Carbondale

Paperback edition 2013

Printed in the United States of America

16 15 14 13 4 3 2 1

The Library of Congress cataloging-in-publication data for the hardcover edition is as follows:
Writing histories of rhetoric / edited by Victor J. Vitanza.
p. cm.
Includes bibliographical references and index.
1. Rhetoric—History. I. Vitanza, Victor J.
PN183.W75 1994
808'.009—dc20 92-46300
ISBN 0-8093-1902-0 CIP

ISBN-13: 978-0-8093-1902-2 (cloth)
ISBN-13: 978-0-8093-3212-0 (paper : alk. paper)
ISBN-10: 0-8093-3212-4 (paper : alk. paper)
ISBN-13: 978-0-8093-8504-1 (ebook)
ISBN-10: 0-8093-8504-X (ebook)

The paper used in this publication meets the minimum requirements of American National Standard for Information Sciences—Permanence of Paper for Printed Library Materials, ANSI Z39.48-1992. ♾

Contents

Editor's Preface, Dedication, and Acknowledgments

. . . "casuistic stretching" is indigenous to historicism.

—Kenneth Burke 1984, 307.

Etymology of farce: stuffing.
Make a farce with livers minced small. Pigge farced with sage. With what stuffe our old historiographers have farced up their huge volumes.

—Norman O. Brown 1974, 42.

This is *not* a preface . . . which amounts to saying that *this is not a lie* (*praefatio*). And therefore, we always already begin here in the midst of a liar's paradox. And realize the absurdity of trying to write a preface, but nonetheless make ways. But this is—or should be by now, after hundreds of years—*old news*. In any case, I will not go into, once again, the impossibility of writing a preface for this collection of essays on writing histories of rhetoric. (We simply have to recall, e.g., Hegel's preface to his *Phenomenology* and its influence on any future [anterior] attempts at writing prefaces from Jean Hyppolite to Jacques Derrida.) What will have become immediately clear to the reader, however, is that every essay in this collection *is* a preface (a lie, a fable, a parody, a farce) or is a statement of predispositions or is an introduction or a beginning or, better put, is a series of beginnings.

And so, as I have been saying, this is no preface, and yet: Sharon Crowley's "Let Me Get This Straight," the first attempt in this collection, begins (from 1982) with a chronicle of recent events and publications on the resurgence of interest in writing histories of rhetoric. By itself, Crowley's essay could, therefore, serve as an introduction. I place it teasingly and perversely in the beginning, but need I say, "reader beware"?

Following Crowley's essay is one by Hans Kellner, in which he takes issue with what historians of rhetoric are attempting in writing their respective histories of rhetoric. Kellner is the only historian in this collection who has been *trained* (and, therefore, suffers from that particular *incapacity*) within the mother discipline of history itself. Kellner is placed in the second position in the sequence of essays so that he might function there as a naysayer.

I am not simply or necessarily suggesting, however, that there is a *yes* in Crowley's position and then a *no* in Kellner's and that somehow or other what follows in the sequencing of articles is an attempt at a synthesis. While Crowley is attempting *to get it straight,* Kellner is attempting *to get the story crooked.* (See his *Language and Historical Represention: Getting the Story Crooked* [1989].)

Yes and no, straight and crooked. I will not explore this issue, or possible confusion, any further. My intention, in this preface that is not a preface, has only been to put an un/certain spin (or whirl) on the first two articles to see what effect such a spin (or possible world) might have on reading what *we* variously have to say about writing histories of rhetoric.

Concerning ourselves, I would only say that we do not form any one school of historical-rhetorical thought: We are not together, by any means, what I would call "traditionalists" or "revisionists" or "formalists" or "poststructuralists" or "modernists" or "postmodernists." At best, we might label ourselves a new "constellation" (Adorno) or a "molecular agglomerate" (Deleuze and Guattari) or a "paratactic aggregate" (Feyerabend). At best, we might say that while we are interested in the past, we are also interested in the future: We are progressively, as arranged here, interested in the future anterior. (In the afterword, "Preparing to Meet the Faces That 'We' Will Have Met," I say some more about us, specifically, about how "we" might differ from other historians of rhetoric.)

I would like to turn now to our dedication: Which is jointly to *George Kennedy* (the classicist) and to *Kenneth Burke* (critic and polymath).

Let me be contrary to my most often stated (already contrary) position and say that if anyone is going to be concerned with writing *a* history of rhetoric, he or she should "begin," so to speak, with Kennedy, but not just begin with him but follow him through his own various contrary developments.

When Kennedy wrote his first history, he cited on the title page the Chicago Platonist Paul Shorey, who said: "We are freed from rhetoric only by knowledge of its history." Recently, Kennedy recanted his use of and belief in Shorey. Kennedy wrote, "I no longer believe that is possible [to be freed from rhetoric] or even desirable" (1988, 232). While Kennedy began a long time ago with, at least, a tacit *no*, he rebegins with an open *yes*. There are other, in my estimation, remarkable attempts on Kennedy's part to say *yes* not just to rhetoric but to rhetorics.

In his translation of and introduction to Aristotle's *Rhetoric* (1991), for example, Kennedy is open to possible ways of reading various troublesome passages. Kennedy attempts to deal with apparent contradictory definitions of *rhetorike* in the text, by assuming that the copy, or copies, being worked from are an accurate copy of Aristotle's copy and not, as some interpreters would have it, an improper copy of a student's.[1] Kennedy deals with the contradictions by simply explaining the possibility that Aristotle himself was exploring, or temporarily saying *yes* to, contradictory viewpoints of what rhetoric(s) might possibly be and that Aristotle saw no immediate necessity to resolve the apparent contradictions (see xi). There are more and other kinds of *yeses* to find in this translation, but I leave them with their open possibilities to others.

Finally, I want to point to the most recent and the most remarkable article, in my estimation, that Kennedy has yet published. I find the article "remarkable" because of its undecidability. The article that I have in mind is Kennedy's "A Hoot in the Dark" (1992). Prior to its appearance, I had heard through the grapevine that Kennedy had written a "wild," perhaps savage, article. And, indeed, he has. Kennedy elaborates on his earlier redefinition of rhetoric as "energy" (1991, 7; 1992, 2), by assigning to it an a priori "function [of] the survival of the fittest" (1992, 10). He further stipulates that rhetoric is (respectively in order) prior to intentionality, to writing, to speech and even prior to *Homo sapiens* and is manifested as well in so-called lower animals and in, yes, vegetables! (As I said, I heard about all of this "through the grapevine.")

Illustrating his point, Kennedy writes of a parliament of fowls: "In the fall, I have witnessed convocations of crows on my university campus. To me, as an uninformed spectator interested in rhetoric, it looked as though they had gathered to debate some important issue. There was much cawing. Some of the crows seemed to become disgusted with the proceedings and flew off; some turned their backs on the center of the group as if to vote 'no.' " He concludes this example by stretching etymologies as far as a Heidegger would: "It is perhaps not a coincidence that the Greeks gave the name Corax, or 'crow,' to the 'inventor' of rhetoric" (1992, 5).

I characterize my reading of this article, "A Hoot in the Dark," as "undecidable," because while rereading its title and the text itself, I cannot still decide if Kennedy (or "energy") wrote it seriously or farcically with beak in cheek. Perhaps both, *yes* and *no*. Perhaps, like Aristotle, Kennedy is exploring the various possible ways, or paths. What is additionally remarkable about the article, however, is that, for Kennedy now, rhetoric is almost identical with Nietzsche's "will to power." Kennedy, indeed, has traveled a great distance.

Similarly, if anyone is going to be concerned with writing *a* history of rhetoric, she or he *must* also "begin" with Kenneth Burke (KB), who epitomizes the very concept of "beginnings."

I will here be brief about KB, for I discuss (redescribe) him at much greater length in the afterword. Everything that KB writes concerns history, that is, concerns various attitudes toward history. He wants to say *yes* to history, knowing all along, however, that it is predicated on *no* (negation). His "most basic of attitudes" are *no* and *yes* and, of course, "the intermediate realm of Maybe" (1984, i).

KB labors—ever historically—with "the miso-philanthropic assumption that getting along with people is one devil of a difficult task, but that, in the last analysis, we should all want to get along with people (and do want to)" (i). And therefore, you or I or we historiographers and historians imagine a plan for saving the world that you or I or we will, only later, turn into some devilish nightmare, because we inevitably "bureaucratize" our acts of the imagination (ii, 225–29).

No mere pessimist, however, KB works and plays hard in his various attempts to solve this problem of bureaucratizing the imagination: Specifically, he gives us accounts of what he calls "comic correctives" (166–75) and "perspectives by incongruity" (308–14). He writes that it is "comedy"—the "attitude of attitudes"—which "meditates upon . . . 'bureaucratization of the imaginative' " (iii); he writes that human beings are not "vicious" but "mistaken." We are all—given the situations that we often find ourselves in—"fools" and, therefore, it is a matter of what kind of fool we want to be (41). From being foolish, which again is inevitable, we can learn. KB writes: "The comic frame should enable people *to be observers of themselves, while acting*. Its ultimate would not be passiveness, but maximum consciousness. One would 'transcend' himself [*sic*] by noting his own foibles. He would provide a rationale for locating the irrational and the nonrational" (171; Burke's emphasis).

Attitudes Toward History continues, suggesting what will come forth eventually in later books on KB's grammar, rhetoric, and symbolic; just as this present book, *Writing Histories of Rhetoric*, must continue, suggesting what will have come forth *event*ually in future (anterior) histories of rhetorics.

Our acts of composition are always collaborative. It is the attitudes (comic or tragic, serious or farcical) of others that always stimulate and inform composing and that should and ought to be acknowledged.

This particular book project—if I can assign it a place on the calendar—began in 1988. I was interested in and took steps toward bringing together, in one critical mass, a group of historiographers and historians that would be interested in discussing both the epistemological-hermeneutical and ethical-political problems of writing histories of rhetorics. The group, which formed a paraconference, achieved critical mass in October of 1989. (It has since then been, on occasion, referred to as "October '89.") When the group met, its format was that practiced during the early days of "The Society for Critical Exchange." Brief position statements were read by a few historians/historiographers and then small and large group discussions (or caucuses) were held. As was typical of the format of "The Society," nothing at all was agreed on or resolved, except to go home and to think and to write. (We, too, made "a farce with livers minced small.")

The contributors included in this volume are some of the people who took their "assignments" seriously, or comically, or (yes) even farcically, and, therefore, wrote about writing histories of rhetorics. (The collection, by necessity, is incomplete.) The influence of the paraconference, we hope, however, goes beyond and will continue to go beyond the pages of this single volume, so as to farce up other huge volumes.

Besides the contributors to this volume, who participated in the conference, I would like to thank others who equally participated: Michelle Ballif, Lorie Goodman Batson, Barbara Biesecker, Carole Blair, Robert Connors, Theresa Enos, Lester Faigley, Rosalind Gabin, S. Michael Halloran, Patricia Harkin, Winifred Bryan Horner, Susan Jarratt, the late Charles Kneupper, C. H. Knoblauch, Michael Leff, Allan Megill, Stephen M. North, Robert Scott, James Sosnoski, Nancy S. Streuver, C. Jan Swearingen, and Marjorie Woods. And there was an even larger group (some eighty others), which, since memory fails, must remain anonymous.

Special thanks for financial assistance goes to the Department of English and Comparative Literature at Miami University, Ohio; to James Sosnoski and The Society for Critical Exchange; and to Wendall Nedderman, past president of the University of Texas at Arlington. In addition, I would like to thank Gary Tate, and Kenney Withers and Curtis Clark of Southern Illinois University Press for their professional support and encouragement and the rest of the staff of SIUP, especially Susan H. Wilson, and freelance copyeditor Ruth Kissell. And finally, for her support in my completing this project and for her help with indexing, I would like to thank my wife, Toni Vitanza.

Note

1. One traditional—perhaps folklorist, but nonetheless stubborn—viewpoint is that the copy of Aristotle's *Rhetoric* that we have must be a student's copy, or a copy of a copy of a copy and so on; for how else explain the "fact" that the *Rhetoric* is apparently in places, in dis/respect to definitions, in such a mess! The "master," some would reason, or insist, could never have nodded.

WRITING HISTORIES OF RHETORIC

1

Let Me Get This Straight

Sharon Crowley

A Litany

1982. James J. Murphy laments writing teachers' supposed ignorance of their professional history. "Since we don't know our own history," he writes, "we don't know whether we are making new discoveries or merely remaking old mistakes" (3).

1984. C. H. Knoblauch and Lil Brannon launch a nasty attack on classical rhetoric, calling it "that old-time religion" (22). Among the horrors supposedly visited on writing instruction by classical rhetoricians, Knoblauch and Brannon count Aristotle's legitimation of the aims of discourse and Cicero's authorization of the The Term Paper (25ff., 30).

1984. James A. Berlin publishes his history of nineteenth-century American writing instruction. Here he introduces his theory of rhetorics as noetic fields: closed systems "defining what can, and cannot, be known; the nature of the knower; the nature of the relationship between the knower, the known, and the audience and the nature of language" (2). Based on this notion, he identifies three nineteenth-century rhetorics, each growing out of its own noetic field: classical, psychological-epistemological, and romantic (3–4).

1986. Not one but four "comments" on Knoblauch and Brannon appear in the back pages of *College Composition and Communication.*

Richard Leo Enos argues that their "rendering of classical rhetoric is largely inaccurate and (consequently) misleading to readers" since it offers "inaccurate and incomplete generalizations" that stereotype classical rhetoric as an inert series of "rhetorical traditions" (502). S. Michael Halloran agrees, writing that Knoblauch and Brannon "view classical rhetoric as nothing more than a formulaic process of encoding preexistent knowledge" (503). Linda Robertson finds a paradox in Knoblauch and Brannon's rejection of classical rhetoric, since "we cannot dismiss with sweeping generalities the seminal texts of our culture while at the same time claiming that writing is fundamental" to the perpetuation of that culture (505). Richard Larson argues that Knoblauch and Brannon's book is "counterproductive" because its authors "dismiss as wrongheaded a major strand in Western thought" (506).

1986. Robert J. Connors reviews Berlin's book in *College Composition and Communication.* Connors accuses Berlin of not being objective enough, of filtering historical events through "powerful terministic screens" in order to make polemical points (249).

1986. John Schilb characterizes the historiography done in composition studies as critically unreflective. He singles out for analysis an essay by Andrea Lunsford, Lisa Ede, and Connors that constructs the 1960s as a period in which a revival of rhetoric occurred in America. Schilb wonders about the accuracy of this narrative, and wonders as well to which rhetoricians it might apply. He remarks that historians "ought to ponder" the constructedness of historical discourse (16). Schilb also notes James Kinneavy's uncritical location of the "sources" of Marxism and existentialism in classical rhetoric; Sharon Crowley's untheorized use of the term "grounding" in one of her histories; and Knoblauch and Brannon's "veering toward ahistoricism" as a way of justifying their "cultural lag theory of writing instruction" (28, 30).

1986. Christine Oravec publishes a history of a nineteenth-century American rhetorical tradition practiced by members of the Democratic party and based on utilitarianism. She notes that most of the work on nineteenth-century rhetoric has been done by historians of composition studies and, apparently because of this, feels the need to justify her attention to a popular political rhetoric that she identifies as "an alternative tradition." She argues that rhetorical history "should be seen in the context of the dominant traditions that generate alternatives in response" (421).

1987. Kathleen Welch critiques what she calls "the Heritage School" of rhetorical history, whose members include Knoblauch and Brannon and the compilers of the *Bedford Bibliography*. Historians from this school, Welch avers, flatten the complex seven-hundred-year history of classical rhetoric into an intellectual and pedagogical monolith. They also indulge in nostalgia for a "golden age of rhetoric" and, as a result, write elitist histories that prefer the good old days to the present. Welch will expand and strengthen this critique in her 1990 book *The Contemporary Reception of Classical Rhetoric*. There she demonstrates that Knoblauch and Brannon's dismissal of classical rhetoric depends on a dichotomizing logic as well as a thorough decontextualization of its genesis. Indeed, their "Heritage School" depiction of classical rhetoric relies not so much on primary sources as it does on accounts by other "Heritage School" rhetorician/historians.

1987. Victor J. Vitanza publishes the first of two ground-breaking essays on the historiography of rhetoric. Vitanza argues that literary theory and composition studies are branches of rhetoric and that the reason nobody acknowledges this fact is that composition studies are mired in a philosophical rhetoric while literary theory draws on a "post-philosophical rhetoric" (1987a, 43). Vitanza posits further that "we" resist writing histories of rhetoric that assume its nondisciplinarity because such histories would entail the construction of pedagogies that "would *dramatically change* the activity of what we call 'teaching writing'" (44).

1987. Berlin's history of twentieth-century writing instruction appears. Its opening chapter takes issue with Connors's version of historiography, as extrapolated from his review of Berlin's earlier volume. Berlin charges that Connors believes that "it is possible to locate a neutral space, a position from which one can act as an unbiased observer in order to record a transcendental object, the historical thing-in-itself" (1987b, 17).

1987. An issue of *PRE/TEXT* appears, containing essays by Berlin, Susan Jarratt, Schilb, and Vitanza, plus a colloquy among the four. All of these essays outline proposals for historiographical methods.

Berlin (1987b) accuses George Kennedy, E. P. J. Corbett, Knoblauch and Brannon, and Wilbur S. Howell of writing teleological histories and charges that Crowley and Don Stewart write "great man" history (49). His preferred method is a more sophisticated, neo-Marxist, version of his earlier notion of noetic fields. For Berlin, rhetoric is now "a set of strictures regarding the way language is used in the service of power," and the job of its historians is, of course, demystification (52).

Jarratt (1987b) proposes a sophistical historiography that will (*a*) redefine and expand the field surveyed by rhetorical history, thus doing history "on the margins of traditionally conceived disciplines"; (*b*) deny the traditional historical myth of continuity, which implies that history gives "a complete and full chain of events with a *telos* in the revival of rhetoric in the twentieth-century"; and (*c*) create antithetical and/or paratactic narratives "distinguished by multiple or open causality, the indeterminacies of which are then resolved through the self-conscious use of probable arguments" (11).

Schilb's historiography (1987) would (*a*) pay attention to the deconstructive notion that reality is mediated through texts; (*b*) incorporate awareness of social differences such as gender, race, and class; (*c*) and (*d*) engage deconstructive and social critiques in dialectic in order to illuminate the strengths and weaknesses of each; (*e*) discover how "simultaneous awareness of deconstruction and social criticism can eventually help make a difference in society" (32). In this essay Schilb seems confident that connections can be made between the writing of history and social or institutional change: "If everyone gave up the hope of writing [history], legacies of social oppression would be unaddressed and might even be actively denied" (34). More recently, however, he has expressed doubt about any easy connection between history-writing and social change.

Vitanza's essay (1987b) continues the critical work of his earlier effort and includes as well his descriptive/polemic classification of historiographical possibilities (traditional, revisionary, and sub/versive). Vitanza's writing is replete with typographical experimentation, sloganeering ("better schizoid than fascoid"), asides and autobiographical puns ("to the Victors . . ."; "after all, I am 'vv'"). But he seems nevertheless serious about the possibility of instaurating a sub/versive historiography that despairs of effecting social change because it "understands that the overthrow of a political position . . . is only a capitulation to eventual recapitulation" (107). Given the "truth" of this inevitability, Vitanza celebrates, incarnates, "drifting," comedy, carnival, performance, as the appropriate modes for intellectual work.

1988. Crowley reviews Berlin's new book (1987b) in *College Composition and Communication*, complaining that Berlin's categorizing impulse has gotten the better of his historicizing impulse. She allows as how Berlin's schema lumps together some pretty inhospitable bedmates and argues as well that the schema assumes that "the practice of rhetoric always involves a search for truth" (246).

1988. Schilb publishes an essay in which he laments that "historians of rhetoric" have "wound up concentrating on 'lessons' from 'the past' instead of confronting the often conflict-ridden nature of historiography" (15). He takes lengthy issue with the historiographical assumptions implicit in an essay on *Phaedrus* written by Stewart. This time Schilb does not conclude that Stewart and his ilk ought to write more self-conscious history; rather, he argues that conflicts among historians ought to be foregrounded in rhetoric/composition instruction, à la Gerald Graff's suggestion vis-à-vis literary studies.

1988. James J. Murphy chairs a panel, or octalog, at CCCC called "The Politics of Historiography," which includes Berlin, Connors, Crowley, Enos, Jarratt, Nan Johnson, C. Jan Swearingen, Vitanza. Murphy jokes that the panelists are seated along a representative spectrum: Vitanza and Berlin on the far left, Enos and Connors on the right. A transcription of this panel is published in *Rhetoric Review*, along with retrospective comments by each panelist. In the retrospectives, Berlin charges Connors and Crowley with conservatism; Connors wonders if we're all not suffering from an "intellectual multiple-personality disorder," being unwilling, on the one hand, to admit we believe in the truth and, on the other, taking "certain stands and writ[ing] as if we knew the truth"; Jarratt ponders the gendered aspects of the argument; Vitanza registers suspicion of Connors's utopian vision ("I write history to try to make my world a better place") as totalizing and exclusive (35, 36, 42). Barely disguising her exhaustion with the whole project, Swearingen laments our warring over versions of historiography: "Polarization begets polarization," she says, and "confrontation should be a last resort. No one wins wars—or revolutions—because when one side wins, everyone loses in the end" (48).

1988. Scholars from Speech Communication escalate Swearingen's war as some of their Biggest Guns lay down a retaliatory barrage to Vitanza's 1987a essay. Michael Leff tries to beat Vitanza at his own game. He accuses Vitanza of an excess of attention to "the logic of contradiction" and performs his own rehearsal of the "comic elements inscribed within the rhetorical tradition itself" (239). Unlike Leff, Kennedy won't play by Vitanza's rules, reminding us, not-so-subtly, that he, Kennedy, invented the rules of this game in the first place. He consigns Vitanza to the camp of those who would reduce rhetoric to style or stylistics, accusing him of espousing a particularly virulent sort of *letteraturizzazione*, "a kind of linguistic herpes" (231). Robert L. Scott suspects that, despite his comedic posturing, Vitanza has submitted to a transcendentalizing impulse and, worse, that he harbors a fondness for persons and positions currently residing "on the margin." That is, Scott suspects Vitanza of trying to rout insiders so as to replace them with outsiders. He confesses he can't imagine what "all of this" has "to do with composition and its teaching" (237). Undaunted, Vitanza counter-responds in a piece called "Cackling With Tears in My Eyes."

1990. Edward Schiappa tries to maintain a distinction between "historical reconstruction" and "rational reconstruction" in the historiography of rhetoric. He complains that John Poulakos's essays (1983b; 1984) on the Older Sophists "require correction if viewed from the standpoint of historical reconstruction" on the ground that "Poulakos makes a number of claims about historically held doctrines that cannot be supported by the available evidence" (198, 201). Poulakos responds (1990b) with a withering attack on Schiappa's "deep hydro (logo) phobia" and unquestioning respect for the historiographical method adumbrated in classical philology: "Unconscious of the ways in which he (Schiappa) influences the text by virtue of the preconceptions he brings to his reading, and unsuspecting of the influence the text exercises on him, he asserts, in effect, that the text is inhabited by certain truths which he, as an objective reader, untainted by the impurities of perspective and bias, can recover" (219, 220).

1990. The *Western Journal of Speech Communication* devotes a special section to "Rhetoric and Historiography." In its introduction, Carole Blair and Mary Kahl opine that while "choices of perspective, goal, and procedure in rhetorical criticism have been subject to a great deal of explicit evaluation in our literature . . . these same choices in writing histories of rhetorical theory have received remarkably scant attention" (149). Like Jarratt, they address the matters of what "materials" should be identified as "rhetorical theories," arguing against a stable meaning for the term "rhetoric" across time (151). Again like Jarratt, Blair and Kahl consider the traditional organizations of rhetorical histories as either continuous or discontinuous, arguing that to limit historical narratizing to these two options "tends to eliminate what Vitanza calls 'inter-textual' analysis, more or less foreclosing the question" of how our readings of, say, Aristotle's texts influence our reading of Plato's texts (151). Last, they argue, à la Berlin and Schilb, that the history of rhetoric ought to be located in reference to the histories of other disciplines, as well as to social, political, and cultural concerns (153).

1990. Berlin, Jarratt, and Vitanza revisit the issue of historiography in yet another issue of *PRE/TEXT*. Berlin argues that historians of rhetoric must realize that in every historical period there are competing rhetorics and that these "are often indicators of competing power formations, of opposing groups forwarding different economic and political agendas" (177–78). Thus, he writes, "Historians of rhetoric—Kennedy, Howell, Corbett, [Brian] Vickers, [Thomas] Conley—are not inadequate in what they say. They are inadequate in what they leave out"—that is, they overlook the political and economic agendas of those who put forward or support rhetorics and rhetorical theories (178). Jarratt's historiography is now straightforwardly feminist: she writes here "as a woman" and asks "how feminists writing histories of rhetoric can take up the challenge . . . to create histories aimed at a more just future" (190–91). Vitanza offers a critique of traditional ethics, delineates his concept of "paraethics," and shows how it might be used to disrupt dominant discourses.

1991. Schiappa returns to the fray over the Sophists, citing John Poulakos, Jasper Neel, Roger Moss, and Crowley as representative writers who espouse a "sophistic turn" in contemporary discourse theory (5). This time he argues that "sophistic rhetoric" is, for the most part, a mirage—something we see because we want and need to see it—which vaporizes once carefully scrutinized." By the time you read this, no doubt one or more historians of rhetoric will have risen to defend sophistry against Schiappa's charge that it is "an incoherent historical concept" (see Vitanza 1993b).

I want to make four observations about this litany. First, I've just written a history. It's fairly lengthy, but still I'm uneasy about its selectivity, about my ability to represent the positions of all participants, about my inability to resist making more ado about some things than others (e.g., disciplinary affinities), about the arbitrariness and misrepresentative character of my use of chronology (e.g., publishing schedules being what they are, an essay published with an earlier date may actually represent later developments in someone's thinking). Second, all the persons taking part in the conversation I've just rehearsed represent a discipline and its related practices that are hoary with age but now in serious disrepute. Third, the conversation is taking place among a small group of people, all of whom know each other's work (and each other). Fourth, many of these people want their scholarship to reach beyond the people to whom they seem always to be talking. Some even want to participate in bringing about an end to, or changes in, various oppressive cultural practices. They are, however, more or less mystified as to how this might work.

A Historiographical Schema

You may have noticed that there are two fairly distinct historiographical positions represented among the voices in my litany. For purposes of clarification, I label them "essentialist" and "constructionist." Discussion of essentialisms and their uses has recently been brought into focus by historians of sexuality and gender.[1] Here I bypass discussion of the theoretical difficulties and insights entailed in this work and use it instead to illuminate differences among historians of rhetoric.[2] I will end by advocating the composition of constructionist histories of rhetoric/composition. I do this for political reasons. This does not mean that I scorn essentialist historiography. Nor do I mean to denigrate the great traditional histories or historians of rhetoric who have in part made possible the limited scholarly respect that rhetoricians and compositionists now enjoy.

I borrow my definition of essentialism from Diana Fuss (1989): "Essentialism is most commonly understood as a belief in the real, true essence of things, the invariable and fixed properties which define the 'whatness' of a given entity" (xi). This sort of essentialism appears in the historical practice of George Kennedy, for example, who claims that "traditional or natural rhetoric occurs in all societies" (1980a, 6). Kennedy makes this assertion despite his awareness that most societies do not conceptualize their rhetorical practices as "rhetoric," if at all. (Of course, I do not mean to imply that a practice has to be conceptualized in order to exist.)

Much less do all societies conceptualize their discursive practices in terms familiar to Western rhetoricians. Fuss notes that historians can make essentializing assumptions only if they also "theorize history as an unbroken continuum that transports (categories) across cultures and through time . . . without in any way (re)defining or indeed (re)constituting them" (1989, 3). Like Kennedy, many traditional historians of rhetoric assume that their fundamental terms are stable linguistic (ontological?) categories that remain relatively unchanged over time or through space. For example, the chronological stability of the term "writing instruction" is taken for granted in the cover graphic of Murphy's *Short History* (1990) of same, which shows a river (of time?) connecting an Egyptian pyramid to a contemporary student writing desk. The geographical and cultural stability of the term "rhetoric" is assumed by Robert Oliver in the preface to *Communication and Culture in Ancient India and China* (1971). Oliver supposes that what Westerners mean by "rhetoric" existed in ancient Eastern cultures: he asserts that the "rhetorical views" of ancient Indian and Chinese people are "intrinsic in their religio-philosophical writings and in their political and social practices" (ix). Schiappa (1990) comes close to this sort of essentializing when he looks for the originary uses of the term *rhetorike* in the fourth century B.C.E., as if these usages would tell us something authoritative about the term's core meaning, or when he argues that "sophistry" can be a useful term only if it can be made to refer to some coherent historical doctrine (1991, 8).

Some essentialist historians make a more profound assumption: history is a force that stands outside history. As Fuss puts it, for some essentialist historians "history itself is theorized as essential, and thus unchanging; its essence is to generate change but not itself to be changed" (1989, 3). In other words, this stronger version of essentialism transmogrifies discrete human actions into the "movement of history"—a primary and transcendental category that is unaffected by its own movement.

In the bad old days, of course, the transcendental version of essentialism informed classical Marxist historiography. Before Althusser and Gramsci (not to mention Stalin), Marxist historians grounded their work in the inevitability of class struggle and the coming workers' revolution. In these bad new days, historians who subscribe to new-right fundamentalism also begin from a postulated *telos*: the Second Coming. Despite their very different politics, both sorts of radical historians subscribe to a deterministic, idealist, essentializing historiography.

Most teleological histories of rhetoric, however, place its golden moment at the beginning rather than at the end. Kennedy (1980a) locates the originary moment in Homeric discourse; Murphy (1972), following some classical doxographers, locates it in the legendary quarrel between Tisias and Corax; many modern historians, like Knoblauch and Brannon (1984), assume that rhetoric begins with the publication (such as it was) of Aristotle's Saturday afternoon lectures. It is surprising, really, how many histories of rhetoric assume that classical rhetoric, whether viewed in a negative or positive light, dictates the shape of all its future conceptualizations. A weaker version of teleological history asserts that the perfection of the beginning can be repeated, either in a different or the same configuration. At least two "new rhetorics" have emerged in modern times: the first, in the eighteenth century, was inaugurated by an explicit rejection of classical rhetoric; the second, in the 1960s, attempted to revive it.

Unlike essentialist historians, constructionists do not assume that human nature has remained stable across time, nor do they assume that linguistic or cultural categories represent natural, transhistorical realities. Since reality is mediated through language, constructionist historians posit that categories such as "human nature" and "rhetoric" are produced and modified within the discourse of a given community or culture in accordance with current social or political requirements. Theoretically, such categories could carry the same meanings across human time and space although, practically speaking, this is not likely given the complexity of human history and human language.[3]

Constructionists also argue that since categories like "rhetoric" are inventions, they are tied to, and are complicit with, the social practices and relations that produce them. That's why the cultural referents named by such categories change over time and from place to place. Last, constructionists assume that human behavior is configured, to some extent, by whatever cultural constructions are operative in a given historical period. This dialectical feature of constructionist historiography renders moot the essentialist notion that history transcends itself.

Constructionist histories of rhetoric are not yet easy to come by. Jarratt (1987a), John Poulakos (1990a), and Welch (1990) have written what Vitanza would call "intertextual analyses" that deconstruct modern or contemporary appropriations of classical rhetorics. Essays like these help to dislodge the myth that received readings (or translations) of older texts are somehow "essential" or "inevitable" by showing how they were constructed to serve social or political or institutional ends.

Jarratt's feminist-sophistic historiography is decidedly constructionist insofar as it challenges the continuity and coherence of rhetorical history, theory, and practice. In *Rereading the Sophists* (1991), Jarratt writes that her historiographical practice may be described as "a search for historically located and politically significant difference" (xxiii). In the course of the book, the Older Sophists become a sort of first locus of the play of such differences within Western history, and their history is made analogous to those of contemporary groups who are marked as "different"—women, composition teachers—by people who speak a dominating discourse. The constructionist bent of her work is made apparent in her remark that sophistic histories are "frankly imaginative reconstructions, instruments of *psychogogia* granted assent through their reception by the whole person who reads or hears them . . . and adopted because they serve social needs" (28). Such embodied and partial histories are, avowedly and deliberately, a far cry from so-called objective histories; according to Jarratt, they "argue their theses . . . self-consciously and without false modesty . . . holding them up for applause and revision" (28).

Aside from these few pieces, rhetoricians have produced more programs for constructionist historiography than constructionist histories. Vitanza is working on a volume of sub/versive historiography that might more properly be called "performative" than constructionist when/if it appears; no doubt he would identify my description of constructionist historiography with the category of revisionary history he calls "self-conscious critical practice."

John Schilb's deconstructive/critical program is constructionist insofar as it foregrounds the role of language in the shaping of history and historical understanding. However, Schilb's criticism of traditionalist historiography is not fully constructionist (at least not yet); he typically calls for the composition of so-called social, as opposed to intellectual, historiography. I'm not sure what Schilb means by this. If he is calling for alternative histories of rhetoric that privilege the voices of persons not typically heard, this is not necessarily a constructionist move, however laudable such work may be. Nonconstructionist histories of heretofore-silenced rhetorics and rhetoricians may certainly be written; for example, Karlyn Kohrs Campbell's two-volume collection and analysis of nineteenth-century woman rhetoricians (1989) is a major contribution in this category.

If Gramsci (1989) is correct, all humans are intellectuals; only some persons are paid to do intellectual work. Thus, another way to distinguish intellectual from social history, in rhetoric and composition studies at least, would be to distinguish those who are paid or otherwise rewarded for doing work in rhetoric or composition from those who are not. The distinction would then operate between histories of teachers such as Quintilian or orators like Jeane Kirkpatrick, on the one hand, and histories of unpaid practitioners such as Sojourner Truth or itinerant preachers, on the other. The intellectual/social distinction still poses a problem for the history of composition studies, however, since that field could not afford intellectuals, defined in this way, until very recently (unless we count persons who made fortunes by writing textbooks). On the other hand, there were, and still are, enormous numbers of teachers and students of composition whose histories remain to be written. I would hesitate to call histories of their work "social," if this term is to be opposed to "intellectual." When one is writing the history of an academic discipline, in other words, the distinction between "intellectual" and "social" history may not be helpful, unless it applies to teachers' scholarship, lesson plans, and syllabi, on the one hand, as opposed to their working conditions or gender or class affiliations, on the other.

Using Schilb's distinction this way, one could call my *The Methodical Memory* (1990) an intellectual history of composition studies, since it explicitly omits consideration of the professional lives of the authors considered within it. On the other hand, while Susan Miller's *Textual Carnivals* (1991) does consider such issues as the gender of composition teachers, I would hesitate to call it a social history, since Miller is concerned with the institutional status of compulsory writing instruction. For work like hers, we need a term like "institutional history." Interestingly enough, both works claim to be constructionist (or deconstructionist) in their orientation. Thus, it seems likely that the intellectual/social/institutional distinction works on a different level of generalization than does the essentialist/constructionist distinction.

Consider also histories of rhetoric and composition studies informed by neo-Marxist historiography. When neo-Marxist histories of rhetoric call attention to the role played by class or institutional discourse in the production and dissemination of texts, they are constructionist to the extent that they attempt to reconstruct the class or institutional structures operant during the period they examine; to the extent that they do not assume that discursive strategies are always in the service of a supposedly single, dominant class that is somehow akin to a contemporary, single, dominant class; and to the extent that they do not assume that "domination" works through identical or similar configurations across history.

The first criterion seems to hold for the histories of classical rhetoric now being published by John and Takis Poulakos. Take, for example, Takis Poulakos's essay on classical funeral orations (1990), which explicitly rejects Kennedy's assertion of the shared essence of such texts, based on their formal similarity (172). Poulakos demonstrates that the production of these occasional discourses was tied to their institutional function of glorifying the Athenian state. As a result, the genre was not monolithic across the time of its use; rather, it underwent changes "as the object of its glorification (the state) also changed" from "the most powerful city-state in Greece to one of four equipotent city-states" (176). Poulakos is aware that another constructionist history could be built around these texts, one that "would describe the shifts this type of discourse underwent as the political formations of Athens changed" (181).

However, as T. Poulakos begins to theorize the constancy of "the political institution of the city-state" as "an overarching continuity against which changes in political formations can be made discernible," or when he does not theorize his casual reference to "the politics of domination and control" and "the structures of imperialism," I wonder whether he is not participating in a peculiarly neo-Marxist brand of essentializing (181, 185). I realize that I am imposing very large theoretical burdens on a short essay. Nevertheless, it is the case that if historians take the position that certain structures of domination are historical constants or if they assume that class distinctions alone determine the production and circulation of texts, their histories are essentialist. They are essentialist as well if they assume that class structures—like anything else constructed by humans—do not change over time or that class is a fundamental, natural, organizing category of human activity.

Construction as Criticism

Whether or not constructionist historiography explicitly targets essentialism for critique, as T. Poulakos suggests, it is certainly the case that constructionist histories raise serious problems for more traditional readings of familiar historical materials. To give a rather spectacular example: David Halperin (1990), a classical historian, argues that sexual behavior was constructed in fifth-century Athens as an expression of power relations. Sexual acts between older and younger citizen males, as well as those between citizen males and women of all classes, constituted graphic affirmation of the ability of adult citizen males to impose their wills, and their bodies, on the bodies of whomever else they pleased. That is to say, in fifth-century Athens, same-sex behavior carried much the same cultural weight for free citizen males as did any other sexual behavior in which they chose to engage. Modern readings that give exclusive (and highly romanticized) attention to the same-sex behavior between citizen males depicted in texts such as Plato's read these texts through modern lenses that tie a person's identity to her sexual preference.

If we accept Halperin's reading of male sexuality in fifth-century Athens, then, that acceptance will modify our readings of histories that filter the sexual behavior of Plato and his cohorts through a later construction called "Platonic love." Today, the behavior that Halperin reads into the lives of these historical figures is construed as an abuse of the social authority invested in older men vis-à-vis their relations with younger men, particularly if the older men in question are teachers of the younger. If you doubt that Halperin's reading of Athenian men's *behavior* will require adjustments to traditional interpretations of their *texts*, I ask you to reconsider the setting of *Phaedrus* in the terms he outlines or, for that matter, Socrates' discussion of love and its analogy to rhetoric.

The potential of constructionism as critique helps me to see how essentialist readings work to reify contemporary cultural values. Constructionist historians argue that essentialist historians work backwards from current descriptions of reality, classifying similar but chronologically isolated or culturally diverse activities by means of contemporary categories. To put this another way: essentialist historians use currently privileged narratives to make sense of historical data that otherwise might seem unsavory, inconsistent, or unimportant. This fact accounts for the dominance of the current rhetorical canon by texts written by males, as well as male versions of women's lives and work.[4] The canon was constructed, after all, by persons whose ideologies were powerfully shaped by patriarchal discourse.

Since essentialist historians do not theorize the constructedness of their own narratives, they naively write the narratives of historical figures so that their behavior accords with contemporary cultural constructions, eliding behavior or beliefs that do not. And since they fail to historicize the constructedness of their narratives, it follows that the values essentialist historians impute to historical figures such as Plato (which are their own values as well) are either above history conceived in its vulgar sense as a record of various human acts, or else they are consonant with history conceived in its transcendental sense. Essentialism, thus, has a vested interest in maintaining an image of Plato and his cohorts as persons whose intellectual work was somehow outside of and uncontaminated by the social and ideological practices of a culture that was, after all, class-ridden and often brutal to those who were not citizens. Ironically enough, then, essentialist historiography (at least in its transcendental version) indulges in a kind of presentism that validates contemporary cultural constructions as transhistorical and thus natural and thus free of ideological content.

And so, constructionist historiography critiques the stance of objectivity itself (Novick 1988). This notion is politically loaded, insofar as "objectivity" (ideological neutrality) is just another name for history as told by those who have the power to impose their stories on others. The illusion of ideological neutrality is a luxury available only to those who espouse a dominant ideology. Persons who subscribe to dominant ideologies do not have to take account of competing ideologies, although persons who subscribe to alternative or subordinate ideologies are always aware of at least one other: The dominant one. This double perspective characterizes feminist historiography, whose historians can critique the male-centeredness of traditional historiography precisely because their authors have learned to speak both the dominant language and an "other" language by virtue of their experience of exclusion.

So What?

Essentialist histories of rhetoric/composition studies seem, then, to buy into certain dominant discourses promulgated in the academy and in the culture at large. Rhetoricians may not wish to support the discourses of neutrality, of patriarchy, of conservatism. At the very least, rhetoricians cannot validate the status quo and remain employed, unless of course they confine themselves to the composition of epideictic discourse. Indeed, given the current status of rhetoric in the popular imagination, perhaps it is fair to say that essentialist histories of rhetoric have been composed in just this mode—as praise of a discipline in disrepute.

Halperin (1990) argues that constructionist historiography offers a couple of other advantages, in addition to its critique of essentialism. If historians can bracket their assumptions about what is "natural," they may achieve access to

> the salient particularities of . . . life in a given society, particularities that might have gone unnoticed—or, if noticed, unexamined—in the absence of a research program that called for scrutinizing them. It also helps the interpreter resist the temptation to integrate alien or exotic phenomena into a plausible discourse of the known, into a picture whose appeal derives largely from its familiarity to its viewers. (42)

Here Halperin seems to claim greater accuracy for constructionist historiography, insofar as it calls attention to the "particularities" of a given historical moment and insofar as it discourages historians from using currently privileged narratives to make sense of historical data that otherwise might seem inconsistent or unintelligible. As far as I can see, however, the constructionist program offers no superior guarantee of historical accuracy since it assumes that historical materials are always read through contemporary lenses. Its self-consciousness, in other words, is not a guarantor of its representational validity.

The point of constructionist historiography, I take it, is that history is useful insofar as it reminds us of the variousness and mutability of human behavior. Constructionism prefers difference to identity; it reads the particulars of history rather than its general sweep; and it situates historical events in cultural constructs that may seem exotic and/or foreign to today's readers.[5] Constructionism is a profoundly rhetorical view of historiography because it foregrounds difference, variety, and change. (What it currently lacks to become fully rhetorical is a theory of how social change comes about, something that some classical rhetorics did have.)

But the rhetoricity of constructionist historiography is not the only thing that ought to appeal to those who would write histories of rhetoric and composition studies. Constructionist historiography attempts to dislodge narratives that privilege the natural or the unchanging; it follows that constructionist narratives of the history of rhetoric also dislodge standard interpretations of our disciplinary past. Constructionist histories of rhetoric will no doubt jettison two narratives that dominate our current thinking about that past: the popular narrative that pictures rhetoricians as having fallen from our ancient greatness; and the academic narrative that pictures composition studies as having arisen from the sterility of current-traditionalism into its recent glorious multiplicity. I am particularly concerned about the pernicious effects of this last story. For one thing, it assumes that thousands of persons (who were mostly women) taught college-level writing during the first seventy years of the twentieth century without raising a whisker of resistance to the aridity of the dominant paradigm. For another, it assumes that we have thrown off the fetters of current-traditionalism and that we have finally arrived at something like the glory that was rhetoric in Greece and Rome. Neither of these assumptions holds, of course.

Obviously, the scholarly flap I have been reviewing and analyzing has been, if not generated, at least accelerated, by the current reemergence of rhetoric as a discipline. Perversely, one could construe this whole flap as a sidebar to the real game in town: the impending institutional legitimation of rhetoric, a legitimation that will necessarily redraw the turf lines laid down by some powerful neighbors who now live on the right side of the academic tracks: Literary studies, the humanistic branch of speech-communication, philosophy, and some of the human sciences—history, sociology, and political science, maybe even anthropology (Nelson et al. 1987). As rhetoric moves toward disciplinarity and (perhaps) institutional respectability, we become concerned about how, exactly, to write its histories in order to make rhetoric and its practitioners (seem to) fit within the disciplinary discourse that currently dominates the academy.

One route to disciplinary independence is, of course, the construction of histories that at once define the range of activities that fall under the disciplinary umbrella, and at the same time distinguishes those activities from those conducted in related disciplines. Thus, we find sophisticated constructionist historians, like William Covino (1988) or Susan Jarratt (1987a; 1991), making colonizing gestures similar to those made two decades ago by a more essentialist Robert Oliver (1971). The texts of philosophy, literary theory and criticism, anthropology, political theory, ethics—all are now the province of rhetoricians. At the same time, a complementary gesture of exclusion works to define a particularly rhetorical attitude toward texts and practices, as opposed to, say, a philosophical or idealizing stance toward the same materials. Interestingly, this gesture is made more frequently by constructionist historians than by essentialists, who seem comfortable with a historical disciplinary narrative that features Plato and Aristotle, Campbell and Whately, Weaver and Perelman rather than Gorgias and Isocrates, Nietzche and Marx, Cixous and Wittig.

Can it be that rhetoric itself is constructionist, at least when it is compared to a more essentializing philosophy?

Notes

1. For theoretical discussions of the construction of homosexuality, see Greenberg (1988), Halperin (1990), Padgug (1989), Plummer (1981). For discussion of the construction of sexuality in feminist discourse, see Butler (1990), Caplan (1981), Fuss (1989), Ortner and Whitehead (1981), Phelan (1989).

2. At this historical moment, the categories *essentialist* and *constructionist* are not mutually exclusive, nor are they simply opposing binaries. Rather, each term requires the other for its deployment: constructionists hold up the inevitability of change as an essential principle; essentialists must defend their essentialism within the current constructionist climate that contests it. Fuss makes the point that there are no pure versions of essentialism and constructionism and urges us to deploy each as political strategies. Furthermore, the categories cannot always be applied to all of the work of a given historian. Nor is this essay a brief for this way of cutting up the historiographical pie. For a different classification, with a very full explanation and lots of examples, see Vitanza (1987b).

3. Although they are sometimes charged with doing so, constructionists (like postmodernists) do not necessarily deny that language can refer to something outside itself. They simply doubt its capacity to refer with perfect equivalence. They doubt further whether reference is the chief role played by language, although they do not doubt the pervasive force of the politics of representation. Actually, reference to some preconstructed reality doesn't interest postmodern thinkers very much, since it is within discursive constructions that the important power games are played. Traditional historians sometimes compare the essentialist/constructionist controversy to John Locke's distinction between the real and the nominal. This is misleading, though, since Locke's distinction presumes an unchanging nature that underlies even those categories discriminated by nominalists. Constructionism is not simply a process whereby new categories are discriminated in nature and then given new names.

4. We can all recite the canon, but since I've never seen it admitted to in print, I want to write it down here: Tisias and Corax, Gorgias, Isocrates, Plato, Aristotle, Hermagoras, Cicero, Quintilian, Augustine, a medieval scholiast or two, Ramus, Wilson, Vico, Campbell, Blair, Whately, a couple of current-

traditional types like Bain or Hill, Richards, Burke, Weaver, Perelman, Toulmin, amen. Two kinds of history are available that contest male-centered canonical lists. For examples that reclaim lost works by women, see Campbell (1989) or Spender (1982). For examples that demonstrate the male-centeredness of historical accounts in science, philosophy, history, and literary studies, see Harding and Hintikka (1983), Grimshaw (1986), Riley (1988), or Spender (1989), among many many others.

5. Since some of these preferences are also prominent features of postmodern theorizing about language and its relation to reality, the constructionist position is validated, in tautological fashion, by its current use. That is, constructionism is possible and popular at this moment in time because a sizable segment of the scholarly population is trying on ways of postmodern thinking that are, precisely, those of constructionist historiography. We see what we can.

2

After the Fall | *Reflections on Histories of Rhetoric*

Hans Kellner

From a survey of the recent disputes regarding the writing of histories of rhetoric, I surmise that the territory is not only so broad that no one dare claim to command it but also that its boundaries, never very clear, are less distinct now than ever. Confident appeals to the essence of rhetoric take the form of ancient formulas about persuasion, discovery of arguments, instrumental use of language, but these appeals do not close the case because what is at issue in the first place is the right of certain privileged texts to determine what rhetoric *really* is. From a historian's perspective, the first problem is one of definitions.

Now, none of this is completely unfamiliar to me because historical discourse finds itself in a similar situation of fragmentation and contention about fundamentals.[1] Most discussions of methods and goals in historical study wind up as debates about what is *really* historical and, more to the point, what is not. My own concerns with the force of language and how it creates the sense of normal, properly constituted, historical questions seems to be a reversed image of the topic of "Writing Histories of Rhetoric." If, as I have maintained in *Language and Historical Representation* (1989), language and its rhetorical resources are the "hidden sources" of historical texts, locked in a sort of underground combat with the documentary evidence to establish what shall be the fundament, the "immortal part," of history, where may one begin to ponder the writing of the histories of rhetoric? It is difficult to ascertain which is the chicken and which the egg, history or rhetoric, even assuming we have our barnyard priorities theoretically established, which is by no means a safe or reasonable assumption. History would seem to be utterly chicken-like, and hence prior to any possible offspring, if we accept for the sake of argument the plausible feminist contention that the chicken is always first. Any event or discourse must appear in recorded time to be known, and such time is the realm of history, isn't it? Yet the small flaw in this reasoning is the word *recorded,* which clearly cracks the shell of the rhetorical egg to reveal that it had feathers in there all along.

It may well be that this dilemma was bequeathed to us by Vico and his Renaissance humanist forebears. We generally assume, since them, that history and rhetoric are both human discourses, neither natural nor, certainly, divine. Yet, if history and rhetoric were both natural *and* divine, the problem would be greatly simplified. Consider, for example, the precise agreement of human rhetoric in its classical form and world history as inaugurated in the Hebrew scriptures, as demonstrated by a well-known professor of rhetoric, speaking at my own alma mater a few years before my time.

> To show you how exact the arrangement of Aristotle is, you will find on opening the bible, that it corresponds precisely with the process of the Creator in making the world. "In the beginning God created . . . (to void)" Invention.
> "And God said . . . (to light)" Elocution.
> "And God divided . . . (to night)" Disposition. (Adams 1810, I, 175)

This discovery by Professor John Quincy Adams that the Creator behaved in the normal course of things divine according to the precepts of Aristotelian discourse may have had a certain irony to Adams and his students, but I suspect that he was perfectly serious. The certain providential path of history *ought* to accord with the inevitable and timeless naturalness of classical rhetoric. If the humanists assumed that the structure of history resembled the structure of discourse, particularly in the order revealed by the *topoi* as principles of organization for all human activity, ancient and modern (Struever 1970, 125.), then Adams's witty illustration to the Harvard undergraduates of 1810 has some substance.

Another professor who, like Adams, went on to more notable pursuits, clearly saw rhetoric as prehistoric. Friedrich Nietzsche notes that "rhetoric arises among a people who still live in mythic images and who have not yet experienced the unqualified need of historical accuracy; they would rather be persuaded than instructed" (Nietzsche 1989, 3). First rhetoric, then history; first persuasion, then instruction. Yet Nietzsche cannot let this simple formula stand for long. Rhetoric has no proper beginning. It is, so to speak, always already there. "But, it is not difficult to prove that what is called 'rhetorical,' as a means of conscious art, had been active as a means of unconscious art in language and its development [*Werden*], indeed, that the *rhetorical is a further development*, guided by the clear light of the understanding, of *the artistic means which are already found in language*. There is obviously no unrhetorical 'naturalness' of language to which one could appeal; the language itself is the result of audible rhetorical arts" (Nietzsche, 21).

It was *all* rock 'n' roll to Nietzsche. So rhetoric is always there in language, which has no innocent state, just as history is always there, long before the concern for historical accuracy mandates a discourse of history.

Both Adams and Nietzsche, who are otherwise vastly different minds, find rhetoric somehow present at the Creation, perhaps already debating priority with history herself. This conundrum of priority is a political struggle, given the authority that foundational priority is accorded in most discourses. It is not, however, an insuperable paradox, as we are all aware. A good deal of the theoretical and practical confusion about history, rhetoric, and any possible interaction of the two discourses arises because both exhibit an endlessly bewildering double nature. Because each of these words, history and rhetoric, embodies a very real and analogous confusion, it could hardly be otherwise than that their wedded life, either as the history of rhetoric or the rhetoric of history, depending upon who gets the top spot in their connubial preposition, should bring forth questionable offspring? Common speech has a way of dictating morality, even to the sophisticated, and common speech refuses to clarify the crucial distinction between history as past event and history as discourse drawn from the traces of past events. Everybody knows this, and most practitioners of literacy crafts readily acknowledge that the past is gone, yet again and again a new book will appear under the banner "back to history," discussing novelists, poets, playwrights in some contextualized fashion without mention of a single historian's name, let alone serious study of any historian's text. For all the self-proclaimed theoretical sophistication of the various "new historicisms" that appear from time to time, historians to them are nevertheless like the drivers from UPS, who drop their parcels and vanish in their brown trucks; in this discourse, literature, not history, is the rich and complex interaction of subject, language, and imagination. New historicisms always come to this (cf. White 1989, 293–302).

Rhetoric is in a boat similar to history's, a craft with two prows and no stern. When it is sighted in the water, it is not easy to ascertain the direction of its motion, if any. On the one hand, rhetoric is a series of texts, a "strand of meaning" as Nancy Struever put it, which describe the instrumental uses of language, more or less, and prescribe a pedagogy in linguistic performance. Yet rhetoric also means the routine, unschooled practice of communication. Common speech strikes again, but in a way that reverses the problem of history. In history, it is the *textual* meaning of the word that is linguistically "marked," and thus in danger of being repressed. In rhetoric, it is rather the nonformalized linguistic *practice,* as limitless in scope as history itself, that recedes behind the traditional "strand" of texts from ancient Sicily to modern Arlington, from Corax to, say, Vitanza. The announced task under consideration in this volume, "Writing Histories of Rhetoric," splinters the historical while essentializing the rhetorical; the issue, however, is clearly "Writing Histories of Rhetorics." Essentially contested concepts both, history and rhetoric each have deep ambiguities that never are entirely absent from any discussion of them.

For reasons of which we are all aware, the modern rhetorician finds himself in the position of the father in the insurance commercial, who has just learned that the kitten is up a tree, the kids need orthodonture, and the plumbing is clogged. At long last, the realization comes: "They NEED me!" At this point, we historians have learned, discourses always become passionately interested in their own histories. What starts to look like a pie will have to be carved up. But how? "Writing Histories of Rhetorics" is a struggle for power over the discourse. Rhetoric has become another "burden of history."

A parable may put the matter into a sort of focus. Imagine the death of a beloved mother, and the sad, difficult, and irksome task of clearing out the family home. Most of the decisions are easy, determined by law and expediency. However, there is a large chest of old papers and what are called "personal effects"—letters, deeds, accounts, photographs, on top of old clothes, military uniforms, and the like. One of the three grown children looks at this mass of material as treasure, suggests ways to preserve the oldest papers from time, wishes to consult curators and archivists to learn more about the materials, and suggests that a special place be set up as a family museum for all of their own children. The second child refuses. The material is worthless; no one cares or will ever look at it. Besides, the world—let's face it—is already drowning in old stuff like this. To preserve it will cost a good deal, might well use up the entire cash inheritance. It is the future that counts anyway, and this child has very earnest and costly plans for it. The third child has an entirely less serious approach to this chest, an approach we may call the Mickey Rooney/Judy Garland approach. (Remember? "My dad's got a barn! Let's put on a Show!!!") Why not give the old stuff to the kids for fun, to dress up in, to put on little travesties, and perhaps to see how much better things are today, what with Velcro, diet pop, and all. Irreverence is what we need, right? Or we'll all wind up like Mom and Dad, truly dull old fuddy-duddies.

After a bit of argument, they decide to look more closely at the papers at the top of the chest. They discover facing them a letter, addressed: "To My Dear Children." And they read.

> Many of the papers here were left to me by my mother, and some were left to her by hers. I could not learn much from these letters and documents when I first inherited them at Grandmother's death, but with the years they have come to mean more and more. Some are still mysteries, and I hope that someday one of you will understand and learn from these. Believe me, their meaning will grow with the years, until in your last years, you will find as I have that they are just about all you have to go by.
>
> You are all grown up, and all have families of your own now. Still, you must learn to keep growing. The only way to do this, I have learned, is to ponder what is here, and to pass it on to your children with what you have learned in life.
>
> Your loving mother

The first child, as you have already concluded, was in tears by the time this was read. The second child was also moved, if a little skeptical. After all, their children were only cousins—seven of them, maybe more coming. They lived in different states. What would they have in common, even if the archaic idea of a family reunion would work, which seemed doubtful. The third child had the tact to keep silent. The matter seemed settled. And so they spent the rest of the day reading.

They read their great-grandfather's noble letter to his mother as he marched off to save the Union in 1862; the nineteen-year-old's style, drawn from Walter Scott, amazed them with its fluid eloquence and sophistication. His spelling was another matter. An uncle's letter from Korea was more like Hemingway in tone, tough and cheerful, better spelled, but less effective, they agreed. Then the material began to turn sour. Drafts of letters from Grandmother, whose silver-blue hair and sweet powder they all remembered so well, to a man who was not Grandfather. It was a letter of alarm, breaking off a liaison. The old lady was pregnant—and obviously not an old lady—and God was apparently speaking to her in no uncertain terms. She and her husband would love the child as their own. . . . That was mother, the date on the letter verified. More letters from throughout the family past, more embarrassment: betrayals, dishonesty, unpunished crimes. And they had hardly made a dent in the material.

The second child saw a great opportunity. "This is terrible stuff! I don't want to look at any more. We come from evil stock, like in Hawthorne or something. Let's sell what has value and burn the personal papers and never tell anyone." The third child readily agreed to burn the personal papers, but wanted to keep the clothes and funny hats because they were ridiculous. The first child, obviously the most shaken of all, was quiet at first but then came forward insistently. We owe a debt to the family, such as it is; if we suppress who we are, what can we ever become?

I honestly don't know how it came out.

It takes no special insight to realize that this commonplace dispute is an allegory of the current historiography of rhetoric. The first child, the faithful, steadfast one, is the traditional historian, with a clear preference for the classical "strand." The purpose of history is to monumentalize, to create a museum so that the heritage will not be lost. This is not to say that the tradition is sacrosanct nor that it is put out of reach in glass cases. On the contrary, the museum is to be a family, "hands-on" sort of place, especially aimed at the kids. Nevertheless, rhetoric sometimes seems out of place in such a history of rhetoric. To take an outstanding example, George Kennedy's classic *Art of Persuasion in Greece* is an antirhetorical history of rhetoric. The author is at pains to suppress any voice of his own. In place of a conclusion, he offers us an appendix, the "Introduction to 'On the ancient orators' by Dionysius of Halicarnassus." This begins by expressing precisely the "gratitude" Kennedy, as first child, would have us feel; yet the cited Dionysius goes on to state that his real goal is not a passive thanksgiving but an active inquiry into how his subject may become still stronger. He closes his introduction (which, you will recall, is the actual end of Kennedy's book) with the phrase "the time has come to turn to the real matter at hand" (Kennedy 1963, 340). What is introductory for Dionysius is conclusive for Kennedy, a neat piece of ventriloquism that is characteristic of his book as a whole. It is a certain historical voice. All the voices in Kennedy's book seem to come from the sources themselves. *They* speak; the authority is theirs, not the author's. Reverence, indeed!

I wonder, however, whether our first child may not be masking a certain hostility in this self-effacing rhetoric. The epigraph of the book is "We are freed from rhetoric only by the study of its history." I find no evidence of irony here. The faithful offspring has an oedipal ambivalence, a yearning for freedom from the "art of persuasion." He lets others persuade for him. His faith in the tradition is a sort of faithfulness to its authors, but he claims no authority that is not first theirs. Has their message, whatever it be, been killed with respect? Most tellingly of all, his presentation of their work avoids the texts almost entirely. The rhetoricians, it seems, have no rhetoric worth examining through a close and patient reading. The standard tactics of the most antirhetorical intellectual historian—paraphrase, summary, and survey—do the trick. What is persuasive (and valuable, to be sure) in Kennedy's *Art of Persuasion* is the freedom from rhetoric that is its stated goal.

The second child, we recall, had other things to do, different aims and allegiances from the first, goals that had nothing to do with the family legacy. With the awful revelations that resulted from studying the family papers, after all, one can hardly say who is legitimately family. *Our* differences from *them,* our putative ancestors, should be firmly established. We are in a position to know and to judge. Is this not James Berlin, a historian who begins with a sweeping rejection of the very concept of descent and of the great individuals who inhabit official family genealogies? Following Foucault, who followed Nietzsche, Berlin champions a carnivalized genealogy that undermines a series of "traditional" stances. Rhetorics, like families in Gothic romances, are infected with blood guilts. Origins determine value, and are usually as tainted as the lineage of our three aforementioned friends. Thus, "to write rhetorical history in a way that valorizes Aristotelian rhetoric, for example, may be to encourage in the writing classroom an ideology originating in an agrarian-mercantile economy that relied on slavery" (Berlin 1987a, 49–50).

By the same token, the historian of rhetoric must identify with the losers as well as the winners, the Sophists as well as the Platos and Aristotles. The logic goes something like this. Dominant rhetorics tend to express dominant social forces. Repressed rhetorics, the losers, tend to represent repressed or oppositional social forces. Since all known societies have been based upon oppression of one sort or another, identification with repressed rhetorics offers a pretty decent guide to being on the side of the angels. Well . . . Identifying with the rhetoric of Mithra, forcibly displayed by Christianity, may be no easier than identifying with the rhetoric of the Nazis and other losers, but will it be worth the trouble? All losers, I mean to say, are not as lovable as the Chicago Cubs. Because history will always award the laurel to the wicked, it is a perfectly reliable guide to activity in this world, we are told. Hegel has been set right-side up. The last shall be first.

Consistently, this demystified position shows little respect for the power of language; as an "ideological state apparatus," it seems instrumental all the way, a case of your interests and your rhetoric versus my interests and my rhetoric. To be sure, when he speaks of the total vision that his dialectical approach to the history of rhetoric affords, Berlin immediately draws back, citing Adorno's caveat about the failure of all totalization. His concern, however, is with the "unreliability of our evidence," not the nature of linguistic representations (Berlin, 59). Although his entire view of history, with winners, losers, and so forth, is drawn rather obviously with a "master template," we are urged to resist all temptations to totalizing systems. In small ways, however, Berlin's prose demonstrates how something can slip through the cracks. When, for example, Berlin writes about "bourgeois" historiographers as opposed to those on "the left," the nonparallelism of the antithesis surfaces; he is unwilling to place the former on the right and unable to find a class appropriate to the latter. If we consider Kenneth Burke's crack that Marx's theory of class was actually a theory of classification, the strains on both become apparent here.

It is, of course, always easy to pick at matters of detail in this or any work. Berlin, after all, is unquestionably correct when he notes that there are always competing rhetorics, that these rhetorics may represent competing interests, and that a presentation of the rhetorical "strand of meaning" as a single thread is fashioned with a particular goal in mind, just as, Berlin confesses, his own differentiating genealogy has a particular ideological goal in mind. All forms of historicization, and their number is legion, mythologize their subjects, either by showing how unnatural a discursive system is in order to transform it, as in the case of Marx, or to show how adequately it conforms to the "order of things," as with Ranke or John Quincy Adams (White 1978, 103–4). If Kennedy finds *rhetoric* burdensome, for Berlin it is *history* that weighs upon us like an alp. He believes that a proliferation of positions will best lead to assent for this ideology of his historical work. When we understand the world, we shall want to change it. If only it were so! A proliferation of positions produces a proliferation of positions.

The third child can be none other than Victor Vitanza—the wise Socratic gadfly spritzing selzer water like Clarabel (Vitanza 1987a 41–66; 1987b, 63–125). Vitanza wants us to begin every discourse, at least implicitly, with a proem that must go something like this, if I am not mistaken.

> Accustomed as we rhetoricians are to public speaking, we all know that discourse is biased to its roots, and that reason and coherence are ideological tools long since unmasked, and that any historical object lacks a necessary form (being only one among any number of others that could be fashioned and presented), and that all historical subjects are equally imbricated in a series of rhetorics of class and profession and nation and so forth, and that both time-organized narrative and serially organized analyses are both traditional forms that have been shown repeatedly to contain their own hidden ideological agendas, and that the sense of cause or explanation in history is part of a discredited drive to mastery/mystery that undermines and violates that sense of real freedom that a rhetorical sense of language gives us, *so consequently* the following discourse can be nothing other than a free-style

performance based insofar as possible upon a constant recognition of its own baselessness. So listen closely!! And "go and do thou likewise."

To be sure, this set of protocols (which I, not Vitanza, have phrased above) touches all the Gorgianic bases, responds to all the current miseries of the rhetorical tradition, while heralding the coming splendors of a "Third Sophistic." Most of the strictures are justified. As so often happens, what passes for clowning is nothing more than following rigorously the strictly logical consequences of quite serious notions.

If I am correct in maintaining that every use of language exacts a cost, however, the costs incurred by this subversive sort of discourse are steep. First, it assumes a rhetorically questionable stance, if rhetoric is to retain any connection with the means of persuasion. All that is at stake in such a performance is the quality of the performer. Since nothing follows (the concept of "following" invoking sequentially ideological thinking), it is also a hard act to follow, in both senses of the phrase. Theoretically, it always starts in the same place and has nowhere to go. Argumentatively, it depends utterly on opponents (usually made of straw) whose bases for discourse have been dismissed in advance. If any audience were to listen to such an orator with nods of affirmation, it would be a nightmare for him.

Second, precisely like the dogmatic discourses it counters, this sub/versive rhetoric becomes a rule-governed antinomianism not unlike that of the Puritans. Such hectoring in this "let-it-all-hang-out" discourse! And after the ground-clearing is done, what remains as the tail end of the discourse is a path so narrowly defined, so unexemplified, that one can hardly perceive it, let alone walk it. It seems a tightrope over a chasm that no one has yet conquered, for heroes only, like Victor Vitanza. Evel Knievel as historian of rhetoric! Virtuosity is magnificent to watch and bracing to read; if we tell the truth, it must always be welcome in a sea of academic dreariness. Still, we should not fail to note that, whatever its flaws, the victorious antirhetorical professionalism of the mid-nineteenth-century historiography won out because it made it possible for scholars of very limited gifts to make usable (or, as historians like to say, "solid") contributions to the enterprise. Rankean history was not all built by masters like Ranke. Nor were all Ciceronians geniuses like Cicero. A program needs a method; charismatic sub/version, although it can be imitated, cannot be built upon.

Let me make clear that I have cited these three particular authors precisely because I greatly admire their work and have learned from each of them. My point is simply that *all uses of language exact a price, and trying to avoid paying the price may be very expensive indeed.* The allegory of the three children has, in fact, led me into paths of iniquity. How quickly we categorize! Is it Aristotle who leads even the most self-conscious historian of rhetoric into *divisios:* traditional, revisionary, sub/versive; or classical, expressionist, epistemic, and so forth? Ironically, the more one assumes the sophistic posture, in order to celebrate the materiality of language, to stress independence from any preexisting reality, and to play with words in as unconstrained a manner as seems prudent, the more one depends for authority on categorical lists of *kinds* of rhetoric, and on evidence of bibliographical mastery, once again in the form of lists of works cited, names dropped. In this there is little of the joy of the epic catalogs of Homer such as the catalog of ships in the *Iliad,* which assures his hearers of the fullness of the world in a great series, nor the carnival of the Rabelaisian list, which mocks its contents and the discourse they authorize by violating any known principles of order and categorization. No, the categories of the manifestoes for the new histories of rhetoric are serious and instrumental. They create allegorical persons to be fleshed out and manipulated, persons not of straw, but recognizable and usefully derived from the discourse under discussion. If this procedure creates a sense of mastery, albeit only within one's own treatise, the enormous bibliography has the same purpose, to establish authority through mastery.

There is nothing wrong with this. It is a characteristic of no one party in this debate; all who venture into the writing of histories must play the game and buy a ticket. It comes with the territory. Historians do it all the time to render manageable the chaos of forms that face them. The end is control and categorization: the means is paraphrase. Let us look at an example from Jacqueline de Romilly's splendid lectures on *Magic and Rhetoric in Ancient Greece.*

> What Isocrates called "philosophy," which meant learning how to be a reasonable and useful citizen, consisted, for him, in learning how to speak well. For Plato, we have the reverse: what he calls "rhetoric" (which does not yet exist) was but a low and second-rate offspring of philosophy, which meant learning the truth by means of dialectic. Both words (*rhetoric* and *philosophy*)

> have changed level. Isocrates gives a lower meaning to philosophy in order to make it synonymous to rhetoric; Plato gives a higher meaning to rhetoric in order to bring it nearer to philosophy. (De Romilly 1975, 51–52)

A telling historical point, this passage is also a showpiece of rhetoric, employing as it does an antithesis developed into a chiasmus built upon the common topic of high/low degree. De Romilly's rhetoric shows more technique than magic—it cannot stir our souls or passions—but that is her point: to codify the enchantment of speech is to create a *dis*enchanted discourse, even if the effects are magical. She has formed pictures of Isocrates and of Plato that are consistent and persuasive, then demonstrated how those images may be compared, once they have been read aright: once, that is, she has gotten them straightened out. Given these identities, her account as I have excerpted it could hardly have turned out differently. It need only be well told. A certain sort of reading, aimed at accurate paraphrase and plausible categories, makes for an inevitable sense of history. However, the one thing Mme. de Romilly has ignored in her work, and she is not alone in this, is her *subject,* insofar as that subject is a rhetoric of texts. While she analyzes the precise uses of key words and metaphors, her purpose is always to discover the intent of her authors, who are in complete control of their language. It is this assumption that makes it possible for her to pin them down like butterflies, "getting the story straight."

Now, Dominick LaCapra has suggested that "historians are professionally taught not to read." Please notice the position of the "not." He doesn't maintain that they are not taught to read well or thoroughly through some professional negligence; on the contrary, the professionalization of historians is an active and demanding regimen, which usually has as its goal a mode of reading that absolutely facilitates their difficult work. This mode of reading sees a text as a document, a piece of information in a mass of knowledge, a thread in a "strand of meaning" that must be untangled, straightened out. To do this, the first step, almost inevitably, is to repress the textuality itself, to eliminate the rhetorical joker from the deck (LaCapra 1983, 339).

Rhetoricians pondering the writing of histories of rhetorics might want to consider such a charge. Your own past has made you suspicious of rhetoric itself in much the same way that modern historical discourse must repress its own historicity, its goal-oriented engagement in circumstance and discourse. The "Harvardization" of English departments, as Donald Stewart (1982) persuasively argued, marks the split that drove rhetoric from its traditional and proper home. It was Francis Child in Cambridge, with his focus on literary criticism, and not Fred Newton Scott of Ann Arbor, who set the agenda for most American colleges, beginning a trend so powerful that even continental adepts of structuralism and its wake lament that the profundities of their concepts are too easily absorbed and digested by the strong stomachs of American practical critics (see Gasché 1979, 177–216). What happened, it seems to me, is that reading conquered writing. What had been a productive mutual relationship between author and reader became *Consumer Reports*.

Learning to write new histories, histories worthy of the remarkable revival of rhetorical consciousness at the present moment, means above all, *to devise new ways of reading,* which will look at the texts as texts, not merely as documents, which will look for the "other" sources of historical discourse in constant tension with the evidence. What is called for, I think, is "getting the story crooked," looking into the various strands of meaning in a text in such a way as to make the categories, trends, and reliable identities of history a little less inevitable. James J. Murphy has pointed out that the rhetoric-based Roman educational system assumed that linguistic ability, *facilitas,* was one, whether for reading, speaking, writing, or hearing (Murphy 1982b, 6). I am not so sure this is any longer the case. The marginalization of American rhetoric by the belletristic, Harvardized forces of literary studies may have produced lingering antagonisms that serve rhetoric ill. To note that a semiological approach is limited to internal structures, while a semantic approach relates a text to the outside world, as a prominent rhetorician has done (Kinneavy 1982, 24), suggests, at least to me, that the real reality is out there, that the real sources are documents, and that a real history will find the story and get it straight. What else but rhetoric will make a claim for the "other" sources, and show a deeper respect for reality by reading texts in crooked ways?[2]

Reading, like writing, takes place first of all for a purpose. The straight story, the plausible pigeonholing paraphrase, makes it possible to handle large amounts of information, but the economics of reading are inexorable. Every gain in scope is won at the cost of the text. Straight readings are also rhetorical inventions, allegories of intention, reflecting a vision of the world that stresses our sense of mastery, our ability to recognize and represent the world. Richard Lanham has called this "Pastoral Humanism" (Lanham 1986, 138). We need this humanism for many reasons, not least of all because it and it alone makes possible our other activities as readers and writers. Historians always talk about their *sources,* and mean their documents, the evidence, what makes up the "strand of meaning" the past has left behind. There are, however, *other* sources than these, hidden sources of language and rhetoric for which we must look crookedly, a bit out of focus, in order to see what is familiar in a different way, in many different ways.

In what is still, after forty-five years, the best history of rhetoric known to me, Erich Auerbach's *Mimesis* (1953), one chapter seems quite apt for my consideration of the historiography of a venerable discourse like rhetoric. I am thinking of chapter 4 titled "Sicharius and Chramnesindus." As you may recall, in this chapter Auerbach considers a passage from the *History of the Franks* by then-bishop, now-saint, Gregory of Tours. The era is the middle 500s. The place is the Merovingian Frankish kingdom, in Gregory's own city of Tours, to be precise. The story Gregory has to tell is a nightmare episode of brutal, random violence, wholesale murders, and a complete lack of a civic or humane ethic. Even innocent cows are not spared! Families act like gangs, and the state, in the form of the Merovingian king, seems impossible to locate. The only force of order is Gregory's own episcopal authority and the wealth of the Church, which for a time can buy off the aggrieved parties, but in the end is itself powerless before the untamed impulses of these barbarians.

Auerbach reads this passage like a master. The breathless, simplified, almost childlike Latin that Gregory has been bequeathed by his education—the best to be had in post–Roman Gaul—has been invaded in its syntax by the crude language of the people, the proto-Romance vernacular, which is centuries away from a written form, but which is nevertheless the tongue that he must use as bishop in shepherding his flock toward peace and salvation. His written language itself, in its diction and syntax, is a struggle between the old and the new social worlds. Remember that "the Dark Ages . . . was a time when people read textbooks and thought they were literature" (Charles Horton Cooley, cited in Lanham 1974, vi). This fallen language, inadequate to any of the subleties available to the Latin historian of previous centuries, bespeaks the fallen world of Rome and its imperium. And yet, Auerbach asserts, the tone of Gregory is a positive, almost an optimistic, one, compared with that of Ammianus Marcellinus, whose history had recorded similar civil unrest in Rome two centuries earlier. Ammianus's overloaded Latin style, in contrast to that of Gregory, knows too much, is swamped with information. The sentences are snake-like monsters, so complicated and strung with clauses as to be virtually impenetrable. The late Empire was so large, so complex, so sophisticated, that any statement was obliged to take it all into account. Compared to this, Gregory's style is Dick-Jane-and-Spot, just as his vision of the world is generally limited to a local, a spot, perspective.

My fondness and respect for this chapter comes from a sense I have as a reader and a student of historical writing that it must contain an implicit image of Auerbach himself, and may reflect on his own circumstances as the historian of realistic rhetoric since the Old Testament. I have a hunch, for which I can offer no documentary evidence whatever, that this chapter had a personal meaning for him; if not, I, at least, can suggest one. The story of the writing of *Mimesis* is well known. Auerbach, one of the foremost Romance philologists in Germany, was displaced by World War II. He found himself in Istanbul, outside the world of the Western culture that he exemplified and professed, and lacking the sort of research facilities necessary to work in the philological tradition. As he tells the story, Auerbach undertook his momentous task under peculiar circumstances, and these circumstances shaped *Mimesis*. Rather than a library-derived treatise on treatises, taking into account the enormous complexity of the philological tradition, Auerbach wrote the history of a number of selected passages from a number of selected texts. In so doing, he produced a work of such scope that it has not been challenged in four decades. It threatens to become a classic. Historiographical progress does not take place through the amassing and ordering of an ever-broader mass of information, or ever-more-refined theories of social or political development. Historical discourse progresses, if that is the right word, by producing classics, in all their individuality and, often, wrongness.

What has this to do with Gregory of Tours? Isn't Auerbach an old traditionalist, praising representationalism, insisting that realism only comes into its own when Christianity makes possible a merger of high moral meaning and everyday life? Doesn't his philosophy of history follow a suspiciously Hegelian course? Wasn't this philological-historical tradition the ball and chain from which the New Critics liberated us? And isn't the canon that *Mimesis* celebrates daily attacked as a wicked plot, reeking with all sorts of fill-in-the-blank "centricities." Sure. It is all true. Nevertheless, it is Auerbach's radicalism, his self-conscious barbarism, that I see in this text. *His* world, the world of the cosmopolitan European, the German scholar of the Romance languages, their change in time, and of the history of their speakers, had collapsed with the Nazis. *His* culture, broad and universal in a sense that is not only unavailable to us today but that is sometimes a subject of scorn, was shattered, sending his peers, Ernst Robert Curtius, Karl Vossler, and Leo Spitzer, into exile. *His* book, which seems to its admirers a miracle of sensitive learning, was in a sense a barbarism, a recognition that in a fallen world the old standards are impossible and can never be regained.

Old Gregory also knew that his *History of the Franks* could never match the great Latin histories, either as reports of momentous events or as great rhetoric. The tale of Sicharius and Chramnesindus is of no world historical importance, being little more than murderous local unrest in very violent times; no Roman historian, Auerbach tells us, would have bothered with it because it told them nothing about what mattered. Gregory might have felt small indeed, pondering the ruins around him, above all the human ruins, devoid of any civic sense. But Gregory did not feel this way. Unlike his predecessor Ammianus, both historically and textually in Auerbach's book, Gregory was living after the fall. The agony was over, the worst had happened, there was nothing more to be feared. It was, or seemed, as bad as it could get. And with this realization, a huge weight was lifted from the shoulders of the few educated, responsible individuals of this "dark age." The ruins were to be picked up again, and rebuilt on better terms; this was ever so much less depressing than trying to hold things up just a little longer. The tradeoff, quite frankly, was barbarism, the brain-smashing warriors—Sicharius, Austrighiselus, Chramnesindus—whose very names are barbarisms, despite their Latin endings. Gregory, his eye on a vision of the future that would come to pass, the Christian Middle Ages, had no reason for despair. It was a necessary fall, a fortunate fall, like the first Fall, the big one. Auerbach must have noticed the similarities of his position to that of Gregory. He chose to reread an unimportant passage in a little-read text of a dark age, and found a great deal. He found his evidence in the language, reading crookedly, because in his exiled condition, it was all he had to go on.

Why should I see Auerbach's *Mimesis* as a history of rhetoric?

What does a history of rhetoric look like today? I use the term "today" advisedly, since the book was published when I was only two years old, but given the longevity of self-conscious rhetorical discourse (which is my cowardly way of avoiding speaking of the "rhetorical tradition"), taking too short a view is a distinct tactical mistake. The subtitle of this book says, "The Representation of Reality in Western Literature." Not very promising, on first glance. Representation is the traditional domain of poetics; and even if poetics and rhetoric have become rather conflated of late, the term must remain suspect as a rhetorical one. "Literature," of course, is worse still, but *reality* is the catastrophe. Rhetoric and reality, as everyone knows, are oil and water; rhetoric is precisely the existential projection of our inability to apprehend reality. If we had reality, if we could hold it and share it, why would we need rhetoric at all? Or history?

We cannot have reality, but we can *claim* it and we do claim it, with rhetoric. Rhetoric is the political discourse, always, because it is our only claim against reality. It is always an appeal to authority and a bid for authority. Since history is the discourse that claims, among all the others, to represent the reality of human affairs, the submersion of rhetoric, its ostensible disappearance into the underground of discourse, coincides with the crisis of authority that gave rise to modern historical discourse. The French Revolution, or rather, the great Atlantic Revolutions of the eighteenth century, create a situation in which a fatherless society, "headless," as Linda Orr has put it, faced the problem of historical representations as a problem of political representation, a family struggle (Orr 1990).

Why undertake writing the histories of rhetorics? To serve the past with gratitude, respect, and, perhaps, hope for the resurrection? To right the wrongs of past exclusions (righting them by writing them) and afford the unspoken a belated voice? To exercise a jolly and nimble will to power? Our three children are with us again, haggling over the family archive. In the remote chance that you are curious, they won't kill one another, but neither will any of them be converted, not in this life anyway. Still, they are a family.

The "strand of meaning," which is the rhetorical tradition, has no meaning until it has been lent a form by the historian. Which form? Which reality? One answer, I think, is found in a general way in an old definition of rhetoric itself: to find "in a given case, the available means of persuasion." Seen large, historical discourse is not the arbiter of politics, society, culture, or righteousness. To look to history for these things, as many people still do, is to be continuously amazed and disappointed with the endless procession of oedipal revisionisms and changes of direction. The only purpose the discourse of history can legitimately claim is to designate and transform the field of evidence into *as many persuasive models as can possibly be fashioned;* history tests the rhetorical and creative foundations of the culture (White 1978, 92; 1987, 45).

So, please, whatever you do, remember that you are rhetoricians first. After all, historians today have more to learn from the rhetoricians than the rhetoricians have to learn from the historians.

Notes

1. Peter Novick's comprehensive and brilliant book (1988) chronicles the "collapse of comity" in historical discourse, leading to the point at which there is no authoritative body to adjudicate matters of basic definitions.

2. We should note here Richard Lanham's reference to "a 'rhetorical' reality always, in one way or another, standing opposite the 'serious,' 'literate' reality of the stable central self, the 'soul' that finds its external counterpart in a really real society really out there for realistic fictionists to describe and tough-minded historians to record *wie es eigentlich gewesen,* as it really happened" (Lanham 1986, 135).

3

Interpreting the Silent "Aryan Model" of Histories of Classical Rhetoric

Martin Bernal, Terry Eagleton, and the Politics of Rhetoric and Composition Studies

Kathleen Ethel Welch

In this essay on the historicizing of rhetoric, I begin an interpretation of Terry Eagleton's "A Small History of Rhetoric," a breathless construction of rhetoric that occurs in his book *Walter Benjamin: Or Towards a Revolutionary Criticism* (1981), by reading it across Martin Bernal's historicizing of ancient Greece in *Black Athena: The Afroasiatic Roots of Western Civilization,* vol. I, *The Fabrication of Ancient Greece, 1785–1985* (1987). The hermeneutic principle with which I approach Eagleton's historicizing of rhetoric is Bernal's Revised Ancient Model, a way of historicizing that offers unusual potential in overcoming tacitly racist constructions in many areas of language studies. I want to place in dialectical juxtaposition the Eagleton historicizing (a piece that lies embedded in a larger text on revolutionary criticism) and portions of the first volume of Bernal's projected multivolume work. (Volume 2 of *Black Athena* was published in 1991 with the subtitle *The Archaeological and Documentary Evidence.*) My position as a white, female North American places me in some hermeneutic situations that are obvious to many readers but not at all apparent to other readers. "White" North Americans are not ordinarily discussed as "raced"; this group's colors, in other words, are made invisible and assumed frequently to be the "norm" against which other colors, shades, or hues are arbitrarily measured, often unconsciously.[1] This situation places me in the tenuous hermeneutic situation of desiring to resist the further colonizing of African cultures, a hermeneutic strategy with which we are all familiar. The prose style I choose, part of any hermeneutic, is that of the academic narrative, privileging logos with references to "appropriate" scholarship; however, at the same time I try to rob logos (in the limiting sense of traditionally Western "logic"[2]) of some of its usually unquestioned power. I would place my rhetorical/compositional/historicist stance, then, somewhere between the scientific prose of a journal such as *Research in the Teaching of English* and the call to action Fredric Jameson writes with in *The Political Unconscious,* a book he begins by exclaiming "Always historicize" (1981, 9) and qualifies by explaining that the historicist does not necessarily have to cite every text written on the subject at hand. My placement does not fit between these categories because I write also as a woman working in an academy that continues to marginalize groups de facto (although not de jure) according to race, gender, and class.[3] As an academic, I am writing from the socioeconomic comfort of the middle class.

Embedded in the second half of Eagleton's book, between sections called "Marxist Criticism" and "On Textuality," appears "A Small History of Rhetoric," the title of which does not appear in the text but in the Table of Contents. The first five pages of this history construct classical rhetoric, while the subsequent seven pages read rhetorical chronology as the diminution of the social power that defined rhetoric in the seven hundred years from, in Eagleton's construction, Corax in the fifth century B.C.E. to Quintilian in the second century A.D., or what is known both unconventionally and conventionally as classical rhetoric. Eagleton opens his historicizing of rhetoric this way:

> A political literary criticism is not the invention of Marxists. On the contrary, it is one of the oldest, most venerable forms of literary criticism we know. The most widespread early criticism on historical record was not, in our sense, "aesthetic": it was a mode of what we would now call "discourse theory", devoted to analysing the material effects of particular uses of language in particular social conjunctures. It was a highly elaborate theory of specific signifying practices. . . . Its intention, quite consciously, was systematically to theorize the articulations of discourse and power, and to do so in the name of political practice: to enrich

> the political effectivity of signification. The name of this form of criticism was rhetoric. (1981, 101)

This construction of classical rhetoric remains a deeply refreshing one for writers frequently spoonfed the pablum that Greek and Roman classical cultures are wholesome, innocuous, and essential. These familiar beliefs promote the "fount" metaphor in a traditional presentation and reception of so-called Western civilization, or, more specifically, in the liberal arts tradition. It is as common in our own late twentieth-century cultures as the air we breathe; and it is just as invisible and powerful. Eagleton's appropriation of this material as a center of power remains an important text in the continuing dialectic of how academic writers construct the past, and in this case the past of language and power, and how we communicate these interpretations in our scholarly work and in our work as teachers.

At least two contexts dominate Eagleton's construction of rhetoric in general and classical rhetoric in particular. The first context presents some of the writings of Walter Benjamin and his response to 1930s' European fascism. The second context relies on Benjamin as a harbinger for the establishment of a revolutionary criticism. Eagleton continues Benjamin's work, which was shortened by the ideological circumstances that led to his early death. "A Small History of Rhetoric" occurs as the second of six sections in the second half, "Towards a Revolutionary Criticism." This early placement by Eagleton is central to his strategy of energizing parts of the language past that apply to our own discourse situation, even though conventionally the same material has been pablumized, an issue that Eagleton has been instrumental in teaching us, as his *Literary Theory: An Introduction* (1983) illustrates.

"The Rhetoricians' Wrangling"

A symptomatic reading of some of Eagleton's constructions in "A Short History of Rhetoric" might yield some helpful subtextual designs. For example, his designation of classical rhetoric as the "cradle of ancient rhetoric" (1981, 104) or his revision of Aristotle's definition of rhetoric to "the discovery of possible means of persuasion with regard to any subject whatever" (103) rather than the ability or faculty to discover in the particular case the available means of persuasion (the definition that was written down—perhaps by students—and so codified and the one readers can point to with the authority of the printed word) lead to some textual problems in Eagleton's construction. However, these blips that enter Eagleton's narrative can be regarded or disregarded as the factual nonthoroughness Jameson writes about and sometimes practices.

The narrative whole that Eagleton builds in this historicizing comprises a narrative of rhetoric that has a beginning, a middle, and an end. The beginning occurs with Corax in Sicily, divorced from his conventional twin/student Tisias (101). The middle of Eagleton's story centers on the eighteenth-century continuing "wrangling," which he interprets as the battle between morality in rhetoric and persuasion toward any ends whatsoever. The ending of Eagleton's story brings attention to the contradiction faced by academics now: "Universities are now precisely such sites of contradiction: the conditions required for them to reproduce ruling-class skills and ideologies are also in part those which allow them to produce a socialist critique" (109).

More powerful in Eagleton's construction of rhetoric would be a rewriting of his interpretation using the definitional categories established by Bernal (1987), categories that were not of course available to Eagleton when he wrote the Benjamin book. Volume 1 of *Black Athena* (the first of four projected volumes by Bernal on, among other things, the historicizing of ancient Greek cultures) changes the possibilities with which Eagleton was working. We can now reinterpret Eagleton's important historicizing of rhetoric as part of a revolutionary critique with the new construction that Bernal has provided. We can reread Eagleton more thoroughly and take fuller account of and action against the "fount" concept of so-called Western civilization. The fount of Western civilization has been the dead metaphor of choice among the conservatives taken to task by Bernal and Eagleton. Bernal's work gives us compelling evidence with which to refute this formative metaphor whose literal level is rarely analyzed.

Taking the Pulse of the Liberal Arts

Bernal dives deeply into pre-"golden age" Greek history (2100–1100 B.C.E.) and the reception of narratives already very old for Athenians of the dominant culture in, say, fifth and fourth century B.C.E. Athens. Bernal, who comes at this material as a scholar in Chinese studies working in a department of government (in other words, as a disciplinary outsider, a point he emphasizes), establishes two models (he does not want to use the word *paradigm*) for the construction of the sanctified Greece that many of us learned to base interpretations on or have been conditioned to accept as "factual" even if we resisted it as "truth." The first model he calls "the Ancient Model," the one that fifth and fourth century B.C.E. people relied on for their own constructions. Bernal writes:

> *Black Athena* is essentially concerned with the Egyptian and Semitic roles in the formation of Greece in the Middle and Late Bronze Age. . . . The first volume of *Black Athena* is concerned with the development of the Ancient and Aryan Models, and the first chapter, "The Ancient Model in Antiquity," treats the attitudes of Greeks in the Classical and Hellenistic periods to their distant past. It considers the writings of authors who affirmed the Ancient Model, referred to Egyptian colonies in Thebes and Athens, and gave details of the Egyptian conquest of the Argolid and the Phoenician foundation of Thebes. I discuss the claims made by various 19th- and 20th-century "source critics" that the Ancient Model was concocted only in the 5th century BC, and I cite iconographic evidence and a number of earlier references to demonstrate the scheme existed several centuries earlier. (1987, 22)

Bernal's second model, the Aryan Model, appeared in the eighteenth century and gained particular power in the nineteenth. Bernal writes:

> Since the 1840s Indo-European philology, or study of the relationships between languages, has been at the heart of the Aryan Model. Then, as now, Indo-Europeanists and Greek philologists have been extraordinarily reluctant to see any connections between Greek—on the one hand—and Egyptian and semitic, the two major non-Indo-European languages of the Ancient East Mediterranean, on the other. (4)

Bernal sets forth as "plausible" the idea that Egyptian and Semitic aspects of pre–"golden age" Greece were suppressed because of ideological agendas that connected to a kind of academic-pop-faux-anthropologic-scientific stance among the historians who, according to Bernal, dispensed with the Ancient Model and bequeathed truth on the Aryan Model. Bernal contends that the "fundamental bases of 'Western Civilization' " have been formed by what he calls "racism" and "continental chauvinism" (2). He finds that the two hundred years of the presentation of "Western Civilization" from 1785 to 1985 came about because of the reluctance to see the "mixture of native Europeans and colonizing Africans and Semites" (2).

For those readers conditioned to accept the liberalism of academic writers since the United States domestic revolutions of the 1960s (and earlier), Bernal's assertion and his subsequent laborious setting forth of his thesis of racism in familiar constructions of Western civilization create discomfort and frequently resistance. Matthew Arnold has, of course, been the usually unacknowledged source of the arid "best that has been produced in literature" and the famous touchstone metaphor.[4] Bernal, who devotes an entire section to "The Arnolds" (347–50), shows that Matthew Arnold's own "sweetness and light" rest partly on racist assumptions. Citing texts that frequently do not appear in curricula in English departments (units that appear to revere Arnold's "best ever" category), Bernal writes:

> The contrasts between Thomas and Matthew Arnold provide an instructive example of the changes that were taking place in English racism in the 19th century. Dr. Thomas Arnold was preoccupied in the 1820s and 30s with the conflicts between Teuton and Gael—including Gallo-Roman—and notably those between the English and the French and Irish. He was proud to be known as "that Teuton of Teutons, the Celt-hating Dr. Arnold." His son Matthew in the 1850s, 60s, and 70s favoured both the Irish and the French, believing that he had transcended his father's narrow-mindedness. Fully aware of linguistic advances, he was a systematic supporter of Indo-Europeans and Aryans. He loved them all. (347)

Bernal recasts characters familiar to people trained in what Richard Ohmann (1976) calls "literary chronology." Using Victor J. Vitanza's construction (1987b), Bernal would appear in the Sub/Versive category because he reconstructs the bases of traditional and revisionary rhetorics, the other two categories Vitanza establishes for the historicizing of rhetoric.

Bernal subverts partly in the ways we have come to expect, by looking at suppressed ideological/rhetorical stances. In addition, he examines the ancient reception and then the 1785–1985 reception of the one thousand years from 2100 to 1100 B.C.E. He examines "Greek cultural borrowings from Egypt and the Levant in the 2nd millennium BC." (17)

It is useful to focus on Bernal's analysis of the Arnolds, particularly Matthew Arnold, whose pedagogical influence in the discipline of English continues unabated. "On the Study of Celtic Literature" is one text in which Arnold establishes cause-and-effect relationships between racial characteristics and national literatures. For example, the Germans are said to be great poets who have no "style." Similarly, the Celts have a lot of "style" (1904, 107–111).

Bernal, as the outsider he declares himself to be, goes to work with the knowledge of philology, languages, dialects, and the disciplines that have transmitted this knowledge. Few people in any discipline have the training with which Bernal works. He blasts open the prison bars of disciplinarity from within. Whether or not traditional classicists or philologists (the latter frequently found among traditionalists in departments of English, cordoned off into their own groups) will be changed by Bernal's research will be discussed later. My focus is the reception that Bernal's work will receive in what is arguably the most powerful subdiscipline in the discipline of English, rhetoric and composition studies. Bernal compels people working in the so-called humanities to take the pulse of the liberal arts tradition that declares the Europe whose "source" or "fount" is said to be a "purified" Greek and Roman ancient beauty and light. He has changed the nature of dialogue/dialectic that rhetoric and composition writers and teachers have with this weighty past, whether it is mentioned explicitly or more powerfully maintained as an invisible presence.

We must wait to see if Eagleton will rewrite his breathless history of rhetoric after considering Bernal's plausibilities. If Bernal's thesis is taken up by enough writers and teachers, if radical pedagogy will actually treat it, then the cloying wholesomeness of the Heritage School of classical rhetoric[5] and of other subdisciplines can become part of inert history (texts treated as valuable commodities, or as attractive antiques) rather than a part of its formative present. The problem with wholesome historicizing is that no one really takes it seriously. Pablum is dull.

A Map for Redrafting by Eagleton Relying on Bernal

What would happen if Eagleton rewrote "A Short History of Rhetoric" with the power that Bernal has given us to combat tacit racist constructions that help to maintain the racist status quo in U.S. culture? I will suggest three possibilities.

First, Eagleton could marshal Bernal's evidence and his ethos as a reputable scholar who has expertise in many dialects (that is, his scholarly ethos is established in "nonwestern" studies). Bernal's book is being taken seriously by many classicists, as a recent special issue of the journal *Arethusa* demonstrates. In "The Challenge of Black Athena," scholars from various related fields analyze Bernal's book from different points of view and from different disciplinary stances. Molly Meyerowitz Levine, the editor of the issue, writes:

> This special volume of *Arethusa* is both a record and an extension of "The Challenge of Black Athena: The Classicists' Response," an interdisciplinary dialogue which was first presented as the presidential panel of the 120th meeting of the American Philological Association in Baltimore, 1989 . . . this volume offers a preliminary response to the case against classics and classicists set forth in Martin Bernal's *Black Athena* . . . [in which] Professor Bernal, scholar of Chinese history and government, professor of New Eastern Studies, and self-avowed "outsider," lays serious and sweeping charges against what he sees as the "classics establishment," the "insiders," i.e., the natural constituency of both the APA and this journal. We, it is claimed, owing to residual racism, anti-Semitism, sheer scholarly inertia, and/or exaggerated respect for authority, have suppressed or ignored the weight of what Professor Bernal considers to be overwhelming evidence for substantial semitic and Egyptian roles in the development of Greek language civilization. (7)

Some traditional classicists are responding, and responding with great persuasive power, as this volume indicates repeatedly. The effect that Bernal's challenge will have on pedagogy will take longer to gauge.[6]

A second question that Eagleton could engage for the redrafting that I recommend for "A Short History of Rhetoric" is the role that disciplines play in the formation of knowledge in the United States. Bernal points out that disciplines create as well as transmit our constructions of knowledge. Ample and rich research in rhetoric and composition studies could strengthen Eagleton's thesis.[7] How we know what we know is determined largely by the construction of disciplines in higher education, a Germanic model that acted as a powerful reformer and has also acted as a powerful maintainer of the intellectual status quo.

Third, Eagleton could examine his own language in his brief history. The cradle metaphor is probably one he would like to delete, one surmises from reading his other work. In addition, a rethinking of the presentation of eighteenth-century rhetoric could be done with the growing research in that field.

Fourth, Eagleton could benefit from Bernal's work by examining his own distinction between the "literary" and the "rhetorical." Certainly Eagleton's explication of various interpretations of the literary in *Literary Theory* (1983) and elsewhere are powerful constructions. But what if Eagleton more self-consciously joined the intrepretive community of rhetoric and composition scholars and continued to acknowledge, as he does so effectively in "A Short History of Rhetoric," the continuing power of rhetoric and, to go further, include composition in his constructions?

I close with two current historicizers who respond in the inclusive spirit that Bernal presents as a rhetorical stance toward the not-too-golden golden age of Greece. They are James Comas (1990) and Edward Said (1979). Comas writes on a topic closely related to issues in historiography: "It might be best to take *theory* as referring, today, not only to the epistemological emphasis of traditional theory or to the challenges of the new 'theory,' but to the site of a struggle between the two attitudes toward knowledge (and the political values behind them)" (7). Said writes: "Ideas, cultures, and histories cannot seriously be understood or studied without their force, or more precisely their configurations of power, also being studied" (5). Both Comas and Said recognize and acknowledge, as Bernal and Eagleton do, that historicizing must act as a force in shaping general perceptions and not only professional perceptions within the academy. The inclusion of Africans in the construction of ancient Greece changes the conceptual bases that the traditional liberal arts frequently work under and through. As the United States undergoes self scrutiny about the failures of education (conceded for different reasons by the lefts, the rights, and the middles of American cultures), the integration of Bernal's shattering but also constructive presentations offer all of us in the academy a powerful new way to attack racism where it may be least suspected of residing: in the disciplines that have transmitted what we know and how we know and, at least in the discipline of English and probably in other fields as well, continue to bind us to ethically bankrupt ways of transmitting to our students what and how we know. The discipline of English continues to thrive on elitism, nostalgia for various pasts that I believe never existed, and a crusty Arnoldian stance that states at every turn that we, the holders of the gates of the kingdom of Culture with a capital "C," are necessarily superior to everyone else. When the majority of the people working in English can say to ourselves that we are not a priestly caste busy with the guardianship of Culture, then we can continue the project that both Bernal and Eagleton have promoted so effectively. It is, perhaps, the kairotic moment to ask, after the union song: "Which side are you on?"

Notes

I thank the National Endowment for the Humanities for a summer stipend that enabled me to write the first draft of this essay. I also thank the University of Oklahoma Office of Research Administration for support.

1. "Color," of course, is given different meanings in different historical periods and cultures. See, for example, Finley (1973).

2. See Welch (1990) for a more detailed examination of the *pisteis* (*ethos*, *pathos*, and *logos*) and how they function in discourse.

3. See Davis (1981) for analysès of the intertwining of these issues and the maintenance of the status quo in virtually every area of culture. For a book-length discussion of women in ancient Greece, as well as a reading of traditional masculinist presentations of this group, see Keuls. A less persuasive but nevertheless important treatment occurs in Pomeroy. See also Nussbaum (1990) and Winkler (1990). Michele Wallace (1990a; 1990b) has discussed in numerous places the intertwining of gender and race. I agree with various other critics that all discussions of race and gender involve class issues. I focus in this essay on race issues as they are excavated by Bernal.

4. See Applebee's recent study (1989) of high school English curricula for an example of the canon problem as well as Robert Scholes's analysis (1985) of the Arnold-to-Frye critical canon that continues to dominate the thinking of many people in the discipline of English.

5. See Welch (1990), "The Heritage School of Classical Rhetoric in the United States," 3–67.

6. I incorporated Bernal's first volume into a graduate seminar called "Historicizing and Theorizing Classical Rhetoric and Composition Studies" in the spring of 1990. My experience with the book in the graduate rhetoric and composition course persuaded me that Bernal's work can act as a powerful basis for a reexamination of unspoken and unacknowledged premises about the nature of classical rhetoric. Bernal offers teachers and students ways to rehistoricize classical rhetoric and composition studies by including the forma-

tive and crucial participation of African cultures. This theoretical basis for an opening up of traditionally "purified"-race (that is, monolithically white) presentations of classical rhetoric is a powerful way of demonstrating the centrality of African cultures in the received canons of various disciplines. See Ong (1982) and Welch (1990). The hierarchy that print has enjoyed over sound (one kind of literacy over one kind of orality) has led to the marginalization of, in the United States, African-American aspects of our cultures and Native American aspects of our cultures. See *Harper American Literature*, vol. I (1987), for an outstanding example of a standard literary anthology for the so-called first half of the "American literature survey" course, a text that demonstrates the centrality of oral texts in constructions of United States writing history. A comparison of this text with many other standard anthologies shows how far we have come in expanding the canon to include the usually marginalized or suppressed voices of the groups that compose cultures in the United States.

7. See, for example, Berlin's two volumes that deal with nineteenth- (1984) and twentieth-century (1987b) writing instruction in the United states; see Connors's (for example, 1981) essays on aspects of the teaching of writing in the United States; Crowley (1990); Johnson (1988); Rose (1989); Applebee (1989); Braddock, Lloyd-Jones, and Schoer (1963); Hillocks (1986). I do not know of another subdiscipline that has excavated its own history as rigorously and as thoroughly as rhetoric and composition studies in the United States.

4

Alchemizing the History of Rhetoric | *Introductions, Incantations, Spells*

William A. Covino

In *Novantiqua* (1980), Paolo Valesio recalls Kenneth Burke's proposal that "every question selects a field of battle." Valesio would take this further: "It is not only a question that selects a field of battle, but *any* statement, in *any* shape, on *any topic*. We can express reality only through selection or stylization. This is the root of rhetoric" (32). The first part of this essay offers a number of possible introductions to the essay, in order to array—in a tentative, fragmentary way—some "fields of battle" that the revisionary historian might enter as he tries to express what he thinks he is doing.

Introduction 1

I am not a historian anymore. Never was, really. I began writing about the history of rhetoric because of my concern, as a composition theorist, with invention; because of my antipathy toward assembly-line heuristics that were being urged in classes and textbooks in the names of Aristotle and Cicero. I constructed a history that would invalidate this pedagogy, by reinterpreting some hallowed texts and trying to hallow some others, eventually producing *The Art of Wondering* (1988). What I did and do—marshalling evidence in the service of a predisposition—is what we all do.

This introduction would preface a plea for self-conscious historicism, with the recognition that all history is subjective history, and that a revisionary history is one which admits *this. As I propose in the introduction to* The Art of Wondering, *all historians bring to their writing a "special narrow-mindedness" (3); the question is not whether a history is narrow-minded or not—it is. The question is, how is it special? How does it offer what Kenneth Burke calls a "new stressing" that is in some way "corrective" (e.g., 1968, vii–xvi)?*

Introduction 2

The history of rhetoric that Kenneth Burke trails through his *Grammar* (1969a) and *Rhetoric* (1969b) begins as a theory of comedy (1969a, xvii) and is full of transitions that are self-conscious pratfalls ("Whoops," Burke seems to say as the discussion takes a turn, "how did I land *here*?").

This introduction brings in the importance of a comic sensibility for the revisionary historian, his grinning alertness to the burlesque so essential to his job. An honest *history, one that admits what it is about, is necessarily comic.*

Introduction 3

Valesio says, "In dealing with the classics and their statements . . . we often must be more imaginative than their terminology would seem to allow. It is not a matter of philological irresponsibility. . . . When we dare to move freely we usually end up discovering that the term in question is richer and more ambiguous than its canonical translation." At the same time, "no dedicated and continuous observation is free from ultimate beliefs" (1980, 16–20).

This introduction sets up a warning, that the revisionary historian who would avoid imposing ultimate beliefs must abjure both dedication and continuity, leading further to a discussion of a deconstructive historical stylistics that adopts paralogy as its grammar (see Lyotard [1984b]; Vitanza [1987a, 1987b]; Kent [1989]).

Introduction 4

One student in my department writes something like this in the introduction to his dissertation, an ethnography: "This method is bound, in some measure, to distort the facts. I have tried to minimize such distortion, but have not been able to eliminate it." Lamenting the impossibility of omniscience and objectivity is a convention in academic prose, a convention this student knows he should demonstrate as part of his graduation into the profession.

This introduction invites a phantasmagoric meditation on the value of distortion, with advice to critics and historians that the only revealing *observations are* distorted *observations.*

Introduction 5

The whole is the false.

—Theodor Adorno 1974, 50

Adorno, trusting only fragments, inverts Hegel's "The whole is the true," in this dialectic of reflections on intellectual and political history, and lets us go on to say that a trustworthy history is an emphatically fragmentary one.

The Conclusion of the Introductions

Revisionary histories should be self-conscious, subjective, comic, distorting, narrow-minded, fragmentary, and lacking in both dedication and continuity.

This has already been said. The postmodern debate, between those who insist upon an ethical or "factual" *center* and those who jeer that the center should not hold, is pretty well established. This collection on writing histories of rhetoric reestablishes the debate, by setting traditional historians "against" revisionaries; thus, it takes another initial step toward incorporating revisionary history into the academy, just as we in English departments have recently incorporated composition theory and literary theory. Eventually, ABDs in the history of rhetoric, interviewing at MLA, will not be asked to tell what they know about Aristotle; instead, they will be quizzed on historiographical hermeneutics, by tenured revisionaries. It won't be long before every graduate program in rhetoric has a "revised" historian, who, like the literary theorist and the composition theorist, will seem to have always been there.

Gerald Graff (1987), speaking of the acceptance of literary theorists into English departments, suggests what the revisionaries can expect:

> If history runs true to form once more, then we can expect [revisionary historiography] to be defused not by being repressed but by being accepted and quietly assimilated or relegated to the margin where it ceases to be a bother. . . . In either case, pressures are relaxed all around: the innovators are appeased, having become insiders with their own positions or programs, while the university gets to congratulate itself for its up-to-dateness and tolerance without having had to ask the established insiders to change their behavior significantly or to confront their critics. (249–50)

It is unlikely that "revisionary history" will shake the technocratic pseudo-Aristotelianism that has made this country and its universities great.

If, as rhetorical historians, we want to move "beyond" the modern/postmodern debate and its assimilation of revisionaries, if only to resist curricular entrenchment, where do we go from here?

The Answer: A Spell

> Take hieratic papyrus and write the prescribed names with Hermaic myrrh ink. And once you have written them as they are prescribed, wash them off into spring water from 7 springs and drink the water on an empty stomach for seven days while the moon is in the east. But drink a sufficient amount.
>
> This is the writing on the strip of papyrus: "KAMBRĒ CHAMBRE SIXIŌPHI HARPON CHNOUPHI BRINTATĒNŌPHRIBRISKYLMA ARAOUAZAR BAMESEN KRIPHI NIPTOUMI CHMOUMAŌPH AKTIŌPHI ARTŌSE BIBIOU BIBIOU SPHĒ SPHĒ NOUSI NOUSI SIEGŌ SIEGŌ NOUCHA NOUCHA LINOUCHA LINOUCHA CHYCHBA CHYCHBA KAXIŌ CHYCHBA DĒTOPHŌTH II AA OO YY ĒĒ EE ŌŌ." After doing these things wash the writing off and drink as prescribed.
>
> This is also the composition of the ink: myrrh troglitis, 4 drams; 3 karian figs, 7 pits of Nikolaus dates, 7 dried pinecones, 7 piths of the single-stemmed worm-wood, 7 wings of the Hermaic ibis, spring water. When you have burned the ingredients, prepare them and write.
>
> —Betz 1986, 9.

Magic spells are nothing new. Memory spells, refinements of this one from the fourth century C.E. that directs us to actually drink our writing, are particularly important today, in the current celebration of cultural literacy as the memorization of information bits. Information bits that function themselves as spells and incantations: a graduate student scrawled me an anxious note just following her written Ph.D. exams, confessing her distress at "forgetting to say *ethos* even once." The budding magician/priestess of rhetoric had left out a magic word and knew that it could mean the end of her charmed university life.

History is a memory spell, an attempt to invoke and consort with the "demonics" and "angelics" of events that are continually receding. In this sense, writing history is a magic act. Histories of rhetoric are doubly magical, if we concede that rhetoric *is* magic, agreeing with Jacqueline de Romilly (1975) that the goal of both magic and rhetoric is illusion, and with Kenneth Burke that "the magical decree is implicit in all language," and that both magic and rhetoric operate as *strategies* calculated to address a *situation* "in the name of" a certain *power* (1957, 5–8). Given the equivalence of magic and rhetoric, making a history of rhetoric is meta-magical, magic about magic.

The hermeneutic filter of every era through the Renaissance explicitly included magic, and magic implicitly informs our modern institutions and habits (O'Keefe 1983; Covino 1991, 1992). If magic was and is a foundation of understanding and interpretation, chronicling rhetoric and/as magic—more fully than de Romilly, and more recently, John Ward (1988) have done—would seem to be the rhetorical historian's next task. However, getting us thinking of rhetoric *in terms of* magic seems unlikely, because our theories and histories of rhetoric are so relentlessly pragmatic; they must point us toward utility, and any history of rhetoric that tries to lead college teachers to think of themselves as magicians teaching magic will be dismissed as spacey (of course, what else is "writing in the disciplines," the newest curricular application of theoretical and historical rhetoric, but a program for teaching institutional incantations?).

The synonymy of magic and rhetoric has not been much addressed because we don't believe in magic but do believe in rhetoric. We might acknowledge that until very recently everyone believed in both, and even now, many still do (even though those who read the horoscopes every day don't admit what they're doing).

A history of rhetoric and/as magic might address several areas:

1. The transformation of the pre-Enlightenment, explicit rhetoric of magic into the current, implicit rhetoric of magic (Covino 1992).

2. The prospect of defining rhetoric as "the study and practice of manipulating phantasms," as suggested by Ioan Couliano's *Eros and Magic in the Renaissance* (1987), which establishes the centrality of the phantasm—from antiquity forward—in the processes of perception and cognition (1–27).

3. The possibility that *eros* is the force that connects magic and rhetoric. Consider Couliano's definition of magic as a definition of rhetoric as well: "Magic is a means of control over the individual and the masses based on a deep knowledge of personal and collective erotic impulses" (xviii). This is the definition of *rhetoric* that is implicit, for instance, in Plato's *Phaedrus*, when Socrates is unable to dissociate his appeal to Phaedrus's soul and mind from a sexual appeal.

4. The history of rhetoric as a continual reaction *against* magic, thus a counter spell. Edward Peters (1978, 21–62) suggests that a fourth rhetorical art in the Middle Ages is the denunciation of magic. The duty of medieval rhetoricians to combat pagan magic led to elaborate descriptions of corrupt magic that were also pedagogical demonstrations of rhetorical conventions (Peters cites the *Rhetorimachia* by Anselm of Besate). Thus, we have the blurring of the presentation of magic and the presentation of rhetoric.

5. The "origin" of rhetoric at the juncture of magic and writing, in the person of Hermes Trismegistus, or Thoth, the Egyptian magician who "invented" writing, and whose pronouncements were cited widely and seriously through the Renaissance, when he was wrongly regarded as the mystic contemporary of Moses and augur of Christianity (Yates 1964, 1–19).

6. The consequences of a lexicon of terms from magic to describe rhetoric. What happens when we think of tropes as spells, or when we rename processes such as "revision" as, for instance, "exorcism?"

7. The coincidence of the politics of magic and the politics of rhetoric. Both Peter Brown (1972) and John Ward (1988) have noticed that the dominant magic of a culture is the expression of *articulate* power, as set against the inarticulate, marginalized power of the disenfranchised magician.

8. The Enlightenment reformations of both magic and rhetoric as twin censorships that sterilized the human imagination (Couliano 1987, 197; Covino 1992).

9. The lives of rhetoricians and philosophers who were also magicians, or who believed in magic. These number so many, from Plato

to Isidore to Descartes to Francis Bacon. Those with explicitly magical theories of suasion, such as Pico, Ficino, Agrippa, and Bruno, deserve new attention.

As an indication of how this last area might be explored, imagine a new reference book titled, shall we say, *Magical Rhetoric in Its Christian and Secular Traditions*. In it we find the following entry:

Cornelius Agrippa von Nettesheim

Agrippa (1486–1535) is the model for Christopher Marlowe's Dr. Faustus and Mary Shelley's Victor Frankenstein. A legendary Renaissance *magus* whose *Occult Philosophy* was standard reading for students of magic through the nineteenth century, he is also an important philosophical skeptic, whose *Of the Vanity and Uncertainty of Arts and Sciences* influenced Montaigne's central statement, the "Apology for Raymond Sebond" (Nauert 1965, 314n). Agrippa's uneven and inconsistent body of writing, together with his variegated and restless career in a number of professions, allows us to consider how a belief in magic may—perhaps must—coincide with philosophical skepticism. Also, in contrast to developing scientific beliefs in the separateness of language and reality, words and things, Agrippa recalls the belief that informed classical conceptions of rhetoric and *logos*, that words *make* reality.

A contemporary describes Agrippa as one "who all his life had wandered about the world, and spoke all languages, and had studied in every science"(Nauert 1965, 157). Born in Nettesheim, near Cologne, Agrippa learned astrology from his parents, and pursued a general course of study at the University of Cologne, where he joined a secret brotherhood of occultists. His claim to doctorates in law and medicine has never been proven; however, he practiced both subjects, working for a time as *orator-advocatus* (both lawyer and official speechmaker) for the German city of Metz, where he successfully defended a woman accused of witchcraft; and as a court physician in French Lyons. A miscellany of stints in political and military service and an occasional university lecture on magic filled Agrippa's life of travels through Italy, France, Germany, and Switzerland.

Agrippa's itinerant life coincides with his itinerant *intellect*. He completes his *Occult Philosophy* by 1510, but does not publish it until 1533, *after* writing an ostensible *refutation* of magic, and rhetoric, and "any kind of learning" in *Of the Vanity and Uncertainty of Arts and Sciences* (1974, 10). In 1509, just prior to completing the *Occult Philosophy*, Agrippa writes a feminist tract, not published until 1532, and later translated into English as *Female Pre-Eminence, or the Dignity and Excellency of that Sex, above the Male* (1980). Agrippa's advocacies of occultism, skepticism, and feminism, intersecting and contradicting each other through a career of temporary professions, shifting religious and political allegiances, and failed appeals for patronage, constitute a rhetoric of unsettled propositions consistent with belief in the magic, invocatory power of words, and the willingness to "explore provisionally any approach to reality" (Nauert 1965, 241).

As both Nauert and Vickers (1984) have pointed out, Agrippa—in concert with the Renaissance magical tradition—believes that words have the power to remake reality:

> Words therefore are the fittest medium betwixt the speaker and the hearer, carrying with them not only the conception of the mind, but also the virtue of the speaker with a certain efficacy unto the hearers, and this oftentimes with so great a power, that oftentimes they change not only the hearers, but also other bodies, and things that have no life. (*Three Books of Occult Philosophy* 1651, 152)[1]

This belief informs Agrippa'a continuing interest in Cabala, which is treated extensively in his *Occult Philosophy*, and considered in both *Female Pre-Eminence* and *Vanity*. *Female Pre-Eminence* (1980) begins with the argument that "Eve" is a more sacred name than "Adam": "Let us at least affirm from the mysterious learning of the Cabalists, that the woman's name in the original language, has a much nearer affinity with the ineffable Tetragrammaton, or sacred name of the divine essence, than the man's, which bears no resemblance thereto either in characters, figure, or number" (7). In *Vanity* (1974), while he dismisses as fraudulent the whole of arts and sciences, including some varieties of magic, Agrippa maintains his interest in discovering a true (Christian) Cabala: "I doubt not that God has revealed to Moses and other of the prophets many mysteries not to be disclosed to the ignorant people, which were covered under the bark of the words of the Law" (137; see also Nauert 1965, 212).

Along with Cabala, Agrippa maintains the importance of *natural* magic. He devotes one-third of *Occult Philosophy* to the magic powers of earthly elements and the incantations that materialize such powers; in *Vanity*, where he finds fault with all else, Agrippa reaffirms natural magic:

> Natural Magic then is that, which having intentively beheld the forces of all natural things, and celestial, and with curious search sought out their order, does in such sort publish abroad the hidden and secret powers of nature: coupling the inferior things with the qualities of the superior . . . by a natural joining of them together, that thereof oftentimes do arise marvelous miracles. (1974, 124–25)

In his advice on incantations, Agrippa implicitly aligns magic with rhetoric by admitting that magic words have the potential to create evil as well as good spirits. Just as the major statements of classical rhetoric (especially Quintilian and Augustine) admit that rhetoric has the power to advance morally corrupt arguments, and warn against its abuse, Agrippa (following Ficino) describes "songs and prayers to attract the power of *any* star or divinity" (Agrippa in Nauert 1965, 246; emphasis added), allowing repeatedly that the magician can invoke evil, and proposing (perhaps too weakly, according to Yates 1964, 132–33) that he should not. In sum, the traditional call for the "good man speaking well" in classical rhetoric finds a parallel in the tradition of magic that Agrippa compiles, with his attention to the good magician invoking well.

Relegation of Agrippa to minor status in Renaissance philosophy and the history of magic seems to be based on his inconsistencies, which irritate critics. Couliano is annoyed with Agrippa's ambivalent attitudes toward magic and religion; setting *Occult Philosophy* alongside *Vanity*, he complains that "ambiguities pile up within [Agrippa]" (1987, 195–200). Nauert devotes a full chapter and more to "the odyssey of Agrippa's mind" (1965, 194–221), to defend against a critical tradition that has dismissed his importance, concluding that Agrippa "personified . . . his epoch": "He was the magician, the cabalist, the Faustian doubter, the living embodiment of many of the enthusiasms and most of the gnawing doubts and uncertainties and fears of his age" (330- 31). Mindful that magic, skepticism, and rhetoric were all objects of wholesale *reform* by the end of the seventeenth century, we can locate Agrippa in the postmedieval, pre-Reformation moment when (as proposed in Vickers's *Defense* [1990] and "Analogy"[1984]; Couliano [1987]; Nauert [1965]) intellectual enthusiasm for the imaginative and expressive possibilities of figurative language, skeptical philosophy, and occult "sciences" was high.

One Final Conclusion

Any history of rhetoric, all of which command the spirit(s) of the past to materialize, is also always the invocation of a text of invocations: I give you Agrippa, in the context of a larger proposal for a history of rhetoric and/as magic; to present Agrippa, I materialize—I write—Agrippa's and Agrippan pronouncements. This is how we do history, the traditional historian no less than I: "I call Cicero to the page," he intones, "to reveal to us his talismans and conjurations for making knowledge and inducing action in the public mind." Recognizing magic as the source-ery of rhetoric and histories of rhetoric, a collegium of revisionaries can alchemize the most reactionary appeals for canonical histories and the most radical appeals for pluralism into their common essence—as spellbooks for making a Western icon of Cicero's *De Oratore,* for making a philosophical rhetoric of Agrippa's shifting stances, for making something out of nothing.

Note

1. Quotations from Agrippa's works are based on my comparison of conscientious sixteenth- and seventeenth-century English translations with the Latin version of Agrippa's *Opera* (1970). Page numbers are given for the English sources.

5

Human Agency in the History of Rhetoric | *Gorgias's* Encomium of Helen

Takis Poulakos

This essay attends to the problem of recovering human agency in the history of rhetoric. It joins other scholarly efforts in rhetorical studies aimed at recuperating voices of opposition and alterity and at incorporating such voices into the canon of rhetoric.[1] And it underscores the principle underlying these efforts, namely, that diversity is essential to a rhetorical tradition aspiring to uphold democratic ideals. Yet the aim to establish diversity as a central feature of our tradition obliges us, it seems to me, to do more than merely demonstrate how past rhetorics provided a counterposition to this cultural norm or to that hegemonic discourse. Our inquiries into otherness, I argue, need be guided by the additional task of demonstrating how opposition and diversity have in fact played a constitutive role in rhetoric's history, how the very body of our tradition has been built on a history of contestatory discourses and heterogeneous voices.

The essay also seeks to extend the project of recuperating otherness by focusing on a segment of our tradition whose oppositional discourses are no longer part of the historical record. In other words, the essay seeks to advance the current theoretical discussion by problematizing the notion of recuperation. As I hope to make clear, however, what makes recuperation problematic in this case is not theory but history—especially the kind of history that was either never recorded at all or was once part of a record now irretrievably lost. Anyone working on rhetoric in the classical period knows that the hope to recuperate alternative voices has long been abandoned: there are simply no oppositional texts awaiting to be recovered, no extant papyri to be retrieved, no manuscripts by women or slaves to be reclaimed. Unlike other, more recent segments of our tradition, the classical period does not afford us the opportunity to incorporate into the rhetorical canon alternative discourses—discourses that have been available all along but that, for one reason or another, have been neglected. When recuperation aims at recovering alternative discourses that have not survived the obliteration of time, the effort to recuperate otherness is necessarily reconstructive. This essay, then, attends to the problem of recovering oppositional voices, when the act of recovery can be set into motion only by means of historical reconstruction.

Indeed, when the only surviving texts are by elite writers, the question of otherness must be raised not in terms of which texts we choose to read but in terms of how we choose to read extant texts. Yet how are we to reconstruct oppositional discourses while reading discourses of the elite? How is one to hear the voices of women, wage-laborers, or slaves while listening to the voices of the upper class? One option available to the historian of rhetoric is to engage theories of reading developed outside the discipline of rhetoric and designed to address precisely these kinds of interpretive problems. Especially relevant to the present discussion are theories of reading advanced by Marxist and poststructuralist models of historiography. Their differences in assumptions, methodological procedures, and conclusions notwithstanding, both historiographical models are compatible with the principal premise of this essay, namely, that it is possible for the interpreter to reconstruct the voice and identity of the "other," even from discourses in which that other voice remains silent and that other identity remains absent.

I say the historian of rhetoric can "engage" rather than "borrow" theories of reading in order to dramatize the necessary tension that results from any such interdisciplinary exchanges. A crossing over of the disciplinary divide typically commits one to more than he or she had bargained for—presuppositions that pull the interpreter in unanticipated directions or resist with unexpected resilience the user's appropriative purposes. While encouraging a move outside the discipline of Rhetoric, therefore, I am not suggesting that answers to our disciplinary questions lie elsewhere. What I am suggesting is that it may be profitable for us to engage models of historiography that have had a larger investment in textual interpretation and a longer tradition of theorizing acts of reading. Still, we must proceed cautiously, with a view to problems we will be importing from the outside as well as to solutions we will be called upon to provide. Indeed, while Marxist and poststructuralist models of historiography can give us sophisticated methodological procedures for reconstructing voices of opposition and alterity, they cannot also help us come to terms with the pronounced differences between them. As will soon become evident, these two models of historiography will inevitably pull the historian of rhetoric in two opposing directions: on the one side, toward determinate political identities and, on the other side, toward indeterminate processes of signification. But even as the historian of rhetoric will be obliged to follow both tracks, it is possible that he or she may succeed in negotiating their persisting differences productively and in orchestrating their divergent aims effectively. This, at least, is the hope underlying the present discussion: that rhetoric can provide viable ways of resolving an important historiographical debate and of reconciling a current theoretical controversy. Rhetoricians, after all, do belong to a discipline that historically has had to reconcile the tension between the contradictory demands of politics and signification, albeit at a somewhat different level of interpretation: the tension between rhetoric as persuasion and rhetoric as figuration.

Marxist and Poststructuralist Historiographies

Within the framework of Marxist interpretation, the reconstruction of otherness is not only feasible but requisite to the historical formulation of class struggle. At the social horizon of interpretation, says Fredric Jameson (1981), the individual text can be understood as an utterance within a larger class discourse and as an expression within a broader, antagonistic dialogue between classes. Given that in this horizon of interpretation "class discourse . . . is essentially *dialogical* in its structure" and the form of that dialogue is "essentially an *antagonistic* one" (84), the text under question must be apprehended as a collective expression constituted by an antagonism or by a dialogue "in which two opposing discourses fight it out" (84). But if a given text is to be understood as articulating only one side of the antagonism or as expressing merely one half of the dialogical exchange between classes, that understanding cannot materialize without the interpreter's reconstruction of the other side of the antagonism or the other half of the dialogue. Jameson explains: "Indeed, since by definition, the cultural monuments and masterworks that have survived tend necessarily to perpetuate only a single voice in this class dialogue, the voice of a hegemonic class, they cannot be properly assigned their relational place in a dialogical system without the restoration or artificial reconstruction of the voice to which they were initially opposed, a voice for the most part stifled and reduced to silence, marginalized, its own utterances scattered to the winds" (85). Within this interpretive framework, the text preserved by the tradition and monumentalized by the canon is situated in direct opposition to the silent voice of its antagonistic other and positioned in antithetical relation to its absent, dialogical partner.

In the Marxist model of historiography, then, the historian is obliged to proceed along the contours of a dialogical system and posit a dichotomous relation between dominant and oppositional discourses, present and absent voices. Because, as Jameson points out, "class struggle is always dichotomous" (83), the inaudible voice and absent identity of the "other" can be made audible and visible respectively, so long as the logic and values expressed by the text under investigation are understood to comprise the voice of the dominant class and to represent the identity of the oppressor. In such a reconstructive procedure, the voice of the silenced "other" and the identity of the society's oppressed will always turn out to be the inverse of the voice expressed in and the identity represented by the canonized text. The "other" will invariably turn out to be the text's "political unconscious."

The process of reconstructing oppositional voices from within a poststructuralist perspective is infinitely more complex. For poststructuralists question the very premise on which the typical reconstructive process depends, namely, the premise that the text is the effect of a determinate expression, be it an individual's or a group's. Derrida's by-now-famous proclamation that "there is nothing outside the text" (1974, 158), that there is "nothing before the text, no pretext that is not already a text" (1981a, 328), questions the legitimacy of any interpretive attempt to reconstruct a given text in terms of some prior or originary cause. Interrupting the text's relation to the real, poststructuralists have shown that representation is the effect of difference and that difference marks not only the text's relation to the real but also to the signification process that makes the text meaningful. In a system of signification where "every signified is also in the position of a signifier" (1981b, 20), a given sign is meaningful not by means of its reference to the outside but by means of its difference from other signs operative within the semiotic code in which that given sign functions.

Poststructuralism complicates the issue of historical reconstruction and problematizes the task of locating human agency within a given text, by providing us with theoretical knowledge about representation in general. Such a knowledge opens up the pathway for a critique of all forms of subjectivity discerned and all forms of identity constructed by the interpreter. For any claim that something or someone is being represented in the text can only be made through the interpreter's abrupt interruption of the signification process. The question of human agency involves, in other words, a decision on the interpreter's part to arrest the free movement of the signifier, to pin down what is ceaselessly moving, and stabilize what is perpetually at play. And while some Marxists have used the poststructuralist insight about the signification process as indicative of the latter's inability to read texts politically (Anderson 1983, 32–55), we can see how this same insight may be used to indicate something quite different: that any "cut" into the signification process is an interested gesture and, as such, a gesture that is motivated by the politics of the interpreter. The dilemma between Marxism and poststructuralism, therefore, is not so much a dilemma between a political and an apolitical perspective, as it is a dilemma between a perspective that authorizes a political reading and one that negates the grounds that would authorize any one particular reading or any one particular politics. Within the poststructuralist framework, then, the reconstruction of subjectivity or otherness requires an intervention that is feasible but suspect, crucial to the reconstructive process but always subject to a critique.

I mentioned earlier two opposing pulls exerting themselves on the historian attempting to reconstruct otherness, and the sketch I have offered above, though too brief to capture all aspects of the current debate on historiography, suffices to demonstrate the dynamics of that opposition. On the one hand, Marxist historiography pulls the historian in the direction of determinate politics and charges him or her with the task of representing "the irrepressible voice and expression of the underclasses" (Jameson 1981, 105). On the other hand, poststructuralist historiography pulls the historian in the direction of signification and charges him or her with the task of recognizing the constructed character of all forms of identity discerned. As a result, the historian is caught in a bind, a situation where political and epistemological demands collide—almost to the point of canceling each other out—and where the stable ground needed to carry out the former task is called into question and made indeterminate by the latter. For the kind of knowledge produced by poststructuralism—the knowledge that identities are discursively constructed and, as such, always putative—does not offer the ground required to sustain a political will or to legitimate its authority. Is the historian to proceed politically, anyway, and simply ignore the deconstructive lessons of poststructuralism? Or to adhere to an epistemology that refuses to sanction determinate identities and, consequently, abandon all political projects?

I have also hinted at the possibility of negotiating this dilemma in a rhetorically viable way. But in order to pursue this possibility at all, we will have to grasp the poststructuralist conception of the constituted character of subjectivity as knowledge about the subject's limits rather than as a proclamation of the subject's "death." To speak about the author in terms of a "function" and of the subject in terms of an "effect" is to limit but not altogether deny the constitutive character of subjectivity. When the poststructuralist inquiry becomes refocused in this way, as inquiry into the limits of agency, the above dilemma between politics and epistemology can be redescribed—this time, in the terms provided by the rhetorical tradition—as the familiar dilemma of deliberative rhetoric: having to act in the face of uncertainty without the requisite knowledge that would sanction the act. To be sure, there are crucial differences here. For uncertainty in the latter case is due to the subject's inability to know how things will turn out after the fact, that is, by the subject's partial knowledge, while uncertainty in the former case is due to the subject's cognizance of its own constitutedness, that is, by the additional theoretical knowledge of the subject's own complicity with structures that constitute it. Thus, whereas the unease with deliberative rhetoric lies in not knowing enough, the quite different unease with poststructuralism lies in knowing too much. And these irreconcilable differences will continue to persist unless we are somehow capable of imagining, on the one side, a situation that is not positivistically oriented (where the determination to act does not derive from presumptions about "right" and "wrong" action) and, on the other side, a situation that does not conflate intention with results (where the determination to act is made with the cognizance that action will somehow exceed the actor's intention). From that dual perspective, the imperative to act involves, at one and the same time, the knowledge of having no definite control over the processes that shape history and the quite different knowledge that the act about to be taken will in fact shape history in some unforeseen and unanticipated way.

To reconcile the tension between Marxist and poststructuralist models of historiography through rhetoric, then, is to approach the historian's intervention in terms of a political commitment, a commitment that is both necessary and necessarily provisional. Such an approach understands the historian's effort to reconstruct otherness as a rhetorical strategy.

Historiography as Strategy

A theory of reading poised to negotiate the tension between Marxist and poststructuralist historiographies by shuttling between politics and epistemology would begin by examining the text's relation to the semiotic field of signification operative during the time of the text's production. As poststructuralists have shown, such a relation is always double, a repetition and a change.[2] For a text to mean anything at all, it must repeat the dominant system of signification; but since no two repetitions are ever identical, the text changes the signification system in its very attempt to repeat it. This double relation can be specified further through the logic of *supplementarity*. The text supplements the semiotic field with an added function, but this addition is placed in the service of displacing the signification system. Initially, then, the historian proceeds along the tracks of a well-known poststructuralist procedure: any change in signification function is a supplement, at once an addition and a displacement. In Derrida's words, "The movement of signification adds something . . . but this addition . . . comes to perform a vicarious function, to supplement a lack on the part of the signified" (1978, 289). Following this double movement of supplementarity, the historian takes note of the dominant signification system and its repetition through the text, but also of the text's effort to displace the dominant sign-system and to effect, as Derrida put it, "a rupture with its past, its origin, and its cause" (291).

The double logic of supplementarity, then, directs the historian to observe not only how a given text repeats the dominant system of signification but also how it attempts to displace it. Now the very act of reading a given text as a site of duplication and displacement may itself provide us with a way of shifting the registers of interpretation and with a manner of turning the analysis from the semiotic to the social. As Gayatri Spivak has shown (1987), the historian can use the text's relation to the semiotic field as a pathway to the social and, assuming that a similar logic of supplementarity also governs the text's relation to the social, can read the text as a site where the social is at once duplicated and displaced. After noting, in other words, how the semiotic field is being tapped, the historian may infer a similar tapping going on with the social and, on the basis of this inference, may go on to grasp the text under question as a gesture of conformity to and confrontation against networks of power operating in the social. Simultaneously a site of repetition and rupture, the text is read, at this juncture, both as the effect of networks of domination and oppression and as the condition of possibility for their crisis.

It should be obvious by now that the stage has already been set for reconstructing otherness along the double axis of repetition and rupture. And it is on this axis that the historian will eventually graft the twin narratives about the "other," first, as the effect of networks of power and, second, as the agent of opposition to them. Yet neither narrative will be satisfactory unless somehow the process of reconstruction follows a procedure that meets adequately the opposing demands of Marxist and poststructuralist historiographies. Irreconcilable though they may be, political and epistemological demands can nevertheless come together strategically.

Indeed the historian can follow up on the political route opened up by Marxist historiography without also being obliged to duplicate the continuist narrative insisted upon by Marxists. To tell the story of the "other" as the effect of networks of power, one need not rely necessarily on the macro-narrative of a class struggle. As Foucault has shown, power is multidimensional, and one's interest in recording the operations of power must yield to one's cognizance of power's multiple networks and their simultaneous coexistence—as well as their ongoing and oftentimes indecipherable transformations. And we do not have to accept Foucault's own historical project wholesale in order to make use of his important insight: that power is discontinuous and, as such, it manifests itself in ways that cannot always be recorded along the lines of some invariable reference point. In order to tell the story of the "other" as the effect of multiple and changing configurations of power, then, the historian needs to fix that which is constantly in a state of flux. In order to examine the forces controlling the text under investigation, the historian needs to arrest the shifting configurations of power. Yet, how is this to be accomplished without recourse to the kinds of formations that power will eventually come to assume? How is the historian to proceed without invoking some future horizon of interpretation or without focusing on some subsequent configuration of power against which the forces controlling the text may be determined? From the very outset, therefore, the political impulse guiding the historian runs up against the limits of knowledge: knowledge does not help because it cannot tell how things will turn out.

And these limits will become more pronounced still, when the historian follows up on the epistemological route opened up by poststructuralists. For what is bound to emerge from this perspective is the recognition that the story about the "other" as agent of opposition can only be told on the authority of the assertion that oppositional voices are fully constituted—an assertion that, unlike Marxists, poststructuralists will not grant the interpreter. Yet, as Spivak has shown (1987), it is still possible for the interpreter to affirm human agency without fully constituting otherness. Without positing the presence of society's "other" in the text, the historian can nevertheless project the "other" onto the networks of power and constitute human agency by virtue of the changes which these networks have had to assume. It is possible, in other words, to conceptualize otherness as a trace—not a presence but a having passed through, not a thereness but a having been there. Asserting that human subjectivity can manifest itself by virtue of the crisis it produces, the historian can constitute otherness on the basis of the changing configurations that networks of power have had to undergo. And this assertion is in line with the general poststructuralist conception of identity as never fully recoverable, as always under erasure. In this manner, the poststructuralists' insistence on the putative character of identity, and hence of its nonrepresentability, is partially met. It is met because the historian neither asserts a presence nor claims to have discerned who the "other" was. It is met only partially because the historian's reconstructive claim, "given the changing configurations of power, this is who the 'other' might have been," does require the positing of a negative consciousness and, as such, the postulating of an essentialism. In Spivak's words, the historian cannot but make "a *strategic* use of positivist essentialism in a scrupulously visible political interest" (1987, 205).

The process of reconstructing the "other" on the basis of a procedure that takes into account both routes opened up by Marxist and poststructuralist historiography lead the historian to impasses that must be negotiated and risks that must be taken. The epistemological impulse checks the historian's impetus to fix the changing configurations of power and to represent otherness, by underscoring the precarious character of his or her claims and assertions. There will always be more knowledge about the operations of power, additional insight about the covering over of difference. In turn, the political impulse checks the historian's impetus to rely too much on the indeterminacy of a future knowledge and a future difference, by underscoring the need to ascertain in the face of uncertainty and to affirm in the here and now. Together the two impulses create a space wherein it becomes possible for the historian to make tentative assertions and take up provisional positions. And it is for this provisional affirmation that we have reserved the term *strategy*. In this context, *strategy* translates political impulses into provisional affirmations and epistemological impulses into affirmations that are liable to error. Strategy is the name for taking up political positions and for keeping our positions open to the possibility of error.

The *Encomium of Helen*

As a way of concretizing the procedure outlined thus far, but also of considering some of its implications, I turn to Gorgias's *Encomium of Helen*. Constructed around a series of plausible alternatives (it was divine fate, or human force, or speech, or love that caused Helen's departure from Greece), Gorgias's famous defense of Helen follows a familiar pattern of dicastic argumentation: the enumeration of a series of probable causes, each one of which rules out the probability of the defendant's guilt. We have already encountered this pattern in Antiphon's *Tetralogies* as well as in Gorgias's *Defense of Palamedes* written some twenty years or so before the *Helen*. It is a type of defense that derives its significance from a very basic form of dicastic rhetoric—argument from probability—a form that, ever since Corax and Tisias, had become part and parcel of oratorical practices in Athenian courtrooms. Insofar as Gorgias's text advances arguments appealing to reason and makes inferences based on probable causes, the *Helen* works within and perpetuates further the system of signification that underlied dicastic oratory during the mid fifth century B.C. Yet, even as the text repeats the dominant system of legal signification, it charges it with a new function: the display of the advocate's own linguistic virtuosity. Indeed, the entire section characterizing *logos* as a powerful lord, who subjects the souls of hearers to forcible impressions and holds auditors captive to persuasion (8–13), works not only as a probable cause of Helen's abduction but also as an exhibition of the speaker's rhetorical ingenuity.

In addition to their ordinary, inferential coding, then, arguments from probability in the *Helen* are invested with a performative function and acquire an ostentatious and playful dimension. The net result of this added function, this supplement in signification, is a confusion as to what falls within and what falls outside the auspices of legal argument proper, what constitutes evidence and what constitutes play. "I wish to free the accused of blame," says Gorgias, "and, having reproved her detractors as prevaricators and proved the truth, to free her from their ignorance."[3] In the original, the phrase "reproved her detractors and proved the truth" links together two procedures typically followed by the defense: exposing the falseness of the accusers and proving the truth, *psebdomenous epideixas kai deixas talethes*. But of the participles used, only the latter (*deixas*) belongs to the purview of legal argument, the former (*epideixas*) being more closely associated with "self-display" or "showing off." The conjunction *kai* linking *epideixas* with *deixas* creates the impression that the act of self-display is as necessary to the case for the defense as is the act of proving. Basing the investigation of falsehood and truth on the advocate's self-display, the phrase above makes exhibition and performance a substantive part of dicastic oratory.

How are we to interpret this effort made by the text to supplement the legal function of arguments with the function of self-display? How are we to read this change in the connotative range of legal discourse, such that dicastic arguments no longer exclusively signify probability but may additionally connote virtuosity and playfulness, exhibition and display? And how are we to understand this new function if not as a supplement, at once an addition and a displacement? To be sure, the work's experimentation with signification has been noted by commentators who, throughout the history of the work's reception, have decoded this supplementarity as a textual contradiction or as a failure to keep apart two distinct types of discourses.[4] The new chain of signification put into motion by the *Helen* has thus been explained away in terms of a "generic blunder" committed by a rhetorician who did not quite know the difference between the dicastic and the epideictic kinds. Hence, Isocrates' response to Gorgias: "Nevertheless, even he committed a slight inadvertence—for although he asserts that he has written an encomium of Helen, it turns out that he has actually spoken a defence of her conduct" (*egkomion peri autes . . . apologian uper ton ekeine pepragmenòn*).[5]

As I have already suggested, my own strategy is to interpret the crisis in signification effected in the work as a sign of a social crisis, and to plot the text's effort to supplement the dominant sign system as a double gesture of conformity to and confrontation against networks of power. From within the first perspective—a perspective generated by the interpreter's understanding of "supplement" as an addition, a filling of a lack—the *Helen* would be read as a gesture signaling a crisis in the aristocratic networks of power and as an effort taken to fill the lack that had caused this crisis. Such a reading would not be incompatible with familiar narrative accounts of the disastrous effects that the democratization process at Athens had had for the aristocrats. Nor would it alter traditional accounts attributing a gradual but steady decline of the aristocrats' stronghold on the Athenian economy to the legislative changes of Solon, Cleisthenes, and later on Pericles, and to the eventual transformation of Athenian courts into public arenas where the ownership of land could be challenged and where huge fortunes could change hands from the propertied few to the propertyless many.[6] But it would permit the historian to invest these accounts with a stronger sense of urgency and to entertain the possibility that, even as the *Helen* was being written, the decline of aristocratic power had reached a point of crisis.

And it is this same sense of urgency that would similarly permit the historian to entertain the possibility that the aristocrats might have looked to rhetorical education as a way out of the crisis and might have sought to use their sponsorship of the Sophists in order to redirect the art of rhetoric away from the probable and toward the performative. Such a turn admits to the failure of dicastic rhetoric proper to serve aristocratic interests as it once had served them, and gives us reason to believe that the aristocrats might have grown impatient with sponsoring an art that could no longer prevent the public's use of the courts as a covert mechanism for the outright redistribution of wealth. In this context, the *Helen*'s effort to generate a confusion in legal signification by mixing up the registers of probability and display would be understood as the effect of a new tactic on the part of aristocrat sponsors: to develop dicastic argumentation along the lines of the rhetoric of self-display. It is a development fueled by the aristocratic conviction that the courts can still be won over to their side—if only a new dicastic art was found, an art as capable with seduction as it had once been with persuasion. The *Helen* gives us the initial but definite signs of instruction in this new art. Under the pretext of a myth and the pretense of an exercise in mock-trial, a new textbook emerges complete with new goals and overt instructions: how to seduce the crowds of jurors by the brilliance of eloquence rather than the probability of argument, how to elicit their verdicts on the basis of a performance rather than an appeal to reason. To the extent that this art would develop successfully, the courtroom would become a forum for applauding staged performances rather than serving justice, and, with it, the value system of aristocracy would be certain to acquire prominence once again.[7]

Indeed, the rhetoric in the *Helen* stages the courtroom as a festival and articulates dicastic arguments in terms more closely associated to the festive situation of an athletic competition than to the sober occasion of a trial. Replete with images of combat and metaphors of rivalry, the text launches the power of traditional forces (*tuche, bia, logos,* and *eros*) against the accused, and lets each one have a go at Helen's will. At the center of the stage lies *logos*, a polymorphous power that manifests itself now as sheer materiality (*ten psychen etuposato*, 13) or a brute force (*bia erpasthe*, 12), now as a might impossible to guard against because slippery and unstable (*abebaios*, 11). Is there not here the makings of a vocabulary to theorize persuasion in a novel way, and does not this vocabulary steer persuasion away from the logic of the probable? Indeed, partly expressed in the metaphoric language of a combat in war, partly in the spirit of a wrestling match in the palaestra, arguments in the text enact symbolically the rituals of competition. And it is undoubtedly a tribute to this text, as well as to several other texts (including perhaps the earliest practice of "contests in arguments," *logon agonas*, attributed to Protagoras), that the later generation came to describe oratorical practices in the courts nonchalantly in the language of wrestling (*Republic* 405c) and to equate skill in dicastic oratory with skill at the pancratium (*Euthydemus*, 271c–272b). Thus linking the courtroom to the celebratory occasions of an exhibition, a display, a spectacle, the *Helen* establishes a connotative domain between dicastic discourse and competitive ideals.

In the meantime, the stylistic conduct of the text, with its obsession to divide all matter at hand into oppositional halves and antithetical pairs, records the motions of a performance that, as Roger Moss has shown, is perpetually driven by the two extreme attributes that characterize Gorgias's use of language: violence and play. It is a performance propelled by the excesses of both, making play by doing violence to language and violating the referential order of language by presenting itself as a mere plaything, a *paignion*. It is a performance that, in Moss's apt terms, "is no more than that, a virtuoso appeal for recognition and applause, not a necessary condition of communication" (1982, 214). In this festival-like competition and spectacle-like performance in *eu legein*, the courtroom defense of Helen manages to address the jurors not as *theoroi* (discerning audiences who must render a judgment) but as *theatai* (onlookers or spectators of a spectacle).

But there is an additional sense in which the text takes dicastic argument further away from the probable and recognizably closer to the performative. Suspending all references to events involved in the case, refusing to recount pertinent facts—on the grounds that well-known facts bring conviction (*pistis*) but no pleasure (*terpsis*) to hearers—the advocate for the defendant neither interprets on the basis of some legal principle nor builds a probable case on the basis of the known facts. The speech for the defense is animated instead by a desire to create a fantastic world, a world where superhuman forces like *eros* and *logos* hold human agency captive and render insignificant any interpretive efforts to establish human motives. It is a world created not by reasonable inference but by magic, and sustained by a familiar conviction: that the doorway to hearers' persuasion is none other than the production of pleasure.[8] Untersteiner (1954) and de Romilly (1975) are correct to insist that the trademark of Gorgias's rhetoric is magic, but we should also note that the precondition of magic is the disruption of the logic of the probable. And that disruption obtains, as Rosenmeyer has said of the function of *apate* in Gorgias, in two ways: both in the relation of *logos* to a subject matter and in its effects on the audience (1955, 233).

The specific recommendation made by the *Helen*, then, may be reiterated as follows: legal argumentation must be reconceptualized along the lines of seduction. The art of dicastic rhetoric should no longer develop exclusively along the lines of the probable,[9] for such a development has not been successful at arresting the redistribution of wealth effected by verdicts in the courts. It must, on the contrary, be developed along the lines of display and, drawing on the earlier spectacles of tragic performances and cultivating its affinities with the poetic tradition, be put in the service of delighting the crowds in the courtrooms.[10] In this manner, the new rhetoric of the courts will undoubtedly begin serving a function similar to that already served by aristocratically sponsored activities outside the courts: a festival, an athletic competition, a staged spectacle.[11]

But even if the text is regarded as occupying a position created by the new intersection of economic, legal, and educational strands, and intended to uphold aristocratic interests, it cannot assume this position without also making evident the vulnerability of aristocracy it was meant to fortify, without somehow also exposing the lack in the networks of power it was designed to fill. It is precisely this lack and this vulnerability that the *Helen* replicates and these fears that it revives as it recasts the familiar story of Helen's abduction in terms of a drama whose main protagonist is seduction. In this retelling, Helen remains the signifier of a dear possession that can be stolen away by any outsider versed in persuasion and, as such, provides an unmistakable reminder that the circuit of economic exchange is not closed to aristocrats but remains instead vulnerably open to outsiders. And what a better way to underscore this vulnerability than represent the outsider as the intruder par excellence and place the most prized possession of Hellas in the hands of a persuasive barbarian. There is a good deal of jesting here, for the Greeks knew all too well that barbarians could not have been educated in the art of persuasion. From Protagoras's great myth to Isocrates' famous hymn, *logos* continues to be singled out as the quality that best distinguishes civilized from primitive societies, the cultural trait that separates Greeks from barbarians. Though it is quite fitting to blame Helen's abduction on a barbarian's brute force, since *bia* is, after all, the essential attribute of his identity, how plausible is it to portray the barbarian as eloquent, seductive, and persuasive? Not at all—unless, of course, the persuasive power of speech is itself depicted as a force comparable to that of *bia*: "What cause then prevents the conclusion that Helen similarly, against her will, might have come under the influence of speech, just as if ravished by the force (*bia*) of the mighty" (12). It is a conclusion well prepared for by the earlier discussion about the magical potency of *logos*, a discussion that suspends the socializing character of speech and links the workings of its power with the practices of sorcery and witchcraft (10). The characterization of the barbarian as a persuasive speaker, therefore, is a jest that nevertheless sparks the most dreaded fear: that the enslaving power of persuasion may be turned against its aristocratic practitioners, render them indefensible, and strip them of their possessions.

Yet, even though *bia* refers to an external force that can only come from the outside, the associations of *logos* to the power of magic and the effect of drugs displace the stark oppositions between the outside and the inside, the persuader and the persuaded, and suggest that the workings of seduction are at once external and internal. Thus, incantations are shown "to beguile [the soul] and persuade it and alter it by witchcraft" only after they have been successful at "merging with opinion (*doxa*) in the soul" (10). Because *doxa* refers both to something external and internal, at once the opinion of the speaker and the counselor of the hearer's soul (11), the effect of persuasion does not obtain until the magic spell cast from the outside meets up with the unstable (*abebaios*) opinion of the soul directed outwardly to physical reality. The overall pattern of the persuasive process in the text is, as Segal has shown, "a cyclical one, from physical stimulus to emotional reaction and back to physical manifestation" (107). According to Segal, the cyclical process does not only explain Gorgias's conception of persuasion but also provides the entire basis for his defense of Helen: "an external sense-datum . . . creates an impression upon the psyche which in turn results in a physical action" (107). Understood in this way, persuasion emerges as a force that works at one and the same time from the outside and from the inside, both forming the soul as it wishes (13) and securing the soul's consent (12), both coercing listeners and obtaining their willing submission.[12] The net result of this unstable locus of persuasion, this shifting back and forth from the outside to the inside, opens up an added possibility, namely, that the enslaving power of persuasion cannot be thought exclusively as aggression coming from the outside but also as manipulation originating within. It is a possibility that was soon to be transformed by Plato into an explicit suggestion and to be spoken (by Gorgias) in reference not to strangers but to Athenians: "And I tell you that by virtue of this power you will have the doctor as your slave, and the trainer as your slave; your money-getter will turn out to making money not for himself, but for another,—in fact for you, who are able to speak and persuade the multitude" (452e).

In this line of reading, the outsider who threatens the aristocratic order can now be seen not as a foreign intruder but as a local antagonist, the enemy within. It is a reading further supported by the analogy of the art of persuasion to the art of medicine. For the effect of *logos* on the soul is linked to the effect that drugs have on the body through a double potency, at once harmful and beneficial. Speech and drugs are additionally linked together through their common capacity to act as antidotes. As Derrida has shown in his detailed study of *pharmakon* in the *Phaedrus* (1981a, 61–171), in the same manner that drugs can function as antidotes to poison, *logos* can also provide the counterspell to the enchanting spell of *peitho*. And while, according to Derrida, "the counterspell, the exorcism, the antidote" for Plato "is dialectics," and the capacity for this "surest incantation" can only come with "training in dialectics" (121), the locus of resistance to the power of *logos* lies for Gorgias in *logos* itself: since the human psyche has no better guide than opinion, one speaker's *logos* can counteract another's *logos* in exactly the same way that the words of astronomers "substitute[] one opinion with another" and the verbal disputes of philosophers "make[] the belief in an opinion subject to easy change" (13). With this analogy, the text leads to the suggestion that opposition to aristocracy does not really come from foreign outsiders but from Athenians—outsiders to the group in control of the economy—capable of resisting the uses dicastic oratory is made of by members of the elite who had been formally educated in the art of persuasion. Through this suggestion, the text points to the alarming prospect that those excluded from rhetorical training may somehow pick it up on their own and master the practice of counteracting one argument from probability with another, through mere exposure to formal argumentation in the courts or hearsay about the art in the agora. And it also opens up the frightening possibility that opposition to aristocracy can consolidate itself around any occasion wherein argumentation can be put to different uses, and indeed on any occasion wherein economically destitute Athenians may find recourse in the language of persuasion and successfully translate personal desire into an expression of public demand.

In such a plotting, dicastic oratory by the Sophists can now be seen as having had an effect not calculated by the aristocrat sponsors—an effect that outstripped their intention and exceeded their purpose. What aristocrats had not been able to foresee was that the art that they had mobilized, this same art they had helped perfect through their sponsorship—in order to counter the democratization of the courts and to defend their interests from legally sanctioned and state-endorsed lawsuits that were constantly brought against them—would somehow disseminate too quickly and make its way to the very people it was meant to protect them from. Nor could they have anticipated that the closed educational system they had channeled rhetorical instruction into would fail to maintain the art in its original form—a specialty or a technical knowledge that could only be kept alive by being passed down exclusively from teacher to student within the private boundaries of a tutorial structure—and keep it from becoming public knowledge. In such a plotting, then, the determination to introduce the rhetoric of display into the courts, a move that we have so far attributed to changing tactics of aristocratic sponsorship of sophistic rhetoric, can now be seen as a strategic response to the new uses dicastic oratory was being put to and, hence, a move made necessary by the uneducated Athenians. Put differently, the decision to blend the rhetoric of probability with the rhetoric of display suggests that the antidote to the rhetoric of probability has already been found. The changing configurations and practices of aristocracy must in this new light be seen as carrying within their very texture the indelible mark of society's "other."

Even as the *Helen* tells the story of changing configurations of power generated by the aristocratic drive for continued domination, it implies at the same time the cause that made these changes necessary to begin with. Even as the work is read as the effect of a crisis, it also manifests the trace of those who produced the crisis, that is, the agents of change. Naturally, we cannot know who these agents were, and any inferences we choose to make about their identity must remain provisional. The *Helen* can be used neither as a source of the "other's" voice nor as an origin of the "other's" presence; it can only be used as a springboard from which to construct who the "other" might have been by virtue of the crisis it produced and the changing configurations of power it necessitated. My reading of the *Helen* both as an effect of aristocratic domination and a condition of its crisis leads me to produce a historical account in which the "other" figures as a collectivity who, confronted with a series of interrelated cultural changes, took advantage of these changes and challenged the power of the propertied few. Such a collectivity may have included members of a rising middle class, merchants and manufacturers without inheritance of land, who seized the opportunities availed to them by their encounters with the art of rhetoric (perhaps through their own encounters with powerful speakers) and used it to advance their own economic and social interests.[13] It may also have included young wage-laborers or old unemployed people whose frequent participation in the large juries of Athens may have brought them in direct contact with experienced advocates' invocations of new laws and convincing arguments that they could eventually make use of in their own litigations against the rich. Finally, it may have also included women and slaves who, though unable themselves to bring legal charges against any citizen, could have acted as informants and supplied crucial information to citizen-friends.[14]

Conclusion

Key to the role played by human agency in the historical account I have produced has been the limited character of its revolutionary potential, a potential and a limit dramatized by the twin perspectives on the text as a reflection of and a confrontation against networks of aristocratic power. Even as the *Helen* reinscribed aristocratic ideology in a new manner, by reconfiguring power around desire, it validated the desire to own in a system where ownership was closed, exposing the existing system of ownership as arbitrary. Even as the text opened up a subject position from which to critique culture, it placed limits around that subject position by validating the desire to own only as pertaining to those permitted to speak in the Athenian courts. Yet neither aspect of human agency will make itself felt unless the historian underscores the retrospective character of his or her investigation. For it is only from the present horizon of interpretation that we can find the *Helen* to be both revolutionary (as regards equality among citizens) and not revolutionary enough (as regards equality between citizens and noncitizens). It is only from the horizon of a future difference that the gift and the limit of the text may be discerned.

And it is this same horizon of a future difference that must guide our present attempts to rewrite the history of rhetoric and to turn the study of the past into the study of human agency. Such a horizon keeps our findings tentative and checks our inclination to congratulate ourselves each time we produce women-sensitive or minority-sensitive readings of our tradition. From within the indeterminate horizon of a future difference, our efforts to give agency to those who do not have it are supplemented with questions about how much agency we have ourselves. Similarly, our endeavors to break away from the discourse of Humanities and to insert voices of opposition into the rhetorical canon are supplemented with the possibility that our historiographical approaches may be perpetuating the very structures of domination they are seeking to disrupt. Indeed, the danger exists that, in the same way that there is always continuity in rupture, our critical reformulations of our discipline may somehow play into the hands of a larger, but indiscernible as yet, institutional logic. It would not be too difficult to imagine, for instance, how the recent emphasis on oppositional voices may well coincide with the interests of institutions of higher learning and, more specifically, with their aims to expand their consumer base by appealing to culturally diverse students, that is, to more consumers. Even as we try to disrupt the logic of Humanistic Studies and its approach to the past as a storehouse of knowledge, the danger always exists that the "other" will be eventually inserted into the discipline and will ultimately become part and parcel of the storehouse of knowledge. The possibility always exists that our efforts to reconstruct voices of opposition and alterity may one day lose their critical edge and become canonical rather than transformational.

The historical account I have produced was erected on the premise that historiography can be thought along the lines of a strategic enterprise, an enterprise driven by the Marxist commitment to human agency as by the poststructuralist commitment to the provisional character of subjectivity. Historiography as strategy accepts the radicality of poststructuralist difference and alterity but seeks to historicize this radicality by way of a provisional affirmation in the here and now. Rhetorically understood, historiography as strategy partakes of the entire range of meanings given to rhetoric by the Sophists: critique and possibility, deliberation and improvisation. It suggests the need to choose strategically one's own essentialisms as a necessary way of inaugurating people's provisional entrance into the arena of cultural politics.

Notes

I am grateful to Barbara Biesecker and John Poulakos for their generous comments and suggestions on the various drafts of this essay. An earlier draft of the essay was presented at the Canadian Society for the History of Rhetoric and was included in the Society's 1989–90 Proceedings. A more recent draft was presented at the 1992 Rhetoric Society of America Conference.

1. See, for instance, Susan Jarratt, *Rereading the Sophists* (1991); two special journal issues on historiography: *PRE/TEXT* 8 (Spring-Summer 1987), and *Western Journal of Speech Communication* 54 (1990); and a collection of essays on historiography edited by me (1993).

2. The procedure laid out in the following pages finds its theoretical backing in several of Gayatri Spivak's works but most visibly in her essay "Subaltern Studies: Deconstructing Historiography" (1987, 197–221). And it is to Gayatri that I wish to dedicate this essay.

3. The *Encomium of Helen,* (2), Kennedy's translation (Sprague 1990). The original appears in Diels and Kranz 1959.

4. For a discussion on the interpreting difficulties posed on commentators by the text's generic ambiguities, see John Poulakos 1983b.

5. Isocrates, *Helen* (14). Original text and translation are in the Loeb Classical Library edition (trans. Norlin, vol 1 and 2, and Van Hook, vol. 3).

6. For a detailed account of legal changes in the fifth century B.C., see MacDowell 1978.

7. For another discussion of epideictic rhetoric as a carrier of aristocratic valuations, see my "Classical Epideictic Oratory" 1988.

8. Indeed, Charles Segal has shown that Gorgias' theory of persuasion in the *Helen* duplicates an earlier associative link, already established by the poets, between *peitho* and *terpsis* (1962, 122–24).

9. According to both Plato and Aristotle, the earliest handbooks of rhetoric had to do with inquiries into the probable. For a detailed account of probability in early rhetorical theory, see Goebel 1989.

10. Loraux's observation (1986) that Gorgias used a discourse of glorification that was completely emptied out of aristocratic valuations and that solely reflected the democratic valuations of Athens (42–56) goes contrary to Garner's observation (1987) that even during democratic Athens "the language of the democratic courts was peculiarly tied to a traditional aristocratic value system which at times placed competitive ideals above justice" (3). For Gorgias's ties to the poetic tradition, see Gronbeck (1972) and Verdenius (1981).

11. For institutional similarities between Athenian courts and festivals, see Garner (1987), 97–99.

12. In Segal's words, there is the suggestion here "that the process is not simply the conquest of a weaker subject by a stronger force, but that the persuaded is himself an accomplice to the act of persuasion" (122). At a later passage, Segal similarly refers to "a psychic complicity to the emotive action of the *logos*" (126).

13. The notion of a middle class in classical Athens has been debated intensely. Ste. Croix's position seems to me most tenable: that there were a number of people who made a living through manufacturing or shipping (i.e., outside the ownership of land) but that their number is hard to calculate—and hence difficult to imagine as constituting a distinct class—since any fortunes

made through manufacturing and shipping were almost certain to be invested immediately in the acquisition of land (1981, 124–25).

14. This possibility is clearly indicated by the frequent litigation cases invoking the law of *apographe*, which encouraged the prosecution of anyone who retained in his possession property belonging to the state (usually involving cases of people born to a non-Athenian parent). If the prosecutor (any Athenian citizen) won the case, he was awarded three-quarters of the value of the property. See MacDowell 1978, 53–66.

6

Nietzsche and Histories of Rhetoric

John Poulakos

During the last decade and a half, the issue of the history of rhetoric has attracted a great deal of attention from many people and many disciplines. Since 1977, the year the International Society for the History of Rhetoric was founded, the number of works addressing some aspect of rhetoric's past has grown considerably.[1] While the urge to explain this phenomenon is undeniably strong, the impulse to take part in the formulation of a new historical consciousness about rhetoric is stronger still—during times of intense activity, one is usually caught in what is happening while reflection on what has happened, or why, generally takes place once the intensity has subsided.

As one might have expected, the recent "historical turn" in rhetorical studies has generated renewed interest in the work of past historians and philosophers of history. If there is one author most responsible for such an interest, that author is Hayden White (1973; 1978). But White and other contemporary historians are indebted to Friedrich Nietzsche, in particular to his "On the Uses and Disadvantages of History for Life" in *Untimely Meditations* (1983a). Unlike other philosophers, Nietzsche is especially noteworthy to students of rhetoric in the light of his lecture notes on classical rhetoric and his writings on the rhetoricity of language (see Nietzsche 1989). Together, these three specific parts of his corpus make him one of the most provocative thinkers that students of the history of rhetoric can read. Nietzsche is provocative not only because he interrogates relentlessly his predecessors and contemporaries but also because he takes a close look at the history of Western thought and transforms it critically, that is, against the prevailing understandings of his time. That this is so is evident in his feelings about ancient and modern rhetoric. Writing in opposition to the hyper-historicist consciousness of nineteenth-century historians, he hides none of his admiration for the ancient Hellenic culture, which held rhetoric to be "the highest spiritual activity of the well-educated political man," and none of his contempt for his contemporaries, whose best application of rhetoric "is nothing short of dilettantism and crude empiricism" (1989, 3). But Nietzsche is not only noteworthy and provocative; he is also relevant to those attempting to escape the dilemma of the history of rhetoric: trying to relive the greatness of bygone rhetorical epochs, on the one hand, and seeking to discover how rhetoric was "really" practiced and taught in the past, on the other. Insofar as neither alternative of this dilemma pays enough attention to existential exigencies in the present, both are limited and troublesome. The one alternative offers an escape from the "crude empiricism" of the present by fixing its gaze on glorious but *dead* epochs while the other displaces the present by means of factual trivia about the past. Neither alternative takes the bold step of shaping a great rhetoric *from* the past and *for* the present.

In this essay, I turn to Nietzsche because the question of the historiography of rhetoric is still an open one and because his writings on history and rhetoric promise to prompt us to more sophisticated histories of rhetoric than we have had. I also turn to him because his view of historiography has mostly been understood in the light of his later work, as genealogy. This understanding, however, lacks the benefit of his earlier essay "On the Uses and Disadvantages of History for Life" and disregards his continuing interest in it even as he went on to write about genealogy (see Foucault 1977, 139–64). In what follows, I first discuss Nietzsche's categories of "monumentalist" and "antiquarian" histories and show that when viewed together they point to the problem of the dialectic of action and historical self-knowledge. Then, I present his "critical" histories as a solution to the problem posed by the monumentalist and antiquarian kinds. Next, I illustrate Nietzsche's monumentalism, antiquarianism, and criticalism with his treatment of sophistical rhetoric, his acknowledgment of his indebtedness to some of his ancient predecessors, and his critique of the rhetorical conceptions of

depredations on peasant moral economies. In a 1753 letter to the Company of the West Indies, French administrators informed the directors that "the lack of provisions has prevented Sir Aussenac from trading more than one hundred captives that were presented to him by the kings of Cayor and Sin who are at war; this [latter] département for more than 3 months cannot even supply itself with cattle; the famine obliged this country's people to eat them and they have become so rare that we are forced to furnish them from here." The same year, Estoupan reaffirmed this point, attributing the paucity of cattle in Gorée to "three years of consecutive famine, which have obliged the negroes to eat their cattle; but the country will refurbish itself after a few years of abundance, since, the herds being the negroes' principal article of wealth, they will doubtlessly apply themselves to recoup their losses by acquiring cattle." Considering the historical qualities of cattle in the region as symbolic capital stores of collective value and collective wealth—the stuff of social contract, relations, and identities—the repercussions of this particular episode on local social logics must have been consequential.[97] What happens when things people normally hold onto and only part with under duress—inalienable things—must suddenly enter the circuits of consumption and maybe even exchange?[98] One wonders how the instability accreting during the eighteenth and nineteenth centuries altered social reproduction in peasant communities. In turn, the strategies devised by villagers to cope with violence and insecurity are bound to remain obscure. The reality of fluctuations and reversals in regimes of value becomes all the more apparent when we consider that a short hundred years after the episode described above the decline of slavery and rise of the peanut trade may have combined to revive the importance of cattle as capital investment. Determining the fate of cattle, that prime emblem of social wealth, would be particularly crucial in unwrapping local practical logics of exchange and social construction. Livestock, however, remain frustratingly elusive in Siin's archaeological contexts, though work in other parts of the world on faunal size and culling patterns strikes a promising note for historical understanding.[99]

In the course of this chapter, I have attempted to conjure up some of the historical fragments scattered by the turbulence of Atlantic history and its representations. I have drawn on material, written, and oral sources to plot the historical arc of different object classes across a variety of contexts. Even within a small province such as the Siin, and despite evidential disparities, it is possible to show that different fields of practice, production, and consumption changed differently with the introduction of foreign commodities. This speaks to the plasticity of local

his time. Finally, I suggest that Nietzsche's three kinds of history allude to three corresponding characteristics of rhetoric: action, particulars, and change. In the course of this discussion, I argue that Nietzsche asks today's historiographers of rhetoric to forego attempts to reenact the great moments or imitate the great men of the past, and to stop accepting fatalistically the implications of deeds done and discourses uttered long ago. Instead, he asks that they see between these two dispositions toward the past (imitation and acceptance) a productive tension, a tension that can motivate critical histories that attend to the demands of the present and, by expressing previously unexpressed perspectives, inspire new actions necessary for life. In effect, Nietzsche asks historians of rhetoric to appreciate the rhetoricity of their enterprise.

Nietzsche's notion of history is firmly tied to his view of life: so much so, that history without regard for life's "charmless needs" is a useless commodity. Nietzsche begins his "Uses" by demanding that history serve life. In his words,

> We need history, certainly, but we need it for reasons different from those for which the idler in the garden of knowledge needs it, even though he may look nobly down on our rough and charmless needs and requirements. We need it, that is to say, for the sake of life and action, not so as to turn comfortably away from life and action, let alone for the purpose of extenuating the self-seeking life and the base and cowardly action. We want to serve history only to the extent that history serves life: for it is possible to value the study of history to such a degree that life becomes stunted and degenerated. (1983a, 59)

In what can be taken as a counterforce to the force of excessive historicism in his own culture and times, Nietzsche rejects the idea of history for its own sake or for the sake of knowing countless but ultimately useless facts from distant epochs. For him, knowledge of the past has no intrinsic worth, and history in itself has no merit. If there is value in historical knowledge, that value issues from its impact on contemporary living, the experiences it sustains or destroys, the actions it propels or impedes, and the meanings it grants or denies to existence. Accordingly, the past should function neither as "a ghost" that always comes back and "disturbs the peace of a later moment" nor as "a dark, invisible burden" that encumbers one's steps (61). Rather, it should contribute to the growth, the vitality, and the strength of a living thing, "whether this living thing be a man or a people or a culture" (62). In other words, the materials of the past should be used by the historian so as to sustain and enrich life, not to impoverish and destroy it. But if this is so, the challenge facing historians is not finding out how things "really" were in bygone times but discovering ways in which to address the present meaningfully and announce the near future insightfully.

Nietzsche discusses the relationship of past and present by juxtaposing two modes of consciousness: the historical and the unhistorical. Although he acknowledges that both are "*necessary in equal measure for the health of an individual, of a people and of a culture,*" he insists that the unhistorical is "more vital and more fundamental, inasmuch as it constitutes the foundation upon which alone anything sound, healthy and great, anything truly human can grow" (63; Nietzsche's emphasis). By contrast, the historical keeps people from being happy by disallowing them to forget: "It is always the same thing that makes happiness happiness: the ability to forget" (62). When one forgets, one puts aside, even if temporarily, the awareness that his thoughts, sentiments, and actions are nothing more than predetermined outcomes of the thoughts, sentiments, and actions of previous generations. Unless one can forget, one becomes paralyzed, left seeing himself as an impotent agent or an inactive observer of an already prefigured course of life. Forgetting, which is a form of oblivion to the past, is significant because it focuses one's attention to the ongoing happenings in one's existence and because it actively screens the past, which often constitutes an obstacle to the kinds of actions required to carry on the business of life. In *The Genealogy of Morals* (1969), Nietzsche notes: "There [can] be no happiness, no cheerfulness, no hope, no pride, no *present*, without forgetfulness" (58).

A precursor to modern existentialism, Nietzsche places a premium on the supreme *value* of existence and insists on a philosophy of "life" that acknowledges the capacity of human beings to make their experiences, thoughts, and actions count. In so doing, he affirms the blind passion for living and endorses a person's anticipation of and thrust into the future. In short, he says the great Yes to life. Time and again, he asks, Does our view of the past contribute to the value of our existence? Can historical knowledge help human beings organize their lived experiences profitably? Can it facilitate their drive to live their lives and expand their freedom of self-determination? To the extent that these questions are answered affirmatively, history is useful; but to the extent that they are not, history makes a person too knowledgeable to appreciate the present and too feeble to desire the future. In a remark apparently directed against Hegel and his disciples, Nietzsche notes:

> Historical men believe that the meaning of existence will come more and more to light in the course of its *process* and they glance behind them only so that, from the process so far, they can learn to understand the present and to desire the future more vehemently; they have no idea that, despite their preoccupation with history, they in fact think and act unhistorically, or that their occupation with history stands in the service, not of pure knowledge, but of life. (1983a, 65)

Clearly, the subordination of history to life leaves no room in Nietzsche's mind for objectivist historians and their claim that history is, or should be, a disinterested enterprise. A purely objective approach to the past is neither possible nor desirable. It is not possible because a historian cannot situate himself outside history or divorce himself entirely from the present interests that motivate his concern with the past; and it is not desirable because objectivist historical knowledge always stands severed from the activities of life, emptied out of all pertinence to the present, and bereft of any chance to generate actions of moment to the present or of consequence to the future. Nietzsche wrote about objectivist historians a few years after the "Uses", "Modern historiography . . . claims nowadays . . . it is a mirror of events; it rejects all teleology; it no longer wishes to 'prove' any thing; it disdains to play the judge; it ascertains, it 'describes.' " These historians are like "lonely arctic explorer[s]," the kind of history they produce is lifeless, and the kind of claims they make is fraudulent: "Here is snow; here life has grown silent" (1969, 157).

Even though Nietzsche insists that history must serve life, it would be too simplistic to view history as the means and life as the end. To be sure, historical knowledge must enhance the value of existence. However, the value of existence is itself, at least in part, a result of historical knowledge. In all its potentialities, the horizon of being has already been circumscribed by the past. At the same time, the range of possibilities for acting in the present has been demarcated by those who lived and acted before us. Accordingly, it is not enough to place history in the service of life; one must also understand life as historically determined. Put another way, an existential view of becoming must be coupled with a historical view of being. For Nietzsche, these two dialectical opposites, will and fate, freedom and determinacy, must be considered together if one is to address adequately the problem of human agency.

Having established the interdependence of life and history, or the link between the unhistorical will and the historical sense, Nietzsche proposes three species of history, each corresponding to a mode of being human: the monumental to acting and striving, the antiquarian to preserving and revering, and the critical to suffering and seeking deliverance. Monumental history springs from the human aspiration to greatness and to power. When one finds models of neither in the present, one turns to the past looking for those rare individuals who, through their inspiring words and bold deeds, influenced the course of events and thus affected generations to come. The monumentalist glorifies the greatness he discovers in the past and, through this glorification, seeks to awaken in his contemporaries the awareness that their age and personal existence may not be as grand as they might think it is. On the contrary, it may be smaller and more impotent than they realize or are willing to admit.

Monumental history is the history of "great actors." It looks at the past as a theatre of personal conflict, a drama of will and power, a play of effort, tenacity, and triumph. Because success in this theatre results directly from personal resoluteness, monumental histories view the few rare individuals they study as creators of their own destiny and as makers of their future and the future of others. Indeed, the entire course of history from within this perspective is nothing more than the sum total of *effects* caused by unique individuals. When these effects are turned into the materials of history, they provide generations of present readers with examples of human greatness and attempt to spur them toward grandiose undertakings. In this capacity, they function as models for action and as sources of inspiration; and in so functioning, they can be said to serve life. By singling out legendary individuals whose daring actions soar above the frivolous doings of most people, monumentalist historical narratives seek to inject the present generation with powerful drives, to expand its horizon to lived experience, and to present it with new possibilities for action at a time when such possibilities seem absent. In effect, monumentalist histories call upon a generation to assert its will against the stifling conditions of the age, to affirm its agency against the constraints of the society, and to set its goals above the goals allowed by the predetermined march of destiny. Contesting the societal limits placed on self-understanding, challenging prevalent notions of selfhood, and announcing new versions of identity, the monumentalist historian has faith in the everlasting durability and imitability of "that which in the past was able to expand the concept 'man' and make it more beautiful" (1983a, 68). In turn, the reader of monumentalist histories stands to learn that "the greatness that once existed was in any event once *possible* and may thus be possible again; he goes his way with more cheerful step, for the doubt which assailed him in weaker moments, whether he was not perhaps desiring the impossible, has now been banished" (69).

Monumental history, however, is not without dangers and disadvantages. To begin with, it says nothing about the criteria against which past greatness was measured and is silent about the conditions that made the rise of strong individuals possible. As a narrative of effects, it ignores the causes—all those circumstances, contingencies, and accidents that paved the way for great actors. Moreover, it prompts present generations to act in the manner of the great actors of the past without telling them whether imitating those actors is possible today, without addressing the dissimilarity of past and present conditions. Because past conditions cannot be replicated exactly in the present, monumental history is forced "to deal in approximations and generalities, in making what is dissimilar look similar" (70). Moreover, insofar as the past is never quite the same as the present, the monumentalist historian runs the risk of mistaking distortion for duplication and consequently inspiring foolish acts. Nietzsche warns: "Monumental history deceives by analogies: with seductive similarities it inspires the courageous to foolhardiness and the inspired to fanaticism; and when we go on to think of this kind of history in the hands and heads of gifted egoists and visionary scoundrels, then we see empires destroyed, princes murdered, wars and revolutions launched and the number of historical 'effects in themselves', that is to say, effects without sufficient cause, again and again augmented" (71). Finally, monumental history can be used as an argument against the emerging greatness of one's contemporaries, an argument that says: to be great, one must possess the authority only history can confer; therefore, what you are now doing is condemned to be a poor approximation of past greatness. In these senses, monumental histories can and often do produce undesirable results that place history not in the service but the disservice of life.

The second kind of history Nietzsche discusses is the antiquarian. This kind stems from the human need to preserve the past from which one has come and is driven by the very desire monumentalist history disregards, namely, the desire to circumscribe human existence. Trying to account for rather than inspire by past events and actions, the antiquarian historian pays close attention to the conditions that made possible the events and paved the way for the great actors whom the monumentalist portrays as exemplary. The antiquarian approach to the past produces narratives that explain why events turned out the way they did. These narratives purport to establish causal links among events and to depict past deeds as necessary manifestations and inevitable outcomes of what came before them. Emphasizing causes rather than effects, antiquarian history connects not one great individual to another but a set of conditions to a set of subsequent outcomes. The antiquarian's insistence on causality, necessity, and inevitability removes accidents and chance from the course of history and, in so doing, eliminates the splendor of individual greatness that monumentalist history seeks to highlight.

Antiquarian history places the past in the service of life by giving people a sense of their own historicity. Situating human action within specific contexts, antiquarian accounts of the past bind human experience to recognizable forms of human activity and endow human existence with the kind of stability that continuity affords. Driven by a sense of gratitude for the people, materials, and conditions that helped shape current practices and forms of life, the antiquarian historian attempts to preserve lovingly the wherefrom of existence. In so doing, he confers "dignity and inviolability" to whatever is regarded "trivial, circumscribed, decaying and obsolete" (1983a, 73). As such, his narrative accounts provide present generations with a sense of belonging, in effect making them "contented with their own homeland and its customs" (73). At the same time, they offer them a self-reflective sense of themselves, that is, the gift of self-understanding, the recognition that "one is not wholly accidental and arbitrary but grown out of a past as its heir, flower and fruit, and that one's existence is thus excused and, indeed, justified" (74). Such a recognition becomes possible when the past is constructed along the lines of a familiar context, a background against which human identities can be discerned. In the words of Mark

Warren (1988), "The antiquarian understands that contexts allowing recognition are rooted in the continuity of the present with the past, that they grow within and through traditions which in turn come to define a people's horizon of existence" (84).

If the risk of monumentalist history is that it can lead to unwarranted and misplaced action, the risk of antiquarian history is that it can lead to an uncritical acceptance of the past as the reservoir of all meaning for human existence, the source from which all forms of self-understanding spring, and the necessary context within which human experience can be recognized as such. More specifically, the danger with the antiquarian approach to the past lies in its readiness to confer respect to whatever is old, dead, or past at the expense of what is new, living, or present. In the words of Nietzsche, "Antiquarian history itself degenerates from the moment it is no longer animated and inspired by the fresh life of the present. Its piety withers away, the habit of scholarliness continues without it and rotates in egoistic self-satisfaction around its own axis" (1983a, 75).

Despite their differences, both the monumental and antiquarian approaches to history have at least one thing in common: they stand in contrast to the "objectivist" approach. As narrative accounts of the past, they make no claims about verifiable data and entertain no illusions of mirroring "the real" or capturing its essence. Rather, they acknowledge the capacity of language to mediate between observer and historical "fact," recognize the constitutive function of narrativity in reconstructing past events, and admit the active presence of personal interest and investment on the part of the historian. In this regard, monumental and antiquarian historical narratives furnish us with knowledge not of "the real" but of the self and its capacity to construct the real. As such, they have more to do with self-understanding than with forms of "objective" knowledge.

Thus far we have glanced briefly at the benefits and dangers of the monumental and antiquarian kinds of history. Taken together, they inform the dialectic of historical self-knowledge and action: although I see myself as a historical being, I act; or, I act despite my understanding of myself as historically determined. Acting alone, without a historical sense of myself (monumentalism), is not only foolish but it leads nowhere. On the other hand, understanding myself only as the product of the past (antiquarianism) robs me of my sense of freedom and reduces me to inactivity. Clearly, neither approach is in itself satisfactory; the monumentalist underscores action while the antiquarian stresses a historical sense of oneself. But insofar as self-knowledge and action are two different things, the problem becomes one of translating knowledge of the past into action in the present. If putting history in the service of life means anything, it means turning the past into a resource for the practice of living.

The solution Nietzsche offers to the problem posed by monumental and antiquarian approaches to the past is critical history. This kind of history arises from the occasional need "to break up and dissolve a part of the past" (1983a, 75), specifically that part that interferes with present living. This need is not a function of one's sense of justice or one's feeling of mercy but of "life alone, that dark, driving power that insatiably thirsts for itself." The verdict of life against the past is "always unmerciful, always unjust, because it has never proceeded out of a pure well of knowledge." Time and again, the critical historian suspends the search for greatness in the past as well as the effort to preserve reverently the artifacts of earlier times and "cruelly tramples over every kind of piety" (76). The critical conception of the past operates from the assumption that much of what the past has produced is dysfunctional and useless because it was not, indeed, it could not have been, produced with our present predicament in mind. Therefore, if we are to place history in the service of our life, we must rid ourselves of the burdens of the past and strive to create from them materials that are useful, that augment our capacity to live joyfully.

Critical history is especially called for in times of failed or failing practices, cultural inertia, and nihilistic sentiments. During such times, whole generations can be overtaken by a sense of powerlessness before the all-determining character of the past and, as a result, resign themselves to their inability to shape their existence actively or to have some say on the direction and significance of their own life. Insofar as one turns this state of affairs into an object of investigation, in effect searching for those strands of history that have caused this particular present, one practices critical history. The critical historian, in other words, accepts neither the verdict of destiny nor the impotence of the subject in creating its own identity. In and through this refusal, he begins the process of looking for a historical explanation of a problematic situation in the present. The thrust of this kind of history, according to Nietzsche, is to put "the past on trial, by painstakingly investigating it, and finally condemning it. . . . The same life that needs forgetfulness sometimes needs to destroy this forgetfulness; for should it ever become clear how unjust the existence of something is, a monopoly, a caste, or a dynasty, for example, then this thing deserves to fall" (76). In other words, what one has inherited from the past is not simply a set of determining factors that have once and for all prefigured the present but rather a set of traditions that must be subjected to critical scrutiny. If done well, critical history can enable its readers to begin acting once again in historically informed and existentially relevant ways.

As in the case of monumental and antiquarian histories, critical history, too, has potential dangers. To begin with, it "destroys illusions and robs the things that exist of the atmosphere in which alone they can live" (95). Moreover, it disregards our connection to the errors, aberrations, and crimes of our ancestors without altering "the fact that we originate in them" (76). Further, it denies us the ability to "regard ourselves as the heirs and successors of the astonishing powers of antiquity and see in this our honor and our spur" (103). For Nietzsche, "The best we can do is to confront our inherited and hereditary nature with our knowledge of it, and through a new, stern discipline combat our inborn heritage and implant in ourselves a new habit, a new instinct, a second nature, so that our first nature withers away" (76).

In the next part of the essay I argue that Nietzsche's historical work on rhetoric exhibits features of the three kinds of history he discusses. His monumentalism is apparent in his treatment of the Hellenic culture and the Sophists against the rhetorics of his time. Embarrassed by the pedantry and crudeness of his own age, Nietzsche in *The Will to Power* looks at the remote past and finds in the pre-Socratic culture of Hellas "the highest self affirmation and transfiguration of existence that has yet been attained on earth. Here we have a standard by which everything that has grown up since is found too short, too poor, too narrow" (1967b, #1051). All subsequent cultures can be said to have been unable to comprehend and appreciate Hellenic antiquity: "What do any latter-day men, the children of a fragmentary, multifarious, sick, strange age, know of the *range* of Greek happiness; what *could* they know of it!" (#1051). With "an excess of powers at its disposal," the Greek culture of the fifth century B.C. became "a hothouse for the luxury cultivation" of exceptional individuals like the Sophists, whose greatness is attributable "to the free play and scope of [their] desires and to the yet greater power that knows how to press these magnificent monsters into service" (#933). Unlike the fourth-century philosophers, whose rational moralism reflects "the decadence of every kind of Greek excellence," the Sophists "developed out of all the Greek instincts." As such, they advanced "the first *critique of morality*" (#428) in which they attack morality-in-itself as nonexistent. Seeing in morality the worst enemy of life, Nietzsche admires and praises the Sophists for possessing "the courage of all strong spirits to *know* their own immorality" (#429). Apparently, Nietzsche finds inspiration from the Sophists' project of subjecting their inherited morality to criticism. Himself a critic of Christian morality, he depicts the Sophists as courageous and strong spirits whose rhetorical enterprises he finds worthy of imitation in the latter part of the nineteenth century.

Nietzsche's admiration for the culture of the Greek Sophists extends to rhetoric, which he calls "the breath of this artistic people" (cited in Ijsseling 1976, 107). Contemptuous of his contemporaries' interest in books, factual accuracy, and pseudolearnedness, Nietzsche praises the Greeks for their persistent industry in perfecting rhetoric: "To no task did the Greeks devote such incessant labor as to eloquence." Their accomplished orators were quite aware of their power to "control 'opinion about things' and hence the *effect of things upon men*" (1989, 213; Nietzsche's emphasis). Through their eloquent performances, they not only amazed their listeners; they also prompted a whole nation to appreciate elegance in the sound of words and to find pleasure in speaking (214). Put to magnificent practice by Homer, the tragedians, the forensic orators, Thucydides, Isocrates, Demosthenes, and so many others, rhetoric can justifiably be called "the most tenacious element of Greek culture" (213) and the culminating point of one's education in that culture (3). Clearly, Nietzsche's admiration of Hellenic rhetoric constitutes a call to action for his intellectual contemporaries. The "great actors" of Greek rhetoric have produced rhetorical "effects" that have become standards of excellence for contemporary rhetorical actions. Therefore, subsequent rhetoricians, and certainly those in the nineteenth century, would serve and be served well if they would strive to imitate the rhetoric of the Greeks.

Nietzsche's antiquarianism is apparent in two texts, his "What I Owe the Ancients," the concluding statement of his *Twilight of the Idols* (1968), and in his lecture notes on rhetoric. In the first text, he expresses gratitude to select people and ideas from antiquity. For example, he attributes his fascination with style to Sallust and Horace: "My sense of style . . . was awoken almost instantaneously on coming into contact with Sallust" and "no poet has given me the same artistic delight as I derived from the very first from an Horatian ode" (105). In the sophistical realism of Thucydides he says that he finds his "cure" for the decadent moralism and idealism of Plato and the Church (106–7). In the pre-Socratic Greeks' festivals and arts he reveals that he discovers "their strongest instinct, the will to power" (107) and in their religious mysteries "that wonderful phenomenon which bears the name Dionysus" (108).

While Nietzsche's indebtedness to the above people and ideas is an example of antiquarianism-as-reverence, his lecture notes on rhetoric take the form of antiquarianism-as-preservation. In and through these notes, Nietzsche preserves not only names, dates, events, and *topoi* familiar to historians of rhetoric but also parts of the work of some of his contemporaries, for example, Richard Volkmann, Gustav Gerber, and Friedrich Blass (see Vickers 1990, 459). With the exception of a few personal asides, these notes were canonized material he borrowed for the purpose of conducting class. As such, they tell us precious little about Nietzsche as a historian of rhetoric. However, had he written a history of rhetoric as such, one can be sure he would have left no stone unturned in his path. Understanding himself to have been in part determined by those who came before him, Nietzsche acknowledges his debt to a few predecessors but is not immobilized by their influence. Rather, he goes on to put his heritage into productive uses. Specifically, he establishes telling links between himself and the Sophists, Thucydides, the Greeks' festivals and religious mysteries, Sallust, and Horace. In so doing, he actively shapes himself as a historical being whose actions bespeak of a man determined by and indebted to antiquity yet living in modernity.

Nietzsche's criticalism is obvious throughout his writings. Whether one reads his condemnation of Christianity, his rejection of Platonism, or his repudiation of metaphysics, one witnesses an irrepressible and tireless critic smashing all icons whose worship had twisted, dwarfed, and disfigured the human personality in the nineteenth century. His critical remarks pertaining to rhetoric are mostly directed against the insensitivity of his culture to the study and practice of eloquence. Aware that the art of discourse during his age was held "in some disrepute" (1989, 3), Nietzsche refers to his contemporaries as "unrefined speech empiricists" (21) and in "Schopenhauer as Educator" decries the lack of rhetorical training in his country: "Anyone who seriously wanted to train in Germany as an orator . . . would find that school nowhere" (1983b, 131). Nietzsche attributes this lack of feeling for eloquence to the perverse love of learned people for theory that has no connection to life. In the posthumously published *We Philologists* (1964), Nietzsche writes: "Antiquity was acquainted only with theories of oratory . . . that formed real orators . . . 'while at the present day we shall soon have theories upon which it would be as impossible to build a speech . . . as it would be to form a thunderstorm upon a brontological treatise' " (60). Trampling over such pieties as objectivist historical claims, "the idolatry of the factual" (1983a, 105), moralistic blueprints by the improvers of mankind, and the epistemological doctrines of hyperrational philosophers, Nietzsche sought to bring down the establishments of factual truth, the castes of the priests, and the dynasties of the metaphysicians. True of his own criticalism, he did all this in order to open a space for historically informed action and a new transvaluation of inherited values.

As we have seen, the three kinds of history Nietzsche discusses find simultaneous expression in his own works. In his unreserved admiration of the great Sophists, he is being a monumentalist; in his awareness of his debt to the ancients, an antiquarian; and in his denunciation of the discourses of Platonism, Christianity, and nineteenth-century historicism, a criticalist. In all three cases, however, the problem remains the same: how to address the past adequately without falling into the traps each historical attitude hides. What makes this problem especially difficult for us is the fact that it posits two contrary conceptions of the past with each conception entertained along three conflicting registers. On the one hand, Nietzsche wants to remember, to consult, and to forget the past as it has been handed down. On the other, he wants to recreate it as a source of powerful motivations, assuring explanations, and burdensome impositions.

The two Nietzschean conceptions of the past are held together by the dialectic of memory and forgetfulness. The great actors of the past must not be forgotten—they inspire us to action, and they enable us to overcome the fears and weaknesses of our modernity. Yet their remembrance must not be permitted to overshadow our will to act in our own times; sooner or later, it must be eased out of our consciousness as we undertake deeds demanded by our present predicament. Likewise, the historical causes whose partial effects we are cannot be forgotten for they help explain an otherwise inexplicable and nonsensical present. Even so, these very same causes must be forgotten, if only temporarily, for they tend to derail us from attending to our principal task, the task of living regardless of the factors that have determined us. Finally, one cannot afford to forget that life is meant to be lived in the present, a time that needs to be freed from the bondage of established truths and traditions. Yet, if the present is to be made meaningful, the truths and traditions from the past cannot be eradicated from our memory entirely. Entertaining some illusions is necessary for life.

Although Nietzsche's three histories can be said to be held together by the interplay of memory and forgetfulness, they are driven by the dissatisfactions of the present—if one is overly content with the way things are, one does not feel the need to interrogate and overturn them. But these dissatisfactions cannot be addressed adequately by simply remembering the life and works of our progenitors. Such remembering often debilitates us because it explains; and what is explained time and again along the same lines achieves justification and respect even when it deserves dismissal and contempt. Remembering also disables because it can take the form of indulgence in idle admiration, the kind that prevents new versions of greatness from ever emerging. Finally, it cripples because it stifles the development of a healthy sense of selfhood and because it keeps the door to unprecedented critical actions shut. The same, however, can be said about forgetting. Individual or collective amnesia incapacitates because it denies us the great examples from the past, thus leaving us uninspired, pessimistic, and inferior. Alternatively, it harbors in us the illusion that we are the sole architects of our fate, untouched by the outcomes of our ancestors' actions. Last, it deprives us of the possibility of acting in historically informed ways.

If the above analysis is correct, how are historians of rhetoric to address the Nietzschean problem? I have already suggested that Nietzsche's own example argues for an orientation that combines all three kinds of history. In what follows, I contend that each type of history alludes to a corresponding characteristic of rhetoric: monumentalism to action, antiquarianism to particulars, and criticalism to change. Proceeding analogically, I maintain that historians of rhetoric can serve us well by complementing Nietzsche's threefold historical orientation with a rhetorical awareness that accounts for action, particulars, and change.

Traditionally, rhetoric has been linked to action. Orators always suggest ways of acting to combat a crisis, to raise the consciousness of the masses, to end intolerable conditions, or to stop injurious practices.

Alternatively, they recommend action in order to improve a situation, to better the lot of the audience, or to augment the pleasures of living. But despite the prospective outlook and hopeful dispositions behind all action, arguments advocating action always involve some aspect of the past. As a rule, orators invoke the past to motivate their listeners to imitate or surpass it in its magnitude and to prove themselves at least equal to the excellence of their predecessors.

Another traditional characteristic of rhetoric is its affinity with the particularities of life, the urgencies of everydayness, and the specificities of the world. Unlike philosophy, which is interested in abstractions and the general case, rhetoric attends to unique situations, singular happenings, and unreplicated events. In their attempts to make such occurrences meaningful, orators employ a particular approach that combines present and past events. But from the myriads of happenings at their disposal, they always choose some and ignore others. In so doing, they highlight certain explanations about the present while putting others in the shade. But because no choice is in and of itself necessary, what is chosen and what is not depends on the orator's purpose. But if this is so, every rhetorical purpose can be viewed as an amalgam of remembrance and forgetfulness.

Yet another feature of rhetoric is its interest in change. Occasionally, orators do speak to preserve the inherited status of things, especially when it is threatened. However, they most often speak either to make sudden changes meaningful or to bring about new changes, to effect a new world, or to affirm this one but in other words. Their guiding supposition has always been that the way things are is mostly unnecessary and nearly always undesirable. But since the way things are has partly been determined by the past, that past needs to be undone. But because change is always *from* something *to* something else, the undoing of the past requires a thorough understanding of what is being undone. Paradoxically, a certain mention of the past is often necessary, even if we are directed to bury and forget that very past.

These three characteristics of rhetoric are not exhaustive. However, they are so central that they should not be left out of account in any history of rhetoric. Accordingly, historians of rhetoric need to go beyond identifying great rhetorical epochs and specify the kinds of action they wish us to undertake. Further, they need to go beyond preserving and transmitting our rhetorical traditions and identify particular linkages explaining why current rhetorical practices are as they are. Last, they need to go beyond reevaluating our rhetorical heritage in the light of our present conditions and point to the specific changes they desire to see happen. In effect, historians of rhetoric need to realize that their task of writing history is a rhetorical enterprise, an enterprise telling us to act this way rather than another, to apprehend our present condition under a certain kind of light, and to change the world we inhabit in specific ways. But if this is so, historians of rhetoric need not do to rhetoric what Nietzsche wanted to do to history—rhetoric has always been in the service of life. However, they do need to make sure they do not turn to history in order to be freed from its rhetoric.

Note

1. In addition to *Rhetorica: A Journal of History of The Rhetoric,* whose first issue appeared in 1983, consider also the issue of *PRE/TEXT* on Historiography and the Histories of Rhetoric (Spring/Summer, 1987) 8.1 2; George Kennedy (1980a); Brian Vickers (1990); Renato Barilli (1989); Terry Eagleton (1981); Thomas M. Conley (1990); Patricia Bizzell and Bruce Herzberg (1990); Thomas Cole (1991); Susan Jarratt (1991); Mark Backman (1991).

7

Contingencies of Historical Representation

Janet M. Atwill

In *The Differend* Jean-François Lyotard confronts what has come to embody a set of standard questions in historiography: reevaluations of the Third Reich that question not only the "uniqueness and moral meaning" (Nolan 1988, 51) of the Holocaust, but its very status as historical event.[1] Lyotard summarizes the argument of one such member of the French *nouvelle droite*, Robert Faurisson:

> The plaintiff complains that he has been fooled about the existence of gas chambers, fooled, that is, about the so-called Final Solution. His argument is: in order for a place to be identified as a gas chamber, the only eyewitness I will accept would be a victim of this gas chamber; now, according to my opponent, there is no victim that is not dead; otherwise, this gas chamber would not be what he or she claims it to be. There is, therefore, no gas chamber. (1988, 3–4)

Lyotard contends that Faurisson's interpretation of the Holocaust is a kind of performative act: it both negates the referent "gas chambers" and silences surviving victims, transforming them into defendants, who, according to the rules of evidence required by the plaintiff, have been "divested of the means to argue" (9). Lyotard calls this situation a "differend"—both a silence and an injustice that result when "the 'regulation' of the conflict that opposes them is done in the idiom of one of the parties while the wrong suffered by the other is not signified in that idiom" (9).[2]

I take Lyotard's discussion of the differend as a starting point for historiographical inquiry for the way in which it underscores the complex contingencies of historical reference. The conflict Lyotard describes between idioms might also be characterized as a conflict between genres, in this case a conflict between the genres of forensic and historical discourse. As Lyotard describes it, the differend is the momentary recognition of a silence effected by the impossibility of translating from one genre to another. On one level, the differend is a "feeling" that " 'one cannot find the right words' "; however, at a more strategic level the differend is an "unstable state and instant of language wherein something which must be able to be put into phrases cannot yet be" (1988, 13). In Faurisson's case, the differend results from the rigorous enforcement of the laws of forensic discourse, rules of evidence that have never been confronted by crimes of the magnitude of the Holocaust. According to the rules of discourse defined by Faurisson, surviving victims are negated and gas chambers "disappear." For this reason historian Vidal-Naquet calls Faurisson a " 'paper Eichmann,' " whose " 'attempt at extermination on paper runs relay for the actual extermination' " (1988, 32). It is the strategic incommensurability between genres, the deliberate failure to effect a linkage between the discourse of law and the discourse of human suffering, that allows Faurisson to claim a momentary discursive victory.

At the heart of Lyotard's analysis is the argument that "reality is not what is 'given' to this or that 'subject' " (1988, 4). Instead, reality is a "state of the referent," a state produced by "establishment procedures," which he describes as a complex network of contingencies capable of both stabilizing and destabilizing referents (4). Consequently, what is at stake in historiographical method is not simply getting the story "straight" or "crooked," right or wrong, but rather giving voice or creating silences.

It is my purpose to outline some of these contingencies in historical representation as they are discussed in the work of Lyotard and Barbara Herrnstein Smith. I shall use, admittedly somewhat loosely, the disciplinary distinctions in discourse theory between semantics, pragmatics, and syntactics to describe three different genres of history writing.[3] In this scheme, the semantic genre relies on the relationship between sign and referent (in this case, historical events, characters, etc.) to convey meaning, or what Lyotard will call "sense." We generally identify the conventions of the semantic genre with "traditional" historiography. The pragmatic genre focuses on the contexts and uses of discourse. In outlining this approach to historiography, I will focus, in some detail, on Barbara Herrnstein Smith's analysis of the construction of disciplinary exemplars. Finally, in exploring a syntactic perspective on historiography, I will return to Lyotard's metaphor of the linkage of phrases, genres, and idioms to explore the syntactic relationships not only *within* a text but also those constructed *by* the text between addressors and addressees. Clearly, pragmatic and syntactic perspectives on history have much in common. Both contrast with the semantic/referential genre of history writing, and both relocate the focus of historiographical inquiry away from signs and referents and onto addressors, addressees, and historical and institutional contexts. It is precisely this relocation of the problematic that makes Lyotard's discussion of the differend so relevant. The referent is only one dimension of discourse, one instance in the "universe of a phrase," which he maintains is composed of four "instances": (1) the referent, what a phrase is "about" (2) the sense, "what is signified about the case" (3) an addressee, that "*to* which" the sense is addressed and (4) the addressor, that "*through* which" the sense is addressed (Lyotard 1988, 14; emphasis mine). As Lyotard argues, only by the strategic enforcement of discursive laws governing the authority of addressors and addressees is Faurisson able to put the referent "gas chambers" into question.

This discussion requires several qualifications. First, I take the semantic genre of history writing as something of a "straw-man" theory. Few histories of rhetoric hold to a rigorous referential contract to match sign to historical event by which the semantic genre is defined here. Second, the genres of the semantic, pragmatic, and syntactic are as much reading strategies as textual conventions. Though I will offer examples of histories of rhetoric that might be placed is these categories, the conventions that distinguish them are better defined as reading signposts than inherent textual features. Finally, reading these texts as exemplars of historiographical perspectives is very different from reading them "for" histories of rhetoric. While this analysis will foreground some of the complexities in these texts, it will necessarily obscure others.

The Semantic Genre

Traditional semantics, as defined by Umberto Eco, is concerned with meaning that results from the "correct" correspondence of sign, referent, and object (1979, 62).[4] James Kinneavy defines semantics as "the study of the signals of a language as having meaning in the sense of being referrers to reality" (1971, 22). In Lyotard's terms, the semantic genre would focus on the first two "instances" of language: referent and sense. This genre is generally characterized by at least three sets of conventions: (1) it foregrounds itself as a reconstruction of historical figures and chronologies; (2) that reconstruction suppresses its own historicity; neither the historical exigencies that prompt such a reconstruction nor the institutional functions such a history would perform are marked problems; (3) in fulfilling its promise to deliver only signs and referents, the semantic genre obscures addressor/addressee relationships. Indeed, the authority of both addressor and addressee is established by the very absence of its discussion. Thus, on the whole, semantic histories place their own rhetorical situations in the background.

Since my primary argument is that histories always embody specific cultural contexts and institutional exigencies, the notion of a genre that could altogether suppress those contingencies is more of a hypothesis than a reality. Even those histories that would seem to hold most firmly to the conventions of the semantic genre situate themselves in ongoing institutional debates. For example, the opening paragraphs of George Kennedy's *The Art of Persuasion in Greece* admit the history's own rhetorical function, despite the fact that it proceeds with very traditional historiographical techniques. At least one dimension of Kennedy's project is to secure rhetoric as a legitimate subject of scholarly inquiry, particularly in the classics:

> One of the principal interests of the Greeks was rhetoric. Classicists admit the fact, deplore, and forget it. . . . But we will never understand the Greeks unless we understand what is peculiar about them. . . . In its origin and intention rhetoric was natural and good: it produced clarity, vigor and beauty, and it rose logically from the conditions and qualities of the classical mind. (1963, 3)

Similarly, Brian Vickers (1990) employs traditional historiographical techniques in his *Defense of Rhetoric*. However, his history of rhetoric from Aristotle to Derrida is also an argument: Vickers challenges rhetoric's identification with "insincerity, mere display, artifice, or ornament without substance" (xi). Charting what he sees as rhetoric's historical fragmentation as a discipline, he argues for its resituation as a coherent field of study that acknowledges "the relevance of history" (xi). Thus, even the most traditional histories acknowledge in some way their own historicity. In the semantic genre, however, these contingencies are more likely to frame the text than to form part of its narrative.

The Pragmatic Genre

In *A Theory of Discourse,* Kinneavy gives a traditional definition of pragmatics as the study of the "use of signals by encoders and decoders" (1971, 22). Since pragmatics focuses on the relationship between discourse and its "users," rather than that between sign and referent, the concerns of the "pragmatic" historian are rhetorical rather than referential. To the extent the historian's audience values "objective" history, the pragmatic historian will follow the conventions of the semantic genre. At the same time, the pragmatic historian admits that history is written to be "used." Either by foregrounding a particular institutional debate or theoretical perspective, the pragmatic historian explicitly acknowledges both the rhetorical and historical nature of his or her account. A pragmatic approach is thus implicitly nonobjectivist: language, meaning, addressors, and addressees exist in mutually constitutive relationships, which are themselves subject to a wide range of contingencies.

Smith brings the pragmatic perspective to bear on two levels of discourse. On one level, she offers a pragmatic account of how "objects" themselves are constructed in discourse; but at another level she approaches the construction of texts, themselves, as "objects," cultural artifacts that perform critical institutional functions. Her objective is to explode the myth of the "object"—whether it be a text or a supposedly discrete historical event—by rigorously interrogating the binary oppositions of fact/value and subject/object.

At the first discursive level, Smith maintains that referents are established by complex classificatory procedures that define "entities" according to the functions they perform in particular contexts. She explains:

> A subject's experience of an entity is always a function of his or her own personal economy: that is, the specific "existence" of an object or event, its integrity, coherence, and boundaries, the category of entities to which it "belongs," and its specific "features," "qualities," or "properties" are all the variable products of the subject's engagement with his or her environment under a particular set of conditions. (1988, 31–32)

Classificatory processes, according to Smith, "implicitly isolate and foreground" *not* inherent properties of objective entities, but rather their "possible functions" (32). Thus, neither the status nor the value of an object is contingent on its identity as a discrete object (its semantic or referential function); rather, both are measures of the extent to which entities perform "desired/able" (or pragmatic) "functions" (47).

The "personal economy" of the "subject" described above may suggest that Smith is invoking an autonomous agent with a private system of values. The "self" she describes, however, is not a static construct; rather, it is variably constituted in a variety of changing roles and relationships.[5] Moreover, economies can never be truly "private," since, as she points out, the "market economy" itself is made up of the "diverse personal economies of individual producers, distributors, consumers" (Smith 1988, 31). Most important, since objects are defined not by their intrinsic properties but by their functions for variably defined subjects and communities, objects and agents are mutually constitutive rather than autonomous. Discursive objects reaffirm and reproduce both classifications and attributions of value; in effect, they "produce the needs and interests they satisfy and evoke the purposes they implement" (32). Consequently, in this discursive terrain, referents are instituted and re-formed in a "continuous process of mutual modification between our desires and our universe" (32); and one identifies both subjects and objects by the strategies through which they constitute their dynamic boundaries rather than by their coherence as discrete entities.[6] In other words, "objects" may be said to constitute subjects as much as subjects constitute objects.

Though this nonobjectivist theory of discourse focuses on the shifting contingencies in the construction of discursive "objects," it also accounts for the ways discursive stability is secured. Once we move from the semantic to the pragmatic axis of discourse, we no longer have necessary relationships between signs and referents, but rather networks of contingencies, which, according to Smith, will appear noncontingent to the extent that they remain consistent. In other words, if a discursive object results from its success in performing a needed function for subjects in particular situations, then the stability of that object will depend on the stability of that community's needs, conditions, and subjects. It is that very stability that transforms contingencies into intrinsic properties.[7]

At the second discursive level, Smith examines textual exemplars, themselves, as signs. Though she focuses on the means by which the academy constructs literary exemplars, her analysis is also applicable to histories as disciplinary exemplars. Smith argues that the relationship between disciplines and exemplars is as mutually constitutive as that between subjects and objects. Exemplars "incorporate" the values of a disciplinary community, reinforcing the community's own referential status by reproducing its values and affirming its practices. Disciplinary exemplars are secured by three sets of contingencies: functions, conditions, and subjects—all of which are inextricably tied. Functions only exist, for example, in relation to specific subjects and conditions.

The first contingency of "conditions" is multilayered, including not only a community's social and historical situation but also its "materials, technology, and techniques" (Smith 1988, 47).[8] In particular, "conditions" include canons, theories, and methodologies—in other words, texts and instructions for reading them. Thomas Kuhn's description of an exemplar as a concrete "puzzle-solution" is helpful in defining the relationship between functions and conditions. According to Kuhn (1970), a disciplinary exemplar defines the state of a community's inquiry and methodologies by reproducing specific disciplinary problems and solutions.[9] Exemplars "exist" for a disciplinary community to the extent that they "answer" certain questions and delimit others. Moreover, specific methodologies ensure that a community will continue to find the same questions answered in a particular exemplar. For example, when particular histories of rhetoric no longer answer a community's important questions, or when new questions arise, these histories will either lose their status as exemplars or be reconstituted to answer questions a community has found more pressing. Thus, the longevity of an exemplar is contingent on its ability to persist in delimiting a range of standard questions.[10]

The third contingency, that of subjects, is particularly critical in the construction of exemplars. Though that contingency will be examined in more detail in the discussion of "syntactic" histories, one of the chief merits of Smith's analysis is her careful highlighting of the inextricability of functions and conditions from carefully demarcated constituencies. Again, since functions are not intrinsic properties of self-contained objects, a pragmatic perspective on discourse displaces notions of discrete subjects and objects since both exist only in a mutually constitutive relationship. However, if function defines an object, that object will endure only as long as the community of subjects who define those functions remains relatively stable. Smith explains:

> Some aspect, or perhaps many aspects, of a work may be constituted in similar ways by numerous different subjects, *among whom we may include the author*: to the extent that this duplication occurs, however, it will be because the subjects who do the constituting, *including the author*, are themselves similar, not only or simply in being human creatures (and thereby, as it is commonly supposed, "sharing an underlying humanity" and so on) but in occupying a particular universe that may be, for them, in many respects recurrent or relatively continuous and stable, and/or in inheriting from one another, through mechanisms of cultural transmission, certain ways of interacting with that universe, including certain ways of interacting with texts and "works of literature." (48)

In other words, the longevity of a disciplinary exemplar is dependent on the longevity of a particular community. Consequently, the "test of time" is largely a test of the sustained homogeneity of a particular constituency—a homogeneity that is secured by both self-selection and strategies for inculcating members into a community. These strategies are effective to the extent that new members resemble the old by the time they are given the community's full privileges. Thus, if histories of rhetoric, as disciplinary exemplars, answer new questions, it is likely that different subjects are asking them.

While Smith would contend that all texts are written in what I have called the "pragmatic genre," I would like to use this category to examine several histories of rhetoric that foreground, rather than obscure, their functions and conditions—and, in so doing, effect shifts in disciplinary values and methodologies. Clearly, pragmatic histories will appear on a continuum with regard to their foregrounding of functions and methodologies. More explicit pragmatic approaches are found in histories that proceed from the perspectives of feminism,

Marxism, and cultural studies. These examinations focus in a more radical way on the role of functions and conditions in both the interpretation of history and the determination of what subjects and events merit historical analysis. For example, Pierre Vidal-Naquet's examination of women, slaves, and artisans in *The Black Hunter* (1983) focuses attention on subjects and events generally neglected in ancient histories. Martin Bernal's *Black Athena: The Afroasiatic Roots of Classical Civilization,* volumes I and II (1987, 1991), reconstruct neglected Egyptian and Semitic intellectual traditions and documents biases in classical studies that effaced those traditions. Susan Jarratt's *Rereading the Sophists: Classical Rhetoric Refigured* (1991) explicitly appropriates the Sophists as a paradigm for reframing contemporary issues in rhetoric and composition from a feminist perspective.

James Berlin's work is well known for its pragmatic, "revisionist" orientation. His *Writing Instruction in Nineteenth-Century American Colleges* (1984) and *Rhetoric and Reality: Writing Instruction in American Colleges, 1900–1985* (1987b) both reflect and induce shifts in what Smith calls the "conditions" of a disciplinary matrix. On one level, Berlin's histories work to demarcate rhetoric and composition as a legitimate domain of inquiry. As Donald Stewart notes in his foreward to *Writing Instruction in Nineteenth-Century American Colleges,* Berlin's book "joins an astonishingly small list of works of serious scholarship which attempt to give teachers of English composition a sense of history about the one course which has, for decades, been taken by more American college students than any other" (1984, ix).

On another level, Berlin alters institutional values and methodologies by making the social practices of writing and teaching the subject of scholarly analysis. *Rhetoric and Reality*'s express purpose is "to vindicate the position of writing instruction in the college curriculum" (1987b, 1). The basis of this vindication, however, is not traditional categories and referents in the history of rhetoric. Instead, Berlin proceeds from the perspective of the analysis of culture, which he explicitly locates in the work of Clifford Geertz, Sacvan Bercovitch, and Goran Therborn (4). Berlin spells out the terms of his contract with the reader: he begins with the thesis that "transformations that occur in a society's rhetorics are also related to larger social and political developments" (4). This perspective disallows a semantic contract with the reader. Berlin admits that his taxonomy of objectivist, subjectivist, and transactional rhetorics is heuristic rather than referential: "None of the categories is monolithic;

each offers a diversity of rhetorical theories. . . . This taxonomy is not meant to be taken as exhaustive of the entire field of rhetoric, but is simply an attempt to make manageable the discussion of the major rhetorics I have entered in examining this period" (6). From Smith's perspective, such a foregrounding of the historian's theoretical orientation could only scratch the surface of the dense matrix of values and practices that constitute a discipline's objects of study. However, this foregrounding of assumptions and intentions is a tacit admission that the demarcation of a "history" is always partial and strategic.

The Syntactic Genre

Carnap described syntactics as the analysis of "relations between . . . expressions" (1942, 9). As an analysis of such relations, a syntactic genre of history writing foregrounds the rules governing what Lyotard calls phrases, idiom, and genres. For Lyotard, these rules invariably determine the authority of addressors and addressees. Like Smith, Lyotard challenges the subject/object opposition in discourse. In his refiguration, however, subjects are posited with each new linkage of phrases; and every act of turn-taking—every new linkage—constitutes a different subject.[11] Thus, from a syntactic perspective, subjects are "instances" of discourse rather than its source or end.[12]

Lyotard contends that discourse is not simply shaped by context; rather, discourse is constitutive of contexts, subjects, and objects. Addressors and addressees are "instances," which are "presented by a phrase"; they are "situated in the universe the phrase presents, as are its referent and its sense" (1988, 11). A "phrase universe" inevitably suppresses certain instances and foregrounds others; and it is this suppression and foregrounding that either creates or prevents particular linkages.[13] The laws that govern these linkages, according to Lyotard, are generic laws—or what we might call generic conventions. What is important, however, is that these conventions invariably include standards by which the authority of both the writer and the audience is judged. In other words, a particular genre can either confer legitimacy on an addressee or deny it. From Lyotard's perspective, the conventions that create a textual genre are less important than the conventions that create writers and audiences.

A syntactic approach to history writing would foreground the construction of both author and audience. A syntactic history, in Lyotard's lexicon, would focus on the linkages a genre creates between addressors and addressees; and those linkages may either solicit new audiences or transform old ones. Though the "addressors" to which I shall point, C. H. Knoblauch and Lil Brannon and Victor Vitanza, would seem to be on opposite extremes of an ideological continuum, their histories are similar in their attempts to effect new linkages with addressees.

In *Rhetorical Traditions and the Teaching of Writing* (1984), Knoblauch and Brannon make an explicit attempt to create a linkage between the academy and teachers of writing. Their audience is invoked in the role of teacher rather than researcher, and their general argument is that classical rhetoric has little to offer to a contemporary philosophy of composition. Maintaining that classical rhetoric is grounded in an epistemology completely at odds with modern thought, they argue that the philosophy that must underwrite a contemporary theory of composition has its roots in the seventeenth century, "when ancient faith in the probity and completeness of traditional lore about the world gave way before a newly skeptical habit of mind" (1984, 51).

In one sense, their history has a very pragmatic cast. They insist that "the history of rhetoric is an enigma to English teachers, its texts unread and its evolution misunderstood" (3). Their cursory treatment of the history of rhetoric is aimed at demystifying that enigma in order to find a tradition and a philosophy that may be used by composition teachers. But their account is also an attempt to invoke different addressees and thus create a linkage between rhetoric and composition as a "sophisticated and intellectually respectable enterprise" and a relatively disenfranchised constituency of writing teachers (2). Judged by traditional standards in philosophy and history writing, their account of rhetoric's history is likely to fare rather poorly. However, as a syntactic history of rhetoric that attempts to create a linkage between the research university and writing teachers, their history fares significantly better.

Vitanza's treatments of the history of rhetoric are similarly concerned with the construction of new linkages. Those linkages are effected largely by the invention of genres that require us to constitute ourselves as very different readers. His subversive genre of history writing persistently focuses attention on the relationship between addressor and addressee. At the beginning of " 'Notes' Towards Historiographies of Rhetoric," Vitanza invites readers to "indulge themselves by entering the text at any point" (1987b, 64). Readers are instructed to customize the text to their dispositions: "For those more comfortable with a genus-species, arboressent style, there's *The* middle" (1987, 64). It is precisely this type of customizing, however, that forces us to become different readers. To the extent that we cannot use traditional reading strategies for Vitanza's texts, we are forced to be complicit with his attempt to deform what Smith calls institutional "conditions."

Vitanza's interest in this deformation is explicit. The conventions of subversive histories are inversions of traditional historiographical conventions; subversive histories are directed "against reality" and rationality (112). Moreover, he is aware that such a history will effect a similar deformation in the relationship between its addressor and addressee. Vitanza's subversive histories aim at breaking the "bondage" of the academic "polis" (111). The subversive historian is a Deleuzian schizoid, whose genre attempts to resituate both addressor and addressee on a different discursive, ideological, and epistemological plane: "If not a dweller in cities, then a nomad. A schizoid is a nomad. S/he has geography without a state, without a map. She has lexical territory without a dictionary or a grammar (*la langue*)" (111). Thus, if we allow ourselves to be invoked as addressees of Vitanza's subversive histories, we must become a very different player in a very different language game.

Conclusion

These summaries of both theories and histories do small justice to the texts; and my discussion of them has certainly been a pragmatic gesture, directed toward multiplying our terms for discussing historiographical method. Smith and Lyotard point to two specific contingencies of historical representation, institutions and subjects, which I would argue deserve closer scrutiny as we both write and write about histories of rhetoric. First, any inquiry into historiography is a tacit admission that histories function as both cultural and institutional signs. Histories do not simply provide windows on the past; rather, they perform signifying functions in the present. Lyotard's conception of generic rules and Smith's notion of institutional conditions provide two ways of discussing those signifying functions; and both Lyotard and Smith point to the necessity of interrogating the standards by which these rules and conditions are secured.

The one contingency to which they point most decisively, however, is that of subjects. At the simplest level, alternative histories of rhetoric will not be written until alternative subjects begin both to define the functions of those histories and to alter the conditions in which they are produced. In other words, we will only begin to redress the silences created by histories when we are willing to allow our own disciplinary idioms to be challenged. "To give the differend its due," Lyotard maintains, "is to institute new addressees, new addressors, new significations, and new referents" (1988, 13). While race, gender, and class are necessary means of defining these new addressors and addressees, these classifications are not exhaustive. They do not account for the infinite ways differences may be described (demographic differences, for example) or for the many roles that supersede race, gender, and class. Thus, alternative histories will require not only multiplying our standards for adjudicating the value of exemplars but also the value of their addressors and addressees. These histories may not perform the stabilizing function of more traditional exemplars—indeed, they will be more prone to produce controversy than consensus. However, it is only through such conflict that we are able to interrogate our own historiographical assumptions and rules of discourse—and write new histories of rhetoric.

Notes

1. The issue of *New German Critique* in which Nolan's article appears is devoted entirely to recent attempts to normalize, historicize, and reinterpret the Third Reich. See also Katz (1992).

2. Lyotard describes another example of a differend: "A Martinican is a French citizen; he or she can bring a complaint against whatever impinges upon his or her rights as a French citizen. But the wrong he or she deems to suffer from the fact of being a French citizen is not a matter for litigation under French law. It might be under private or public international law, but for that to be the case it would be necessary that the Martinican were no longer a French citizen. But he or she is. Consequently, the assertion according to which he or she suffers a wrong on account of his or her citizenship is not verifiable by explicit and effective procedures" (1988, 27).

3. The distinctions between semantics, pragmatics, and syntactics are treated by Kinneavy (1971) and Eco (1979), though Eco raises them largely to critique them.

4. Eco (1979) distinguishes traditional semantics from structural semantics; instead of isolating a sign, structural semantics places it "in a system of other cultural units which are opposed to it and circumscribe it" (73).

5. Smith explains, "It must be emphasized that any particular subject's 'self'—or that in behalf of which he or she may be said to act with 'self-

interest'—is also variable, being multiply and differently configurable in terms of different roles, relationships, and, in effect, identities (citizen, parent, woman, property owner, teacher, terrestrial organism, mortal being, etc.), in relation to which different needs and interests acquire priority (and, as may happen, come into conflict) under different conditions" (1988, 31).

6. "Because our purposes are continuously transformed and redirected by the objects we produce in the very process of implementing them, and because of the complex interrelations among human needs, technological production, and cultural practices, there is a continuous process of mutual modification between our desires and our universe" (Smith 1988, 32).

7. Put another way, "a co-incidence of contingencies among individual subjects who interact as members of some community will operate for them as noncontingency and be interpreted by them accordingly" (Smith 1988, 40).

8. Smith elaborates: "It is assumed or maintained . . . that the particular *conditions* (circumstantial, technological, institutional, and so forth) under which the members of the group typically interact with those objects are suitable, standard, or necessary-for-their-proper appreciation, all other conditions being exceptional, peculiar, irregular, unsuitable, or substandard" (1988, 41).

9. Kuhn (1970) argues that exemplars as "concrete puzzle-solutions" can "replace explicit rules as the basis for the solution of the remaining puzzles of normal science" (175).

10. Smith describes an exemplar's "dynamics of endurance": "An object or artifact that performs certain desired/able functions particularly well at a given time for some community of subjects, being perhaps not only 'fit' but exemplary—that is, 'the best of its kind'—under those conditions, will have an immediate survival advantage; for relative to (or in competition with) other comparable objects or artifacts available at that time, it will not only be better protected from physical deterioration but will also be more frequently used or widely exhibited and, if it is a text or verbal artifact, more frequently read or recited, copied or reprinted, translated, imitated, cited, and commented upon—in short, culturally re-produced" (1988, 48).

11. For another elaboration of subjectivity as "turn-taking," see Bakhtin (1986).

12. Lyotard's critique of subjects as the source and end of discourse explicitly challenges the communication model of discourse: "The human and linguistic sciences presuppose that the human beings they are supposed to know are in possession of something they communicate. And the powers that be (ideological, political, religious, police, etc.) presuppose that the human beings they are supposed to guide, or at least control, are in possession of something they communicate. Communication is the exchange of messages, exchange the communication of goods" (1988, 12).

13. " '*X's* phrase, *my* phrase, *your* silence': do *we*, identifiable individuals, *x*, *y*, speak phrases or make silences in that sense that we would be their authors? Or is it that phrases or silences take place (happen, come to pass), presenting universes in which individual *x*, *y*, you, me are situated as addressors of these phrases or silences?" (Lyotard 1988, 11).

8

Revisionary Histories of Rhetoric | *Politics, Power, and Plurality*

James A. Berlin

Our "official" histories of rhetoric—the formulations of George Kennedy (1980a) and Edward P. J. Corbett (1990) and Brian Vickers (1990) and Wilbur Samuel Howell (1971), for example—depict rhetoric's historical trajectory as a march of ideas, ideas characterized as unified, coherent, and rational. Rhetoric has a life of its own in the aerie realm of the intellectual firmament, transcending the play of economics and politics and power. From this lofty perch it serves as a mighty helpmate to those who would serve truth and virtue and a demystifying foe against illusion and self-interest. The tradition of rhetoric is one, and its authentic exponents are united in a common language and purpose. Plato speaks to Aristotle and Aristotle to Cicero and Cicero to Quintilian and Quintilian to Augustine and Augustine to himself until Aristotle and Cicero and Quintilian are again given their due respect in the Renaissance, when the word of words, "rhetoric," is again taken forward. This traditionalist account, furthermore, is accepted with appropriate modifications even by those who disagree about the foundation and objective of this transparent conversation. Whether the one, true, holy, catholic, and apostolic rhetoric is situated in the golden age of the past or anticipated in the golden age of the future, there is no disagreement about its monolithic character, even though the two constituencies—the traditionalists and the progressives—disagree about the elements that make up the monolith and their trajectories. The role of women, subordinate classes, and other subaltern groups in these narratives does, however, remain consistent: they are conspicuous by absence.

For Kennedy, Corbett, and Vickers, the eternal rhetoric is located at the source of the dialogue, among the ancients who set the fundamental terms of the discussion in motion. (Vickers has even recovered for us the Sophists and their anticipation of contemporary developments in rhetoric, although not without reservations about the consequences [1990, 121–28].) Subsequent events in the narrative of rhetoric thus build on this solid foundation, or, alternately, they cultivate seeds first planted at the origins. Disruptions in this trajectory, of repeating the past while discovering the already prefigured new in it, are historical aberrations, temporary displacements. These are to be explained away as the products of failed cultures—the most frequently named being that of the Middle Ages and the nineteenth century.

Thus, in Corbett's scheme Aristotle is the foundation of all future rhetorics: "With his philosophic treatise, Aristotle became the fountainhead of all later rhetorical theory" (1990, 543). Unfortunately, during the Middle Ages, rhetoric became a "scholastic exercise" rather than a "practical art" so that during this time "the art of rhetoric stood still, if it actually did not retrogress" (548–49). And although the authentic tradition is eventually restored, it again undergoes so precipitous a decline in England in the nineteenth century that Corbett must conclude: "The history of English rhetoric might well terminate with the end of the eighteenth century" (569). Still, as he explains in the conclusion to his history, "the long and honorable tradition that classical rhetoric has enjoyed" may have "risen and fallen periodically in public prominence," but "it always stages a comeback" (578). George Kennedy admits that rhetorical theories and practices other than the classical merit study (1980a), yet he cannot resist portraying departures from this tradition in a narrative of degeneration, describing the movement of the eighteenth century away from classical rhetoric as "The Decline of Neoclassical Rhetoric" (240). He also announces with approval a return to rhetoric's classical sources in the twentieth century, explaining that at Cornell and Chicago, in Kenneth Burke and Chaim Perelman, "the classical tradition in rhetoric seems to have entered a new phase in its long and distinguished history" (241). And in the concluding chapter of his study, a section in which he stages a dialogue pitting the ancients against the moderns, Kennedy finally comes down firmly on the side of "the old eloquence" (245), this time "Plato's ideal rhetoric," which, his spokesperson explains, "has never really been worked out in all its implications" (244). Finally, Vickers (1990) confidently announces that rhetoric has undergone "two great breakdowns," one in the Middle Ages, the other in the nineteenth century. Both have been short-lived, however, as the first is followed by "rebuilding and rediscovery in the Renaissance" and the second creates the occasion today for "the beginnings of a second renaissance in rhetoric" (215).

In contrast, Howell (1971) argues that the historical conversation of rhetoric has been a mistaken, formalized, and repetitious parlor game, with each voice reproducing the errors of its predecessor, the ancient sources of rhetoric finally setting in motion error and repression. Rhetoric, however, is too powerful for its false servants, those who set up foolish idols in its place, so that at last the genuine progressive unfolding of the one, true, holy, etc. rhetoric is inaugurated. For Howell, Locke is the bringer of great tidings, through induction able to transcend at a single bound the falsehood of the Aristotelian syllogism, freeing us from the hollow forms of the classics: "The history of an intellectual revolution would not normally have a hero, but it is tempting in the present instance to pronounce this dictum inapplicable and to confer the title of hero upon John Locke. . . . So far as its dominant thrust may be said to be embodied in the works of one man, the movement under examination here is hardly anything more than the expression of Locke's influence in this or that of its many ramifications" (7). Howell's history, like its antagonistic traditionalist counterparts, sees the action as the conflict between the good guys and the bad guys (but not women, since there are none in these scripts), the good guys finally arriving to save the day.

For both the traditionalists and the progressives, rhetoric has, despite its corrupt opponents, been restored to its holy mission, to serve truth, justice, and the rhetorical way.

When I encounter these reverential readings of the history of rhetoric, my first impulse, I must confess, is to resist, to portray the heroes as villains and the villains as heroes. For example, some Sophists were indeed fast-buck artists, selling their knowledge to the highest bidder, but many were also opponents of Greek slavery, misogyny, and a "democratic" *polis* that enfranchised only male descendants of native-born Athenians. As Eric Havelock (1957) has argued, some Sophists supported a radical democracy in economic and social as well as political arrangements. In contrast, Plato—the darling of the conservatives—was an unremitting enemy of democracy in any form, allowing rhetoric into the republic only to enable the philosopher-monarchs to manage the lower orders. (To give him his due, he did allow women into his ruling elite.) After all, since the soldiers and workers could not discover the dictates of reason and pursue them disinterestedly, they would have to be manipulated through psychological appeals to desire what their betters knew to be best for them (see Kauffman 1982). Aristotle, the great defender of reason and the democratic polis, was convinced that some of us are born slaves and that all women are inherently inferior and incapable of citizenship. Dying one of the richest three hundred men in Athens, his politics favored an educated and wealthy elite, and his rhetoric teaches this elite to dominate and control their inferiors (see Berlin 1992). Cicero was a dirty politician among dirty politicians, supporting in his intellectual and political work one of the cruelest, most violently repressive governments ever to exist (for a summary of these charges, see Dorey 1964). Progressives who would take comfort in my vilification of the ancients, however, ought to recall that Locke, himself always wise to the ways of financial investment, encouraged an epistemology whose main use has been to dominate nature and human beings in the service of economic gain for the few, meanwhile denying reality to any experience that cannot be commodified and exchanged in the open market.

But I realize my response is unjust, serving as a simple reversal of the binary oppositions on which the histories I have mentioned are formulated, oppositions repeated in more extreme forms today in our general discussions of rhetoric. Thus, the enemies of rhetoric argue that it is inherently corrupt (usually because they want to conceal or naturalize their own rhetoric) while we defenders of rhetoric too often take the opposite tack, insisting that it is inherently good. The problem with this dichotomy is that it is ahistorical. It argues that rhetoric is a practice that can somehow transcend the historical conditions of its own time, speaking in its essential purity (or, alternately, corruption) to all ages. It forgets that the formulation of a rhetoric is a product of the economic, social, and political conditions of a specific historical moment. The mission of the revisionary historian of rhetoric I have in mind is to resist the notion of rhetoric as a unified, coherent, and univocal collection of texts stretching over time, texts that support either truth and virtue on the one hand, or error and vice on the other. The revisionary historian must instead locate the variety of rhetorics that exist at any particular moment and examine their interaction with each other and with the conditions of their production. This will require seeking out the suppressed rhetorics of women, workers, and other marginalized and silenced groups. In this study, some rhetorics will prove noble and good, but some will inevitably prove quite the contrary.

This synchronic investigation will often lead to a diachronic one. There is no question that throughout history earlier rhetorics were studied with a view to discovering their contemporary relevance. Rhetorics often do carry on an intertextual correspondence with the rhetorics of other times and places. These relations are of course important considerations. Those who construct rhetorics, on the other hand—however much they may keep before them the example of one or another rhetorical tradition—are first and foremost concerned with addressing the play of power in their own day. Plato, Aristotle, Cicero, Augustine, Margaret Fell, Locke, and Mary Wollstonecraft were all concerned with the uses of language in the economic, social, and political institutions of their own times. When Cicero appropriates Aristotle, he does so in a way that serves his political purposes in the Roman senate, not the Athenian assembly (Douglas 1964). Indeed, his very reading of Aristotle is conducted through the terministic screens of his own historical conditions; just as when we today attempt to recover Aristotle, we focus on those features that most reinforce our desires for our own society—his privileging of the rational appeals and his apparent endorsement of democracy, for example—while conveniently overlooking what we find less admirable—his class and gender bias and his advocacy of the wealthy.

The examination of historical rhetorics, then, must be historicized. This means finding their differences from us as well as their similarities. Revisionary readings, however, must acknowledge that locating these differences is only possible through situating rhetorics within their unique economic, social, political, and cultural conditions. Rhetorics never answer only to themselves: they reflect and, of equal importance, refract the conditions of their creation and functioning. Rhetorics provide a set of rules about the dispositions of discourse at a particular moment. They codify who can and cannot speak (the wealthy but not the poor, men but not women, the certified expert but not the ordinary citizen); what can and cannot be said (the wealthy must be protected from the poor, the expert always knows best); who can and cannot listen and act (men only, the propertied classes only, the certified experts only); and the very nature of the language to be used (the register of the ruling class, the parlance of technocracy, the narratives of patriarchy). Rhetorics do not make these decisions on their own. They are constructed at the junctures of discourse and power, at the points at which economic, social, and political battles are waged in public discourse. To paraphrase Marx, it is within rhetorics that humans become aware of ideological battles and fight them out (Marx 1970, 21).

This is why there are always at a given moment a plurality of rhetorics, even during the most repressive times. This is hard for us to see because our traditional histories have insisted upon creating a monolithic tradition. Thus, until recently, even the Sophists were banished from the engulfing folds of the one true tradition, a result of the judgments made on them by the canonical Plato and Aristotle. The Sophists indeed belong outside of the tradition descending from these two powerful figures, but not because Plato and Aristotle are truly rhetorical and the Sophists are not. Certain Sophists represented a set of discursive practices that stood for another economic and political order, an order that their more established and popular rivals found dangerously subversive. As Havelock (1957) has taken pains to demonstrate, these Sophists argued for democratic and political arrangements that denied slavery and the inherent inferiority of women. Fortunately for us, this sophistic rhetoric achieved enough currency in its own day to require resistance by its opponents. Thus, although we know it almost exclusively through the denials of it by its adversaries, at least its existence was thereby made a part of the historical record. The revisionary historian of rhetoric must realize that there are also numerous rhetorics of the past that never attained enough currency in their own day to offer a serious challenge to the powerful. It is her business, then, to attempt to recover these rhetorics—for example, the rhetorics of slaves and women in Athens and Rome and the United States, or the rhetorics of the working class when a Neo-Ciceronian bourgeois and elitist rhetoric was shaping the formation of our constitution. This involves looking for lost and neglected documents attesting to these formulations. Since the texts of these marginalized rhetorics were often not formally recorded or were destroyed by their oppressors, finding the past will often mean examining the fragments of documents in which a rhetoric is demonstrated or discussed, in which the adversarial position is articulated. Nancy Streuver (1970) and John Poulakos (1984) and Richard Enos (1976) and others have done this for the Sophists, Eugene Genovese (1972) has carried out this project for African-American slaves of the last century, and E. P. Thompson (1963) has demonstrated it in writing about the working class in England. Today, many are attempting to locate the suppressed rhetorics of women—Karlyn Kohrs Campbell (1989) and Susan Jarratt (1990) and Sue Ellen Holbrook (1991), for example.

This revisionary/subversive position does not, as I said earlier, preclude a diachronic treatment of rhetoric. There is no question, for example, that Aristotle and Cicero and Locke can be made to speak to our conditions today. We must realize, however, that they are first addressing the situations of their own cultures, cultures that in many ways, and probably most, constitute our other. We must realize that inscribed in these historical texts are the power relations of their day, complete with all of their cruelties and injustices. Victor Vitanza has reminded us of the cognitive and psychic shackles these rhetorics impose (1987a; 1987b). I would remind us that they enforce ideological conditions as well—for example, brutalizing relations of race, class, and gender—that are difficult to resist, often because they are so much like our own. I do not wish to deny that readers finally construct texts rather than simply surrender to them. I wonder, however, if we can construct texts so unmistakably concerned with power in a way that resists their inequities, particularly when we canonize them as exceptional and exemplary, doing so because we find in them our own failures validated. We are also situated in politics and power, and our awareness of this inevitability must be self-consciously included in our investigation. We must own up to our own political agendas.

There is a final reason for writing histories (the plural intended) along the lines drawn here—lines that are crooked and subversive of narratives of peace, order, and harmony. Our search for alterity, for rhetorics other than the familiar, can reveal to us alternative possibilities in conceiving discursive practices and their power formations. Thus, the departure of an age from a dominant rhetorical tradition is a strong argument for its receiving special attention—as Michael Leff (1983) and Marjorie Woods (1990) have shown us in treating the Middle Ages, as Susan Jarratt (1985) has demonstrated in discussing the nineteenth century. We must look for the dangerous other, the subversive silences of earlier ages and our own.

But does my proposal involve a categorical refusal of other kinds of history, as some have suggested? Could I ever in my wildest flights of Leftist frenzy wish the histories of Kennedy and Corbett and Vickers and Howell be banished from consideration? I would have to answer an emphatic no to both questions. As I have reiterated throughout this essay, I see rhetorical history in pluralistic terms. Corbett's history did not foreclose Kennedy's nor did Kennedy's foreclose Vickers's. Despite their sharing a dominant narrative plan, they each make a unique contribution. Each, however, is incomplete, as is obvious from the fact that Kennedy's treatment followed Corbett's and Vickers's followed Kennedy's and Corbett's revision then followed all three. None considered that its predecessor had exhausted the field. As I said earlier, these three excellent studies demonstrate the contention that rhetorics arise in response to their predecessors, and their authors do an admirable job of articulating this conversation, showing the influences and cross-influences. These studies have been valuable if only because they have placed much of the materials of rhetoric on record, or at least the materials favored by the professional middle class, the group represented most recently by the likes of E. D. Hirsch and Allan Bloom and William Bennett. They also display an intelligent and insightful reading of the materials of rhetoric, offering a rich array of observations. And the same could be said for Howell's different kind of history.

The problem is not their strengths, however: it is their weaknesses—not what they do so well, but what they do not do at all. The final impression one is left with in examining Kennedy and Vickers is that their method is unproblematically exemplary: all that is genuinely important in pursuing the history of rhetoric has been here presented, and the reader need look no further. (Corbett acknowledged the incomplete nature of his history.) I wish that each had been more self-conscious about his methods, explaining them and acknowledging their limitations. Admittedly, this would have been difficult for Kennedy writing when he did. The same, however, cannot be said for Vickers. Nonetheless, I will agree that all the histories I have criticized in this essay are worthy and necessary reading for anyone interested in the history of rhetoric. Readers must, however, be made aware of their incompleteness, their gaps and fissures, in both omitting other rhetorics and other ways of reading the rhetorics included, and in failing to foreground their own methods. I suspect that given the recent concern for historiographic method, it will be more difficult for anyone to make a similar mistake in the future. (But obviously it will not be impossible since the faith in the "definitive" history, despite its very denial of historicity, not to mention rhetoricity, remains strong in certain conservative quarters.)

I would also like to comment on another criticism of the position I am forwarding. As I have already indicated, my proposed historiographic method does not prohibit other methods: all it asks is that these others foreground their intentions with all their implications. If, for example, a historian decides that politics is not a part of rhetoric despite all the evidence to the contrary, then she ought to say so, explaining her reasons for taking her position. In other words, my comments are especially intended to discourage unreflective accounts—not simply accounts that disagree with my own. I am also offering, of course, what I take to be a more productive approach. (I will be the first to acknowledge that what I am proposing is difficult since it requires an interdisciplinary method, looking at rhetorics in relation to culture in its most expansive formulation, but that is not really at issue here.) I would at the same time emphasize my openness to other historical accounts, accounts that inevitably provide me with materials for my own formulation. But of course I reserve the right to continue to criticize what I take to be their errors and inadequacies.

I also feel constrained to make one other peace offering. I have been told at conferences (but never, to my knowledge, in print) that my recommendations would preclude the normal appropriations of historical rhetorics that are a continuing part of theory building, as Kenneth Burke has done with Aristotle. My objection is not to such uses—a necessary strategy of writing rhetorics—but to its unreflective operation. As Burke calls upon certain key concepts in Aristotle in *A Rhetoric of Motives*, for example, he not only does so selectively, but he also makes no extravagant claims about the historical authority of his reading. A typical case occurs early on when Burke calls on Aristotle's contention that rhetoric "proves opposites" in support of his own more expansive assertion that identification and division appearing together make for "the characteristic invitation to rhetoric" (1969b, 25). In the section in which this appears, Burke undertakes this gesture with the appropriate recognition of the differences between the political conditions of the past and the present; he even includes specific reference to differences in "the purely technical means of communication," meaning here the contemporary use of journalism. The differences finally are more important than the similarities, even though Aristotle does prove useful in making the point. Mining the rich storehouse of historical rhetorics for their contemporary applications in this way will continue and ought to continue. It should not be undertaken, however, without striving to understand the full political and cultural implications of the appropriation: differences are here as important as identities.

Finally, I would like to say a last word about the complex relation between the past and present in writing the contextualized history I am recommending. As I have suggested repeatedly, objectivity is out of the question. All historians are interested, writing their narratives from a particular ideological position. It is impossible to become a *tabula rasa* innocently recording the raw data of the historical record. For one thing, the raw data is simply too overwhelming to be dealt with without selection, and some ideological principle will always guide the selection. As I have argued (1987a; 1987b) both the data selected and formulations about the significance of this data are interpretive gestures. My position here is that the historian must acknowledge the principles—primarily ideological in nature—that are to govern this interpretation. The historian studying the nineteenth century, for example, is working from her position in the twentieth century, and it is impossible to transcend her historically formed consciousness in order to enter innocently into that of another historical moment. Instead, she must strive to understand as much as is possible her own situatedness, primarily by realizing her decisions in writing history will be based on her own loyalties in economic, social, political, and cultural considerations.

Writing history involves judgments about which scenes and actors and events are important and which are not. These judgments engage the historian in a critique of historical records, a criticism of their relative value and importance. This in turn is a product of the historian's own ideological predilections, her own vision of preferred economic, social, and political arrangements. The historian who sees no reason to search for the rhetorical texts of those out of power at a particular moment because these are not important in the unfolding of historical events has made an ideological decision, not a choice of fact. The contention here is that history is the record of great and conspicuous events and great and conspicuous people—the winners of history, however ill-gotten their gains. All else is mere backdrop, mere stage and setting for this more significant action. These interpretive decisions, furthermore, are based on a utopian gesture, a vision of the world as it ought to be. My conception of the significance of past events will be based on my conception of the perfect society, and it will be from this vantage point that I will select data and offer an interpretation of those data. Thus, historians will sometimes agree about the significant texts—as do Corbett and Kennedy, for example—without agreeing on the interpretation of them: Corbett valorizing Aristotle while Kennedy enthrones Plato. And the difference will be in their conceptions of the world as it ought to be, as well as in their conceptions of what it actually is. In the case of this example, I would disagree with both, looking to certain Sophists as the most fruitful demonstration of rhetoric in ancient Greece because they offer the best precedent for a modern democracy.

I would also argue that this historiographic method encourages a dialectical reading of past and present that will encourage a variety of conflicting readings, even among those who share ideological loyalties. A commonplace of historical studies is that the past is studied in order that we may not repeat its mistakes, encountering in it lessons of value for the present. While this formulation cannot be rejected out of hand, it is often employed in the service of a historical conception that sees the past and present as identical. For instance, those who see in Cicero's *De oratore* a discussion of argument that "serves as a good index to the subsequent history of rhetoric" (Sloan) somehow overlook the obvious differences between the violently antidemocratic Rome of Cicero and the contemporary commitment to democracy found in most Western states (however much the commitment remains unfulfilled). As I have said repeatedly, the historiographic method I am suggesting foregrounds difference over identity. This difference, furthermore, is useful not simply because it offers new conceptions of the past not yet entertained. I am also convinced it offers new interpretations of the present.

To see the past as different is often to render the present disparate and strange, offering the defamiliarization of tacitly maintained truisms about our own time. Once again, I will insist that the past is not always better than the present, as classicists will argue, nor is it always worse, as progressives maintain. Often it is both at once. Aristotle reveals the inevitably probabilistic nature of political decision making and the centrality of the *polis* in the decision-making process, while simultaneously preferring the wisdom of the wealthy and educated over the judgment of the ordinary citizen. In his complex divergence from us, then, Aristotle can underscore our own distrust of communal decision making, as well as our denial of contingency in favor of scientific certitude even in areas where such certitude is simply not possible. He can also remind us of our failures in democratic representation that so much resemble his—in our methods of financing political campaigns or in the subtle devices we have devised to discourage citizens from voting. I am arguing finally for a dialectic between past and present. Our conceptions of the present guide us in looking at the past, but in looking for our other we discover disruptions in our conceptions so that past and present are simultaneously reconceived. Thus, my position is not doctrinaire—not a privileging of economic universals over cultural universals, or vice versa, for example—but a search for interpretations that cast the past and the present in new conceptual formulations. And this dialectical process is never finally ended, since the relation of past and present will continually change through time, each generation needing to reformulate its historical understanding.

In the closing section of this essay I want to offer a more detailed description of the historiographic method I am proposing. I want especially to address the challenge to history writing posed by the postmodern disruption in our confidence in grand historical narratives, a challenge that has been constantly kept in mind in what has already been said. (I have also discussed this issue along somewhat different but related lines in Berlin 1990.) Jean-Francois Lyotard (1984b) has been the central figure in denying the possibility of metanarratives of history, of accounts that exhaustively elucidate the significance of the entirety of human conditions in the past or present. He has disputed the totalizing discourses of such schemes as Hegelianism and Marxism or the faith in scientific progress and the invisible hand of economic law. All are declared language games that are inherently partial and interested, intended to endorse particular relations of power and to privilege certain groups in historical struggles. Against this totalizing gesture, Lyotard argues for a plurality of particular narratives, limited and localized explanations that attempt to address features of experience that grand narratives exclude. This requires (as I have underscored in this essay) looking for what has been left out in ordinary accounts, searching for the events at the unspoken margins of a culture. This moves attention to such categories as class, race, gender, and ethnicity in the unfolding of historical events. This is often history from the bottom up, telling the stories of the people and events normally excluded from totalizing discourses.

Against this plea for the complete and entire rejection of comprehensive historical accounts, however, I would argue for the necessity of provisional, contingent narratives in explaining the past and present. While history may be without an inherent plan or progression, it is the product of the complex interactions of people, social institutions, ideologies, technological conditions, and modes of production. To relinquish the comprehensive attempt to make sense of history is to risk being victimized by it. Meanwhile, those who have the most to gain from totalistic historical explanations that validate present economic and political arrangements, the most recent victors of historical battles, will continue to sponsor histories from their point of view, framing master narratives that authorize their continual power and privilege. The attempt to make sense of history will always be undertaken by dominant groups, at the very least to account for the justness of their access to power. These histories of course deny the ideological commitments of their master narratives, usually in the name of an innocent empiricism, and insist that the facts of the matter, not any ruling narrative codes, are making the case. As we have seen, the mediating role of language in all human activities challenges this formulation. After all, past events that contributed to the formation of social and political arrangements are simply too numerous to be presented in their entirety. Some principle of organization and selection must always be invoked, and it is in these choices that the ruling narrative is to be located.

The postmodern turn demands that the role of such narratives be acknowledged, while preventing the move to forward any as essential or universal: all are provisional and contingent, always subject to revision and possible rejection. Cornell West has recently offered a similar proposal and in distinctly rhetorical terms, looking upon provisional and contingent notions of the total as a necessary heuristic and synecdochal way of proceeding: "Without 'totality,' our politics become emaciated, our politics become nothing but existential rebellion. Some heuristic (rather than ontological) notion of totality is in fact necessary if we are to talk about mediations, interrelations, interdependence, about totalizing forces in the world. In other words, a measure of synecdochal thinking must be preserved, thinking that would still invoke relations of parts to the whole. . . . It is true, on the other hand, that we can no longer hang on to crude and orthodox 'totalities' such as the idea of superstructure and base" (Stephanson 1988, 270). Despite their conditionality, these provisional narratives are always preferable to the atomistic responses that, in the words of Stanley Aronowitz and Henry Giroux, "run the risk of being trapped in particularistic theories that cannot explain how the various diverse relations that constitute larger social, political, and global systems interrelate or mutually determine and constrain each other." Contingent narratives then become heuristics that open up "mediations, interrelations, and interdependencies that give shape and power to larger political and social systems" (1991, 70).

To use Fredric Jameson's formulation, such narratives provide cognitive maps that at the simplest level are indispensable to daily experience, providing "that mental map of the social and global totality we all carry around in our heads in variously garbled forms" (1991, 415). For projects as complex as the estimation of history, complex cognitive maps that serve as provisional heuristic devices for responding to the vast array of data are indispensable. Indeed, in a remarkable departure from Marxist traditions, Jameson even concurs with Cornell West in placing the concept of the base/superstructure relationship in this category, identifying it as "a starting point and a problem, an imperative to make connections, as undogmatic as a heuristic recommendation simultaneously to group culture (and theory) in and for itself, but also in relation to its outside, its content, its context, and its space of intervention and effectivity" (1991, 409). The directing narratives to be invoked in writing history here recommended similarly offer this capacity to provide connections while never determining in advance exactly what they will be. The narrative and the facts it discovers engage in a dialectical interaction in which the two terms of the encounter are always open to revision, the narrative revealing and deciphering data while the data revise the narrative.

Teresa Ebert has recently offered an instructive conception of this use of a provisional totality within a postmodern frame. Her model is feminist and resistant, what she calls "resistant postmodernism" in contrast to the indefinite play of difference found in "ludic postmodernism": "There are two radically different notions of politics in postmodernism. Ludic politics is a textual practice that seeks open access to the free play of signification in order to disassemble the dominant cultural policy (totality), which tries to restrict and stabilize meaning. Whereas resistance postmodernism, I contend, insists on a materialist political practice that works for equal access for all to social resources and for an end to the exploitative exercise of power" (1991, 887). While Ebert is thoroughly appreciative of the critique offered by feminist ludic postmodernists, she finds it wanting in its politics. It is not enough for postmodernism to examine difference and the excluded other in an effort to reverse or displace hierarchical binaries, however valuable this may have been at an earlier historical moment: "Instead it needs to inquire into the power relations requiring such suppression" (1991, 889). Ebert poses a scheme for regarding the central role of signifying practices in the formation of subject and society that makes for a coherent commentary on the position I have offered in this essay. For her, language, the sign, is "an ideological process in which we consider a signifier in relation to a matrix of historically possible signifieds. The signifier becomes temporarily connected to a specific signified—that is, it attains its 'meaning'—through social struggle in which the prevailing ideology and social contradictions insist on a particular signified" (897). Language is thus the arena of struggle for determining the meaning of key signifiers, signifiers that then operate in the formation and maintenance of economic and political conditions, as well as in the very construction of the consciousness of the subjects of history. The important addendum is that resistance is always possible since the contradictions between signified and signifier—for example, the promises of supply-side economic policies and the actual living conditions of what is now being characterized as "the bottom ninety percent" of the population—continually provoke opposition to hegemonic ideologies.

Ebert also offers a reading of difference that leads to a conception of the inevitability of provisional and contingent notions of a constantly changing totality: "But a postmodern materialist feminism based on a resistant postmodernism, I contend, does not avoid the issues of totality or abandon the struggle concept of patriarchy; instead, it *rewrites* them. Totality needs to be reunderstood as a system of relations, but such a system is not a homogeneous unity as the Hegelian expressive totality proposes: *It is an overdetermined structure of difference*. A system—particularly the system of patriarchy—is thus always self-divided, different from itself and multiple; it is traversed by 'differences within,' by differance." Difference here becomes the conflict of social and material conditions conceived as a totality of shifting relations of the economic, political, and cultural: "If totalities are structures of differences and thus multiple, unstable, changeable arenas of contradictions and social struggle, then they are open to contestation and transformation. But such transformations are themselves contingent on analyzing the ways in which the operation of power and organization of differences in a specific system are *overdetermined* by other systems of difference, because systems of difference are also situated in a social formation—which is itself a structure of differences made up of other systems of differences, including the social, economic, political, cultural, and ideological" (1991, 899).

All of this means that any category of investigation—whether gender, class, race, ethnicity, or age—must be considered in its complex relations to other mutually influencing categories within a complex and shifting totality of differences. For example, at the most obvious level gender relations in the United States during this century can be characterized as consistently inequitable in the distribution of political power between men and women. This inequity, however, has manifested itself differently among different classes and races, and even these differences have varied greatly from decade to decade as economic and social conditions have changed. This shifting totality requires that any investigation of human behavior must be historically specific in its methods and materials, never resting secure in any ahistorical, universal mode of thought.

The historiographic method recommended here, then, demands honesty of the historian, a candid acknowledgement of her ideological stance, her conception of perfect economic, social, and political arrangements, her vision of utopia. The historian is never simply writing an account of the past. She is also writing an account of the present and, of equal importance, a hope and vision of the future. In telling us what happened, the historian is telling us what ought to happen now and tomorrow. These are matters too important to be left to the silently implicit, to be obscured in the insistence on history as facts and only facts. Acknowledging the postmodernist critique of all totalistic thinking, furthermore, the historian realizes the provisionality of any conception of the good life and the good society. She must always reserve the right to revise and refigure her position. The historian then owes it to us and to herself to tell us where she stands so that we can know whether we want to stand with her.

9

Future Historiographies of Rhetoric and the Present Age of Anxiety

John Schilb

In recent years, I and several other scholars have focused upon the rhetoric of the history of rhetoric.[1] This trend reflects a more widespread awareness that rhetoric always infuses knowledge claims.[2] But as we seek to consolidate and institutionalize our work, we face a thorny issue. On the one hand, if even histories are marked by rhetoric, then the authority of any field seems vulnerable—including that of rhetoric itself. On the other hand, if rhetoric is pervasive, it seems an ideal basis for a discipline—indeed, for a metadiscipline that will supervise others. Yet although this second possibility is bound to enchant those of us who deem ourselves rhetoricians, we should choose the first. Being aware of the rhetoric of the history of rhetoric should make us perpetually consider how our knowledge is limited, rather than leading us to consecrate ourselves as a 1990s' version of Kant's "tribunal of reason." If we seek to become a discipline, let alone a metadiscipline, we may utterly indulge in certain habits that already slight the complexity of texts, institutions, and cultures.

Let me cite these habits by invoking Hans Kellner's book *Language and Historical Representation: Getting the Story Crooked* (1989). One of its main themes is that "each academic tribe produces and harbors a system of anxieties that, perhaps more than anything else, identifies a scholar as a member of the group" (12). Of course, more than simply fear drives our ambitions for rhetoric as a field. We sincerely (and rightly) believe it can illuminate human thought, action, and relations. But I want to identify here some anxieties that rhetoricians, including historians of rhetoric, have shown even as their work has gained status. For each reduces the complexity I feel we should pursue, and each might get ignored if we seek merely to safeguard our new prestige.

First of all, many of us exhibit an unfortunate zeal for classification that I call "taxonomania." That is, we attempt to map a whole field of study by dividing it into neat, distinct parts, often assigning them varying degrees of worth. This habit was crisply affirmed at the 1990 Conference on College Composition and Communication, when a journal editor compiling a bibliography of composition scholarship implored his audience, "Send me your categories!" Certainly this impulse has long characterized rhetoricians; it dates back to Aristotle. And it would be ridiculous to do away with classifying once and for all, even if we could. But the current rage to segment and rank objects, methods, histories, epistemologies, and ideologies of rhetorical study risks obscuring too much to protect our own theoretical security. Emphasizing the differences *between* the items so classified can lead us to ignore the differences *within* them. For one thing, we might wind up attaching the same label to texts or worldviews whose family resemblances are superficial at best. C. H. Knoblauch (1988) underscores the suspicious versatility of composition's present god-term when he observes that "roving, and normally warring, bands of cognitive psychologists, text linguists, philosophers of composition, historians of rhetoric, Marxist critics, post-structuralists, and reader-response theorists all wax equally enthusiastic about 'the social construction of reality' " (146). Note, too, that a person's epistemology or ideology can itself be a heterogeneous, even contradictory mixture of beliefs. An additional problem looms when we naturally strive to keep our categories small, limiting them if possible to the mystical number three: traditional, revisionary, and sub/versive histories (Vitanza 1987b); cognitive, expressionistic, and social-epistemic rhetorics (Berlin 1988); expressivist, transactive, and poetic discourses (Britton 1978); the major "methodological communities" of scholars, researchers, and practitioners (North 1987); the rhetorical motives of play, game, and purpose (Lanham 1986). Probably these theorists would argue that they ultimately want to get beyond rigid conceptual distinctions, being committed instead to fluid, dialectical study of how discourse and society relate. Indeed, each of them brilliantly demonstrates how to conduct such inquiry.[3] But the act of classifying might come to *appear* an end in itself, seeming to offer other scholars the convenient labels they are shopping for in their effort to establish rhetoric as a simple quasi science. Although perhaps we cannot eliminate categories altogether, we can ask ourselves in specific instances whether we need to invoke them. If we do set them up, we can ponder how they might prematurely fix our own or someone else's research agenda.

Second, even if we strive to discredit philosophy in favor of an antifoundationalist rhetoric, many of us still consider arguing within or against this discipline a valid way of confronting social circumstances. We thus fall prey to what I call "epistemologia." Perhaps I can make this point best by referring first to Richard Rorty (1989), whose elegant demolition jobs on epistemology have inspired Kenneth Bruffee (1986) and others in composition and rhetoric. Although Rorty repeatedly attacks epistemology as misleading and irrelevant, he himself works within a traditional history of ideas as he does so, instead of undertaking a detailed analysis of worldly conditions. He just redeploys the traditional prestige of philosophers when he speaks as if his skill in critiquing them qualifies him to pronounce upon global matters. When he attempts to make a case for liberalism, he barely refers to historical events and hardly deigns to pinpoint the current dynamics of power; instead, he suggests that one should become a liberal because neo-pragmatists have effectively critiqued their philosophical forefathers.

Rorty's would-be disciple Kenneth Bruffee shares his proclivity for intellectual history and also champions liberalism as its inevitable product. When forced to acknowledge leftist movements, both have breezily chastised them, not addressing their empirical research but simply deeming them rotten with metaphysics. Not only does this approach merely wrest the prestige of epistemology for its critics; it imparts to epistemology so much continuity and attributes to it so much responsibility for our present ills that other historical developments seem incidental.[4]

A preference for analyzing epistemologies rather than conjunctures also threatens to haunt those of us drawn to "postmodernism" as a possible rubric for historiography. For example, Gregory Ulmer (1985), Richard Lanham (1986), and Louise Wetherbee Phelps (1988) invoke the term to denote a wonderful emerging *Zeitgeist*, rather than carefully exploring possible differences in people's current situations and considering how not everyone may benefit from so-called postmodern trends. Again, despite new lingo, a traditional history of ideas winds up being promulgated at the expense of larger social research. Rather than follow these examples or settle for parroting Jean-Francois Lyotard's now-famous designation of "postmodernism" as a welcome "incredulity toward metanarratives" (1984b, xxiv), we need to probe the relation between the *various* senses of "postmodernism": its designation of an epistemological critique, a set of artistic practices, and an ensemble of global conditions. This should involve considering texts like Andreas Huyssen's *After the Great Divide* (1986), an account of postmodernism's role in the whole history of the avant-garde, and Fredric Jameson's essay "Postmodernism: Or, The Cultural Logic of Late Capitalism" (1984), an analysis of our present conjuncture that has sparked much comment by literary and political theorists. Whatever resources we ultimately draw upon, we should recognize how focusing upon epistemology—even if only to vilify it—can block more intractable issues that we must team with various disciplines to confront (Schilb 1991).

The third anxiety that we display can be termed "canononia." This is the impulse to boil rhetorical history down to a particular set of cherished texts, an official heritage. Conceivably, rhetoric encompasses a wide range of discourse: not only scholarly texts, but also the transactions of everyday life. This open, democratic, pluralistic aspect of the subject can make it the most effective counterbalance to Allan Bloom's dogmatic revival of the "Great Books" (1987). Yet a tendency to concentrate upon certain masterworks has also marked the rhetorical tradition, and disciplinary ambitions can exacerbate it, just as they have in literary studies.

The main problem with a canon, of course, is that it threatens to exclude other works that challenge our conventional notions of rhetorical history. We are only beginning to acknowledge the voices of women, minorities, and entire cultures missing from the paideia. Just as feminist critics have warned against a simple "add women and stir" approach to the literary canon, so these missing voices might alter our whole sense of rhetoric's past. They also throw into question our impulse to canonize at all.

Again, even invocations of "postmodernism" or other new theoretical trends can rigidify our objects of study. Take the case of the Sophists.

Traditional histories of rhetoric have often accused them of unethical manipulation. Lately, however, they have been glorified as precursors of various "posts." Yet despite these polar reactions, in both instances they remain cornerstones of rhetorical history, their foundational status abetted by the near-extinction of their actual texts. Instead of viewing them as crucial sinners in the epic of rhetoric's redemption or as forerunners of today's Parisian saints, perhaps we should heed Derrida's own caution about them. In "Plato's Pharmacy," he warns against any "slogan or password of a 'back-to-the-sophists' nature," declaring his interest in "some entirely-other of *both* sophistics *and* Platonism, some resistance having no common denominator with this whole commutation" (1981a, 108). While he does not ignore the Sophists, he strives to displace any focus upon them, favoring theorists and principles that elude the conventional opposition of Sophists and Platonists (also see Olson 1990). One of deconstruction's most illuminating moves is, in fact, to avoid simply reversing classic ethical dualisms and instead to question dualism itself.

Thus, we should not forget the Sophists but instead consider other figures who might disrupt the ethical drama in which we have cast them as villains or heroes. Similarly, we should not jettison any of our canonical texts automatically but instead should cultivate the Burkean "perspectives by incongruity" that other texts might bring to them. Also, we should reflect as self-consciously as possible on the personal desires and institutional forces that drive us to canonize. For example, our efforts to fix the Sophists in rhetorical history might be viewed from a Lacanian perspective, as a desire to cement a gap in our conceptual order so that it boasts a sterling coherence. We should also consider how our efforts to legitimize our field can influence how we receive certain works. As I have remarked elsewhere (1987, 30), the veritable barrage of criticism launched against Knoblauch and Brannon's book *Rhetorical Traditions and the Teaching of Writing* (1984) says more about rhetoricians' professional investment in a certain body of texts than it does about the work's flaws. (Indeed, such a book gives us a blazing opportunity to defend the honor of our traditional archives; if Knoblauch and Brannon had not come along, orthodox rhetoricians would have had to invent them.) On a very practical level, rhetoric programs should be careful not to freeze their reading lists in the name of professional coherence. We have little to gain in emulating the cryogenic habits of many university departments.

Accompanying rhetoricians' "canononia" is yet another anxiety, which might be termed "golden age nostalgia" but which I prefer to call "Brumairism." At the start of his *18th Brumaire of Louis Bonaparte*, Marx (1984) observes that

> the tradition of all the dead generations weighs like a nightmare on the brain of the living. And just when they seem engaged in revolutionizing themselves and things, in creating something that has never yet existed, precisely in such periods of revolutionary crisis they anxiously conjure up the spirits of the past to their service and borrow from them names, battle cries, and costumes in order to present the new scene of world history in this time-honoured disguise and this borrowed language. (15)

While Marx was specifically describing French political activists in 1789 and 1848–51, the passage also applies to the many rhetoricians who want their subject given back the centrality it enjoyed for two thousand years. They respond to the present conjuncture by evoking a prelapsarian state, when students received coordinated, practical instruction in the art of discourse because *the* rhetorical tradition held sway.

I myself feel somewhat drawn to this picture. Certainly a larger perspective on discourse was undermined when Arnoldian aesthetics won out over rhetoric as a guiding principle of English departments. Yet Brumairism even in this context is problematic. For one thing, golden age thinking threatens to reify the canon of rhetoric, stabilizing its texts and the interpretations of its texts so that a vision of lost coherence may be preserved. What Hans Kellner says of historians' anxieties seems especially relevant here. He points out how they nurture related beliefs in the totality of the past, in the unity of the written text, and in the coherence of the present conjuncture that supposedly authorizes their work (1989, 12–13). Rhetoricians bent upon reviving their alleged golden age reinforce these dubious assumptions, slighting the heterogenous forces operating in various eras and documents. If rhetoricians are to rebut the right-wing golden age visions of the Blooms, Bennetts, and Cheneys, espousing the same kind of historiography does not seem the most promising tactic.

When conservatives suggest colleges once offered a coherent, humanistic, disinterested education pivoted around the Great Books, they of course promulgate a myth. As Gerald Graff (1987) has shown, the modern university has always been a site of fragmentation, politics, and challenges to humanism, even if it did not blatantly proclaim itself as such. And as numerous commentators on education have pointed out, American schools today face the challenge of a greatly expanded and diversified constituency. Similarly, it is by no means certain that the golden age of rhetoric's supremacy was all that golden, or would be now. Keep in mind that no one arguing for a return to the good old days of rhetoric lived during them. We also lack any clear evidence that students then actually gained from instruction in rhetoric. Furthermore, consider again how it excluded from the classroom and the curriculum various groups that have only recently been allowed entrance.

Besides cultivating a dubious portrait of past intellectual life, Brumairism often overlooks current academic politics. As I have pointed out (1989), those who champion the revival of rhetoric often ignore ideologies opposed to rhetoric (such as the Arnoldian aesthetic that still lurks in most English departments) as well as differences between rhetorical theories themselves (the neo-Aristotelian concern with "rhetoric" as persuasion versus the deconstructionist concern with "rhetoric" as tropes.) When I noted these conflicting forces in an MLA paper and proposed there a curriculum that foregrounds their conflicts instead of making a single version of rhetoric supreme, an audience member harrumphed that the academy must return to Isocrates. Yet while Isocrates personally interests me, I could not imagine how anyone might convince an English department, let alone a whole university, to adopt him as a presiding deity. Note that in order for the effort to succeed, even current partisans of Isocrates would have to agree upon just *how* to consider him foundational.

When we simply affirm canonical figures of rhetoric and expect colleges to heed us, more is at work than sheer political naivete. We also assume that the rhetorical tradition is an irrepressible tide of history and that we serve as its agents. The professor who simply extolled Isocrates was in effect promulgating the famous slogan from *Star Wars*, "May the force be with you."[5] Yet we need to ponder how cultural authority is actually achieved and which of a great many candidates deserve it. Besides confronting the obstacles to rhetoric in our own institution, we should analyze the historical role of the academy itself and consider how rhetoricians might benefit society more by aligning themselves with other groups than by forming yet another discipline with a set pantheon.[6]

This point brings me, finally, to "heterophobia": the sentiment that all rhetoricians must hang together if the work of rhetoric is to be accomplished. Although being together in a discipline need not require scholars to agree upon everything, it usually pressures them to follow the same mission. But today's rhetoricians are, to use a voguish word, overdetermined. Many affiliate themselves not just with rhetoric but with various fields, movements, constituencies, and blocs. Several historians of rhetoric linked to composition, for example, are more concerned with stopping the exploitation of writing teachers than with building bridges to colleagues in speech. These actions are not mutually exclusive, and both seem worthwhile. But if the first is a priority, forming a general discipline of rhetoric may not be the most expedient way of addressing it. Similarly, rhetoricians committed to feminist, minority, or socialist movements may not serve them best by aligning themselves with certain other rhetoricians.

Furthermore, past experience suggests that some people and ideas inevitably get marginalized when disciplines form around certain core concepts. When, for example, Kenneth Bruffee (1986) draws a host of composition specialists to the notion of "social construction," it is important to note that his bibliographic essay on the subject omitted feminists and Marxists and that later he explicitly scorned the latter. Besides concentrating upon "social construction," compositionists should analyze their field's construction of "the social," insofar as it has pushed away radical theorists instead of affirming them. Similarly, appeals to "the rhetorical" should be probed for what they exclude or de-emphasize as much as for what they encompass.

Alliances of rhetoricians should not always be avoided. When they tolerate diversity and stand as the best available means for a school to foster civic literacy, they of course should be encouraged. Yet we should entertain at least as much the possibility of rhetoric's serving as a storehouse of concepts for various groups to draw upon at various times for various purposes. Faculty might even then achieve curricular coherence, not by reviving the paideia but by juxtaposing these disparate groups and collectively examining how their relations to rhetoric differ.

If my listing of anxieties amounts to any general prescription, then, it is for rhetoricians to study how taxonomies, philosophies, canons, heritages, and disciplines can thwart understanding of historical conditions. Even as I propose this goal, however, I recall Kellner: "When historians ponder the future, even the future of their own trade, the time is, at least in some small and very literal sense, out of joint; the future, that great *generator* of insecurity, must be defused, turned into a special variety of the past, a new sourcebook in the 'lessons of history' " (1989, 267). In other words, visions of the future can stem from yet one more anxiety—a demand that it clearly accord with our sense of earlier times.

Certainly the last few years have shown how unpredictable our own era can be. The sudden demise of Communist governments in Europe leaves me and other rhetoricians on the left facing new pressures to refine and justify Marxist accounts of history. Even if few of us believed in an orderly triumph of the dialectic or equated actual Communist states with the spirit of Marxism itself, we have to ponder the recent change in regimes if our stories of oppressive power relations are not to suffer the "incredulity toward metanarratives" that Lyotard reports. At the same time, recent events should not leave advocates of capitalism feeling *their* version of history has been thoroughly vindicated. When Francis Fukuyama (1989) declared "an unabashed victory of economic and political liberalism" (3) in his much-discussed article "The End of History"—later converted into a bestselling book (1991)—he tried to thwart analogies between him and Daniel Bell (1960), who had announced "the end of ideology" on the eve of a decade of massive student protest. But Fukuyama does seem as willfully naive as Bell in assuming that capitalist institutions heroically advance and resolve history's underlying plot. Not everyone, of course, associates capitalism with "victory"; its impact upon the various populations of the world remains quite varied. Moreover, as Marx long ago pointed out, capitalism itself fosters global instability by seeking to generate new markets and more cost-efficient production centers. In fact, David Harvey (1989) has shown that the availability of computer networks and exploitable Third World labor now drives capitalism to refashion its strategies and remobilize its resources faster than ever—even if its new hyperspeed produces stock market crashes, junk bond swindles, self-defeating corporate takeovers, and massive unemployment. In other words, the really committed deconstructors work on Wall Street, not the Yale campus. Finally, the classic metanarratives of Marxism and capitalism have been increasingly challenged by social movements not exactly coinciding with either paradigm. Note, for example, the resurgence of ethnic nationalism in Europe, the spreading worldwide influence of feminism, and the growing importance of postcolonial discourses.

The complexity of the academic and global scenes in which historians of rhetoric work reminds me of a celebrated "prediction" made by Paul de Man. It appears at the start of his book *Allegories of Reading* (1979). After explaining how a passage in Proust uses metonymy even as it exalts metaphor, de Man observes that "there is absolutely no reason why analyses of the kind here suggested for Proust would not be applicable, with proper modifications of technique, to Milton or to Dante or to Holderlin. This will in fact be the task of literary criticism in the coming years" (17). De Man's statement has since then repeatedly been cited as an arrogant prophecy that has, admittedly, proved true. Yet even though he was certainly apodictic at times, I submit that here de Man is being ironic. Just three sentences back, he wryly notes that through the analysis of Proust he has just undertaken "we seem to end up in a mood of negative assurance that is highly productive of critical discourse" (16). In a manner quite typical of his work, he then questions the reading of Proust he has just accomplished: "The reading revealed a first paradox: the passage valorizes metaphor as being the 'right' literary figure, but then proceeds to constitute itself by means of the epistemologically incompatible figure of metonymy. The critical discourse reveals the presence of this delusion and affirms it as the irreversible mode of its truth. *It cannot pause there however*. For if we then ask the obvious and simple next question, whether the rhetorical mode of the text in question is that of metaphor or metonymy, it is impossible to give an answer" (18; emphasis mine). Undecidability looms because even as criticism exposes Proust's underlying metonymies, it confers an image of authoritative subjectivity upon the narrator, thus reauthorizing metaphor. Instead of resting content, then, with the kind of interpretation that "will be the task of literary criticism in the coming years," de Man pushes for even *it* to be deconstructed. Still, far from believing such relentlessness will be welcomed, he points out that it usually meets "considerable resistance" (19). When admirers or detractors of de Man debate his supposed prophecy, they "resist" his actual problematizing of literary history. To quote the last paragraph of his essay, they try to defuse "an anxiety . . . of ignorance" (19)—a fear that past, present, and future cannot be smoothly joined together.

Ironically, the controversy now generated by de Man's rediscovered collaborationist journalism shows just how disjointed an intellectual career can get. Historians of rhetoric might also reasonably object to his postwar theorizing, finding it too aloof from progressive politics and too committed to a notion of "rhetoric" as the tropological undermining of meaning. But he and Kellner nevertheless usefully remind us that even "revisionary" or "subversive" histories can exhibit undue "assurance," albeit of a "negative" kind. The "task," if anything, is to make *lack* of "assurance" a constructive partner in our work.

Notes

1. See, e.g., 8.1–2 (1987) and 11.3–4 (1990) issues of *PRE/TEXT*, which include articles by Jarratt, Berlin, Schilb, and Vitanza.

2. See, e.g., the Nelson, Megill, and McCloskey collection (1987). It presents a good overview of how rhetoric pervades various fields, although it defines rhetoric more or less exclusively in a neo-Aristotelian sense.

3. When Vitanza (1987b) sets up the categories of "traditional," "revisionary," and "sub/versive" historiographies, he asserts that "naming and categorizing are finally inescapable, just as ideology is" (84). Immediately afterward, though, he declares that he ultimately aims *"to establish a category that would destroy the categorizing, that would unname the naming, that would finally make the activity of categorizing and constructing 'covering-laws' ironic"* (84). Furthermore, he states that "seldom does any one historian function exclusively in any one category of historiography, though s/he may, indeed, for the most part emphasize one over the others. I would (also) hope that my placement of particular historians in particular categories would not become *the* important issue in any (if any) continued discussion of this paper" (85). Vitanza's qualifications and cautions suggest he himself worries that readers will simply embrace his typology. The question thus arises whether his own resorting to it is, in this instance, "inescapable."

4. Anderson (1979) cogently analyzes how a fascination with epistemology has also weakened the political efficacy of Marxist thought in the twentieth century. For further discussion of the relationship between Rorty's and Bruffee's thinking, see Schilb (1990).

5. See Gouldner (1985) for an analogous argument about how certain Marxist intellectuals have at times sought power by identifying themselves with shifts in the *Zeitgeist*.

6. Wilshire (1990) offers a powerful critique of how the disciplinary organization of the modern university encourages scholars to adopt narrow professional identities. Ohmann (1990) stresses the need for intellectuals to affiliate themselves with movements outside the academy if they wish to have genuine social impact.

10

Eating History, Purging Memory, Killing Rhetoric

Lynn Worsham

This essay offers a reading of Roland Barthes' "The Old Rhetoric: An *aide-mémoire*."[1] Barthes' study is not a traditional historical narrative, only an extended outline, or what he calls a "memorandum" presenting "a chronological and systematic panorama of . . . classical Rhetoric" (1988, 11). On first glance, however, his outline has what Nietzsche would call the antiquarian appeal of a traditional history claiming to present and to preserve only the essential and uncontroversial facts (1983a, 72–75). A closer look shows it actually performs what Vitanza calls sub/versive history, produced by a desire to break with the philosophical rhetoric of Plato and Aristotle (1987b, 112–14). Since we have few examples of the sub/versive approach to history (other than Vitanza's), Barthes' sketch of the classical system of Rhetoric[2] has a sort of taxonomic appeal in that it may help to fill out the category of sub/versive historiography and thus may expand our understanding of what motivates this approach and makes it necessary. Beyond its pertinence to historiographical questions, there are other reasons to study his memorandum. Although Barthes is not considered among the major theorists of contemporary rhetoric, *rhetoric* is arguably the critical term in his vocabulary—critical in the sense that it is capable of producing crisis and movement in his thought.[3] While Barthes makes his reputation first as the preeminent French structuralist and ultimately as a postmodern writer, it is to the history and theory of rhetoric that he ritualistically returns to develop his project of *écriture*.[4] His entire oeuvre can be read as an extended dialogue and struggle with the traditions of rhetoric, a struggle that is glimpsed most explicitly in "The Old Rhetoric." My general aim, then, is to suggest a reason for rhetoric's pivotal role in the development of what Barthes considers a subversive practice of writing and thereby to suggest his importance to the contemporary rehabilitation of rhetoric.

To understand Barthes' view of the history of Rhetoric, it is first necessary to understand his view of the rhetoric of history. Although I will argue his perspective is particularly instructive as an example of the sub/versive approach, it is consciously shaped by his reading of Nietzsche's essay on historiography, "On the Uses and Disadvantages of History for Life." Especially pertinent in this context is Barthes' earlier work *Michelet*, a book on France's nineteenth-century romantic historian that begins by stipulating what it is not: "Neither a history of Michelet's thought nor a history of his life—still less an explanation of the former by the latter" (1987, 3). *Michelet* offers, in other words, neither a history of ideas nor a biography of a great man but an essay on history-writing composed in terms of a complex conceit, inspired by Nietzsche, that establishes a relationship, for example, among history, gastronomy, disease, and transcendence. I want to briefly review the terms set forth in Nietzsche's essay on historiography before turning to *Michelet* as a mere aperitif for this rumination on Barthes' history of Rhetoric. A good digestion always requires the proper preparation of the palate.

"On the Uses and Disadvantages of History for Life" can be read as part of Nietzsche's effort to return life to its ground in the aesthetic dimension as an art that must be learned and continuously practiced "if it is not to eventuate in mere babblers and bunglers!" (1983a, 118). In this essay, Nietzsche focuses on what he perceives to be the glut of disinterested historical knowledge that has soured the modern stomach on its true creative vocation. Nietzsche refuses a merely "decorative" modern culture in which content is detached from form, knowledge is liberated from need, and thought is released from its obligation to produce action. Nietzsche works over a set of distinctions and correspondences—between human and nonhuman, the historical and unhistorical, memory and forgetting, sacred and profane. He wonders what differentiates the human being from cattle grazing in a field, and he recognizes humanness in the capacity for history and memory. Unlike the cattle who have no sense of history, the purely human and historical sense ruminates excessively and overstuffs itself with the content of alien ages. Feeding anxiously on the past to retain its monopoly on the meaning of being human, the purely historical being begins to resemble what it fears and hates most—namely, its other, the nonhuman, which is figured in this essay as the unhistorical beast grazing in the field. A thoroughly historical being, Nietzsche writes, is like "an animal that had to live only by rumination and ever repeated rumination" (62). An excess of historical knowledge causes indigestion and paralysis and leads to the diseased condition of modern life—or what Nietzsche calls "*the malady of history*" (120). Specifically, this knowledge "consumed [in excess] without hunger and even counter to one's needs, now no longer acts as an agent for transforming the outside world" (78). With a pure gaze that assumes vision is detached from all personal interest, the historical being ironically cannot apprehend the most obvious fact about human existence—the necessity of forgetting, the necessity of difference or the nonhuman—and thus remains ignorant that "it is possible to live almost without memory" (62). History and memory do not protect us from the fact that life, in any case, will be a savage purge, that knowledge (the sacred) is necessarily a matter of perspective, a simplification by design, and a creative distraction.

The disease of modernity needs only a simple emetic: "Knowledge in the service of life." This is Nietzsche's criterion for a good digestion, for returning knowledge to its ground in life and the immediacy of need. There are three kinds of need corresponding to three different ways of eating history: The monumental historian needs the past and consumes it as a model for achieving something great in the present. The antiquarian needs the past as one who likes to preserve and persist in tradition. In contrast to these two, the critical historian does not need the past but is oppressed by some present misery, understood as a legacy of the past, and wants to throw off the present burden. Critical history is a dangerous and untimely art that acts against the past for the sake of the present and future. It requires a strong stomach to make the judgments and sacrifices necessary if knowledge is to serve life. It must guide antiquarian and monumental history by purging knowledge of its preoccupation with the past and reconnect it with present need and future hope. More important, it must be a self-consuming art, an art consuming itself in action, if it is to alleviate "the true neediness and inner poverty" of human existence.

In *Michelet*, Barthes not only works through the same terms that digest Nietzsche's thoughts on historiography, he takes the idea that critical history is a self-consuming art to the limit of its possibility. "Michelet, Eater of History": This is the title of the opening chapter of a book that muses on the many senses in which history-writing consumes itself while it also consumes the historian. "How does Michelet eat History?" Barthes asks (1987, 20). How does Michelet constitute history as a nutriment or "nutritive habitat"? In a manner reminiscent of Nietzsche's grazing cattle, Michelet "grazes" on history—in Barthes' words, "he passes over it and at the same time he swallows it" (20; cf. Nietzsche 1983a, 60–61). But unlike Nietzsche's cattle, who have no sense of the historical, who do not know what is meant by yesterday or today, who only eat, rest, digest, and eat again, Michelet is a man who wants to feel historically through and through, who lives by repeated rumination, constituting his ideal nutriment as a *tableau*, or overview, so as to forget nothing, swallow everything, and make himself commensurate with the whole.[5]

Historical tableaux (like any classification system) make possible what Barthes calls the "apprehension of a continuity" (1987, 35). Tableaux place the historian in God's position, whose "chief power is precisely to hold in a simultaneous perception moments, events, men [*sic*], and causes which are humanly dispersed through time, space, or different orders. The tableau takes the place of the ancient cosmogonies" (22). This is the function of historical tableaux: To render History-as-God, the historian-as-prophet, and history-as-cosmogony. While Michelet constitutes and receives history as a nutriment, he also abandons his life to it. It is his Passion—his life and particularly his suffering and death, "for it is this death which constitutes Michelet as historian, makes him into a pontiff who absorbs, sacrifices, bears witness, fulfills, glorifies" (19). Historiography, thus transmuted, takes the form of hagiography; the historian, its sanctified body.

For Barthes, the Christological theme will always imply its ironic and vulgar counterpart: Michelet also organizes history the way a parasite would—that is, "he burrows into the heart of historical substance, feeds on it, grows in it, and though existing only by its means, triumphantly invades it" (18). Michelet is the "Eater of History" and also the "ruminant," the Parasite and the Host. In an image exquisitely vulgar, Barthes explains: "History as a delicious, indeed an essential unctuosity, since it is in the warmth of this closed, full History that Michelet will deposit, as an intelligent parasite, his own organism" (38). This parasite also carries the malady of history. He afflicts himself with "the most terrible historical diseases," the only treatment for which is more work, more history. History is a ritual ailment for Michelet, Barthes says, "only because he posited it in its total extension, granting himself the power of communicating by daily manducation with a History-as-God" (25). This disease of excess has no other purpose than "to establish Michelet as the manducator, priest, and owner of History," which he endows with two goals and one direction: "It is to be *consummated*: on the one hand, concluded, fulfilled, and, on the other, *consumed*, devoured, ingested, so as to resuscitate the historian" (25).

Barthes is also an eater of history, no doubt deliciously satisfied that he too has deposited something of himself in his "little book" on Michelet. Yet if he has occasion to feed on history, it is neither the ideal nutriment nor the staple of his diet.[6] The past form and future project of rhetoric are his sustaining nutrition, the substance upon which he feeds, the fertile loam across which his writing spreads rhizomatically rather than parasitically or virally. Rhetoric is the delicious, indeed the essential, unctuosity in which Barthes will deposit, as an intelligent parasite, his own organism in order to resuscitate himself and to think a future for writing.

Barthes' lecture notes on classical Rhetoric must be understood in this context, for his formal study of Rhetoric comes at a critical point in his thought, at a point of transition in which, though still affiliated (afflicted?) with his earlier structuralist practice,[7] he is already searching for a "new semiotics of writing." He explains: "At the source—or on the horizon—of this seminar [on the history of Rhetoric], as always, there was the modern text, *i.e., the text which does not yet exist*" (1988, 11). Barthes is not driven to Rhetoric by an antiquarian or monumental need for history. His passion instead is to bring something new into being, a new practice of language: "One way to approach this new text is to find out from what point of departure, and in opposition to what, it seeks to come into being" (11).

To understand the old Rhetoric in opposition to and as a point of departure for a new rhetoric, Barthes does not need to consume a full history. He needs only a memorandum. The culmination of his research, he says modestly, is "nothing more, then, than an elementary system of information, an introduction to a certain number of terms and classifications" (11–12). He constitutes the history of Rhetoric as a tableau whose divisions and classifications provide an overview and an outline of the ancient regime of Rhetoric. It is the kind of thing he claims he would have liked to find "ready-made" but that did not yet exist (at least in French) when he began his formal inquiry into classical Rhetoric. Though Barthes constitutes his nutriment as a tableau, he does not graze upon it as Michelet grazes on history, for grazing is the kind of rumination that takes time. If Michelet, the romantic, ruminates on the past and makes himself suffer the misery of too much history, Barthes, the postmodernist, samples his entire course in a few distracted bites, tasting the "power and subtlety of that old rhetorical system," relishing "the modernity of certain of its propositions," but, on the whole, preferring a different repast (12).

Barthes has no appetite, no stomach, for a lengthy rumination on the history of Rhetoric perhaps because when he begins his inquiry, Rhetoric is, for him, already dead. With a God's-eye-view, he surveys the old Rhetoric, less from the vantage point of the benevolent or hungry host, still less in the guise of a scavenger feeding on carrion, and more nearly in the guise of the forensic pathologist, dissecting the corpse of Rhetoric, performing a postmortem in order to ascertain the reasons for its demise. Yet there is no murder mystery to be solved here, no hermeneutical code to be broken. This death is evidently a suicide. The questions to be answered pertain to why Rhetoric died, how, by what means, and when. They also pertain to the crimes committed by Rhetoric or through its tutelage.

The account begins with a definition that apprehends or establishes, almost breathlessly, a 2500-year-old continuity. Rhetoric is a metalanguage, a discourse on discourse, involving several practices that correspond to successive and overlapping periods within a history: Rhetoric as technique, the classical "art" of persuasion; Rhetoric institutionalized as a "teaching," and eventually as material for examination (exercises, lessons, tests); Rhetoric as a "science" that treats language as an object and classifies the various effects of language; Rhetoric as an "ethic," a system of rules whose "role is to supervise (to permit and to limit) the 'deviations' of emotive language"; Rhetoric as a "social practice," a privileged technique that permits the ruling classes to gain ownership of speech (13–14). Working together, these five practices constitute a "formidable" and "repressive" institutional system. They also offer an initial answer to the question of why Rhetoric died: "Born 2500 years ago in legal cases concerning property, rhetoric was exhausted and died in the 'rhetoric' class, the initiatory ratification of bourgeois culture" (14). This summation could also be an obituary.

In Barthes' judgment, Rhetoric (as technique, teaching, science, ethic, and social practice) universalizes itself and shapes a super-civilization (the historical and geographical West). The system it has imposed is the only feature shared by successive and various historical groups, a fact that suggests to Barthes that there exists "superior to ideologies of content and to direct determinations of history, an ideology of form" and "a taxonomic identity" uniting diverse populations, practices, and historical periods (15). The formal systematicity that Rhetoric has imposed makes possible the illusion of historical continuity. In opposition to this formidable system of Rhetoric, a counter-rhetoric develops in the form of what Barthes calls a "ludic practice" or "black rhetoric" of games, parodies, ironies, erotic and obscene allusions—whatever within discourse is not mannered, mannerly, or to the manner born. This rhetoric marks a transgressive and subversive site where all social taboos and linguistic rules are lifted or traversed, a site that opposes the very idea of form and "flouts the very concepts of science and historical reflection to the point of calling into question history itself" (14–15).

An account that begins with a tableau of six practices quickly boils down to two opposing rhetorics, the repressive and the transgressive, which further distill into two even more originary rhetorics. First, a *rhetoric of the syntagm* generates a "proto-rhetoric," a political and juridical rhetoric, that then degenerates into the repressive institutional rhetoric charged with policing language and society alike; and, second, *a rhetoric of the figure* generates, on the one hand, a literary rhetoric increasingly cut off from its political and ethical ground and, on the other, a politically dangerous and ethically suspicious rhetoric of transgression. In this familiar structuralist binary is written the birth, flowering, and death of Rhetoric and, ironically, the possibility of a new rhetoric of writing that draws a transgressive practice into a political and ethical rhetoric. I will return to this new rhetoric later.

That Barthes would employ in his autopsy a structuralist binary is only to be expected given his intellectual history. In a comment on the ideology of classification, he offers an early formulation of what we now call, following Adrienne Rich (1986), "the politics of location": "The taxonomic option is an ideological one: there is always a stake in where things are placed: *tell me how you classify and I'll tell you who you are*" (47). Although he offers this comment in the context of identifying the instrument or agent of Rhetoric's death—the way in which an obsession with classification and taxonomy both creates the entity and its identity and then becomes the stake in its heart—his comment applies as well to his own forensic procedure. Barthes, the structuralist, is compelled to make two incisions in the corpse: the first, to show a diachronic movement; the second, to expose Rhetoric's systematicity. Furthermore, Barthes does not work on an isolated existence: "Rhetoric must always be read in the structural interplay with its neighbors (Grammar, Logic, Poetics, Philosophy)," he writes; "it is the play of the system, not each of its parts, which is historically significant" (46). Not surprisingly, Barthes is primarily concerned with Rhetoric and Poetics in both his diachronic and synchronic analyses, for their interplay determines the historical destination of Rhetoric. Though he makes two incisions, two passes over the historical field, both produce the same account of how the death of Rhetoric occurred: Through its passion for the requirements of form and classification, it "exhausted itself trying to hold within a necessarily more and more discriminating network of 'the manners of speaking' "; "trying to master the unmasterable," it simultaneously consummated (objectified and institutionalized) and consumed itself through its taxonomic frenzy; it was swallowed up by a Rhetoric of the figure; and finally died—empty, exhausted, and irrelevant—replaced by the modern study of style (85).

More specifically, the first cut into the corpse reveals what Barthes calls a "journey." It is composed, rather significantly, of seven "days" that offer in summary form a brief chronicle of events and a cast of characters which, in a week's time, created and destroyed the world of Rhetoric as "the only practice . . . through which our society has recognized language's sovereignty . . . which was also, socially, a 'lordship' " (1988, 15). This journey places Rhetoric, not history or the historian, in the position of God. Thus, it is Rhetoric that gives the very possibility of constituting historical tableaux and of holding in simultaneous perception what is dispersed through time, space, and different orders. The journey includes familiar names (Empedocles, Corax, Tisias; Gorgias, Plato, Aristotle; Cicero and Quintilian), and the chronicle presents the events that compose a familiar (canonical) history. In Barthes' journey, then, we see the ratification of one of our most nourishing beliefs—the association of Rhetoric with cosmogony, with the founding of a world.

Though the death of Rhetoric is not in question, the circumstances of its birth generate some speculation, offering what ultimately will be a fertile moment for conceiving a new rhetoric (cf. Sutton 1986). Barthes recounts what is generally known—that the art of speech is born, around 485 B.C. in Sicily, from the social conflicts and political chaos involving property rights and changing governmental structures. Formulated in this context, Rhetoric-as-God intercedes to adjudicate claims of ownership and is quickly incarnated as an object of instruction. What Barthes finds instructive here is not that this is an unmediated birth or even that Rhetoric is born of the labor of sublimation, but that Rhetoric has a *directly* mediated, *purely* ideological origin (an immaculate conception?): It is "as if language, as object of a transformation, condition of a practice, had been determined *not from a subtle ideological mediation* (as may have been the case in so many forms of art), but from the baldest sociality, affirmed in its fundamental brutality, that of earthly possession: we begin to reflect on language in order to defend our own" (1988, 16–17; emphasis added). Here he finds evidence that Rhetoric, from its origin, is part of the ideology of private property and consumption. He also finds evidence that the earliest rhetoric, a "proto-rhetoric," born of social and political need, is not a rhetoric of the figure but a rhetoric of the syntagm, of discourse. This fact allows him to construct a narrative in which Rhetoric dies when the politico-judicial theory and practice is swallowed up or "smothered," as he says, by a rhetoric of the figure—that is, by an aestheticization of rhetoric. In the second to fourth centuries A.D.—the so-called golden age of Rhetoric, or the Second Sophistic, when it flourishes as a literary aesthetic—Rhetoric is already in its death throes (42–46). During this time, the "triumphant and moribund" Rhetoric loses its specificity as a *technè* and begins to encompass everything, a general culture and a national education (43).[8] The process of rigor mortis, already begun in the Middle Ages, simply follows the constriction of the domain of Rhetoric to *elecutio*.

The second incision into the corpse finds what Barthes calls a "network," consisting of key terms forming a systematic and synchronic conception of the *technè rhétorikè* as a "kind of subtly articulated machine, a tree of operations, a 'program' destined to produce discourse"

(16). Rhetoric-as-Tree and Rhetoric-as-Machine: These metaphors give Barthes the means of transportation (*metaphorein*: to transfer or transport meaning) for moving through the network of Rhetoric. One provides a view of Rhetoric as an arboreal (and hierarchical) structure with a singular root system, three main branches (invention, arrangement, style), and many subclassifications, offshoots, and stages. The other provides a cybernetic machine for producing and managing discourse: "In the rhetorical machine, what one puts in at the beginning . . . are the raw materials of reasoning, facts, a 'subject'; what comes out at the end is a complete, structured discourse, fully armed for persuasion" (50). In the discussion sponsored by both metaphors, Barthes makes reference to the familiar elements in the system of Rhetoric: the five arts, the three forms of appeal, the special and common topoi, the tropes, the enthymeme, the rhetorical example.

Interestingly, it is in the second stage of his postmortem—in particular, his ruminations on the ideology of classification and the art of *dispositio*—that his double descent into time and the machine begins to show signs that a new rhetoric might be shaped from the dross of the old. In developing the notion that there is always a stake in where things are placed, Barthes speculates on "the place of the plan," or the concept and implementation of order in discourse: "Either we regard the 'plan' as an 'ordering' (and not just as an order), as a creative act of the distribution of materials, in a word a labor, a structuration, and then we connect it to the preparation of discourse [*inventio*]; or else we take the plan as a product, as a fixed structure . . . a grid, a stereotyped form" (49). On the one hand, order is an active and creative ordering and structuration in which *dispositio* is the art (or method) of invention; on the other, order is passive and created, a ready-made structure linked to style and to a reified notion of the formal features and parts of discourse. According to Barthes, Rhetoric has traditionally understood order in this second sense and linked *dispositio* with form and style. He wants, however, to situate a new rhetoric within the possibilities opened up by the first sense of order: "In its greatest extension, the *technè rhétorikè* includes five principal *operations* [the five arts]; we must insist on the *active, transitive, programmatic, operational* nature of these divisions: it is not a question of the elements of a structure, but of the actions of a gradual structuration" (50). From this formulation, he constructs a two-term system opposing a *rhetoric of production* to a *rhetoric of the product*. Rhetoric thus far in its history has been a rhetoric of the product, of style, and of consumption, but Barthes wants to push this machinery aside and set up a new discursive economy based on a rhetoric of production. This distinction represents an attempt to find in the old *technè rhétorikè* the equipment for formulating a new rhetoric of the syntagm through a reworking of the idea of form and order. Neither a reified rhetoric (an institutional and repressive rhetoric) nor a purely aesthetic rhetoric of the figure, it would be a rhetoric of production whose principal arts—invention and arrangement—would link a new aesthetic practice to political and ethical rhetoric and produce a reconstructed social order.

Barthes ends his formal inquiry into the death of Rhetoric here, but he finds himself ruminating on his findings four years later, spurred on by the desire that launched his historical inquiry in the first place—the desire for a new rhetoric (91–93). The possibility for such a rhetoric cannot even arise, he says, until three questions (points or *status causae*) are judged in the case of Rhetoric.

The first question concerns historiography. Barthes asks: "Neither a technique, nor an esthetic, nor an ethic of Rhetoric are now possible, but a *history*?" (92). Barthes claims that a history of Rhetoric is today *necessary*, one broadened by the critical discourses of our time—specifically, by the ludic or black rhetoric that flouts the very concept of history to the point of calling both history and Rhetoric into question. Both critical and revisionary, the perspective of such a history would not focus on the past as an object of interest for its own sake or as a metanarrative of legitimation for present and future projects, though it would nevertheless reduce the old Rhetoric to the rank of an historical object in order to effect a rupture with that formidable and repressive institutional system that has imposed what Barthes calls an "optimal homogeneity" on social conflicts and cultural differences (91). A revisionary perspective would disclose this ugly truth about Rhetoric, and it would also disclose the sense in which Rhetoric, while it has imposed a taxonomic or formal identity on diverse societies and historical periods, has itself remained unmoved and substantially unchanged—in other words, that while constituting the very possibility of history, it has remained unhistorical and inhuman. The goal of such an endeavor would be critical and sub/versive in its effort to return rhetoric to history, to open it up to history—to the present and the future through a rupture with its past. History thus conceived is wholly sub/versive in its anti-Platonic rejection of history as remembrance (Vitanza 1987b, 112).

The second question to be decided pertains to rhetoric's immediate future as a form of cultural criticism. Barthes observes "a kind of stubborn agreement between Aristotle (from whom Rhetoric proceeded) and our mass culture, as if Aristotelianism, dead since the Renaissance as a philosophy and as logic, dead as an esthetic since Romanticism, survived in corrupt, diffused, inarticulate state in the cultural practice of Western societies" (1988, 92). Aristotelianism survives today—politically, through democracy and, culturally, through an ideology of the "greatest number," through the majority-as-norm, and through the ideology of common sense—and defines a "trans-historical Occident," which is that of "the *endoxa*," or current opinion. Barthes sees an agreement between the ideology of common sense and Aristotle's Rhetoric of probability and argues that although Aristotle's Rhetoric is a rhetoric of reasoning and proof, it is a "deliberately diminished logic" because it is adapted to the level of the "public," which subordinates an ethical/aesthetic rhetoric to the psychology of the public and to a rhetoric of public opinion. Aristotle's Rhetoric of probability survives in the products of mass culture—in films, pulp novels, commercial articles—the production and marketing of which follow the Aristotelian rule: "Better an impossible probability than an improbable possibility" (22). Barthes wants to see a thoroughgoing critique of Rhetoric's complicity with the emergence of nineteenth-century mass culture and the hegemony of twentieth-century consumer culture. This critical project, sub/versive in its anti-Aristotelianism, would continue the demystifying work Barthes began in *Mythologies* (1972), where he delineates the rhetorical figures of petty bourgeois myth. But it might also include a criticism of the whole apparatus of writing instruction as part of the machinery for perpetuating the ideology of common sense and consumption.[9] In this respect, rhetoric's future lies in its ability to turn a self-consuming and critical eye on the relationship of the present to the past and rise, phoenix-like, from its own ashes, completely new and different.

Finally, the third question to be decided in the matter of Rhetoric concerns its complicity with the cultural construction of literature and the ideology of humanism. Barthes observes that literature, formed by Rhetoric and sublimated by humanism, emerges from the most brutal conflicts of money, property, and class—conflicts that are contained, domesticated, and sustained by educational and state institutions. Rhetoric therefore must examine its complicity with literary ideology—for example, with canon-formation, the myth of the author, and the mythical distinction between ordinary and figurative language (cf. Barthes 1986a).

These three judgments, together with Barthes' history of Rhetoric, show what Rhetoric has accomplished and what it has failed to do. In contrast to the narrative of marginalization and oppression that has been constitutive of the modern discipline of rhetoric and composition studies, Barthes constructs a narrative in which Rhetoric not only takes center stage in the history of Western culture but is the central fact in the transhistorical repression and annihilation of difference. Though finally a suicide, Rhetoric was a remorseless serial killer, so to speak, that made no eleventh-hour effort to repent—that is, to critically examine its own history and its relationship to bourgeois society and to mass culture. Barthes' indictment of Rhetoric implies a strong argument for the necessity of a sub/versive practice of historiography, especially one that escapes the romance of marginalization and disenfranchisement that we currently seem to prefer in rhetoric and composition studies. Barthes' final verdict in the case of Rhetoric is as inevitable as it is remorseless: "This is why reducing Rhetoric to the rank of a merely historical object; seeking, in the name of *text*, of *writing*, a new practice of language; and never separating ourselves from revolutionary science [semiology]—these are one and the same task" (1988, 93).[10] With the fate of the old Rhetoric finally settled—consumed and consummated in this tripartite judgment—Barthes will henceforth turn his attention to developing that new practice glimpsed in his descent into time and the machine.

Two additional (and related) judgments remain, however, that are crucial to an understanding of Barthes' indictment of Rhetoric. The more difficult question concerns whether his new rhetoric fulfills his vision of an aesthetic practice reconnected to a political and juridical rhetoric or whether it extends bourgeois ideology and further aestheticizes rhetoric. This is a matter I will set aside here since I address it at length elsewhere.[11] The other judgment, more easily rendered, pertains to his stake in where things are placed—specifically, his choice of metaphors for ordering (and inventing) the history of Rhetoric and his reduction of Rhetoric to the rank of a historical object, placed forever in the past.

God and Machine, one might argue, serve as a kind of *deus ex machina* (or as a "theos-trick," to use Vitanza's term), either imposed by the historian-as-god as a solution to the hermeneutical problem of emplotment or compelled by the machinations of other forms of imperialism. Barthes might counter, however, that although these metaphors are certainly deposits of his own organism, they also derive from the history of Rhetoric—in other words, they are first deposited in him by the Rhetorical education to which he has been subjected. They are doubly constitutive—of both subject and object, knower and known—and perhaps therefore possess some intrinsic or objective validity as well as a certain specular horror and fascination. The issue of validity is not particularly close to Barthes' concerns, of course, and the question of the origin of his terms misses the more germane question of their destination. His decision to construct his history as an outline or tableau (organized by the metaphors of God and Machine) deliberately, though deceptively, participates in and perpetuates the passion for classification that finally kills Rhetoric. His choice, in short, is meant to fulfill a destiny and close a history—namely, that Rhetoric-as-God is dead and that the God in the Machine (the desire for social control exercised through and imposed by language) is exposed for what it is. There is nothing modestly antiquarian in a choice of terms and approach that effectively seals Rhetoric's fate by placing it in the past as the dead art of an equally dead object, to be remembered only long enough to be forgotten. In this light, the title of his lecture notes—"The Old Rhetoric: An *aide-mémoire*"—is pure irony, and his memorandum, his double descent through time and the machine ("as down a double river") is also, and more important, an aid to forgetting. Ingested according to its own directions, this memory-aid serves as a purgative, as it were, for what turns out to be the object of Barthes' disgust.

Disgust is actually the key to this program, as I read it. Disgust is the paradoxical experience of a pleasure that arouses horror, and it results from the removal of the distance between subject and object, or self and other. This means that disgust is the affective response to an identification between self and other and the corresponding loss of difference. It is partner to the fear of homogenization and the loss of distinction. Kristeva has shown this experience, which she calls "abjection," to be the fundamental principle of subjectivity—the means by which we constitute and maintain the boundaries of individual identity (1982). To produce and maintain the boundaries that protect identity from collapse into the other/object, the subject—in this case, Barthes—must assert his distance and difference from the old Rhetoric. His desire to purge Rhetoric from collective memory is a need to purge himself of his identity with Rhetoric. An eater of history, he has been consumed and thoroughly digested by the old Rhetoric. Like Michelet, Barthes burrows into the heart of Rhetoric, feeds on it, grows in it, triumphantly invades it, and exists only by its means. He is part of that optimal homogeneity Rhetoric has imposed on different moments, events, and "men." The disgust he feels for Rhetoric is equally self-disgust and self-loathing for his lack of difference and distinction. He must purge himself of Rhetoric if he is to create a new practice of language and reconsecrate himself in its terms. His desire for a new rhetoric is a desire for the god-like power to create himself anew, to give himself new origins—a new stomach, as it were—and to recreate himself as an individual purified of and liberated from his linguistic and cultural constitution in the old Rhetoric, subject nonetheless to the imperatives of a new rhetorical practice.

In *A Lover's Discourse, Roland Barthes,* and *The Pleasure of the Text,* Barthes works out the terms of his new rhetoric and his new identity that motivated his formal study of classical Rhetoric in the first place. Although Barthes' judgment against classical Rhetoric, specifically as it has been digested by Plato and Aristotle, strengthens the affinity between his history of Rhetoric and sub/versive historiography, it is his effort to create a new expressive, literary rhetoric from a ludic or black rhetoric of theatrics and hysteria that compels a reading of Barthes' new rhetoric across the category of sub/versive style (cf. Vitanza 1987b, 112; 1990). The question I will leave unanswered here is whether Barthes' new rhetoric fulfills the vision of what he glimpsed in his double descent through history and Rhetoric or whether it simply recontains rhetoric in the compass of an aesthetic cut off from political and ethical practice. A thorough investigation of this question will help to clarify the nature of the political and ethical claims of sub/versive rhetoric.

Notes

1. *Autotomy* refers to the spontaneous casting off of body parts for self-protection. Lizards, I am told, will cast off their tails when the circumstances warrant. Their survival is determined, to some extent, by the capacity to autotomize, a knack that must, in some sense, comment on the human capacity to accessorize. While this might be the source of a sound ecological policy (lizard-skin shoes and wallets made only from the abandoned tails of self-sacrificing lizards), I am particularly interested in autotomy as an academic practice. Academic beasts undergo autotomy in a variety of situations, though it is

usually less spontaneous than carefully calculated, as most academic matters tend to be. This essay, for example, is a piece taken from a much longer study of the debate on historiography as it has developed in rhetoric and composition studies in recent years. That study, as yet unpublished, redefines rhetoric as gastronomy, or the art of eating well. My reading of Barthes' outline of the history of classical Rhetoric, as it appears here, has been drastically simplified and reduced in scope to accommodate the requirements of this volume. What this reading casts off, specifically, is the feminist tail that wags the whole beast. This paper, in other words, is missing the most significant (and, to me, the most interesting) part of its body and thus seems almost like an accessory. Though autotomy describes the genre of this paper, it is central to its conceptualization in another sense: Autotomy describes Barthes' relationship to classical Rhetoric and clarifies his motive for studying it in the first place.

2. Throughout this essay, *R*hetoric refers to the classical system of rhetoric; *r*hetoric refers to the field of rhetoric generally (understood synchronically and atemporally) and sometimes specifically to Barthes' new rhetorical theory and practice that he seeks in his study of classical Rhetoric. This distinction is necessary to mark two different referents for the term and to clarify the senses in which Barthes is wholly concerned with the category of "the rhetorical." It also follows Barthes' own usage.

3. Barthes' interest in Rhetoric has not been a focus of scholarship and, when it is discussed, it is incidental to the main argument. See Ungar (1983, 124–25) for the best discussion thus far. See also Lavers (1982, 72–75) and Rice and Schofer (1982). For a superb essay on Barthes and the rhetorical concept of *pathos*, see Blau (1987, 84–103).

4. Barthes distinguishes the poststructuralist notion of *écriture* (writing), or textuality, from the classical notion of work, or *oeuvre*. *Ecriture* is an open, infinite process that simultaneously generates and subverts meaning while the work is considered a closed, finished, and self-contained product of representation. See also Barthes (1967) for his earliest formulation of the distinction between work and text. For a short but helpful history of the concept of *écriture*, see Johnson (1990).

5. Constraints of focus require that this presentation simplify Barthes' view of Michelet. It presents only one level of signification that Barthes finds in the historian's writing. He locates a second level in Michelet's writing that works to undermine the status of facts on which historical knowledge is constituted. Barthes might agree with Vitanza's view (1987b, 96) of Michelet as a revisionary historian.

6. Barthes' comments on history and historiography are scattered throughout his many essays and books. See also Barthes 1986b; 1986c. For secondary sources on Barthes' view of history and historiography, see Ungar (1983), Culler (1983), and Champagne (1984).

7. Ungar (1983, 125) also suggests that Barthes' formal inquiry into the old Rhetoric comes before his break with the scientific project of structuralism but actually anticipates the concerns around which he will shape a critical practice after the break.

8. This observation is especially pertinent to the contemporary context in which rhetoric is increasingly viewed as a metadiscipline or foundation for all other disciplines and knowledges. The contemporary revival or rehabilitation of rhetoric involves diverse domains that seek to rediscover and articulate the aesthetic dimension of their forms of knowledge and knowledge-making activities. This includes both a study of the role of writing in the construction of knowledge and of the tropologic of knowledge. See Nelson, Megill, and McCloskey (1987) and White (1978). What Barthes might warn against in the contemporary revival of rhetoric, then, is a loss of the specificity of rhetoric as *technè* as well as a smothering of the political-judicial practice by an aestheticization of rhetoric. In a related context, he mentions the contemporary "reinvigoration of rhetoric," about which he makes this observation: "To recover rhetoric is inevitably to believe in the existence of a *gap* between two states of language"—that is, "a naked base, a proper level, a normal state of communication, starting from which we can elaborate a more complicated expression, *ornamented*, endowed with a greater or lesser *distance* in relation to the original ground" (1988, 84). Just as inevitably, he says, "rhetoric is always condemned in the name of a rejection of a hierarchy of languages." Again, this is a fascinating observation in light of his own condemnation of Rhetoric. In any event, and following this line of thought, his words suggest that a contemporary reinvigoration of rhetoric must navigate a dangerous course between the belief in the fictions of literal and figurative language, on the one hand, and, on the other, a collapse of all distinctions among the aesthetic, political, and ethical.

9. This is the general subject of a book I am currently at work on.

10. Barthes' outline of Rhetoric (though published previously in the journal *Communication*) is reprinted in *The Semiotic Challenge*, where it is strategically placed as the lead item—as if to announce that the first challenge in what he calls the adventure of semiology is to create a rupture with the old Rhetoric.

11. See note 1. Huyssen (1986) discusses the question of whether Barthes is a postmodern writer or continues the modernist project of French poststructuralism.

11

Structuring the Narrative for the Canon of Rhetoric

The Principles of Traditional Historiography (an Essay) with the Dead's Differend *(a Collage)*

Jane Sutton

> Death as the object of study is the blind spot of any account, hence of any history.
>
> —Paul Ricoeur

Introduction: The History of Rhetoric in the World Picture

Martin Heidegger (1977) portrays the modern age as the age of representation. He tells us that all aspects of life—art, science, religion, culture—exhibit the mark of a human representing. With this description of the human subject as "the representer of all representing," Heidegger laments: "Every relation to something—willing, taking a point of view, being sensible of [something]—is already representing" (150). Before we can begin to understand why Heidegger mourns the representer's position for humanity (*Homo rhetoricus*), we need to recognize that the notion of representation commits the foundation of Being (Truth) to universality (One), not particularity (multiplicity). In terms of rhetoric vis-à-vis Truth and universality, we must realize that, in the same way, rhetoric grounds itself in, at least as Aristotle conceptualized it, "not with what seems probable to a given individual like Socrates or Hippias [particular], but what seems probable to men of a given type [universal]; and this is true of dialectic also" (see Aristotle 1954, 1356b 33–35).[1]

This fundamental philosophical position of universality—arising out of Platonic-Aristotelian metaphysics and cemented by the Cartesian *ego cogito*—already knows what Being (Truth) is, a knowing that obligates all aspects of life, including rhetoric, to an organized unity or system. Within it, each part of life and all aspects of its relationships get to be represented. Heidegger talks about the privilege to be represented. He calls it "get[ting] into the picture," "[literally, to put oneself into the picture]" (1977, 129). To this subjective notion of my "getting into the picture," Heidegger adds the objective concept of our "getting the picture." In his characteristic style, he writes: " 'We get the picture' . . . what is, is set before us, is represented to us, in general, but that what is stands before us—in all that belongs to it and all that stands together in it—as a system" (129).

Representation renders all subjectivity and particularity into a unity. This unity is a problem for Heidegger because it enables any system the (vulner)ability to be objectified as universal knowledge. Maintaining unity or having one picture is a darkening cloud that conceals what may be otherwise or other than as we know it. Subjectivity—that which, rhetorically speaking, is probable to a given individual—is denied truth or any "real" value. A total darkening would mean, in other words, that the individual could only *be* and never *become*. A total darkening has implications for rhetoric's relation to the individual and to the public, meaning "men of a given type" (Aristotle 1954, 1365b 35). At best, in this world picture rhetoric would empower an individual to think, to mean, and to speak within the system of knowledge, and, at worst, rhetoric would manage individuals for the sake of that system.

If we focus on the problem of representing rhetoric's history as a Tradition, we discover that unity—its theory—is created out of diversity of practice. Based on what Heidegger has said, rhetoric, as practiced by particular rhetoricians—for example, Socrates or Hippias, to continue with Aristotle's example—is appropriated into the picture, and each subjective case for rhetoric, that is, each particular practice, is then *made* commensurate with a body of practices that are already organized consistently and systematically as a theory of rhetoric. This unity of organized practices, in return, represents the system of rhetoric as The Tradition. Extending Heidegger's "getting-into-the-picture" metaphor (1977, 129), we can say that the metaphysics of representation surrounds the picture of The Tradition: What can be seen in rhetoric's history, consequently, is only that which is framed as The Tradition. Extending the purview of this idea, Heidegger writes: "The sphere of historiographical research extends only as far as historiographical explanation reaches" (123). Rhetoric's historiography, of course, is no exception. Viewing "representation" and rhetoric together, I will show that the writing of history is driven by "representation," and the rewriting of history is driven by the history of representation.

Today, The Traditional picture is impoverished. Symptoms of its lifelessness are evident in the end of metaphysics and the death of rhetoric. As I have argued, the death of rhetoric is a facsimile of the end of philosophy (Sutton 1986, 203–7; see also Genette 1982, 103–27; Todorov 1982, 60–84, 85–111). The end-of-philosophy talk says that what is at stake in rewriting The History of rhetoric is its origins. That is, in order to write rhetoric's History, it must be represented in relation to some conceptual beginning. Specifically, its origin starts after a power struggle—*logos* versus *pathos* (Havelock 1967), a battle involving the dialecticians/philosophers, poets, and the Sophists. The winning side portrays proof by *logos* as the true representation of the whole of rhetoric. This outcome for rhetoric is signified in the words: Proof by *logos* is *the only true constituent* of the art (Aristotle 1954, 1354a 14; see Sutton 1986, 208–12). This so-called whole picture, ironically, shortens the reach of rhetoric's historiography since it restricts the art to parts that lend themselves to being represented legitimately according to metaphysics or first philosophy. For example, metaphor is invited into the picture only if it acts reasonably (Ricoeur 1977). "Sophistry" is altogether out of the picture. It is not that history forgot the rare, the exception, the unique; rather, it is that each has been systematically excluded from a history that seeks uniformity, consistency, and probability *to the principles of a given type* (universal "man").

Collage

This essay is a provisional attempt to expose the implications of adhering to a Traditional mode of representing a history of rhetoric. What is at stake, therefore, is the *status* of representing rhetoric through the power struggle between Plato and the Sophists. To figure in what cannot be represented Traditionally exposes the system of power that authorizes certain representations while it simultaneously blocks, prohibits, or invalidates others. The risk is that this essay will fall into a unified structure consistent with the narrative of liberation. This essay will attempt to circumvent such a Traditional interpretive maneuver of confinement by using a technique that revolutionized modern art, namely, the collage.[2] Since the power of power cannot be represented, but only felt, a collage seeks to unhinge the reciprocity between a Traditional picture of rhetoric and the system of ordering, selecting, and composing that dominates as well as stabilizes the scene of writing a history of rhetoric.[3]

Even without a philosophical rationale courtesy of poststructuralism (see Ulmer 1983), an essay with a collage is rhetorically appropriate. Writing about the history of rhetoric with an essay and a collage is the kind of writing that makes rewriting The Traditional history of rhetoric possible. Combining scientific and artistic insights with his own tools of the trade, Hayden White (1978) urges us to approach historical inquiry, for example, with psychoanalytic and impressionistic modes of representation. In this manner, White says, historians can dramatize "the significance of the data which they have uncovered but which, they are prohibited from seriously contemplating as evidence" (47–48). Without dramatization, the historian is confined to The Traditional way of representing a subject. Because representation works, White says, by eliminating "certain kinds of data from consideration as evidence" (46), the medium of collage, being a graceful product of scissors and paste, can take apart and put together, as I see it, any "data" in the history of rhetoric. Torn apart, The Traditional *frame* of reference, thereby, no longer systematically excludes.

Questions concerning the artistic merit of collage raise issues with a parallel in rhetoric's history that is too seductive to ignore. Until the beginning of the nineteenth century, collage is decorative garbage, just kids cutting up pictures. By the late nineteenth century, however, the collage lends itself to being, ironically, representational art since its nature is indebted to actual, real fragments—literally "stuff" from the past (Wolfram 1975; Group *Mu* 1978). Likewise is the experience of rhetoric. In the *Phaedrus*, for example, speech writing is composing with a twist—rhetoricians just "pasting together and pulling apart" words (Plato 1963, 279). But again, by the nineteenth century, Nietzsche

(1966, 1969, 1974) writes philosophy rhetorically with a strategy of "scissors and paste," as manifested in his aphoristic style.

Traditionally, a collage and rhetoric are "scavenge" arts, a conception intended to express the neologism formed on scavenger/savage. Rhetoric and a collage are scavengers: Both are accused neither of being able to use nor to have anything that is their own; both are savages, meaning kindergarten, pre-rational ventures in image, language, and thought that continually force contradiction and an anti-system (Plato 1963, 279).

The medium of collage, then, is suitable for understanding what constitutes "doing" rhetoric's history for a Traditional rewriting and for a nontraditional writing. Traditionally speaking, a collage can furnish the viewer with real, literal pieces of past pictures of rhetoric. In the manner of a looking glass, a collage reflects back Tradition in all its multiplicity. In the manner of a mirror, the multiplicity that is reflected turns into a object of knowledge. Nontraditionally speaking, objectifying the past allows the viewer of this hodgepodge to reflect upon and reject writing of the past just as the artist does when he or she takes scissors to pictures. Ulmer (1983) puts it this way: "Something becomes an object of knowledge only as it 'decays,' or is made to disintegrate" (97). The premise here works off the paradox that a subject needs to be objectified in order to be talked about and what is objectified requires a subject to destroy it if there is to be a subjective perspective.

Placing this paradoxical premise within the context of writing an essay with a collage, we understand that what is an object of knowledge in the history of rhetoric is images *of* the Sophists as opponents of politics, ethics, and truth. This negative image is necessary for the continual representation of The Tradition's account of itself as The Tradition of rhetoric. Rewriting the history of rhetoric requires scissors that can destroy certain images and requires paste that can make other images into an object of knowledge. If these images of the Sophists can be destroyed, the image *of* rhetoric-as-bad, in turn, can become an object of knowledge awaiting destruction.

Dis-position

The essay begins, then, with a collage, composed of *fragments in dispute* over the death of the Sophists. Down the left-hand side are ranged a series of fifth-century fragments on the death of Sophists to describe the conditions of practicing rhetoric in Athens, while the right-hand column represents nineteenth-century research that denies the fifth-century fragment, usually in the form of a footnote.[4] In other words, the fragments are in dispute and constitute what Jean-François Lyotard (1988) calls a differend.

> A differend would be a case of conflict, between (at least) two parties, that cannot be equitably resolved for lack of a rule of judgment applicable to both arguments. One side's legitimacy does not imply the other's lack of legitimacy. However, applying a single rule of judgment to both in order to settle their differend as though it were merely a litigation would wrong (at least) one of them (and both of them if neither admits this rule). Damages result from an injury which is inflicted upon the rules of a genre of discourse but which is reparable according to those rules. [The differend] suggests . . . that a universal rule of judgment between heterogeneous genres is lacking in general. (xi)

In the middle—between an ancient fragment and a modern footnote—are postmodern phrases, mostly from Lyotard that illustrate rhetoric's differend.[5] While Lyotard is concerned with the victims of the Second World War, his approach to understanding the history behind silencing victims, nonetheless, reaches all the way to classical Athens. His approach enables me to extend my reach in rhetoric's past and understand The Tradition as a production of readings (broadly defined as the nineteenth-century reading social science reading positivism reading scholasticism reading Cicero reading Aristotle reading the Sophists)—a production of readings strained with the project of having to disable the discourse of the "other" and of turning away from differences in social relations. In sum, a collage, à la Lyotard, juxtaposes translator's footnotes to Sophistical fragments with Sophistical fragments themselves (in Sprague 1990). With The Tradition's footnote to the Sophistical fragment and the Sophistical fragment itself in absolute contradiction, I recreate the conflict in Tradition and expose it as a differend (using Lyotard 1988; cf. De Las Casas in Hanke 1959; de Certeau 1988; Kennedy 1963). These "phrases in dispute" invite us all to reconsider the judgment of the dead as a differend rather than a litigation.

The second part of this paper is a brief discussion of The Tradition as it attempts to unhook the contradictions from the principles of its own Traditional historiography. In so doing, the principles of Traditional historiography are revealed in the wake of the Heideggerian problem of representation—questions concerning the classic assumptions of unity, harmony, linearity, and closure committing history to a model of development.

In sum, the essay seeks to investigate the thoughts and beliefs of Tradition while the collage tries to examine the relationship of these thoughts and beliefs. There are, then, two methods for gaining an understanding of the principles or truths of Traditional historiography in rhetoric, and both of these must be pursued simultaneously in order to yield the final result: understanding the principles of writing, of history, and of rhetoric. In writing an essay and collage, my goal is to see choices made in relationships, decisions coping with each other, and the tension of history when organized Traditionally.

The Dead's *Differend*: A "Gathering" of the Principles of Traditional Historiography in Rhetoric

NAME: sigma, omicron, phi, iota, sigma, tan, sigma

Deathplace: Athens, Rome, After the World Wars
Profession: Rhetoric

The Period of Opacity

The Period of Clarity

The Period of Disparity

Hippias. *Killed*.
While organizing a plot against the state (Sprague 86A 15).

Menexenus says Antiphon and Lamprus are mentioned . . . , but Hippias is not (Sprague 86A 13 N.4).

> It is the nature of a victim not to be able to prove that one has done a wrong. One becomes a victim if one loses these means. One loses them, for example, if the author of damages turns out directly or indirectly to be one's judge. The latter has the authority to reject one's testimony as false or the ability to impede its publication (Lyotard 1988, sec. 9).

Thrasymachus. *Hanged himself*.
After repenting of vain and sterile professorial chair (Sprague 85A 7).

Scholiast said there is nothing to connect this Athenian with our Thrasymachus (Sprague 85A 7 N.3).

> Either the damages you complain about never took place, and your testimony is false; or else they took place and since you are able to [repent] to them, it is not a wrong that has been done to you, but merely a damage, and your testimony is still false (Lyotard 1988, sec. 7).

The Period of Opacity

The Period of Clarity

The Period of Disparity

Prodicus. *Executed.*
Charged with corruption of the youth (Sprague 84A 1).

This is false. Surely the Byzantine encyclopedist has Prodicus confused with Socrates (Sprague 84A 1 N.1).

> Let *p* be: you are the victim of a wrong; *not p*: you are not; *Tp*: phrase *p* is true; *Fp*: it is false. The argument is: either *p* or *not p*; if *not p*, then *Fp*; if *p*, then *not p*, then *Fp* (Lyotard 1988, sec. 8).

Theramenes. *Put to death.*
Under Law of Thirty Tyrants (Sprague 84A 7).

As some report, must take down a notch or two (Sprague 84A 7 N.8).

> The one who lodes a complaint is heard, but the one who is a victim . . . is reduced to silence (Lyotard 1988, sec. 13).

Protagoras. *Banished.*
From all Athenian territory. Drowned. In shipwreck (Sprague 80A 2).

He died in all likelihood [at Delium in 424] not long before his presentation of the *Flatters* of Epolis . . . (Sprague 80A 11).

> . . . the only eyewitness I will accept would be . . . (in Lyotard 1988, sec. 2) slaves under torture (in Aristotle 1954, 1376b–13779–5). The plaintiff . . . should have said . . . since the only witnesses are the victims, and since there are no victims but dead ones, no place can be identified as [Athenian territory] (Lyotard 1988, sec. 6).

The Period of Opacity

The Period of Clarity

The Period of Disparity

Antiphon. *Convicted.*
Of treason and was cast out of city unburied (in

After what Didymus the grammarian said, there follows another version of his

Sprague 87A 3 [11]).
NOTICE: Anyone adopting one of the bastard or wedlock children of Antiphon will be deprived of citizen rights (Sprague 87A 3[24]).

death but this is a different Antiphon. (Morrison 1976).

> The victims, the executioners, and the witnesses at [the trial] enter into the class of human beings; the messages we receive from them are meaningful and offer material for verification, even if they are incompatible with any Idea of humanity (Lyotard 1988, sec. 31). But, what if the opponent strives to hide that he or she does not observe the rules of cognition, and acts as if he or she were observing them (Lyotard 1988, sec. 34)?

Thus
Paving the Way

Of Entropy

From Epilogue

To Prologue

GORGIAS. *Lived*.
To 108 years of age (Sprague 82A 13).

Was Gorgias a Sophist? (Harrison 1964).

> For thought to be modern, doesn't it suffice that it think in terms of the end of some history? Or, is postmodernity the pastime of [man] who scrounges in the garbage-heap of finality looking for leftovers . . . and who turns . . . into . . . promise of change (Lyotard 1988, sec. 182).

For Tradition
Against Tradition

Of Entropy

From Epilogue

To Prologue

Athens

Thus mankind is one, and all men are alike in that which concerns their creation and all natural things, and no one is born enlightened. And the savage peoples of the earth

Rome

The most satisfactory image would be to think of the rhetorical tradition as a great interwoven vine leading from two main trunks, the practical side, was nurtured by a

compared to uncultivated soil
that readily brings forth
weeds and useless thorns,
but has within it . . . natural
virtue . . . Bartolome De Las
Casas's (1474–1566) argument
against Aristotelianism (in
Hanke 1959, 112).

rich culture and put forth an
exceedingly green foliage for
a brief time, supported in
part by its fellow trunk.
Thereafter the other, theoretical trunk alone continued to
grow, drawing strength and
sap from its dying *mate* . . .
(Kennedy 1963, 263).

After World Wars

> We [barbarians] were once the masters of the earth; but since the gringos arrived we have become veritable pariahs . . . we have the hope that the day will come when they realize that we are their roots and that we must grow together like a great tree with its branches and flower (de Certeau 1988, 231).

Conclusion to the Collage: Introduction to Writing Historiography

The "Dead's Differend: A 'Gathering' of the Principles of Traditional Historiography" is a collage of rhetoric, of history, of writing, and of the received tradition. It is a cut-and-paste arrangement using what is available from the stock of various cultural materials. Said rhetorically, the selections from what has previously existed represent "commonplaces" (*topoi*) in that they are used over and over and give shape to a variety of histories. These selections, as they participate within a Traditional framework develop into lines of thought or arguments that shape historical data in a particular way. Under this representation of *Logos* (truth), rhetoric escapes its propensity for distorting the *logos* (proof by reason) with figures of thought and speech. With all of this mind, we can see that not only do the fragments on the death of the Sophists lack a framework to be developed into complete and sound arguments, but also we can see that the subject matter, the death of *Rhetoric*'s predecessors, is mere hyperbole. By looking upon the death of the Sophists as an incomplete, insignificant, or exaggerated notion, the dramatic impact is obscured.

The death of the Sophists, speaking literally and figuratively, is no less dramatic than philosophy's dismissal of rhetoric in the *Gorgias* (see

Plato 1963; Ijsseling 1976, 7–17). In fact, the obscurity surrounding the death of the Sophists creates the principle behind Traditional historiography. A glance back at the collage shows footnotes denying Sophistical fragments. That is to say, a footnote, insofar as it steps over brutality, tragedy, politics—people, keeps The Rhetorical Tradition in a pattern of explanation that excludes Sophistical rhetoric from History and, therefore, does not see the contradictions punctuating rhetoric's past. It is to that underlying pattern—the representation of the history of rhetoric without contradiction—that I want to pursue now. By unmasking this pattern I offer insight into the principle—the transformation of experience into one picture—and the problem of representation confronting the writing of a history of rhetoric.

Content of the Form

The transition from a collection of fragments to a story of The Rhetorical Tradition depends upon the application of the notion of teleology, an idea of development that is attributed to Aristotelianism and, later, Hegelianism.[6] Applying the idea of teleology (*teleos*)—meaning achievement of perfection—to rhetoric's past, Aristotle indicates the art is not perfect. Rhetoric needs to be developed further since past rhetoricians, as Aristotle (1954) points out, "have constructed but a small portion of [the] art" (1354a 13). Seeing Aristotle as the final developer of rhetoric, The Tradition, driven by the desire that rhetoric's *history* also achieve perfection, controls what counts as historical "fact." Contradiction makes Rhetoric's History impure, thus weakening the Tradition's ideal of perfection. For example, as Aristotle (1954) represents rhetoric's past, the earlier version of the art is discourse by *pathos* (1354a 10–15) and needs to be made right with argument or proof by *logos* (1355a 1–30), something that the Sophistical version lacked. And then, Aristotle (1954, 1402a 17, 25) attributes a method of argument to Protagoras (a Sophist). Rather than incorporating this contradiction in the history of rhetoric, an investigation of Protagoras's method of argument in *The Tradition* is absent, except as a footnote (see Sesonske 1979).

At any rate, setting aside issues of textual consistency in Aristotle's *Rhetoric* and focusing on the notion of its development (see Sutton 1993), I see a good example of how The History of Rhetoric operates teleologically. The Tradition lies about or ignores practice by offering an abstract understanding of the development of argument. It is abstract because the idea of the total absence of argument has no roots in lived experience. That is to say, Protagoras never understands himself as practicing rhetoric without *reasoned* argument. When reviewing the past, it is Aristotle, followed by The Tradition, who claims Protagoras's imperfect unreasonableness. Regarding the abstract in history, Ricoeur (1980) writes: "History is a bookish notion and not an existential one; it is the organization by the intelligence of data which refer to a temporality which is not *Dasein's*" (Being [there]; 38).

A view of temporality that is not rooted in lived experience, that is not *Dasein*'s as Ricoeur puts it, is illustrated in the almost obsessional tendency toward classification by which all sorts of distinctions and divisions are made regarding rhetoricians and rhetoric in history. The gap between the early rhetoricians' experience and practice of the art at a particular moment in history (say, in the law courts during the revolution of 411 B.C. [see Antiphon 87 B 18–19 in Sprague 1990; Sutton 1989]) and rhetoric's history of the genre of judicial rhetoric is enormous (see Wilcox 1942; Kennedy 1980b; Sutton 1991). In fact, this gap—between a(n) practice/experience and the classification of it—Ricoeur goes on to tell us, constitutes a blind spot in the history of rhetoric. I want to shed some light on this blind spot so that a principle of The Traditional historiography—the representation of the history of rhetoric without contradiction—can be understood.

I will explicate this principle of historiography by examining three ages: They are (*a*) the age of obscurity, (*b*) the age of clarity, and (*c*) the age of disparity. Following Heidegger's theme of the transformation of experience into the world picture, I will describe how an age manifests the principle of historiography through the problem of representation. With that outline, I can be more specific.

Statement of the Problem, Assumptions, and Method

When Heidegger (1962) describes the principles of Western philosophy, he is revealing the history of Being and its death. Insofar as philosophy and rhetoric have parallel histories, it can be said that when the locus of truth was wrestled out of obscurity and situated for philosophy in reason/dialectic and for rhetoric in *logos*/enthymeme, the settlement of truth in a location or place brought closure to the question of Being and, in turn, produced the foundation on which to build the now-self-evident principles of Tradition for each discipline. Broadly described in a Heideggerian understanding of representation, the principle of Traditional historiography is as follows: "That which the ancient philosophers found continually disturbing as something [a] *obscure* and hidden has taken on a [b] *clarity and self-evidence* such that if anyone continues to ask about it he is [c] *charged with an error of method*" (2; my emphasis).

The principle, then, for rhetorical historiography is this: First in the age of obscurity, the practice of rhetoric was transformed into theory. During this time, only what could be turned into theory or what could be conceptualized out of the practice got into the world picture. Following that, in the age of clarity only theory represents rhetoric because practice is what characterizes obscurity. Then, finally, given this presentation of rhetoric, The Tradition accuses anything outside that theoretical frame as erroneous. And yet, the principle—from practice (the world) to the hyper-authority of theory (world picture)—must be operative in the history of rhetoric; for otherwise, the fluidity of temporality—all is in transit (*rhóe*)—combined with the rhetorical impulse of uncertainty—contingency of situation—would not permit us to grasp and hold on to anything, not a theory, much less a history (Owens 1983, 66). The history of rhetoric is already in despair. The principle is necessary but inadequate.

By addressing the principle—the transformation of the world into one perfect picture—of traditional historiography, I am able to determine "the 'laws' or 'principles'," of which, Hayden White (1973) writes, "a particular age's 'spirit' is . . . a manifestation or phenomenal form" (4). These "laws" or "principles" are manifestated in each of the ages—obscurity, clarity, and disparity. The "spirit" of perfection in each age inheres it to a line of thought disposing it to choose the same specific documents as real, reliable, or significant. Once "chosen," the "spirit" of the age uses these documents to support a plot line for a story on the tradition of rhetoric. Within this teleological-driven narrative is an ideological component that works to ensure that the *form* of Traditional historiography has consensus. This consensus is necessary to the vitality of The Tradition's notion of a canon of rhetoric. The canon controls the business of rhetoric's life.

The explication offered in this essay attempts to incorporate Heidegger's critique of representation and truth in the rewriting of the history of rhetoric. Time, which is crucial to the transformation of experience into a picture, and the temporality of the three ages—obscurity, clarity, and disparity—are different. The assumptions regarding this difference converge on a notion called the "gathering." Heidegger draws memory, language, thinking, Being into the discourse of "gathering."

The "gathering" can be conceptualized as that of *thinking by questioning* the past. Thinking back involves memory whose object is the past and future-possible so that the recovery of memory brings forth a succession of associated ideas that can be completed. This means that memory reproduces the past and processes it for the future. Memory is not a product of representation but a rhetorical cycle of revolution. Memory is not something that designates what is perfect but something that is rhetorically active and seeks completion. As such, insofar as memory aids them, truth and understanding are embedded in linguistic possibilities of temporal moments rather than in a correspondence between past and present established in time. In her conversation with Heidegger about the meaning of "gathering," Joan Stambaugh (in Heidegger 1969) writes: "It is the most fundamental presupposition for anything to be or to happen at all" (17). Moreover, in their work on Heidegger, Michael Hyde and Craig Smith (1979) explain: "Here [the "gathering"] new linguistic possibilities are called into Being (made known) and thus expand a culture's awareness of reality" (352).[7] Here thinking does not seek to attack the existing attitude at every temporal moment. Rather, the distinction is a shift away from "the push-pull belief" of traditional accounts of non/perfect rhetoric existing in time (see Vitanza 1987a, 44). Heidegger's method, as hermeneutics envisions it, is not a test of a claim in time but the interpretation of cyclical meanings regardless of their "timing" in history. Thus, the use of Heidegger's method with which to write an essay is compatible with a collage that mixes up Lyotard's talk about victims of gas chambers with fragments about victims in Athens.

The Principles of Traditional Historiography in the Age of Obscurity

Rhetoric, as it is represented in The Tradition of Western philosophy, is another name for deception, the lie, fabrication, and artifice. *Sophistic,* as it is represented in The Tradition of Western philosophy, is another name for fallacious reason, the dark and dangerous side of a cunning intellect, and mental dullness. *Rhetoric* and *Sophistic* are linked, then, through deception, violence, and persuasion. As H. Sidgwick (1974) claims, the benefits of both rhetoric and Sophistry were "equally hollow and illusory" (78). Sophistry and rhetoric are the dramatic focal point to which Plato's ideas are juxtaposed. A good example of this conflict is illustrated in the analogy of the white and black horses in *Phaedrus* (Plato 1963, 273). A true art of rhetoric is possible once the black horse is bloodied and struggles against emotion to obtain the same state of reasonableness as does the white one.

In a collection of essays centered on the historical theme of a true and a Sophistical rhetoric, Jacqueline de Romilly (1975), like so many others, describes Plato's battle with the Sophists as solely an attempt "to . . . discredit . . . the ways of the [S]ophists" (28). Equally important to this attack is rhetoric's connection with magic and poetry (see Havelock 1967). For example, de Romilly works closely with the *Republic* (Plato 1963) to show that, like magic, rhetoric deceives and plays on "false impression" (de Romilly 1975, 332). For other historians, such as Hegel (1963), the beguiling and the bewitching of listeners is illustrated best in *Protagoras* (Plato 1963, 315–59) where the Sophist is accused of "charming [young foreigners], like Orpheus; and they follow him obeying the charm of his voice" (359). This representation of Sophistical rhetoric as potentially unethical is elsewhere discussed in political terms. In *Politicus* (in Wilcox 1942, 136, 148), for example, the man who deals with politics without possessing political knowledge is the greatest magician of all Sophists.

Traditionally speaking, it is rhetoric linked to Sophistry, that is, the deprivation of clarity, that is *yoeteia* and vulnerable to being charged with an error of method. De Romilly (1975) writes: "Anything that is irrational and deprives [one] of lucidity is witchcraft, *yoeteia*. Anything that suggests an erroneous impression is *yoeteia* too" (36). In the same vein, W. C. K. Guthrie (1969) reports magical qualities are compressed in a difficult word to translate—*deinotes*—which is derived from a noun meaning "fear." Guthrie writes: "It stands for anything terrible or dreadful" (32). What is dreadful causes despair. Eventually, the word *deinotes* became coupled with the word *sophos*, to mean clever or skillful as of some dreadful power. Thus, implied in the phrase "clever" is the notion of *deinos*, sorcerer and Sophist, one who weaved belief akin to Bacchic frenzy or a hypnotic trance (see McNally 1970, 3; Segal 1962, 199; Havelock 1967).

This line of thought about the Sophists is not only well known but became the foundation of the scorn for rhetoric. A truncated version of this antagonistic plot of Western thinking reveals itself most poignantly in the dialogue *Sophists* where these men are degraded in several ways.[8] However, Plato's dialogue *Gorgias* is the most effective denouncement of the Sophistical art and rhetoric (see Ijsseling 1976, 7–17).

The above discussion suggests the age of obscurity understands the history of rhetoric as a footnote to or a preface to Plato. While the dialogues are the principal guardian of the plot of the historical development of rhetoric, rhetoric and the Sophistical art emerge out of a profusion of counterclaims not always consistent with Plato. Rhetoric is about riddles, prophecies, and oracles as in Gorgias's magic and Antiphon's dream interpretation (in Sprague 1990, 82A 32, 87A 12). It is about making enemies with tyrants called Hieron and Geon and turning around and befriending them as in the case of Corax (Farenga 1979). It is mixed up with laws promoting the laws of Draco and the reforms of Solon and then undoing democracy with oligarchy and the Law of the Thirty Tyrants (Wilcox 1942). Rhetoric is about seeking justice and truth in the Aeropagus before 6000 and devouring that aim with the bribes of sycophants (Bonner 1916, 1927; Lofberg 1920). It is all this and more, a multiplicity of inconsistencies.

In The Tradition, the history of rhetoric must be conciliatory and overcome the art's dark, dangerous, and subversive roots in Sophistry. The desire for reconciliation with philosophy allows The Tradition's plot to admit Aristotle's indebtedness to the Sophists (see J. Poulakos 1983a). However, friendly overtures to the Sophists stop with their acknowledgement and The Tradition returns to speak on Aristotle's *Rhetoric*. In other words, with the debt to the Sophists paid off, the history of rhetoric can set the record perfectly straight. The principle of development—the selection of material to reach a perfectly consistent system—chooses "objectively" and slides over or dismisses genuine conflict. In this way, contradictory ideas (as in the case of the method of argument of Protagoras [Aristotle 1954, 1402a 17, 25; see Sesonske 1979, 71–91; Sutton 1991])—are disposed of and the quest for a perfect and consistent *Rhetoric* is maintained. In the contest between the honesty of ambiguity in bits and pieces of Sophistical fragments and logical clarity of a complete text, the latter prevails.

The Principles of Traditional Historiography in the Age of Clarity

I describe this approach, for the most part, under the work of one scholar. The major and most informative writer of a unified treatment of persuasion is George Kennedy.[9] That is to say, Kennedy (1963) offers what Kenneth Burke (1969a) calls "a representative anecdote" (59–61) of why the Sophists are historically important: They allow The Tradition to trace the evolution of rhetorical theory. Kennedy puts it this way: "We must remember that oratory was one of the oldest and most active of Greek traditions, but one which was not *self-conscious* until the fifth century" (27; my emphasis). Viewed as such, The Tradition gives considerable attention to showing how the art evolved gradually. For example, to trace its development, Kennedy begins with the Sophists and demonstrates how rhetoric evolved. He describes how Aristotle transcended the serious problems of the ancients' use of eristic techniques and stylistic devices by systematizing and conceptualizing the theory of rhetoric: "Aristotle is trying to create a systematic art of eristic to replace this unscientific approach; the beginning is difficult, he says (183b 23 [in *Sophistical Refutations*]) but once stated the theory of the art will grow in bulk" (Kennedy 1959, 171). Even though the Sophists are credited with the partial development of rhetoric, the differences between Sophistical and Aristotelian rhetoric are not expounded. According to Heidegger (1962) in the age of clarity, it is *self-evident* that the Sophistical practice of rhetoric needed augmentation. That it is *self-evident* becomes clear as The Tradition passes through the looking glass to track down the "other" side and charge it with an error of method (e.g. Halloran 1976; Scott 1964; Schiappa 1990).

Another example of approaching history as a unity is K. E. Wilkerson's (1982) account of persuasion in early Greece. Extending Kennedy's (1963) claim that "later antiquity found formal rhetoric everywhere in Homer" (35), Wilkerson (1982) points out that "the early rhetoricians, Gorgias, in particular, turned to the Greek poets for techniques adaptable to speech making" (113). In juxtaposing the Homeric conception of rhetoric to the Aristotelian version (1954), The Tradition (à la Kennedy 1963 and Wilkerson 1982) illustrates how a Homeric argument, "the barest of enthymemes," lacked complex development (Wilkerson 1982, 113). Displaying an evolutionary stance toward the art, Kennedy (1963) and Wilkerson (1982) maintain that against a backdrop of political changes and a continual belief in the efficacy of decision making the art of rhetoric was not completed effectively or soundly until the fourth century B.C. when Aristotle formally constituted it. At the most basic level, the age of clarity is one that works within an archaeological disposition toward the Sophists. In this sense, history, because it examines the ancients as one might look upon relics of a few surviving artifacts of a primitive, poor culture, is history *made* clear under the rule of being *self-evident*.

In sum, the writing of history in the age of clarity is evident in two ways. First, the Sophists are viewed as stepping-stones to be stepped over obliquely on the way to a more developed and "grammatized" theory. Because the Sophists have "little or no conscious conceptualization" (Kennedy 1980a, 27; Enos 1976, 37), their contributions are minimized by contrasting them to what is more complete, Aristotle's *Rhetoric*. As such, it is Aristotle and his *Rhetoric* that are being fully restored rather than rhetoric. Second, the argument that Aristotle's *Rhetoric* is the completion of the art blinds the history of rhetoric: It cannot see another perspective even when the story of the Sophists eternally returns, though it returns in different forms. The argument—*Rhetoric* as the completion of the art—starts with the belief that a theory of rhetoric moved from inadequacies, when humans had not yet achieved consciousness, to maturity epitomized by rational thinking (e.g., Kerferd's 1981 reading of Hegel 12–13). This attitude, furthermore, applies a schematization to the history of rhetoric that moves infinitely from no understanding to more and more understanding. As progress is made, concerns that turn up and do not fit this schematization of theory are ignored, forgotten, or hidden (see Wilcox 1942). Paradoxically, the teleological framework opens the Sophists to the study of rhetoric but then closes them off at the same time due to its teleological method, particularly its insistence on what counts as fact, which, in turn, is embroiled in the question, What is progress? Thus, the teleological method furnishes a criterion of admission to the category of fact and contains already future representations of the history of rhetoric. Heidegger (1977) observes: "Historiography as research projects and objectifies the past in the sense of an explicable and surveyable nexus of actions and consequences" (123). Again, this method is not evil but essential to theory building and historical research. But, it does not see.

To plot the age of clarity, then, is very complicated with all of its historical intrigues and theoretical conspiracies involving the Sophists. With blindness to anything but arguments that follow a teleological rationality, these historians "cast in the role of enemy anyone not capable of occupying the symbolic place of power as defined by the system" (Ricoeur 1980, 56). Ironically, in the age of clarity, the more objective the system of rhetoric becomes as in, say Aristotle's *Rhetoric*, the more subjective is its history because at every turning away from the Sophists, its history encounters its *own* projection of rhetoric as deception. The age of clarity is caught, then, in the web of its own historical project. First, blinded to its own deceptive practices, its history deceives itself about events prior to the writing of Aristotle's *Rhetoric*. History has poked its eyes out and cannot see the killing of a Sophist. The death of Sophistical rhetoric and the putting to death of early rhetors loses its importance in Tradition.

And second, the death of the Sophists and their rhetoric cannot be rendered as totally meaningless because that would deprive rhetoric of a point of origin for writing theory and history. Representation, as Heidegger has shown us, needs a frame for there to be a picture. In this way, the age of clarity is bound to the frame of death of the Sophists since rhetoric emerges after the kill. Relating the concept of death to the writing of history, John Campbell (1984) tells us:

> In characterizing history as a strategic, stylized symbolism which emerges from a community's experience of life as a tensional field, I am saying that both proximately in the here and now, and ultimately when life is seen against death, human consciousness is typified by awareness of exigence and constraints; to be an individual or part of a group, then, is to understand oneself as a speaker or listener. (236)[10]

Understanding this passage as coming at the end of the age of clarity, Campbell characterizes, wittingly or unwittingly, the history of the history of rhetoric. His interpretation allows us to see that consciousness of the history of rhetoric is typified by exigence of death and, in this case, death of the Sophists.

The Principles of Traditional Historiography in the Age of Disparity

Beset with the historical iniquities and philosophical inequalities in elaborating what counts as "fact," histories of rhetoric ride the pendulum toward obscurity. The recognition of the inconsistencies regarding "facts" in history helps to extricate the Sophists from what Aristotle and Plato have said about them and, thereby, helps to lift the face of rhetorical consciousness out of the blindness of The Tradition. Mario

Untersteiner (1954) typifies this new orientation when he writes about lifting the veil of Idealism.

> The [S]ophists agree in an anti-idealistic concreteness which does not tread the ways of skepticism but rather those of realism and a phenomenalism which do not confine reality within a dogmatic scheme but allow it to rage in all its contradictions, in all its tragic intensity, in all the impartiality imposed by an intelligibility which will revive the joy in truth. (xvi)

Specifically, what must be unchecked is the meaning of "truth" as certainty that is gained only by detached reflection.

From this perspective, many scholars have recovered or "rehabilitated" the Sophists by arguing that they, and specifically Gorgias, had an epistemology of rhetoric that came from a philosophical tradition opposed to Idealism, the basic tenets of Platonism. Bromley Smith (1921), among others, interprets Gorgias's "On Non-Being" as a Sophistical-philosophical grounding of persuasion with its truth basis in probability (337). Bruce Gronbeck (1972) argues for the possibility of Gorgias in rhetoric:

> He [Gorgias] must be understood as a subtle analyst, a skilled dialectician, a perceptive linguist, and a knower of souls, Plato notwithstanding; his agonistic dualism represented a potent challenge to idealistic dualism. In an age which sought to order man's world through rhetoric and poetic, he offered an analysis of those arts at least as attractive as Plato's. (38)

Gronbeck justifies the removal of the Idealistic forces of Platonism to reveal Gorgias's philosophical perspective in the light of philosophy, specifically existential phenomenology. With the promise of a modern philosophy, the Sophists are relevant to contemporary theory in communication (e. g., Engnell 1973, 175) because they rejected a "formal, logical system of argumentation from universally affirmed and binding first principles" (Enos 1976, 57).[11]

In the age of disparity, therefore, the Sophists can be affirmed because the condition or fact of truth about Sophistical practices is unequal to the truth of Idealism. These scholars rehabilitate the issues of probability, antithesis, relativism, and sense perception not for seeing the Sophists as Sophists but for getting back to a non-Idealistic conception of truth that, ironically, philosophy is seeking to abandon "after metaphysics." The recognition of differences between "truths" is an indirect testimony to the principle—the transformation of experience into one picture—that inaugurated the search for a united rhetoric with The Traditional history. That is to say, even though the locus of truth changes locations, there is still one representation of the history of rhetoric.

Moreover, it is the age of disparity because the choices offered by philosophy for rhetoric only benefit rhetoric abstractly and philosophically. Whether we speak of the Sophists *from* a Platonic voice or *against* the Platonic voice, we are still within that particular structure. For example, one significant objection to Protagoras's philosophy (in Sprague 1990, 80A 19) is that it violates the principle of noncontradiction. This principle holds that "it is a property of being that no being can have and not have a given characteristic at one and the same time" (McIntyre 1967, 547). To defend a Sophist such as Protagoras from either Plato's objection (*Euthydemus* 286c in Sprague 1990 80A 19) or Aristotle's refutation (*Metaphysics* 1062b 13, 1007b18 and 1009a 6 in Sprague 1990 80A 19) is to depend on Plato's thinking and Aristotle's questions and, thereby, to legitimate perpetually what is non-Sophistical. In terms of representation, to entertain the principle of noncontradiction is to assume a certain *frame* of reference within a metaphysical system and to assume that the law of noncontradiction and its axioms of logic are, as Nietzsche (1966) talks about it, adequate to reality.

There is another concern for integrating Sophistical rhetoric as an alternative to Idealism. The representation of The Tradition is strengthened by counterposing what is Idealistic with what is Sophistical. From this point of view, to place rhetoric via the Sophists in conflict with Plato's Idealism is to recognize that the Sophists turned away from metaphysics and toward an epistemology that attacks theories of immutable truth (Jarrett 1969, 15). However, to make this division leaves us with the same despairing choices with which Plato's (1963) Socrates confronts Gorgias: "Shall we lay it down then that there are two forms of persuasion [rhetoric], the one producing belief without knowledge, the other, knowledge" (454e). The Socratic dialogues are reawakened with this reborn exigence and the Sophists risk being put to death again.

Thus, any inquiry into the Sophists that starts with the language of Platonic and Western themes is in a very subtle way to shorten the reach of historiography and to limit the content by adhering to the form of the Platonic dispute. The principle of Traditional historiography is insidious. Severely, Western metaphysics has condemned rhetoric. How can rhetoric be the subject of its own history using the very dichotomy that destroyed it?

Conclusion and Implication

Between the fragments and few lines left by the Sophists and Plato's characterization of them exists a space where clues can be found. It is to that space that the project of rewriting the history of rhetoric gathers. That (re)turn to the Sophists can be said to be decisive and to end the history of rhetoric's relationship with The Tradition, particularly its desire for clarity rather than ambiguity. A praise of ambiguity is best portrayed, as I have figured it within spaces of The Tradition, in Plato's (1963) description of the Sophistical art in the *Protagoras*.

> Now I declare the sophistic art is of great antiquity, but those who practiced it in ancient times, fearing the odium it involved, constructed a shield and veil for themselves, some of them poetry, as in the case of Homer, Hesiod, and Simonides; some religious rites and prophecies, as did Orpheus, Musaeus and their followers, some I have observed athletics, as with Iccus of Trentum and another still living, Herodicus of Selymbria, originally of Megra, as much a sophist as any; and music was the disguise adopted by your own Agathocles, a great Sophist, and Pythocleides of Ceol and many others. All of these, as I say, from fear of ill-will used these arts as screens. (316c5–e5)

The forms that the Sophistical art may take (poetry, athletics, prophecy, music, religious rites, and so on) are screens, that is, masks, or concealments to something not named. What has not been named, and thus never transformed into a picture, has been shielded to protect the nature of the Sophistical art from representation *necessarily* just as it avoids a pure historicism in our knowledge of rhetoric.

Seen in this light, Nietzsche (1974) makes the final point about The Tradition courageously:

> Now something you formerly loved as truth or probability strikes you as an error: you shed it and fancy that this represents a victory for your reason. But perhaps this error was as necessary for you

> then, when you were still a different person—as are all your present "truths," being a skin, as it were, that concealed and covered a great deal that you were not yet permitted to see. What killed that opinion for you was your new life and not your reason: *you no longer need it*, and now it collapses and unreason crawls out of it into the light like a worm. When we criticize something, this is no arbitrary and impersonal event, it is, at least very often, evidence of vital energies in us that are growing and shedding a skin. We negate and must negate because something in us wants to live and affirm—something that perhaps we do not know or see yet. (245, 246)

I have said that the topic of rewriting the history of rhetoric presupposes a consideration of the problem of Traditional historiography. What is uncertain in all this talk is rhetoric's relation to its past. Is rhetoric related to the past in a linear and progressive way? Or is it related to it ironically and subversively? Perhaps rhetoric is caught in either a linear/ progressive or in a(n) ironical/subversive eternal return to ward off the chaos of a New Rhetoric.[12] But, as Nietzsche (1961) would say, rhetoric must have chaos in it "to give birth to a dancing star" (46).

Notes

1. References to Aristotle and Plato are by line, rather than page number.

2. It may be useful to think of a "representer representing" tradition as taking pictures with a camera. The developed picture is judged by standards of aesthetic composition and form. This thinking assumes that rhetoric is out there as object-in-the-world and its picture can be taken. History is reported through good investigative photo-journalism. I am interested in looking at those photos and displaying them in a new way.

3. Harvey (1969) discusses this approach—making the reader see or feel something—as an objective related to a writer's set of values. Applying this method to geography, he writes: "If we wish to convert someone to our own view of the objectives of geography, we can only do so *via* his beliefs. We might play upon his social conscience, for example, and point to the starvation and misery in the streets of Calcutta and seek thereby to convert him to a view of geography that is highly committed to doing something which will be useful in alleviating that starvation and misery. Or we might play upon his aesthetic feeling, take him slowly through the ruins of Rome and convert him to a standpoint that encompasses the 'feel' of the landscape through time. We cannot, however, destroy his beliefs by logical argument, any more than we can support our own by such argument" (4).

4. All fragments are from Sprague's edition (1990) of Diels-Kranz, *Die*

Fragmente der Vorsokratiker, and each collection of fragments on a Sophist has its own translator. Comments on the fragment, which are on the right side of the page, are found in the translator's footnote to the fragment.

5. The prefix *sec.* to Lyotard (1988) entries means section, not page number.

6. I am borrowing from Havelock's (1957) approach and translation to Aristotle's *Politics,* 295–337.

7. See also Versenyi (1965, 17–20) and Rorty (1979) for the discussion of "truth." For the model of how old meanings are dug up for disclosure, see Nietzsche (1969, 15–56). This method as a revelation is also discussed by Ricoeur (1977,280–95) and Hinman (1982).

8. In this dialogue, six definitions of Sophistry are given. Plato's *Sophist*: "First he [the Sophist] was discovered to be a mercenary hunter after the young and rich secondly, a sort of wholesaler of learning for the soul and thirdly, was he not shown up as a retailer of the same goods? and fourthly, a salesman of his own products of learning to us but fifthly, he was sort of a master in the art of combat about words, appropriating to himself the eristic techniques and the sixth instance was disputed, but nevertheless we agreed to assign him the role of purifier, as regards the soul, of opinions that obstruct learning" (1963, 231D; cf. Sprague 1990, 79 2). For a discussion, see Oscanyan (1972), Kerferd (1981), and Scott (1964).

9. Kennedy has numerous books and articles. I do not claim to represent his scholarly activity and published research, particularly his most recent work. In graduate school, I was his student in a Classical Rhetoric seminar at the University of Colorado, Boulder, 1982, and, based on that experience, I see him as a brilliant and thoughtful spokesperson for rhetoric, a guardian of the history of rhetoric. For further discussion of what I "do" with Kennedy in this essay, see Jarratt (1987b, 11).

10. Campbell (1984) ends his characterization by saying, "My formulation shows my indebtedness to Lloyd F. Bitzer's delineation of the rhetorical situation" (236). This is an interesting acknowledgment given what I have said and given the criticism of the objectification of the rhetorical situation (see Biesecker 1989).

11. Another version of this theme of rehabilitating the Sophists concerns logography. Lentz (1982, 66), for example, defends the Sophists against Plato's criticism of writing. Similarly, Enos (1974, 10) makes this case.

12. On why chaos may need to be warded off, Pico della Mirandola (1984) records that Platonists "believe that before [the] orderly motion of the heavens and the present arrangement of earthly things, there existed a disorderly and tumultuous motion, ruled by a soul sick and wicked" (83).

12

Taking A-Count of a (Future-Anterior) History of Rhetoric as "Libidinalized Marx-ism" (A PM Pastiche)

Victor J. Vitanza

Dedication: For "Baubô"

> . . . during his seminars Lacan sometimes mused about how high his analysands could count.
>
> —S. Schneiderman 1983, 2.

> In many languages of the world counting has never been developed. In some languages of New Guinea . . . people . . . count: *one thing, two things, many things,* and then must stop; one man translated his counting system into Pidgin English for me as *one fellow, two fellow, plenty fellow.*
>
> —K. Pike 1982, 23.

> . . . all human . . . Desire . . . is . . . the desire for "recognition."
>
> —A. Kojeve 1969, 7.

> . . . the worst thing is "being ignored."
>
> —Octalog [V. Vitanza] 1988, 33.

Taking A-Count of a (Future-Anterior) History of Rhetoric

. . . language is an operational superstructure on an erotic base.
—N. O. Brown 1959, 69.

"Some More" Difficult Beginnings

Making myselphs accountable to my collig(gation)s: My essay is about many things—too many scattered things—that have been, heretofore, ignored (negated). But which no longer can be ignored. Altogether (but never together), my essay is about *counting* and about what has been and still is *ignored* in writing . . . what is cavalierly referred to as . . . *The* History of Rhetoric. But my essay, which is—as I've said, an essay about many-cum-scattered things—is not an essay, therefore, that easily follows (*poria*); in fact, for the most part, throughout the first half, there will have been, for sure, one difficulty after another in following (*aporia*), what it is that is being said here, if not mostly elsewhere. And why? Because it's an essay subject to *tmesis* (Barthes 1975, 10–11), that is, subject to cutting up, to pastiche effects, to interruptions, to polygraphy. While my essay dis/engages in cutting up, it is nonetheless searching, forever searching, for a locus cum loci of a third person who will *not* negotiate how the pastiche effects might be revised for easy passage, but how they might be recut up and repasted in yet still other (*aporetic*) ways. This task of reading/writing, therefore, will not have been easy. For me or for other readers/writers. And again, Why? For the simple reason that this essay is in search of "the excluded third man" (Serres 1982a, 67) and "third woman" (Berg 1982), who have been excluded not only from *The* History of Rhetoric but also from writing histories/hysteries of rhetorics. Therefore, what this (my) essay is searching for is what has been systematically excluded but when finally included (if it so happens that the excluded third does "show up") will not make my or any other reader/writer's task any easier. In fact, the appearance of the excluded third will make everyone's task more difficult. What my essay is searching for, then, is not *the*, or even *a*, reader cum author who could make sense of a history/hystery that would be finally liberatory, but "some more" readers cum authors, if authors at all, who would be perpetually revolutionary, perhaps anarchistic. (Yes, I use that dreaded word "anarchistic," if only to mislead, misdirect! Yes, once again we're waiting for the early Trotsky!) I'm, then, less a writer and more a *cacographist*. I would turn readers into an *epigraphists*. My essay will be concerned, perhaps then, with the question, How many readers/authors (i.e., interrupters) does it take to re/write, reinscribe, to cut up, the anathema that goes by the so-called proper name of *The* History of Rhetoric? And I do plan (scheme) to cut (it) up!

About counting: A possible answer to this question of How many?, if an answer is needed, is to be un/founded in my view of counting, which is simply: *one, two*, and *"some more."* And no more. I'm using it as a conceptual restarting place. In dis/order to restart *some-more talk* (of mine and my readers) about writing histories/hysteries of rhetorics. I've used it previously in " 'Some More' Notes, Towards a 'Third Sophistic,' " (1991b) in dis/order to ac*count* for what has been displaced—and therefore ignored and held un/accountable—in writing *The* History of Rhetoric.[1] And what has been displaced (held in the clutches of negation)? Un/namely, a phenomenon of nonrationality (i.e., Gorgian, Nietzschean, Hedeggerian, Lyotardian *kairos*) that creates the conditions of (what I call) *a Third Sophistic hystery*, which is radically oppositional and appositional to philosophical-rhetori*k*al history/hystery.

In dis/order to achieve this end (or beginning), relationships between *logos* and *kairos* have to be re/accounted for and then replayed: *Which can and must be done by way of what I have called hystery-writing*. Which, if it can be called "writing" (see note 11), has a profound effect on *logos*. (Or vice versa.) What an "excluded third man" and "woman" would say, then, is that hystery-writing can revive (tease out) that which was repressed in and lost to a Platonized or Aristotelianized *logos*. And again, Why was it lost to *logos*? In order to write *The* History. For some of the pre-Socratics (who were hysterics) *logos* was, on occasion, the ambivalence/confusion of both *physis* and *doxa*. With Plato and Aristotle, however, *logos* is reconceived, with *physis* as privileged and *doxa* as supplement. (What I'm talking about here is repression, suppression, political oppression.) A state of productive confusion, therefore, was lost, and remains lost. And the conditions of the possibilities of hystery-writing (-speaking, -thinking) were displaced, or held (in their nonrational possibilities) unac*count*able. (See Heidegger 1959, 98–114;1984, 59–78. Also, Kofman 1987.)

The kind (or un/kind) of *logos* that I'm alluding to—it must be grasped—is highly problematic. In this view, then, both the so-called pre-Socratic *logos* and the Platonic or Aristotelian *logos* are both highly problematic. In the former, there is the acceptance of the confusion of language, and nothing is to be done to redeem it (hence, a tragic view of knowledge), whereas in the latter, especially the Platonic latter, there is the rejection of the confusion of language, except as practiced by, say, the Sophists, the *demos,* and barbarians, and everything is to be done to redeem it (hence, an optimistic view of knowledge). I'm thinking perhaps of the distinction that Nietzsche makes between the "cheerful pessimism" (the gay science) of the Greeks in the tragic age of philosophy and the "optimism" (of "theoretical man," i.e., Euripides/Socrates) in the post-tragic age of the Greeks (see Nietzsche 1967a). In my view, here and elsewere, in my tragic but cheerful view, I must insist and incite that *logos* (discourse, language) is helpless as "guide" (*hegemoon*) for rational, so-called Enlightenment history.[2] (And I might add that this "guide" is finally helpless in holding back hystery-writing. What has been, heretofore, repressed, eternally returns.) Such a "guide" is not always rational, or trustworthy. Human beings' possession of language is a dangerous possession (cf. White 1978, 265). Some of the pre-Socratics, especially Heraclitus, were well aware of the unreliability of the narrator of *logos* who would interpellate them and us. As a case in point: An agent or ethical subject—such as Gorgias's "Helen"—listens to the *logos* and, in listening, deliberates over whether to act or not to act, but is confronted with a logical dilemma and, therefore, does not act in order "to act or not to act." (Another case is Nikos Kazantzakis's Christ in *The Last Temptation* [1960], who is called *and* not called by God/*logos*.) As Mario Untersteiner says, however, "in every action . . . it must nevertheless be thought that a decision is carried out, even if not always consciously, because the power of one of the two alternatives may have been such as . . . to cancel out the other, as in the case of Helen, who deserves acquittal once it is shown by *a revival of the ambivalence of logos* [as both *physis* and *doxa*] that in any case this famous woman could not have come to a rational decision." What happens, then, Untersteiner explains, is that "epistemology . . . becomes will, decision, which was [for Helen] realised in a *kairos* endowed with the property of breaking up the cycle of the antitheses and creating something new, irrational" (1954, 161; cf. 177).

In relation to counting and accountability: Helen has become overwhelmed by *kairos,* which extends the dilemma/binary, in which she finds herself, into a trilemma of *one,* then on to a *two,* and then finally moves past the dilemma into a destabilizing-nonrational *third* of "some more." The trilemma develops, as we might ac*count* for it in still other terms, from "one"-homogeneity through "two"-heterogeneity systematized finally to "some more"-radical heterogeneities, multiplicities.[3] What *kairos* is, as I would characterize it now, is affirmative desire; it is un/founded on a metaphysic of excess, not lack. (See Deleuze and Guattari 1983.) *Kairos*, here then, denegates the negative informing, that is, suppressing, repressing, politically oppressing, *logos*. What *kairos/logos* would have us do, again then, in writing histories/hysteries of rhetorics, is to be dissatisified with playing the *fort/da* game (the negative deconstructive game), and to search for third ways, which *kairos/logos* are always telling us (it is simply a matter of our learning how to listen, to record, and then to dis/cord).

Let me emphasize: It is the revival of the ambivalence/confusion of (or even deception [*apate*] inherent in) *logos* that is crucial here. As Heidegger says: "For the Greeks appearing belonged to being, or more precisely . . . the essence of being lay *partly* in appearing" (1959, 103). With this view of *logos* in mind, then, we can venture to revive, with the help of Untersteiner (and Kazantzakis [and Heidegger]) again, a hystery-writing and a concomitant subject (or *ethos*) as radically heterogeneous—with these most ethical subjects being engaged in a *dissoi logoi* (see Untersteiner 1954 , ch. 7) that would irrepressibly dis/engage in *dissoi* para*logoi* (see Vitanza 1987a and 1990; cf. Jarratt 1991) and irrepressibly become poly*ethoi* (scattered subject positions).

At this point/less, it is necessary to turn toward a further set of *atopoi* (from *topos, e/utopos,* to *atopos*) that might prepare the future authors (epigraphists) of this article to interrupt *The* History of Rhetoric. The *atopoi* that "I" (the present so-called author) have in mind are "de/negation," "pastiche," and "hysteria/schizophrenia."

De/Negation: Another way of saying ("some more" of) all this about *searching for* a new conceptual restarting place, or a new way of re-*count*ing history in dis/order to revive hystery, is to echo Hegel's but primarily Alexandre Kojeve's view of history—namely, "human history is the history of desired Desires" (1969, 6). (I'm doing this kind of recalling, however, so that I can get beyond Hegel and Kojeve to my "some more.") Therefore, Kojeve says: "desire . . . is . . . a function of the desire for 'recognition' " (7). Simply put, we want to be valued. But how is this desire for desire (i.e., desire for recognition, or to become Master) to be satisfied? Both Hegel and Kojeve answer: By risking our life in order to negate anOther, that is, to create a Slave.

(Master/Slave. Another dilemma, waiting to become a trilemma.) Hence, recognition (value) is based on *denial* (i.e., negation, oppression) *of anOther*, which must be *denegated*, as Kojeve's Slave, in fact, *denegates* (*affirms*) its Being-for-itself (21–22). But is there not yet an/other way, waiting to express itself as a trilemma? From Master/Slave, Teacher/ Disciple, Analyst/Analysand to a third kind of subject position: One, two, cum-a-radical-many subject positions? (I cum we think so, and will return to such thinking.)

However, in reflecting on this view of what drives history, Kojeve writes: "Human Desire [therefore] tends to satisfy itself by *a negating . . . action*" (1969, 6). Now we're getting closer to my point, but without really ever reaching it. Therefore, my point/less. This *tendency to negate is the defining tendency of modernism* (see Lyotard 1984b, 77–82). What is lost to modernism (what is lost is reality, realism!), however, is regained (spoken and heard) by ill-virtue of negation. (Here, *no* means *yes*.) Freud wrote of negation/disavowel as central to his hermeneutic (1955, 19: 234–39). Marx wrote of disavowel/commodity fetishism as well (1977, 163–77). Kenneth Burke tells us that we ("inventors of the negative") cannot say what a thing is, but we can say what it is not (1966a, 9). And thereby, paradoxically, say what it "is." This is a modernist questioning and inventing by way of negation. (Just think of, e.g., Gorgias's "Nothing [of essence] Exists" [Sprague 1990]. Theodor Adorno's *Negative Dialectics* [1987]. Or Existentialism's existence precedes essence. Or perhaps recall Michel Serres's concept of "negentropic" [1982a; 1982b]. Or Jacques Derrida's metaphysics of absence with its posthermeneutic of "negative deconstruction." Or Paul de Man's "negative knowledge" [1983]. The list goes on.) I would desire, however, even beyond Kojeve's rereading of Hegel's Slave (1969, 21–22), or these other modernist-negative ways of reading/writing, a particular postmodern repositioning that would be *a double negative*—that is, a negating of the negative (a denegation) in dis/order to get to some nonsynthetic "some more." (You see, I desire *some-more hystery!*, to which I will have eternally returned.)

Pastiche: In this light of a double negation—or this darkness—my essay is variously about the productiveness of postmodern/Dionysian thought for talking about *The* history, or more so, *hysteries of rhetorics*. My essay dis-counts Fredric Jameson's view of postmodernism and history,[4] and counts on Jean-François Lyotard's and Judith Butler's views among Others'. Specifically, then, along with a practice of double negation, my essay reclaims and practices *pastiche* as a means of getting to what, heretofore, has been ignored. It is not parody that I engage in; for as long as there is a Marxist left (or a Kapitalist right), contrary to what Jameson tells us, there's both a need and opportunity to dis/engage in *pastiche* as a form of drifting. Therefore: While my socialist "colligs" say, "Let's Party," I say: "Let's just-pastiche!" I reclaim/revive pastiche over parody on the same basis as Butler does: "Whereas parody, Jameson argues, sustains some sympathy with the original of which it is a copy, pastiche disputes the possibility of an 'original' or, in the case of gender, reveals the original' as a failed effort to 'copy' a phantasmatic ideal that cannot be copied without failure" (1990, 157). Traditional *history-writing* works with, or suffers from the nostalgia of, an original that can be recovered; *hystery-writing*, however, paratestifies to the impossibility of an original of the real (which is the intractable, the impossible) and how it must be a-voided (denegated). *History-writing* presumes the ideal or actual whereas *hystery-writing* can assume impossibility, therefore, perpetual possibility. Hence, lack (a negative that is *de*negated) becomes excess. But this lack model must be demystified and (again) demystified. (To this point and its attendant problems, I will ever return.) It is assumed, dear reader, that the hystery-writer, or hysteric, simply needs the Master (or analyst) to help recall what was lost. The hysteric subject position, therefore, needs to be further demystified, in fact, perpetually demystified. Hence, the schizo.

Hysteria and Schizophrenia: My essay—which is about *writing* (if it can be called "writing") *hysteries of rhetorics*—is also about hysteria and schizophrenia—but not the clinical kind—and about their perverse/*pharmakonic* value in creating the (future) conditions for the possibilities of history-cum-hystery: For the possibilities of exploding/fragmenting *logos* that would speak such hysteries, for exploding/fragmenting the *ethos* that would record such discord and that would be its "subjects" matter, and for exploding/fragmenting *pathos* that would further dis/engage in such hysteries. (Hysteria and schizophrenia, when combined, are ways of *de*negation.)

Hence, the three *atopoi*, so as to drift. And so . . .

Let's Drift (in atemporality): My essay (transitionally) is about just-linking (Lyotard 1988) this point about hysteria/schizophrenia (timelessness) with the next point about temporality. (Cut and paste, recut and repaste. Where is Brion Gysin when we need him?) Postmodernism, like poststructuralism, generally eschews "temporality/historicism." However, after the grand narrative of *The* History has been—as nonrational desire wishes—*de*negated, fragmented, shattered, scattered, then, multiple provisional temporalities will have created the conditions of possibilities. The dividing/fading of grand temporality is, thereby, the de-struction of symbol, which, as Paul de Man says, "postulates the possibility of an identity or identification" and conversely the deconstruction of allegory, which "designates primarily a distance in relation to its own origin, and, renouncing the nostalgia and the desire [as rational and original] to coincide, it establishes its language in the void of this temporal difference" (1983, 207).

Let's Drift (in the future anterior): But this is only an initial step toward *rethinking time* in relation to history/hystery, *chronos/kairos*. My essay, however, is less about de Man's view of allegory/irony in disrespect to symbolic temporality and is much more about what Jacques Lacan calls the "future anterior" (the tense that heals). After the fall, we must be healed, *but healed pharmakonically*. Lacan writes: "I identify myself in language, but only by losing myself in it like an object. What is realized in my history is not the past definite of what was, since it is no more, or even the present perfect of what has been in what I am, but the future anterior of what I shall have been for what I am in the process of becoming" (1977, 86; also see 1988, 158–59; cf. de Man 1983, 222; Kellner 1991). (I [personally, but socially] am *on the way to* becoming a [future-anterior] nomad. I would be "some more" of a nomad than any of the Sophists ever were. I would be a third Sophist.) What Lacan (and I) are saying is difficult to understand, especially in relation to a "libidinalized Marxism" or "libidinalized hystery," if a connection is not made between the future anterior and the eternal return of the repressed (or suppressed or politically oppressed). What has been negated (repressed) today, therefore, will have returned tomorrow. It is this way, I especially contend, with *The* History of Rhetorik.

Moreover, my essay is similarly about what Lyotard calls "working without rules in order to formulate the rules of what will have been done," which is the paradox of the future (*post*) anterior (*modo*) (1984b, 81). My project is proleptic as well as paratactic and nomadic.

My attempt, therefore—in just-linking timelessness with new, but Third Sophistic, temporalities—is to bring together both aesthetics and politics, to create the conditions of the possibilities of eventually being able to bring together both post-Marx and post-Freud with Nietzsche, that is, the future after Nietzsche, and then being enabled (finally) to talk about *libidinalized marxism*. My attempt, thereby, will have been to approach living within what Lyotard calls the *pagus* (the savage place, "a border zone where genres of discourse enter into [perpetual] conflict over the mode of linking [coupling]" [1988, 151]). We must not forget: "It is necessary to link," as Lyotard says, "but not how to link" (66; cf. 29, 80). (History, rationally founded, links according to rules; hystery, nonrationally un/founded, links to reach for "some more.") And so, let us reach for "some more."

Is this possible? This pastiche? Is postmodernism, without a falling back into the modernist "negative," possible?: My immediate answer is nes/yo. I do not believe that "the negative" can be a-voided, only perpetually resisted—though at times, I will insist, with bravado, that it can be a*void*ed, as when I speak of *denegating the negative*. When thinking *as a modernist*, I believe that things, or the Lacanian *real*, must be seen as "impossible" (Lacan 1978, 167), before we can *realize* states of "possibilisms."[5] This kind of thinking, however, can be—and more often than not *is*—counterproductive. And why? Because it allows capitalism (as well as vulgar socialism) to reterritorialize the flow of desire. The modernist negative is the same sign as the sign of lack. What better propels capitalism than the sign of lack, and especially if it can be planted in the unconscious. "I want, I want, I want." And capitalism says, "*I* will satisfy you." Capitalism, just as vulgar socialism, is afraid of desire and, therefore, appropriates and represses it. Deleuze and Guattari write: "If desire is repressed [via the negative], it is because every position of desire, no matter how small, is capable of calling into question the established order of a society: not that desire is asocial, on the contrary. But it is explosive; . . . No society can tolerate a position of real desire without its structures of exploitation, servitude, and hierarchy being compromised" (1983, 116).

When thinking *as a postmodernist*—resisting-critiquing modernism and its negative-lack model—I believe, like Deleuze and Guattari (1983, 25–29, 295, 311), that the unconscious has no "no" there. (Hence, again, one postmodernist activity is to denegate this negative that modernists, such as a Freud, have planted there in their perpetual acts of colonization.) But what did Freud do? He simply negated consciousness; hence, the *un*conscious. But what Freud did was more complicated, for in fact he *did* say that there is only affirmation in the unconscious: Dora's NOs meant YES (see 1955, 7: 57)! Freud, however, proceeded nonetheless to territorialize the *un*conscious. He specifically said, when he sailed to that country (where Id was there shall Ego be), that he found Oedipus there. Found Castration there. Found Lack there. The Oedipus story is a story of prohibition/of the negative. Of repression. Therefore, in the negative (the *un*conscious), Freud tells us, we have the negative (prohibition, lack). Which leads to negation in infinite regress. (At best, Freud *is* a hysteric! as he himself labels himself. [See 1955, 1: 262.] He is a hysteric, however, who dislikes schizophrenics because he cannot recode and thereby control them.)

But again, when thinking *as a postmodernist*, there is agreement that the conscious state is only, after all is said and undone, an epiphenomenon. But it is also a construct of hegemony, but no more a construct of hegemony than the unconscious itself can be and, indeed, is. As postmodernists, we must, therefore, not plant or find in the unconscious only another negative. Another hegemonic prohibition, or a law. (And to this statement, I have to include that we must not plant or find in the unconscious a universal lack of freedom and, then, politicize it as being realized only in the Master Narrative of class-struggle. [See Jameson 1981.]) We will find, instead, pure affirmative desire.

Let us sail from that country of our naive (conscious) thoughts; it's no place for sub/versives. As postmodernists, however, let us understand that we sail/negate *doubly*: By dismissing the conscious, we *denegate* the *un*conscious and let it flow freely, let it flow as it so desires, into our everyday (heretofore, called "conscious") life. Such a flow of desire lets history become hystery. Let us float and drift on the free flow of desire, as you, my readers, must freely drift through this (my-cum-our) paper.

My approach, therefore, throughout (*a*) will not be a traditional disciplinary approach, nor will it be an attempt that is informed by a grand narrative metadisciplinary approach. Instead, my approach will be a borrowing of Louis Althusser's "wild/savage practice" ("*une pratique sauvage*"), which in turn is a borrowing from and commentary on Lenin's "wild answer," or response, to the "dividing practice" between Hegelian Idealism *and* Marxist materialism, between ideology *and* science. Althusser further characterizes: "A wild practice [is to be taken] in the sense in which Freud spoke of a wild analysis [see 1955, 11: 221–27], one which does not provide the theoretical credentials for its operations and which raises screams from the philosophy of 'interpretation' of the world, which might be called the philosophy of *denegation* [this term is translated as "denegation," but it is here simply "negation"[6]. A wild practice, if you will, but what did not begin by being wild?" (1971, 66).

My wild/savage practice, or response, is in counterresponse to *The* History of Rhetorik, which is depicted (by way of a "dividing practice") as a grand narrative *and* as in conflict with *The* History of Philosophy. (Often the two are blatantly combined—via a Masterful deflection—to form The History of *Philosophical* Rhetorik.) Or my wild/savage practice, or response, is to Plato's "dividing practice" (*diaeresis*) between the party of one *and* the party of many (*Theaetetus* 160d, 180d). This "dividing practice," like all others in our field, only serves to deflect sophistries, magic in language, and all "savage/wild" uses of language (see Lyotard 1988; Cixous and Clément 1986). This "dividing practice" deflects "counter-memory" (see Foucault 1977). This "dividing practice" negates "some more."

Therefore: Playing with Althusser's language—at first substituting my words for his words and then finally using his exact words—I would wildly/savagely say: There are hysteries *in* rhetorik rather than The history *of* rhetorik: Hysteries of the displacement ["negation"] of the bodily, therefore indefinite, repetition of a null trace [a residue] whose effects are, nonetheless, *real* (cf. 1971, 63). Hysteries of rhetorics speak through the savage *silences* of Dora, through the savage *miraculating body* of Schreber and savage *dreams* of the Wolf-Man, through the savage *acts* of Lacan's Christine and Léa Papin—all of which are excluded, through "negation" (repression/suppression) from *The* History of Rhetorik (oppression).[7] If included, they function solely as illustrations of deviant, *a*rhetorical behavior, only as examples of the *pathos of ugliness*, which must be forever excluded from the *polis*. As Catherine Clément says: "Somewhere every culture has an imaginary zone for what it excludes, and it is that zone we must try to remember *today*. This is history that is not over" (Cixous and Clément 1986, 6; Clément's emphasis). And again as Clément says: "The same goes for women as for madmen: in a *manifest* position of exclusion, they keep the system together, *latently*, by virtue of their very exclusion" (1981, 134; Clément's emphasis; cf. N. O. Brown 1966, 160–61). Hence, the power of negation. We know who we are—We men and women of the *polis*—because we are *not* "one of them"! But, I would insist/incite, we are!

My central point/less (!), further developed, in relation to this wild, savage practice of mine, is that though systematically deflected/silenced, *these hysteries* ("counter-memories") of Dora, the Wolf-Man, and the Papin sisters, nonetheless, can profitably be read in *The* History of Rhetorik. (As Deleuze and Guattari say: "A schizophrenic out for a walk is a better model than a neurotic lying on the analyst's couch" [1983, 2; cf. N. O. Brown 1966, 159–60]). As Lenin reads Hegel *as* a materialist, and Lacan and Feminists read Freud *as* a hysteric, we must come to read George Kennedy and James Murphy and Michael Leff not just as historicists but also *as* hystericists, as schizos, as deflectors of the most savage, misshapen forms of *letteraturizzazione* (see Kennedy 1988, 231). Yes, we must become, in an Althusserian-Leninist sense, "partisans" with them (Althusser 1971, 64), so as to "denegate" them, too. Our potential libidinalized comrades in reading hysteries of rhetorics.

Moreover (*b*), my approach will have been a "drifting" approach, from Michel Montaigne (the essayist), and from Lyotard (a drifter [see 1984a]), but not from René Descartes. I am a drifter: The attempt (the essay) is foreign to finishing, completion, reaching a goal. I am a nomad. I'm, in Other's words, as I've said and said, a "cutup" (see Foucault 1977, 154; Copjec 1989).

My approach will have been, as it always already has been, a "hysterical" approach, from Helene Cixous, the hysterical body-politic that laughs (see 1981). It will be a "schizo" approach, from Deleuze and Guattari (the schizo that radically, forever switches codes [see 1983, 15]). But I fear, as Nietzsche, "I am not the mouth for these [my readers'] ears" (1984, part 1, sec. 5). For I'm, for them, an *impropria persona*.

But most of all my approach will have been *the future after Nietzsche*: Nietzsche—the greatest advocate of a pessimism of cheerfulness (*amor fati*) and the most suspicious of thinkers (the aphorism that embodies nomadic thought). Which means? I do not wish to be the Apollonian, "theoretical man" (the harbinger of [historicist] optimism), but the Dionysian, "artistic Socrates" (see 1967a, secs. 14–15). I do not wish to be "the good man speaking," nor "the representative of seriousness," nor the traditional-escetic priest, but the satyr-speaking (see 1969, preface, sec. 6; first essay, sec. 3–6; third essay, sec. 11). And where does the Dionysian go to speak, the satyr go to write?

From the *polus* to a *pagus*: The *pagus* (the savage place of "some more" linkage) is a frightening, threatening place; it is from a Lacanian perspective the pre-oedipal place of primary narcissism, or from a Deleuzian perspective, "affirmative desire"; it is (in either case, but especially the latter) most threatening to the survival of the *polis*. (Father Freud felt the necessity to "negate" it, while brother Norm Brown wishes to revise Freud as a denegator.) *We now must denegate the (de)negation*! Thereby, letting (affirmative) desire flow excessively! We must move from "science/history" to "hystery/fantasy effects." Freud, the scientist-hysteric, struggled with this distinction when writing about Dora. (But what of Marx and the *polis/pagus*? I read *The 18th Brumaire* [1984], and I said: Oh, grandpapa Marx, I must leave you if I am ever to remain [a] revolutionary. And then, I asked for early Trotsky. Which is to say, I asked for "some more." But then, I also recalled what they [Stalin and company] did to Trotsky! But I would still have "some more.")

To use a coined phrase from C. S. Peirce, the *pagus* (the savage place) or "some more" is one of the places of places, of "*esperable uberty*"—that is, the place of the "expected" or "hoped for," the place of "rich growth, fruitfulness, fertility; copiousness, abundance."[8] (The place of "some more" *and* the places of Baubô!!). "Uberty," then—like Heidegger's/ John Poulakos's "Possibility" (1984) and Robert Darton's/my "Possibilisms"[9]—is the "haunting" place of total, but un*count*able freedoms. "Uberty" is (impossible?-)"Liberty." It is, in its/my most hyperbolic radical of presentations, the place of Babel/babble, babylonianisms, the wildest heteroglossias. The f/arting of Baubô! It's a "nightmare" place for, and to be avoided by, Jürgen Habermas and his europocentric thinking (see 1979)! It's a place that Hayden White would call the locus of "the absurdist moment" (1978, 269). It's the place of a *physis* that has not been placed under negation, as Plato and then Aristotle have placed not only *logos* (as I previously discussed) but also *physis* under negation. (That I would also be a follower of a Heraclitian *logos* and a de Sadian *physis* is how I would differ from my sophistic "colligs" who would be followers of local *nomoi*. [Cf. Jarratt 1991.])

In speaking of the absurdist moment, White says that those "critics" who would engage in such a "moment" (as, yes, I would here and elsewhere dis/engage in it) . . . those "critics" would investigate "the dark side of civilized existence—that which, as Nietzsche said, had to be given up or repressed or confined or simply ignored [placed under negation], if civilization was to have been founded in the first place" (1978, 269). This dark, wild, savage side, I would insist and incite, "has simply been avoided by [historians of rhetoric] who define their principal task as the defense of civilization against all of these [savage] things [i.e., people and ideas]" (269). I would return us, then, to this dark side (the *pagus*, where denegated pagans, and *pagani*, gambol and satyr-ize, where *physis* is gat-in-tooth and cleft-in-hoof); and I would return us in dis/order to remind us all of how we have deflected it, and at what costs to Others and to ourselves. Hence, I would search for and perversely celebrate—when writing about hysteries of rhetorics—what White calls "such antisocial phenomena as barbarism, criminality, insanity, childishness" (269). This return I would see as part of the task of a Third Sophistic hysteriography. If not Plato's philosopher-king, then Dora. If not Aristotle's judge, then Schreber. (I make much of all this "return" of the repressed in the second half of this paper.)

Counting "some more" and reaching a de/stabilized third via the Dilemma: Ferdinand De Saussure has given us the *di*lemma of *la langue* and *le parole*, or of *system* (community in language) and *a speaker's expression* (controlled by system-community-*polis*). Noam Chomsky as well has given us "Competence" and "Performance." (And there has been a whole [consecrated] host of analogous binaries/dilemmas, built on these two.)

Lacan (the *pagan* of all *pagani*), on the other hand, has identified the wild (screaming) place of the *third*, which turns the *di*lemma into a *tri*-lemma. (I know, I know, Lacan generally speaks by ill-virtue of the negative, so what?) That wild, screaming place is *lalangue* (the place of Babel/babble, the place of the *pagus*, the place where the most "radical [of] mutiplicities" dis/engage in, heretofore unknown, linkages). Few venture there. (See 1985, 80–82.) But can and does *lalangue* (which I would insist on associating, in this instance, with the *pagus*, and which I associate with *Letteraturizzazione*) really threaten to *destabilize* the *polis*? I think not. (I think that the systematizers of language, such as a Habermas, want us to think that Lacanian *lalangue*, or the *pagus*, is a threat, so that they can be "benevolent," but nonetheless a threat to us all in their dream [i.e., nightmare] of "benevolent," philanthropic ORDER.)

After Lacan, there is délire: Besides the Lacanian concept of *lalangue*, there is the Lecerclean concept of *délire*, which is *yet another* third place of "some more" (but a place that *negotiates for us* [we are passive, but protected!, in its midst]). It's a place situated between *lack* and the laughing face of "schizophrenic" *excess*. It perpetually attempts linkages here. *Délire*, as Jean-Jacques Lecercle says,

> is the frontier between two languages, the embodiment of the contradiction between them. Abstract language is systematic; it transcends the individual speaker, separated from any physical or material origin, it is an instrument of control, mastered by a regulating subject. Material language, on the other hand, is unsystematic, a series of noises, private to individual speakers, not meant to promote communication, and therefore self-contradictory, "impossible" like all "private languages." (1985, 44)

This latter, I would interpolate here, is Nietzsche's *bodily rhythmic* view of language (cf. Cixous and Clément 1986, 93; Lyotard 1984b, 22; Barthes 1975, 66–67). Lecercle continues:

> [Material language] is an integral part of the speaker's body, an outward expression of its drives. It imposes itself on the individual, controlling the "subject": it is not the transparent medium which the instrumentalist describes, nor the means of consensus which the conventionalist conceives, it is, to misquote a philosophical phrase a (material) process without a subject. . . . This is a real contradiction. Neither of the two languages exists on its own, as an independent entity: material language is repressed and returns to the surface as a disruptive force, and the "dictionary" is an abstraction which denies the material expression of instincts. *Délire* is the name for this contradiction. . . . Between the dictionary and the scream, or in both at the same time, délire pervades the text, dissolves the subject, threatens to engulf the reader in its disaster, yet saves him [and her]—and the text—at the last moment, by preserving an appearance of order, a semblance of linguistic organization. Even screams can become dictionary items; and every word, even an entry in a dictionary, can be a scream. (1985, 44–45)

I'm (now) reminded of Cixous's Screams! Cixous's Laughter! And her call: "Let's get out of here" (1981, 255). Her screams, her laughter, her calls *do* get appropriated (in the Kapitalists' or Socialists' dic[k]tionary), don't they? Which invites her, I assume, and others of us, in our individual, private (Imaginary) ways, to return (to retrope) affirmatively even (at times) against *délire*-as-the-Negotiator! And so . . .

As Burke says, "well, where are we now?": Let's get out of here and end, so that we might begin again, on an/other affirmative note, by recalling Lacan's concept of the future anterior. Which is somewhat like délire-as-the-Negotiator, but which is constantly *projecting nomadically* in its search.

It's a concept/tense that is postmodern. Clément, in her book on Lacan, puts it well:

> Lacan . . . fooling around with tenses found in grammar [a] resource, the form whose function it is to span *the gap* between past and future *and link* the two firmly together: the so-called future anterior, the future that comes before like the *poetic life* imagined by Baudelaire. Only one tense is truly *dialectical*: a logical shuttle between past and future. No one pays attention to it. But it is true that the locution 'I will have been,' oddly twisted as it is, contains seeds of the future that one finds retroactively [proleptically]. It is a memory curious about its own future. A memory with a gift for science fiction, which refuses simply to repeat the old saw, "once upon a time," over and over again. Everything is different if we say, "It will have come to pass. . . ." The fairy, whether *good or bad*, wins in advance: the story is already sketched out, *but it changes as it is being told*. As if nothing had happened, *the future anterior alters history*: it is the miraculous tense. *The tense of healing*. (1983, 123; my emphasis)

The tense of a (Third, eternally returning, nonrepressed) Sophistic.

Desire and the Social

Let's begin again: What remains, then, in dis/order to get where we will have desired to venture? What remains is what always remains: The social, with its affirmative desires. (Most of what the reader will now "read" is fairly easy to follow, and so if you, dearest of readers, are still with me, you will be rewarded with "some [easier] more.")

I believe, like Deleuze and Guattari, that "*there is only desire and the social, and nothing else*" (1983, 29; their emphasis). And "In the unconscious there are only populations, groups, and machines" (283; for the influence of Nietzsche, see Thiele 1990, ch. 3).

This view of desire, however, is not colonized by rationality, nor by the negative. It's desire, as Kristeva, points out, that is deeply influenced by rereadings of Hegel, Nietzsche, Freud, and Marx. It's desire that is resistant to linguistic formulation/subjugation and, therefore, is desire that is disruptive of "a logical, normative basis for the speaking subject." It's a view of desire, situated in a *newer ethic* (post-Aristotelian and -Kantian) that "crops up wherever a code (mores, social contract) must be shattered in order to give way to the free play of . . . jouissance" (Kristeva 1980, 23; cf. Rajchman 1986).

And why am I interested in this view of desire with its newer ethics of resistance and disruption? I am focusing on *desire*-in-language (variously Foucaultian "counter-memory" and Lacanian *lalangue* and sophistic *Letteraturizzazione*) so as to ask profane questions (and to ask them perpetually) about the *subjugated social* (i.e., the social, with its desire, made rational, ac*count*able: rationality = the negative; *non*rationality = denegation of the negative). Specifically, however, I am asking (*de*/in*terror*igating) questions about rewriting *The* History of Rhetorik, not in relation to Enlightenment heroes, but in relation to the Other's heroes, if they can still be considered heroes!, like Freud's Dora or Wolf-Man, or Deleuze and Guattari's Judge Schreber and Antonin Artaud, or still Others. (We will return, eternally again, to these uncelebrated [as in PM celibate] embodiments of radical heterogeneities; *for* there's no *epideictic* discourse [*no paignion]* for them. We will return in dis/order to recognize the desire of the Other. [Cf. Deleuze and Guattari 1983, 176; Cixous and Clément 1986, 84.])

In the meantime: Here's something to ruminate on when struggling to let be written, *hysteries of rhetorics*: Lacan muses: "The Life experience of the paranoiac [by which he means, the schizo] and the world view it engenders may be thought of *as a novel form of syntax, which enlists its own peculiar means of comprehension for the purpose of affirming* the community *of mankind*." Lacan is speaking of *"schizographie,"* schizo-speaking/writing, which has been, heretofore, *ex*cluded from the community. He continues:

> Understanding this syntax can, I think, provide an invaluable introduction to the symbolic values of art and, more particularly, to the problems of style—an introduction, in other words, to art's [and I would insist on adding, rhetorik's] peculiar virtues of conviction and human communication as well as to the paradoxes attendant upon its creation. Those problems will always remain beyond the grasp of any form of anthropology [Humanism or ac*count*abilty] that has not yet freed itself from the naive realism of the object. (*Premier Écrits sur le paranoïa*, cited in Clément 1983, 57–58; my emphasis)

To be sure, some people will say, here, that I'm conflating poetics *and* rhetoric. They need that *alibi*. And ah, there's the rub. But what am I to do? other than to insist that poetics *and* rhetoric were artificially separated, for example, by Plato and Aristotle. (And they were separated for reasons of *the game of knowledge, the game of power*!) Political discourse is poetics and vice versa. And it's the *vice* of our political "lives" that has been displaced, and *it's that "vice"* that I'm after! To separate them is to invite *an alibi* (an ex-cuse that provides the conditions) *of not understanding* (as I'm attempting to mis/understand via misprision, or a denegation of the de/negation) *how The History of Rhetorik is The History of Oppression*. (Like Heidegger, it is the end of philosophical rhetorik and the primacy of poetic speech that I am after. [See Grassi 1983, sec. 1; cf. N. O. Brown 1966, 160–61.])

The History of Desire/Power: But what is it specifically that *I mean* (!) when I say that "The History of Rhetorik is The History of Oppression"? I mean (will have meant, let's give "some more" years) two things so as to get on to a sophistic third. (And it will take me a while to get to the second-cum-third, so don't hold your breath! as "we" re*scramble* around.) I mean that the history has been a representation of how rhetors have attempted to define, to obtain, and to keep *power*. And at the expense of Others. Desire/Power is defined across a scarcity (*negative, lack*) model. (In part, this has to do with separating poetic discourse from political rhetoric, to which I will eternally return—to this which has been eternally repressed.) What do I mean by scarcity model? There is this terribly dangerous notion in *The* History of Rhetorik that with the so-called origins of rhetorik, there was simultaneously the origins of *the promise of democracy*—which, in turn, meant the promise of changing the *scarcity/lack model* into a common one of equity, or equal distribution of rhetorical power and determination over one's life within the *polis*. (Except for the slaves and women and barbarians, of course!)[10]

Vincent Farenga, among others (see Althusser 1971, 67), *will have done* much to expel/dispel this dangerous notion. For Farenga, *Rhetoric arose out of the overthrow of tyranny only to return (us all, ironically) back to tyranny*. (That's the way it is when working with the lack/negative model: What is *de*territorialized only ends up being *re*territorialized. Hence, Deleuze and Guattari's and my Trotsky/ite perpetual *de*territorializations.) Farenga's statement about *The* History of Rhetorik is, to be sure, heretical; for the great majority of rhetoricians (both *classical* and *modern*), who tell the story of origins (or reorigins) would, instead, wish us to believe that rhetorik has contributed to and is the primary means of our "emancipation" (i.e., is [potentially] the means of an equal distribution of power through *equal access* to rhetorical deliberation) and that, for example, one *patron saint* of the history of rhetoric is "Korax"—though for these rhetoricians "Isocrates," or "Aristotle," or "Cicero," today, is the most revered.

The "story" (Grand Narrative of Emancipation) goes like this: Sicily was ruled by "Gelon and Hieron," two terrible tyrants, who eventually lost their control over the Syracusans. The two tyrants had forbad the Syracusans to communicate orally, but allowed them to communicate through *sign language*, that is, with their appendages via some sort of *proto-dance-pantomine*, via some sort of *somatic tropings*. (They are forced to be *a*phonic! [Cf. Freud 1955, 7: 39–41; Cixous and Clément 1986, 19–27].) The Syracusans, in hopes of overthrowing the tyrants, prayed to Zeus, who answered their prayers. But fearing a return to tyranny, the people wanted to have absolute control over all things, upon which they fell into a state of *disorder*. However, a person by the name of "Korax," who had been in "Hieron's" service, *used speech to soothe the people back to a state of order* (!). As he spoke, *his speaking taught the people how to control (discipline) themselves*; specifically, as he spoke, he referred to the first part of his speech as "introduction," and the subsequent parts as "narration," "argument," "digression," and "epilogue." By these means, he contrived to persuade (that is, to teach, or as Althusser would say, "to hail/interpellate" [see "Ideology" in 1971], or as Deleuze and Guattari would say "reterritorialize") the people just as he used to persuade one other man—namely, the tyrant! (Farenga 1979, 1035–36).

What are we to think of such a story, such a history *of* rhetorik that has displaced *in* it a hystery? Are we to ask, at last, critically-cynically, who is this Korax? Would not our charge be that *he is* the culprit, or the goat whom *we-the-people* are *to sacrifice in dis/order to prepare (that is, to cleanse) ourselves for the "cure" or for the final solution/emancipation*? Is he not the tyrant behind the tyrant (the source of the dis-ease)? In a sense the answer is "Yes." It is an answer based, *however*, on *re*codification, or *re*territorialization. And, therefore, I think that such an affirmative answer (which proves actually to be another crypto-[displaced]-*negative* answer [simply recall Lenin/Althusser's concept of "de/negation"]) greatly silences an important point—namely, that

"Korax" (or anyone else whom anyone wishes to put forth as "the father" or "the mother" of rhetorik, or as "the liberator" of woman or humankind) is only the narrative function of the will-to-(negative)-authority/power. Still more specifically, I would now say that ("philosophical," i.e., *classical* or *modern*) *rhetorik*, which espouses *a pragmatics of power* and its *control*, is similarly a function of the will-to-extract/abstract *techné* (*the game of knowledge*) from *physis* (see Jardine 1985, 72–73).

From a *postmodern* rhetorical vantage point, however, "Korax" must/ought to, or *will have been*, resisted/disrupted by way of radical (heretical) "little [i.e., radically heterological] narratives" played out by and through the game of (poetics, avant-garde) art. The *strategies* of that game are—in the words of Lyotard, comparable to Lacan's words—a para/activity "without rules in order to formulate the rules of *what will have been done*" (1984b, 81). But then, once the rules are known or ac*count*able, "the future anterior" must be reengaged again, and again, and again, perpetually. (And again, this reengagement is *de*codification and/or *de*territorialization, or *perpetual revolution*.) As Lyotard would say, such a game is *the game of the Just* (see Lyotard and Thebaud 1985). What is important to understand here is that Lyotard is *not-just* advocating the use of *local* (stable) *nomoi*. And why? I repeat: Because by placing "little narratives" in the future anterior (by placing them within the pragmatics of the game of avant-garde art) Lyotard is and I am advocating *non-homogenizable radical heterogeneities/multiplicities*. Or advocating, evoking, provoking, a perpetual drifting toward a Third (forever already destabilizing) Sophistic.

Where are we now in dis/respect to Writing The History of RhetoriK?: I hope that our ruminating *will have been taking* us to the idea of *the dispersion of power* in various ac*counts* and in my *ironic* ac*count*s of writing histories-cum-hysteries of rhetorics. If classical and modern rhetors have attempted to define, to obtain, and to keep power, the new Third Sophistic rhetors (hysterians) *will have found* ways of *re*thinking power altogether, will have found ways of *not-just dispersing* it among all people equally (I hope that the Korax *misrepresentative antidote* disabuses us of this notion, or specifically why this dangerous notion of "equity" has been only a dangerous *displacement* [again, Althusser's "de/negation"] of where power really rests—namely, in the person ["Korax"] who does the "hailing"/"interpellating"). But more so, the new Third Sophistic rhetors *will have found* ways of *placing power in* *perpetual diaspora*. Power! And what is it *if not* at root *the love of fascism*. Have not Nietzsche and Foucault made this abundantly clear to us all? As Nietzsche metaleptically says through Foucault, we must resist "not only historical fascism, the fascism of Hitler and Mussolini—which was able to mobilize and use the desire of the masses so effectively—but also the fascism in us all, in our heads and in our everday behavior, the fascism that causes us to love power, to desire the very thing that dominates and exploits us" (Preface xiii, to Deleuze and Guattari 1983).

Beyond "Local *Nomoi*" as Little Narratives to Schizo Narratives: *BUT* let's complicate this matter even further (with what I'm further attempting), and let's start talking (in Babel/babble) even more on several levels simultaneously. I'm talking about *scrambled-talking*. (Remember: It's necessary to link, but not how to link!) As I've said, I'm *not-just* talking about "linking" local (stable) *nomoi* with conventional poetic play/fantasy; I'm talking—more so, if not perversely—about an aesthetics (poetics) of excesses (see Weiss 1989) that is to be linked to politics. (KB writes: "a system of aesthetics subsumes a system of politics" [1968, 113].) Or I'm talking about . . . well, let's perversely imagine . . . "my writing"[11] epideictic (*paignions*) hysteries for such postmodern, Third Sophistic rhetors as Dora or the Wolf-Man, or Judge Schreber or Antonin Artaud, or Christine and Léa Papin; or better yet, writing hysteries as they will have written them. Which is what I will (not) have been doing!

Such *paignions* would be, at minimum, a step (and, to be sure, a stumble, a stutter in-"our"-languages) toward the hysteries of (affirmative) desires—the hysteries that have been denied legitimacy, locked up, systematically oppressed. *Letteraturizzaziones*! Counter-Memories! These in/famous rhetors (Dora and the Wolf-Man, etc.) are the *lumpen/proletariat* (see Marx 1984; cf. Vitanza 1993a), the *excluded thirds* (see Serres 1982a), that have, heretofore, been rounded up and sent to *the gulags* (they have been silenced [made *a*phonic like the tyrants' subjects], turned into *differends*, victims only furthermore victimized). What is it that I *will have been attempting*? Let us recall that the two tyrants—Gelon and Hieron—had forbad the Syracusans to communicate orally, but allowed them to communicate through sign language, that is, with their appendages via some sort of hysterical or proto-dance-pantomine, via some sort of somatic/se*mantic* tropings. (Let's dance the tarantella!) What is it that *I will have been doing*? I will have been calling on (awkwardly put) what's (far) left over both from and in (heretofore) *the* *writing of The History of Rhetorik*—un/namely, that which still *lies* (buried) *unrestfully silent*. (And buried deep in the "counter-memory" of languages of the body.) I'm speaking of the somatic/mantic-bodily tropings. The hysteries (the body hysterics) that will have been written, but not written, are, as I eternally return to them, epideictic (*paignions*) hysteries of/for such postmodern, Third Sophistic, sub/versive rhetors as Dora or the Wolf-Man, or Judge Schreber or Antonin Artaud, or Christine and Léa Papin. In the Other's words, the question more generally, therefore, that I (will) have been asking and entertaining answers to (it's important, crucial to guard this question, to keep it always forever open) is WHAT WILL HAVE BEEN ANTI-OEDIPAL (De-Negated) HYSTERIES OF RHETORICS? WHAT WILL HAVE THEY LOOKED, SOUNDED, READ LIKE?

But let's further complicate all this discussion with another de/stabilizing allegory, and henceforth make it even more scrambled. When a historian, or "maker of history," like Ronald Reagan (a neo-Hieron) dumps these in/famous (the Doras and Wolf-Men) onto the streets-as-gulag, they still get ignored by us, right *under* our very eyes! We—my "colligs" and I—are Oedipus and in more ways than One! (Thebes is in the midst of *a famine*. We are in the midst of *the negative*. We are in the midst of, and have let *our*selves be defined by, the *LACK*.) I'm talking about the dispossessed, the disinherited, the *barbars* of the *pagus* in the streets of the *polis*! (All projected eighteen to twenty million of them, or us, by the turn of the century. All who have been denied a voice.) I'm also talking about the Anti-Oedipals. I'm talking about those Others who resist the negative by engaging in the affirmative. Desire, no longer as lack, but as affirmation. These are the subalterns whose stories can't be told, but in a nonhumanistic way "will have, nonetheless, been told."[12]

But not with, by, or through political discourse. (There is no longer a Korax who can hail/interpellate them.) If not through political discourse, then through pararhetorics. Such a discourse, political discourse, even in the midst of ideology critique—only displaces the *lumpen/proletariat*. Kristeva (1986) says that the story can be told with, by, or through psychoanalytic discourse. But what kind of discourse is this that she's alluding to? Certainly not Rogerian or Buberian discourses, which only invidiously/insidiously maintain the social bond/age, via reterritorialization. (And certainly not [again] Koraxian discourse.) Let me explain further, and in doing so, let's reexamine the notion of *the cure*, the notion of *philanthropy*. (Which *gives* only with the contractual understanding of getting *a return*.) This all will require going back in dis/order to go forward.

Chapter One (about cure): Lacan tells us that when *psychoanalysis* came into being (because of female and male hysterics), it was unfortunately "discovered" by a medical doctor, a Dr. Freud, whose predisposition or "trained incapacity," was *to cure* (once and forever) the disorder. (See Heath 1978; cf. Schneiderman, who has Lacan against the cure, 1983, 47, 50, 57.) Freud's hermeneutic predisposition, however, prevented him from being suspicious enough, about his philanthropic motives. First, he for the most part withdrew his initial view that both males and females suffered from hysteric symptoms; he backed down because his "colligs" kept (paranoically) insisting that it was impossible for a male to suffer from hysteria (after all, a male has no womb, which can become nomadic!, so let's call it "shell shock" [see Showalter 1987, who speaks of eighty thousand male hysterics in the first war.]). Second, Freud insisted on (perhaps his trained incapacity again) employing only myopic/monological hermeneutical principles, such as the *oedipal complex* and *penis envy* (all based on lack). These first two only perpetuate the master/slave relationship between males/females. And third, Freud, as Deleuze and Guattari tell us, "doesn't [didn't] like schizophrenics. He doesn't like [them because of] their resistance to being oedipalized, and tends to treat them more or less as animals" (1983, 23). Freud, again, does not like schizos because of their resistance to the negative. As exiles, as *barbars*, outcasts from the *polis*, schizos like Artaud resist, disrupt, expel, vomit up "Papa, Mama" and "Korax"[13]—that is, the *Symbolic*—which is, in Deleuze and Guattari's view, a vomiting-as-resistance to being Oedipalized. I insist, as Deleuze and Guattari do, that this "vomiting" can be seen as not an illness, but a paracure! A *pharmakon*. (Therefore, I vomit up *The* History of Rhetoric. Vomit. Vomit. Vomit. Vomit.)

Marx's cure—by which I mean a cure based on orthodox Marxists' readings of Marx's texts—is that the *lumpen/proletariat* ("pauperism," the lowest common denominator, which for me also includes the Jean Genets and Antonin Artauds of the world and includes the aesthetic of language, *Letteraturizzaziones*) will simply disappear, will wither away, with the dawning of (e)utopic socialism. In other words, philanthropy, or the cure, is built into dialectical/historical materialism. For these orthodox Marxists, the concept of the *lumpen/proletariat* is a vulgar-

restricted economic category that defines *desire* exclusively in terms of lack, or the (modernist) negative. My "casuistic stretching" of this *negative concept of economics* is an attempt—on the extreme Left hand of the *a*phonic body—to establish the conditions of the possibilities of seeing what the *lumpen/proletariat* might/could mean for us . . . *if* the *lumpen/proletariat* were *libidinalized*, or viewed in a radically heterodox economic category that defines *desire*, not in terms of "the negative," but in terms of a (postmodernist, denegated) "affirmative." (I'm *not* speaking here of a libidinal economy based on kapitalism, as unfortunately Lyotard [1974], much to his own chagrin, previously has.) If the *lumpen/proletariat* is seen as also including the Jean Genets and Antonin Artauds of the world, we will have begun to understand them not as something that is to be cured, but *as* a cure (a *pharmakon*) themselves. The *lumpen/proletariat*, as I have re/presented them here, will never disappear any more than the irrational/nonrational Doras will wither away. Hence, the modernists' necessity to cart off these people to the Gulags (both the pickpockets and the dissidents—all schizos), so that the rabid, vulgar, orthodox, "romantic socialists" (historians of rhetorik) can declare socialism a success. (At bottom, there's no difference between a logical positivist, in relation to language, and an [orthodox or, at times, heterodox] Marxist!) Again, if I am to remain (a) revolutionary, I must reject but remake Marxism. (Hence, a Libidinalized Marxism.)

But—to be sure, let's turn the whirl even more around here—it's *not-just* "romanticized socialism" that's at fault. As I said earlier it's, *more so*, "romanticized kapitalism." When kapitalism is not teaching us to be political quietists, it's teaching us to be altogether blind to the *lumpen/proletariat* as "we" step over and over (and even occasionally "trip" over) them in the *pagus* in the midst of our *polis*. What is not understood by (orthodox) Marxists but is understood by Fifth Avenuists (and that's what makes the latter especially dangerous, because they are able "to capitalize" off of *and* "*re*territorialize" the *lumpen/proletariat* in more ways than One) is that *some* (a small, perverse percentage of) human beings engage in such "pauperism" and "dissidence" (schizoidness) for reasons *other than* vulgar economics. (It is this few-cum-excess that I speak of! Not all.) The kapitalists are much closer to an understanding of the libido than the Marxists. That is why the kapitalists are so damn frightening. But then again, the Marxists' blindness to the libido is equally, if not more so, frightening.

What can *we learn* from the *lumpen/proletariat*? The *Letteraturizzazi-*

ones? Specifically: What can we learn from how people respond to them? What can we learn from them concerning the cure and philanthropy? (How, in other words, can they be a para-cure?)

This first specific question—what can we learn from how people respond?—is of immense importance. Let us recapitulate: Recall my earlier reference to Kristeva's saying that there is a "Platonistic acknowledgment on the eve of Stalinism and fascism: A (any) society may be stabilized only if it excludes poetic languge." She adds: "The question is unavoidable: if we are not on the side of those whom society *wastes* in order to reproduce itself, where are we?" And yes, let us remember what KB says: We must make "peace" with our "faeces" (1969a, 23). (If it is not obvious by now, when I talk about the *lumpen/proletariat* and *Letteraturizzaziones*, I'm talking about both language and people.) And Clément who says: "Somewhere every culture has an imaginary zone for what it excludes, and it is that zone we must try to remember *today*. This is history that is not over" (Cixous and Clément 1986, 6). (The imaginary zone can be a gulag or a ghetto or a septic tank.) And again she says: "The same goes for women as for madmen: in a manifest position of exclusion, they keep the system together, *latently*, by virtue of their very exclusion" (1981, 134).

I recall now, having read Burke's book review of Hitler's *Mein Kampf*, in which Burke points out how Hitler refers to the Habsburg Empire as a state of nationalities and the parliament, where the representatives met, as Babel/Babylon. (It is necessary that you, dear reader, *drift* with me here.) Burke writes: "The many conflicting voices of the spokesmen of the many political blocs arose from the fact that various separationist movements of a nationalistic sort had arisen within a Catholic imperial structure formed prior to the nationalistic emphasis and slowly breaking apart under its development." Burke continues and now more to my point: "So, you had this Babel of voices; and, by the method of associative mergers, using ideas as imagery, it became tied up, in the Hitler rhetoric, with 'Babylon,' Vienna as the city of poverty, prostitution, immorality, coalitions, half-measures, incest, democracy (i.e., majority rule leading to 'lack of personal responsibility'), death, internationalism, seduction, and anything else of thumbs down sort" (1957, 172). It is obvious where Hitler's vision is going, which is to keep the system together, blatantly, by virtue of exclusion. And as we well know by now, though KB was predicting then what was to come, Hitler did exclude, by silencing all the mixed voices as manifested in both language and people. Burke writes: "The wrangle of the parliamentary is to be stilled by the giving of *one voice* to the whole people, this to be the 'inner voice' of Hitler, made uniform throughout the German boundaries, as leader and people were completely identified with each other" (177; my emphasis).

And so do I need to spell out here what we have learned (but not learned) from how Hitler and his dupes responded to Babel/babble and Babylon? How, for example, the advocates of *The* genre of history (as this genre itself positions subjects and objects) excludes hystery? *The* history is not democratic; only the inclusion of the hystery of Babel/babble can be radically democratic! It is time to reconsider the whole concept of historial genre so that we might move beyond genre altogether.

The next specific question—What can we learn from the *lumpenproletariat* and *Letteraturizzaziones* concerning the cure and philanthropy?—is taken up again by Burke. In his *Counter-Statement* (1968), he makes a distinction between the "practical" and "aesthetic." (Here, I return to conflating the political and poetic.) For Burke, the *practical* favors "efficiency, prosperity, material acquisitions, increased consumption, 'new needs,' expansion, higher standards of living, progressive instead of regressive evolution, in short, ubiquitous optimism." By contrast, the *aesthetic* (the Bohemian) favors "inefficiency, indolence, dissipation, vacillation, mockery, distrust, 'hypochondria,' non-conformity, bad sportsmanship, in short, negativism" (110–11). He continues: "The 'Bohemian,' the 'aesthetic' . . . relegates enterprise to such inquiries and imaginings as serve to 'corrode' the practical—it is concerned with such intellectual vagabondage, such aspects of 'irresponsibility,' as constitute a grave interference with the cultural code behind our contemporary economic ambitiousness" (121). Yes, my dear comrades in *The* history of rhetorik, *I would, indeed, be irresponsible*! (Cf. Enos 1991.)

This all gets worse for better. KB writes (perversely): "A society is sound only if it can prosper on its vices" (1968, 114). "The aesthetic," or "the anti-practical," he continues, "would be driven back to democracy (a system of government based upon the fear that central authority becomes bad authority—democracy, organized distrust, 'protest made easy,' a babble of discordant voices, a colossal getting in one's own way—democracy, now endangered by the apostles of hope who would attack it for its 'inefficiency,' whereas inefficiency is the one thing it has in its favor" (114). But (Oh) let us continue: "The Fascists, the hopeful, the propounders of business culture, believe that the future lies in perfecting the means of control. The democrat, the negativist, the man who thinks of powers as something to be 'fought,' has no hope in perfection—as the 'opposition,' his nearest approach to a doctrine is the doctrine of interference" (115).

In sum, KB writes: "The aesthetic would seek to discourage the most stimulating values of the practical, would seek—by wit, by fancy, by anathema, by versatility—to throw into confusion the code which underlies commercial enterprise, industrial competition, the 'heroism' of economic warfare; would seek to endanger the basic props of industry" (115).

KB, here a postmodernist before his time, espouses resistance to and disruption of the political status quo, and any forthcoming macropolitical activities, left or right.

Let us drop anchor now and listen to what we might hear from critics: I can hear some self-righteous leftist saying, "Victor, see, you are a neo-conservative. You hide behind all this talk about aesthetics, organized distrust, inefficiency, and do nothing at all for the street people, whom you mislabel as the *lumpen/proletariat*." Such a response, I *can* mis/understand, given what is subjectively invested in being a leftist. Which is? Their way—which is their trained incapacity—is *the* way (see, e.g., Jameson 1981).

My point, as previously announced is that we cannot socially engineer either language or people, because there will always be paraelements that will escape being engineered, paraelements that we more likely than not (given that we are, as KB says, "rotten with perfection") have to exclude (in the name of "thugs") in some gods-forsaken way. (We will have to take political prisoners; every *system* must have them.) Therefore, I have suggested that we (the so-called fortunate) not try to help-by-excluding on *our own terms* (because we always expect "a return" on our investment) but that we, instead, listen to and learn from what both (street) language and (street) people, what *Letteraturizzaziones* and the *lumpen/proletariat*, say they want/desire. (To this point, I will return.) Marx, on the other hand, said that we must listen to, learn from, the *proletariat*. There, then, lies our differences!

The *proletariat*, to be sure, are not in *The* History of Rhetoric, except by displacement; hence, they demand their rational inclusion. They point out the logical inconsistency, the inherent contradiction. (The birth of rhetoric and the birth of democracy should not be at odds!) But what of the *lumpenproletariat*? The "Some More"? They, the nonrational, push for even greater, more radical democracies. (Herein is where I differ most emphatically from Susan Jarratt's call for what I see as her liberal democracy, not a radical one at all [see Jarratt 1991].) How much—dear reader, you might ask—can *The* History of Rhetoric bear? My answer: As much as it takes to distend and finally explode *The* (speculative) genre of history. It is not inclusion into *The* history that I desire but radical, countless numbers ("some more").

Let us listen to what Lyotard says: Marx "thinks he hears the demand of the proletariat, which is . . . *an ideal of reason*, namely an emancipated working humanity. The proletariat demands communism, the free linking of phrases, the destruction of genres. . . . This finality is signaled . . . by the enthusiasm which workers' struggles can arouse" (1988, 171–72; my emphasis). Lyotard continues: "Marx understands the feeling of enthusiasm as a request emanating from an (ideal, emancipated) self. The referent of the Idea of communism is transcribed as a subject (addressor) who proscribes communism. The common being wants itself. This can be formulated [however] only within the speculative genre" (172). And, ah, there is the problem. "To let the proletariat 'speak' is to endow it with a historical-political reality. Marx built the International Association of Working Men. He interprets the sign that is the enthusiasm aroused by the Commune as if it signaled the political project of the *real* class and as if it outlined the organization of a *real* party" (172; my emphasis). The proletariat demands the end of genres, but its enthusiasm, if it is to become channeled into a political reality, must be *real*ized through "the speculative genre," or *the economic genre*. What has happened is what KB calls the "bureaucratization of the imaginative" (1984, 225–29). What has happened is what Lyotard calls "central monopoly"—"the party assumes a monopoly over the procedures for establishing historical-political reality" (172). Which, in turn, gives us party-line history and politics. I would have what KB has called "a national 'Art Party' " (1968, xiii). I would be "the representative of 'the aesthetic' . . . who blurted out things in a somewhat violent fashion," while I would have my leftist/kapitalist "colligs" be the representative of " 'the practical' . . . who looked upon [their] adversary as a scandal" and while I would have you, my reader, be "one other figure . . . who suffered the wrangling of the two, . . . feeling that both" of us had our "particular kinds of justification" (xiii).

What I hear, echoing back to Burke, is that we have much to

learn—aesthetically and politically—in respect to writing histories-cum-hysteries of rhetorics. We have to learn what Walter Benjamin learned in the streets of Paris from the *flaneur*, the conspirator, the Boheme, the ragcollector, but also learn what he did not. We must learn that there is more than one economic system at work here. (There are, in fact, some more!) There are more ways than one to call for, or to go on, a strike! There are more ways than one to express desire. (Lacanian *lalangue*, which is embodied in our *polis*, is a perpetual strike, a perpetual expression of desire-as-cure.) Let us, therefore, learn how *to count* the irrational/nonrational number of ways so that we might a*void* the speculative genre of history. Let us set aside, for a while, the negative approach (of a genre of genres) and take up the affirmative approaches of non-ac*count*ability as "the free linking of phrases, the destruction of genres." Which means what? It means, in dis/order to understand, "we" must libidinalize (over-rationalized) Marxist texts! We must *de*territorialize them! After all is said and undone, *I am a libidinalized Marxist*, but by virtue (i.e., a radical ethical *areté*) of both Marx and Freud being "subsumed" within a Nietzschean irrational/nonrational few-cum-"some more." I am a Deleuzian/Guattarian, radically heterodox Marxist, which is a negation of the negative (orthodox) Marxists, so as to reach new perpetual states of affirmation. Which means what, in addition? It means we have more (a great deal "some more") to learn from "minoritarians" (embodied, *a*phonically, in the *lumpen/proletariat* of *lalangue* and in the *pagus*) than we have to give them. We must, then, with the help of the *lumpen/proletariat*, rethink benev(i)olence. (We must find, as Gayatri Spivak says, ways of "negotiating with structures of violence.") As Spivak says: "It is the disenfranchised who teaches us most often by saying: I do not recognize myself in the object of your benevolence, I do not recognize my share in your naming" (1989a, 218).

Chapter Two (another possible cure): Deleuze and Guattari, in their *Anti-Oedipus* (1983), argue against *the orthodox cure*.[14] They write: "What are the most favorable conditions for the cure, it is asked? A *flow* that lets itself be plugged by Oedipus [or any Grand Narrative, Freudian or orthodox Marxist]; *partial objects* that let themselves be subsumed under the category of a complete object, even if absent—the phallus of castration [the negative]; . . . For what is the meaning of 'so *that* was what *this* meant'? The crushing of the 'so' onto Oedipus and castration. The sigh of relief: you see, the colonel, the instructor, the teacher, the boss, all of this meant that: Oedipus and castration, 'all history in a new version' " (67). You see, my "colligs," in this scheme, to be sick *is* to LACK Oedipus, or an Oedipal (Social) metanarrative! (91). (Jameson, in the *Political Unconscious* [1981], says: for society to be sick is to LACK a Grand [Socialist/Marxist] Narrative of Emancipation!) As Deleuze and Guattari say: "Psychoanalysis is like the Russian Revolution; we don't know when it started going bad" [1983, 55].) They also say: "Oedipus [and who/what else? the proletariat?] is a means of *integration* into the group" (103; my emphasis). And then they also say: "Oedipus is something like euthanasia within ethnocide" (169).

Start making some simple substitutions here, folks, and you will begin more clearly to understand what I'm allegorically, ironically alluding to. Need "some more" help? The narrator of *The Unbearable Lightness of Being* tells us—in between discussing Oedipus and an allegory that Tomas wrote based on the myth—that: "Anyone who thinks that the Communist regimes of Central Europe are exclusively the work of criminals is overlooking a basic truth: the criminal regimes were made not by criminals but by enthusiasts [socialist romantics] convinced they had discovered the only road to paradise. [The elimination of all dissidence/dissonance. In the body-hysteric politic! The removal of the *pagus* from the *polis*.] They defended that road so valiantly that they were forced to execute many people. Later it became clear that there was no paradise [great, good place], that the enthusiasts were therefore murderers" (Kundera 1987, 176). As Kundera's character Tomas says, they were like Oedipus and therefore should/ought to put their eyes out and leave Thebes. See all, read all, of this *théorie*-fiction so as in dis/order to see, again. Which will have put "us" in a position to have been able to ask forever again: WHAT WILL HAVE BEEN ANTI-OEDIPALized (de-negated) HYSTERIES OF RHETORICS? WHAT WILL HAVE THEY LOOKED, SOUNDED, READ LIKE? Or to ask affirmatively, WHAT, then, WILL HAVE LIBIDINALIZED-HYSTERIES OF RHETORICS LOOKED, SOUNDED, READ LIKE?

Chapter Three; or "Some More, Some More": What Deleuze and Guattari say about a *cure* is that *schizos are combatants against the orthodox cure* (remember Freud did not like schizophrenics). How do they resist? Deleuze and Guattari say:

> The schizos [have their] own system of co-ordinates for situating [themselves] at [their] disposal, because first of all, [they have at

> their] disposal [their] very own recording code, which does not coincide with the social [i.e., linguistic] code, or coincides with it only in order *to parody* [I would say "pastiche"] it. The *code of delirium or of desire* proves to have an extraordinary *fluidity*. It might be said that . . . schizophrenic[s] pass . . . from one code to the other, that [they] deliberately *scramble . . . all the codes*, by quickly shifting from one to another, according to the questions asked [them], never giving the same explanation from one day to the next, never invoking the same genealogy. . . . When [they are] more or less forced into it and [are] not in a touchy mood, [they] may even accept the banal Oedipal code, so long as [they] can stuff it full of all the disjunctions that this code was designed to eliminate. (1983, 15)

I see this statement as a postmodern *manifesto* for writing (future anterior) hysteries of rhetorics. What must be stuffed full of *disjunctions*—as "I will have been attempting"—is that code, or set of codes, that go by the banal proper name of *The* Tradition of *The* History of Rhetoric (see Bizzell and Herzberg 1990). The *schizophrenic hysteriographer* will have deliberately sought out the very limit of *The* Tradition: S/he will have been its inherent tendency brought to fulfillment, its surplus product, its *lumpen/proletariat* (the somatic tropings of the Doras and Wolfmen), and its paradoxical "exterminating angel." S/he will have scrambled all the codes and will have had been the transmitter of the decoded flows of affirmative (i.e., denegated) *desire*. S/he will have been the eternal return of the repressed "counter-memory."

"De Beginnibus"!

I began this long hysterical/allegorical-personal statement with the affirmative statement, "I believe, like Deleuze and Guattari, that '*there is only desire and the social, and nothing else.*' " Why is it, again then, that I choose to trek with schizos? What do they, after all is said and undone, have to do with the social? What I'm against, as I have stated, is a *subjugated group*, and what I'm advocating at this moment, like Deleuze and Guattari, is a libidinalized *subject-group*.

A *subjugated group* is, in its structure (and everything else), *paranoiac*. It's structured in two ways: Either by *homogeneity* or by *heterogeneity homogenized* or by *both*. It's a group that gets its order from some other group or from "Korax" Inc. Socialist political formations tend to be *homogenized*; capitalist political formations, *heterogeneity rehomogenized* according to the needs of supply and demand (the negative, the lack). Paranoiac political structure is also called *molar*. Deleuze and Guattari write:

> It might be said that of the two directions in *physics*—the *molar* direction that goes toward the large numbers and the mass phenomena, and the *molecular* direction that on the contrary penetrates into singularities, their interactions and connections at a distance or between different orders—the *paranoiac* has chosen the first; [s]he practices *macro*physics. And it could be said that by contrast *the schizo* goes in the other direction, that of *micro*physics, of *molecules* [*micro*politics] insofar as they no longer obey the statistical laws [of a master group or narrative]: waves and corpuscles, flows and partial objects that are no longer dependent upon the large numbers; infinitesimal lines of escape, instead of the perspectives of the large aggregates. (1983, 279–80)

Then Deleuze and Gauttari say: "It *would be a mistake* to contrast these two dimensions in terms of the *collective* and the *individual*" (280).

So where are we? The *molar* (paranoiac) is the *subjugated group*. And the *molecular* (schizo) is the *subject group*, which is *radical multiplicities* or *heterogeneities*. Which resists and disrupts all attempts by the *molar* socialists and capitalist rhetors to make desire conform to their flows, or "Korax's" schema, or disposition, for discoursing. Schizos (as desiring-machines, with heterogeneous parts) in a Marxist economy take the modes of production, distribution, exchange, and consumption and produce an undifferentiated body (politic?) without organs. Schizos radically-heterogeneously disrupt desiring (logical-binary) machines (1983, 5), which are designed, as "Korax" would have them, to control the flow (disposition) of desire. Schizos produce at a *molecular* level. What schizos understand, contrary to "Korax," is that any attempt to return to the past was/is only a return to domination; and any effort to appropriate state control (ISA) is an effort to perpetuate despotism (to be, as Nietzsche says, resentful and then reactionary); and finally any "political program" for *revision* is a potential blueprint for *molar, paranoiac* investment of social desire as lack. What is desired, then, is a *sub/version*, through a schizophrenic process of affirmation (denegation), by rapidly switching codes, so as to shatter the synecdochic (container and thing contained) system. Where are we now? Or, Where *will we have been*? "*De Beginnibus*"!

Theirs/"Ours" should, therefore, be attempts at forming "transverse relations among deterritorialized flows" so as to be able to include, in "our" writing hysteries of rhetorics, those who, heretofore, have been excluded (silenced, made into *differends*) such as Dora and the Wolf-Man *and* Genet and Artaud who have *no papas, no mamas*, who have not been oedipalized. I got no papa, no mama, no "Korax," no Plato, no Aristotle, no Isocrates, no Cicero, no Quintilian, no. . . . Herein, No becomes Yes and Yes, No. Becomes Nes/Yo!

"Some More" radical switching of codes: A Loss of the Personal: We have counted again from 1, 2, and "some more," and it's the schizo-social that I am in flight with. That I am NoMadic with. I would lose/confuse the personal in dis/order to be anOother "perfect hysteric." *Q*: What is hysteria? *A*: It's a confusion concerning gender (and genre). It's not androgyny, which is a synthesis. It's, instead, a productive confusion of such political categories as "male" and "female. " It's gender as "cultural performance" (see Butler 1990). Therefore, like Nietzsche, in his last, *pastiched* letter to Jacob Burckhardt (the individualist, Renaissance historian!), I to you all say: "what is disagreeable and offends my modesty is that . . . *I* am every name in history" (Nietzsche 1984, 686; also, see Deleuze and Guattari 1983, 21–22; Vitanza 1993a).

AnOther Beginning: "*Measure* is alien to us [Be gone Prot*agoras*!]; let us own it [our alienation]; our thrill is the thrill of the infinite, the unmeasured. Like a rider on a steed [let's now affirmatively forget Plato's *Phaedrus*] that flies forward, we drop the reins before the infinite, we [post]modern [wo/]men, like semi-barbarians—and reach *our* bliss only where we are most—*in danger*" (which is *Beyond Good and Evil*, 1966, 224).

And in the beginning: "Even laughter may yet have a future. I mean, when the proposition 'the species is everything, one is always none' has become part of humanity, and this ultimate liberation and irresponsibility has become accessible to all at all times. Perhaps laughter will then have formed an alliance with wisdom, perhaps only 'gay science' will then be *left*" (1974, bk. I, 1; my emphasis).

Or, AnOther Comic Beginning:

Dexter: Oh yes, yes, yes!
Sebastian: Funnier than that?

Dexter: Oh, absolutely. Yes.
Dexter: Now on the St. Louis team we have Who's on first, What's on second, I Don't Know is on third . . .

Notes

I would like to thank Lorie Goodman Batson and Lisa Hill for their corrections of and comments on the original draft of this essay. A recent letter from Hans Kellner, concerning this essay, reminds me of my debt (life?) to Norm Brown (*Life Against Death*, 1959) and, I should add, Herb Marcuse (*Eros and Civilization*, 1962), both of whom I read in my youth. (I must point out, however, that Brown would have nothing to do with my use of the future anterior. See 1959, 92.) The question of "negation" continues to interest me (see Vitanza 1991a).

1. Actually, I have used this approach previously (1987b; 1991b), and have used it in the improper name of "the excluded third" (1993a; 1993c). (I have discovered, just now [7/8/90] that these three roughly correspond to Deleuze and Guattari's three of the celibate machine, the paranoiac machine, and the "miraculating machine" (1983, 17–18.) John Poulakos (1984) similarly counts to *three* ("Ideal, Actual, Possible"). In respect to my paramethod of counting, Poulakos has pointed out in conversation with me that Plato (*The Sophist* 237d-) discounts such counting as mine. Lacan, according to Schneiderman (1983), learned to *re*count to *three* (as in "Imaginary, Symbolic, and the Real") and then to *four* (as in "four fundamental concepts"). Cf. Ragland-Sullivan (1984).

2. I have deliberately (further) confused matters here by using the word *hegemoon* more appropriately associated with Isocrates rather than Plato. I have worked out the implications of this word in relation to Plato, Isocrates, and Heidegger in a chapter on Isocrates in a book that I am writing on historiography.

3. In 1991b, I have asked and answered: "How far could Plato/Socrates count? The answer, I believe, is *One*. they wished to anchor their view of the *logos* and the subject in an indivisible/Parmenidean *One*. How far could Aristotle . . . count? It is a complicated answer, but he does tell us quite explicitly in the *Physics* (bk. 1, ch. 5–6) that he counts *Two* (as 'contraries') and *Three* (as 'substratum'), but 'neither One nor Innumerable' (189a). (This 'Three' is not the same as Pike's 'Many Things,' of which I will refer to as 'some more'/'radical multiplicities'/'Possibilisms'; it is also important to note that Aristotle explicitly says there cannot be a Four +, or an 'innumerable' [189a 20].) Therefore, Aristotle counts: *Two, Three*. But let us not be fooled: Aristotle is playing a shell game with only *One* primary pea, if any at all. His notion of counting to *Three* (as 'substratum') is a generic systhesis/unity of the prior *Two* (the 'contraries'); it is a *Three*-cum-'*One*' that is 'differentiate[d] . . . by . . . means of contraries, such as density and rarity and more and less' (189b 9–10). Hence, while agreeing to the possibility of *Twos*, he still has his crypto-*One*, which he calls a *Three*. Moreover, he says, 'it is impossible that there should be more

than one primary contrariety' (189b 20–25), thus emphasizing Unity/*One*ness again."

4. For Jameson, see "Postmodernism and Consumer Society" (1983); or for a longer version, see 1984; or for the still longer discussion, see 1991.

5. This position, I have ruminated on at great length (1991b). It is, to be sure, a modernist position that reaches for postmodernist radical multiplicities. I nomadically stated: The Impossible-cum-Possibilisms! This is home—i.e., such States of Possibilisms—as much as there can be a home for "the unhappy [nomadic] consciousness" (Hegel).

6. *A Caveat*: For Althusser, "denegation," which is translated from *negation* to *denegation* (see "Glossary," Althusser 1987, 312), is a displacement, a deflection, which, e.g., is "an unconscious denial masked [through ideology] by a conscious acceptance, or vice versa. There is a potential confusion here, however, with what I have already and will again refer to later as "*de*negating the negative," which I borrow recklessly from N. O. Brown (1959). Therefore, *denegating* will mean (hereafter) *the denegating of the denegation, or negation*, so as to let be heard what (heretofore) has been systematically/ideologically negated, silenced, represented as *lack*; to let flow, in other words, nonrational *desires*, and to let them linguistically flow in *excess*.

7. For this cast of characters, see Freud on Dora (1955, 7: 3–122); Schreber (1988); Wolf-Man (1971); Clément on the Papin sisters (1983). They are all variously discussed by Deleuze and Guattari (1983).

8. See Sebeok, "One, Two, Three, Spells UBERTY" (1988, 1). The article is important because of its concentration on stabilizing "threes," which is a concept that I began this article with, but in a contrary fashion. Searching for de/stabilizing thirds in dis/order to breakup the binaries is part of my postmodern strategy of resistance and pastiche (see Vitanza 1993c).

9. Darton discusses the *Possibilism* as "against the givenness of things" (1989, 10). See Vitanza (1991b).

10. By way of explaining the concept of "desire," one must understand, *first*, why it is that we more often than not desire being duped by preferring slavery over freedom. *What is it, at these times, that we Desire*? Deleuze and Guattari see that what we Desire is Our Oppression/Domination. For them, however, Desire should be pure affirmation; they resist Freud, who sees/saw Desire in terms of Lack/the Negative. Freud had defined Desire semiotically across the Oedipus story, i.e., across a prohibition. And therefore attempted to control the flow of Desire. I will discuss this later. But for now here is a passage from *Anti-Oedipus*, in which the authors (and Reich) are wise to the problem of negative Desire: "Even the most repressive and the most deadly forms of social reproduction are produced by desire within the organization that is the consequence of such production under various conditions that we must analyze. That is why the fundamental problem of political philosophy is still precisely the one that Spinoza sees so clearly, and that Wilhelm Reich rediscovered: 'Why do men fight for ther servitude as stubbornly as though it were their salvation?' How can people possibly reach the point of shouting: 'More taxes! Less bread!'? As Reich remarks, the astonishing thing is not that

some people steal or that others occasionally go out on strike, but rather that all those who are starving do not steal as a regular practice, and all those who are exploited are not continually out on strike: *after centuries of exploitation, why do people still tolerate being humiliated and enslaved*, to such a point, indeed, that *they actually want humiliation and slavery not only for others but for themselves*? Reich is at his profoundest as a thinker when he refuses to accept ignorance or illusion on the part of the masses as an explanation of fascism, and demands an explanation . . . formulated in terms of desire: no, the masses were not innocent dupes; at a certain point, under a certain set of conditions, they wanted fascism, and it is this perversion of the desire of the masses that needs to be accounted for" (1983, 29; emphasis mine).

It is, *then*, necessary to understand the differences between the concepts of "Desire-as-lack" (the negative/scarcity model based on acquisition) *and* "Desire-as-pure-affirmation" (the impossible made possible, based on free-flowing production). Deleuze and Guattari (1983, 22–35) are the best in explaining this difference, as they take on that long tradition of dialectics (which creates the negative) from Plato through Adorno to Lacan (cf. Butler 1987).

Elsewhere (1991b), I have extended Deleuze and Guattari's argument, specifically against Lacan, by extending my own rereading (or *de*territorialization) of Lacan, in which I extend Lacan's view of the impossible-as-lack to a view of the impossible-cum-possible-as-excess. (As Lacan writes: "The unconscious is that chapter of my history that is marked by a blank or occupied by a falsehood: it is the censored chapter" [1977, 50]. Or otherwise put: It is the *negated*, modernist chapter. For additional statements by Lacan, on "the impossible," see 1978, ix, 51; and 1977, 331, specifially the references listed under "Epistemology.")

In 1991b, I paradoxically accept/do not accept lack. Which is how I perpetually, hysterically-situate myselphs here, if the reader catches my drift. Sometimes a postmodernist, other times a modernist, but always a postmodern modernist—I have functioned very much as a *bricoleur* throughout as well as a "drifter."

In a paper written a year after this present article, I develop a contemporary genealogy of the negative and discuss two ways toward affirmation; see 1991a. (The paper was presented to the PACT project [The project for affirmation in critical theory, associated with the Society for Critical Exchange].)

11. This kind of "writing" is under erasure. No One can write it; *They*, who are ever catachrestic (without reference), write themselves, or are written by their bodies. But I would, on the left hand, send my reader to Lyotard (1988), in which he talks about how some one of us must bear witness to *differends* (in part, the loci of exclusion) and discover idioms for them, and we must do so "without criteria." (See, e.g., 13.)

12. At this point, we reach one of the *pharmakons* of this my paper. "The street people." What have we to learn from them? (Spivak, whom I will refer to later, would have major reservations, about their being able to speak for themselves; we, for sure, cannot speak for them! Anymore than we can speak/write for the Other. Hence, the statement in note 11. Let me now complicate

the argument: I agree that the "subalterns," as Spivak develops the argument (1987; 1988), cannot speak for themselves, nor we for them. The concept of the *lumpen/proletariat* that I am using, however, in associating it with schizos and body hysterics, can and do speak uncontrollably for themselves, though we cannot speak for them. Here lies my difference with Spivak. Here lies my negation of the negative.

Deleuze and Guattari have much to say on this subject (which I have called with a special sense the *lumpen/proletariat*) and again in respect to desire-as-Lack. They write: "Desire . . . becomes this abject fear of lacking something. But it should be noted that this is not a phrase uttered by the poor or the dispossessed. On the contrary, such people know that they are close to grass, almost akin to it, and that desire 'needs' very few things—*not those leftovers that chance to come their way, but the very things that are continually taken from them*—and that what is missing is not things a subject feels the lack of some where deep down inside himself [sic], but rather the objectivity of man, the objective being of man [*sic*], for whom to desire is to produce, to produce within the realm of the real" (1983, 27; their emphasis). Remember this is the real not as impossible, but as possible, as a paramodel of Desire-as-affirmative-production.

13. Kristeva puts it graphically: "I imagine a child who has swallowed up his parents too soon, who frightens himself on that account, 'all by himself,' and, to save himself, rejects and throws up everything that is given to him—all gifts, all objects. He has . . . a sense of the abject" (1982, 5–6). I have written a lengthy paper on the virtue of what I call "just vomiting" (1993b).

14. E.g., 17, 65–67, 91, 167–68, 332. Limitations of space do not allow me to give an adequate exposition of Deleuze and Guattari. It might be helpful, therefore, to read Bogue (1989) and Holland's (1988) discussions of Deleuze and Guattari and how the para-philosopher and para-psychoanalyst resist Marxist [socialist] and Freudian [say, capitalist] master narratives and hermeneutics. And also perhaps it would be helpful to see Deleuze and Guattari's *A Thousand Plateaus* (1987) and Guattari's *Molecular Revolution* (1984), both of which are helpful and easier to read than *Anti-Oedipus* (1983).

AN AFTER/WORD | *Preparing to Meet the Faces That "We" Will Have Met*

Victor J. Vitanza

> The ambivalence of writing is such that it can be considered both an act and an interpretative process that follows after an act with which it cannot coincide. As such, it both affirms and denies its own nature or specificity.
>
> —Paul de Man 1983, 152.

> . . . *nausea* makes me balk at that milk cream, separates me from the mother and father who proffer it. I want none of that element, sign of their desire; I do not want to listen, I do not assimilate it, I expel it. But since the food is not an "other" for "me," who am only in their desire, I expel *myself*, I spit *myself* out, I abject *myself* within the same motion through which I claim to establish *myself*.
>
> —Julia Kristeva 1982, 3.

> The rôle, or *persona* of the author seems not that of father, or even brother, but of conscientiously wayward son. . . .
>
> —Kenneth Burke 1968, 213.

> Useless to ask a wandering man
> Advice on the construction of a house.
> The work will never come to completion.
>
> After reading this text . . . I realised the absurdity of trying to write a book on Nomads.
>
> —Bruce Chatwin 1988, 178.

Victor J. Vitanza

The Schizophrenic voyage is the only kind there is.
—Deleuze and Guttari 1983, 224.

In the buginning is the woid, in the muddle is the sounddance.
—James Joyce 1976, 378.

"We"

As soon as a reader thinks that he has rid (read [red]) himself of someone, s/he eternally returns. (For those who might still hunger, who might still desire "some more," I have prepared this supplementary stuffing. For those, however, who have had more than enough, then, I would suggest that it's time to close the book, for more than one course yet remains. [What is before us is another dinner with Trimalchio.] I would, dear reader, not have you both bark and barf it all out!)

What I have written here should be read doubly as a continuation of the introductory statement to this book and as a look back that attempts to deal with the forever begged question of "we" and the question of "better," which are most complicated questions.

(It is traditional to get someone else other than the editor to write an afterword; but pray tell, Who might that someone else be? Some reviewer will list, at least, a half dozen ever-so-proper names in response, as s/he continues to look for whatever else is wrong with this collection and afterword. So it goes!)

In what follows I am going to presume to chat (or rather stutter [and paratheorize]) very generally (and *event*ually [i.e., performatively]) of what "we" are *about*. That is, who "we" are and what I think that "we" are *doing*, in particular, in this collection of essays. And, of course, what I presume to say here is *my story*.[1]

Beyond the thin boundaries of this volume, there are yet other stories being told of what "we" are *about*. I would like now to turn briefly to one such story . . . among other stories. (It is, after all is said and un/done, another way of "rebeginning.")

In the second edition of *The Present State of Scholarship in Historical and Contemporary Rhetoric* (1990), "we"—i.e., some of us who have been engaging in rethinking or, as Richard Rorty might have it, "redescribing" (1989) historiographies of rhetoric—find ourselves discussed and appraised. "We" are noted in the last two chapters, respectively by, Donald C. Stewart, "The Nineteenth Century," and James L. Kinneavy, "Contemporary Rhetoric."

Alexandre Kojeve in his *Introduction to the Reading of Hegel* has left us with these words: "All human . . . Desire . . . is . . . the desire for 'recognition' " (1969, 7). I remember having said at a rather in/opportune moment at one of our major conferences that "the worst thing is 'being ignored' " (Octalog 1988). If this statement of mine signals "the worst thing," I now have a better idea of what "the best thing" is. Working with a Lacanian model at this opportune moment, I am well aware that "the best thing" is the realization of the impossibility of "recognition." Though "we" so desire to be recognized, *there is* (and always already) *only "misrecognition."* And so how have "we" been recently "recognized"—that is, "misrecognized"?

In the volume on *The Present State*, Stewart takes particular note of recent interests in historiography. (What is of partial interest is that this information is not included in the book's index, which is only another way of being mis/recognized.) After giving a brief account of the flurry of panels and collections of articles on the subject of historiography, Stewart writes:

> Much of the discussion at these meetings and in these papers is heavily influenced by postmodern critical thought (how anything can be "*post*modern" continues to baffle me except in the world of people for whom the material and conceptual facts of life are all verbal constructs, continuously adapting to their contexts and the shifting nature of language and reality), which makes the not so new or profound discovery that cultural contexts are complex and always in flux and that language which attempts to deal with this phenomenon is inadequate because also in flux.
>
> None of the individuals involved in these "events" seems aware that in 1976 Winston Weathers described a style, Grammar B, to cope with these problems, not even Victor Vitanza, that occasional Paganini of the printed page, who employs some of the devices of Grammar B while writing deconstructed prose. They are also largely unaware of the fact that in insisting on the interdisciplinary nature of rhetoric, they are carrying out the rhetoric program developed by Fred Newton Scott at Michigan in the 1890s.
>
> I cannot leave this subject without an additional note on style.

> In a number of papers which I read, increasingly under protest, I discovered authors enslaved by current literary critical jargon. It is characterized by extensive use of such terms as *privilege, reify, valorize, foreground,* and even an occasional *non-foundational* and *criteriology*. This is "lit/crit speak," a subspecies of "academic/speak," a language greatly inferior to English in both diction and syntax. I suggest that it be avoided. (1990, 174)

It is, indeed, tempting to respond to this general assessment, which is a typical point of view, or "redescription," though with some variations (see especially Connors 1991, 66–68, 70 n14; 1992, 34), espoused by what I have called "traditional" historians of rhetoric (see Vitanza 1987b). And as desire—not need—would have me do it, I will respond, though ever indirectly and very generally. (I pray that my readers will take my counter-response to Stewart as similar to Paul Feyerabend's response to Imre Lakotos [see Feyerabend 1988], who was/is absent, but who in his, now their, absences are ever more so present. *Fort/da, fort/da!*)

Some More "We"(s)

The question that I am going to wrestle with here is Can I better recognize, in the midst of mis/recognition, what "we" are *doing* than Stewart or Robert Connors has or can? (After all, I am trying to write an afterword-that-is-not-a-typical-afterword to this collection of essays written by many of the people to whom Stewart has indirectly referred.)

However, my answer to the question Can I better recognize? has to be from the start *Nes/Yo.*[2] (But, then, I leap too far ahead of myself.)

In ruminating on this question, I begin with the problem of *recognition as impossible* and that all there is, is mis/recognition. (This is my beginning because out of mis/recognition can and do come new productive mis/recognitions or "redescriptions"; or out of the impossible can and do come possibilisms. The impossibility of recognition does not mean, therefore, that Stewart, Connors, and company or "we" in this volume have to fall into silence, anymore than it means that I cannot write an afterword.)

We are rhetoricians: One of the issues that the problem of recognition suggests is that complete recognition of, say, the thing-in-itself *is*—should/ought to remain—impossible. (Any attempt to seize the fantasy of reality, or of the (Lacanian) real, or of the sublime object of ideology, or of a final vocabulary, can only lead to a political-social disaster.) Because we are variously rhetoricians, we accept either a "strong" or "weak" version of this notion of mis/recognition and, consequently, are aware of the dangers of attempting to seize the fantasy of the thing-in-itself (e.g., the Freudian *thing* or Lacanian *real*). It would appear that we, therefore, are together on this point. There should be no quarrel over this issue, unless, of course, another "rhetor" may have a very different notion of what it is to be a rhetorician. (I am occasionally puzzled by the ancillary question, How much can a "rhetor" change and still be, or be mis/recognized as, a "rhetor"?)

And yet, there are quarrels, for there are particular "naive rhetors" among us who still express amazement at a title such as *The Rhetoric of Fiction* (thinking it only an oxymoron, a confusion of "reality" and "fiction"), or particular "leftist rhetors" who express a penchant for grasping the fantasy of the real, or the great, good place (thinking it only within their political *real*ization).

The question (oh, so quickly) becomes a question of ideology: Another issue that the question concerning recognition suggests, however—and it is the more important one for me here—is that the very conditions of the possibilities of recognition—i.e., that any of us can recognize at all—come into being only by virtue of the particular *ideologies* through which we together or separately can see.

My point, therefore, is the point of *ideology*, that is, the whole point of leftist thinking, with which, in great part, I mis/identify. And lest we all forget, my ever-looming point concerns the question of Who is better at recognizing what "we" are *doing* as historians and historiographers.

(The question of "better" is important, for it is all a question here of critique, *though I would rather perpetually drift*. [My inscribed personality/temperament here is split, for this "I," as will have been performed, is both "we" and "I."] This "I" believes that the very act of critiquing [itself or others] can be highly problematic because it is more often than not "reactionary" and, therefore, motivated by "resentment." Performative suspicion is, instead, preferred.)

My tentative answer: One might argue—though I finally would not, however—that Stewart, Connors, and company are less able to assess what "we" are *doing* than "we" (of the various "lefts") are able or possibly than an "I" is, simply because Stewart and company exist in a state of mystification. That is, they are *un*aware, as Louis Althusser would put it, that they are very much within, enveloped by, an ideological space, or that they are occupying "subject-positions" fostered by the ideological-state-(academic) apparatuses.

What is especially mystifying for them is that while they understand how language (*logos*) works through ever-shifting contexts (Stewart himself suggests an understanding of this point), they fail, however, to act on their understanding. They end up, consequently, reacting in the name of something called, as Stewart clearly labels, "English." (I ask, What's 'dis English?) Hence, in this case, mystification always already remains incipient or latent. As Marx says: "They do this without being aware of it" (1977, 166–67; cf. Zizek 1989; de Man 1983, 102–41). Do what? Write *The* History of Rhetoric and assess "us" across a fetishistic misrecognition (see Marx 1977, ch. 1, sec. 4).

I know, I know, the language here *is* remarkable! It is not, however, by any means, as Stewart labels it, "*post*modern." There is, to be sure, every reason in the world/whirl (i.e., the Heraclitian storm) to fear language, that is, to express logophobia. As everyone from Heraclitus to Heidegger has been telling us, we are not at home in language; in other words, we are perpetually in its unhomeliness, or its uncanniness. If the biblical Christian God is *logos*, then, his son, Jesus Christ, is not at home with *logos*. Father and son here are at odds with each other; they are perhaps a personification of unhomeliness. (Freud would read this all very differently, all very Oedipally, but I refuse to impoverish the discussion.) What I am thinking in terms of, however, is Nikos Kazantzakis's quasi-Nietzschean characterization of Christ in *The Last Temptation* (1960), which portrays Christ as a hysteric in the midst of his or her uncanniness. (If Christ is both God and man, then, he is the very embodiment of the unhomely. *Pater Omnipotens Aeterna Deus*.) The four major versions that we have in the other book—that would be *the* book—certainly do not deal with this problem of the *logos* and uncanniness.

I know, I know, this prose with its elusiveness and now allusiveness is still, if not more, unreadable.

(About prose, language, *logos*: I recall what Richard Lanham says: "It may perhaps be fruitful to view style as a self-corrective circuit. . . . A totally serious, referential use of language never lasts long. It becomes stylized, turns playful. Bureaucratic jargons start out as purely denotative, strictly business, but end up as games of euphemism, of obfuscation, of plain verbal nonsense—'buzz words' which can be glued together in any combination. . . . Language cannot last long without returning to its rich resources of play" [1976, 31]. About the so-called plain style, he writes: "Clarity does not lie entirely in the eye of the beholder. It lies in formal properties. . . . Not clarity . . . but formal hunger may determine the shape of symbolic expression. It is generally assumed that language originally tried to be clear and only later degenerated into self-pleasing rituals. Why not the other way around—pleasure first?" [21]. And again: "The real deceiver is the plain stylist who pretends to put all his cards on the table. Clarity . . . is a cheat, an illusion. To rhetorical man at least, the world *is* not clear, it is *made* clear" [22].)[3]

A(nother) reflection on this answer to the question of who is better at mis/recognition: Why did I say (several paragraphs ago, before I got into all this stuff about the *logos*) that I would not argue this point about "being better" at assessing what "we" are *doing* but, nonetheless, carried on, by reporting such an argument? Is this simply part of what a (cross-eyed, Third Sophistic) *rhetor* must do in considering the various standpoints, even if only s/he wishes to report an argument so that s/he can, if s/he so desires, counter it? Perhaps. Or is this so-called tactic merely a guise and a ruse? or a cover-up? Again, perhaps.

If so, then, I am performatively suspicious—when I think as a "Marxist"—of such a motive, this my commonplace motive. ("I may know it, but perhaps I am nonetheless doing it." Such a subject-position, Marx would counter, can lead to cynicism. [Cf. Althusser 1986, 235; cf. Sloterdijk 1987.])

And yet, as I ruminate on my answers and possible motives—without shame or guilt—parenthetically and within brackets, and parenthetically yet again . . . As I ruminate as such, what comes to my mind, at this very moment, is that my answer, nonetheless, is *right/wrong*. (Or it is what I have referred to as *Nes/Yo*.)

(Dear reader, are you still there? Or, were you ever there with and for a me such as a performative "me"? who dis/engages in this essayistic meandering? The ship that I set sail on has the figure of Montaigne attached to its prow. As Deleuze and Guattari say: "The schizophrenic voyage is the only kind there is" [1983, 224].)

Whatever the case, I must lift anchor and (once again) continue to drift.

And so, I have to insist on the "truth" of the matter: I also do think "we" are—or I am!—better at mis/recognizing what "we" are *doing* (or better at mis/recognizing) as historians and as historiographers than Stewart, Connors, and company.

Why? (I *repeat*, for emphasis, and then add a point with a twist or two that my leftist colleagues might not be willing to add.) I repeat: Stewart, Connors, and company do as they do when they do history or assess "our" histories because they exist in a state of mystification, or false consciousness. That is, they are unaware that they are very much within, or enveloped by, an ideological space, or that they are occupying "subject-positions" interpellated and fostered by the ideological-state-(academic) apparatuses. (Stewart, Connors, and company are subjects/agents determined by the discipline, which, in turn, determines what "they" will have said about "us" or about anything.) What they are unaware of is that the "reality" of the discipline of either "rhetoric/composition" or of "composition studies" is a fantasy construction.

Therefore, I would pro-*le-tarot*-ly submit, they are *not* better than "we" are!

What I would now even more perversely add to this statement, however, is that all of us *are* in a similar-mutual predicament of being caught in the mire of dreaded ideological constructions. As it is for Stewart, Connors, and company, so it is for "us."

A perversity, however, can and does mis/lead to yet another more outrageous twisted perversity: For it can and is argued *pharmakonically* here that "we" not only know that "we" are "caught" in ideology, but it is this very negative knowledge that *enables* "us," nonetheless, to resist ideological forces at work in "our" writing histories of rhetorics; in fact, "we" would write with the sole purpose of demystifying previous mystified histories. (It is not necessarily the case, as Marx would argue, then, that this [my] kind of "critical thinking" has to mis/lead to cynicism. [See Althusser 1986, 232.])

And so, "we" sigh with relief.

And yet (will this ever come to an end?) is there not another-'nother possible twist of mis/recognition? (Re/working and re/twisting the exposition of this argument is like searching for a new topological configuration. Sometimes, it is necessary casuistically to stretch people and ideas in dis/order to see around corners.) I think that there is yet another mis/recognition, especially if we all mutually mis/understand here that what is suggested—by assumption in the argument so far—is that there is, nonetheless, a (human/ist) choice based on, or warranted by, this negative knowledge. (It is argued: It is this very negative knowledge that *enables* "us," nonetheless, to resist ideological forces at work in "our" writing histories of rhetorics.)

For me, however, such an assumption of a human/ist choice is an unacceptable mis/reading of possible mis/readings. As it is for Paul de Man (1983, 75), so it is for me: Negative knowledge, therefore, does not simply mean that "we" are enabled by virtue of being aware of ideology and thereby using it as leverage. No, this is not the case! Negative knowledge more importantly means here, however, that when it is extended to "our" very being (as negative essence), *this negative knowledge is "our" un/doing as humanist*. ("We" know that "we" cannot know "our"selves. What has happened is that in thinking reflexively [in the mirror of self-reflection]—that is, having had *thought about thought*—"we" have turned "our"selves into an object, about which "we" can have only negative knowledge. [The dialectical pull toward universal consciousness has been our undoing, whether it be toward the Spirit or material conditions.] As the object dissipates, so do "we." And yet, modernism is born, with all of its terrible problems.)

I will have returned to this view of negative knowledge. I will have had to re/circle in twisting, pretzel fashion around it, before finally re/addressing it as "I" performatively cannot not; I am not only a topologist but also a cacographist.

And so, let us re/begin: And turn to Stanley Fish's idea of "theory hope," which argues (in any case, here) that self-consciousness, or self-reflection, or Marx's humanistic "ruthless criticism" (1978), does not make for a better critical performance *against* ideology, or fetishistic mis/recognition (see Fish 1989). In a nutshell what this means is that, say, Theodor Adorno or Max Horkheimer's critical theory is finally no more effective than traditional theory. There is always "some thing" that critique cannot get to. (All corners cannot be looked around, no matter how much "we" stretch.) Perhaps this "some thing" is *real*ly "no thing." I recall (and re/emphasize again, especially in this context) de Man's view that "demystification [of false consciousness *is*] the most dangerous myth of all" (1983,14). Demystification, for de Man, is no cure; for its goal can never be to get down to bedrock positive knowledge. What can be gained, however, is the "knowledge of the impossibility of knowing," which "precedes the act of consciousness that tries to reach it" (75). This is, as I have said, negative knowledge, which spills over into the im/possibility of humanist thinking, but which causes tremendous problems because we of different persuasions, nonetheless, long nostalgically not only for knowledge but for the subject-position (or agency) of humanism itself so that we might grasp such knowledge.

Where Are "WE" Now?

> Could a historiographer drive on his history, as a muleteer drives on his mule,—straight forward;—for instance, from *Rome* all the way to *Loretto*, Without ever once turning his head aside either to the right hand or to the left,—he might venture to fortell you to an hour when he should get to his journey's end;—but the thing is, morally speaking, impossible: For, if he is a man of the least spirit, he will have fifty deviations form a straight line to make with this or that party as he goes along, which he can no ways avoid.
>
> —Larry Sterne 1940, 36.

Where are "we" now? (Or actually, Where are we various historians of rhetoric now?)

Answered simply: The argument against Stewart, Connors, and company is devastating, but then the argument against either "us" or me is possibly still just as devastating.

Answered ironically: What if there is another form of ideology (a *sublime object* of ideology) behind ideology that is even more insidious and, therefore, even more devastating? (What if: " 'We' think that 'we' know about it, but are still doing it, and don't even know that 'we' are still doing it"? What if: "It's an illusion that 'we' live in, or can even successfully strive for, a postideological condition"?)

What I am suggesting simply and ironically, then, is that there is always the possibility of a "mirror effect" here—which I have "repeatedly effected"—with this kind of reasoning as it trails off into infinite regress. Marx was well aware of "the mirror effect" and warned us about it (see 1977, 144), though he does not—as far as I know—speak directly of the nightmare of ideologies "nested" in ideologies. And Althusser? Well, I will get to him later. (If I have put on an ironic mask here and enacted a "para/noyance's" [or schizo's] vision, Althusser enacts a paranoid's nightmare.)

Let us continue this *dissoi logoi* way of thinking in dis/order to reach for what I have called a mis/status of *"dissoi* para*logoi"* (1987a, 55), which is a detonation of this whole issue in dis/order to drift perpetually. (If I were Jack Kerouac, however, I would rent a skywriting plane.)

I do not desire to get stuck in the now rewritten mis/realization that "either 'we' or I, too, don't know that 'we' are doing it, but still, nonetheless, do it."

(And—readers, if I still have any readers—I am well aware that this twisting-turning, bumping-rebumping dis/course is potentially nauseating. It has a certain-uncertain element of vertigo. It has the same effect as riding in back of mom and dad's car. And *that is* precisely the effect, after all is said and un/done, that I am after. So let us all continue, which requires going back to the future.)

Marx, in his concern for the problem of value, would prevent this ideological blindness (mis/recognition) from continuing by virtue of refocusing on the social relations between individuals, which has been displaced into the relations between things. (See 1977, 163, 165.) But this is not enough of a dissolution, for It reeks of a certain form of *mastery* and all again in the name of *humanism*. (I'm still mindful of the im/possibility of ideologies "nested" within ideologies. I'm mindful of *pre*dispositions that I cannot identify. And it is that "mindfulness" that is being patently-symptomatically-ironically *performed* here.)

Marx wishes to go home, and yet there is only "sinthome" (see Zizek 1989, 71–75), or the unhomely (the uncanny). And I wish for the audience to catch my drift, and yet there are no ears for what desires to be said. And therefore for me as well as for any future audiences, not only irony but suspicion is still forever desired. (As Nietzsche says: We all have a *"duty* to [performative] suspicion today, to squint maliciously out of every abyss of suspicion" [1966, 34; Nietzsche's emphasis. Cf. Kenneth Burke's "democratic mistrust," 1968, 118].)

However, there is here not only suspicion but also perversity and nausea that are desired. And, therefore, I must add (rather damningly) that Louis Althusser writes:

> Marx never believed that a knowledge of the nature of money (a social relation) could destroy its appearance, its form of exis-

> tence—a thing, for this appearance was its very being, as necessary as the existing mode of production. Marx never believed that an ideology might be dissipated by a knowledge of it: for the knowledge of this ideology, as the knowledge of its conditions of possibility, of its structure, of its specific logic and of its practical role, within a given society, is simultaneously knowledge of the conditions of its necessity. (1986, 230)

This statement, of course, is Althusser's attempt to argue against the young Marx as a humanist and to argue for the older Marx as a dialectical/historical materialist. But Althusser (in his extreme, "symptomatic reading") does not speak for, or to, many of my leftist colleagues. Who still *theorize* their collective hopes and fantasies, which they place in the language game of knowledge and in humanism.

A Digression

> Reader, I think proper, before we proceed any farther together, to acquaint thee that I intend to digress, through this whole history, as often as I see occasion, of which I am myself a better judge than any pitiful critic whatever; and here I must desire all those critics to mind their own business, and not to intermeddle with affairs or works which no ways concern them; for till they produce the authority by which they are constituted judges, I shall not plead to their jurisdiction.
>
> —Hank Fielding 1950, 5.

Alluding to Althusser: . . . allows me now to speak of where I—at this very in/opportune moment—am drifting practically/conceptually. (This is a transitional paragraph into a digression, with an announcement!) It is, in part, the direction that Althusser ventured and claims that eventually Marx himself ventured, un/namely, the direction *against* humanism. The eventual strategy behind this transition and un/naming, however, is different when Althusser performs it and I do it. Whereas Althusser becomes—as he says, the mature Marx becomes—an *anti*humanist, I am and, here, will become a *non*humanist.

(Let us all keep in mind simultaneously, dear reader/critic/reviewer, that I am still ruminating on the question of Who is better at mis/recognizing what "we" are *doing* as historians and historiographers?)

And so why would I embrace nonhumanism? in the light or darkness of this question?

"A ruthless criticism" by/of humanism: In ruminating on this question, let us return to Fish's idea of "theory hope." Previously, I said that Fish's idea argues that "self-consciousness does not make for a better critical performance *against* ideology, or fetishistic mis/recognition." (Althusser says the same, or says that Marx says the same.) Criticism as humanism, in other words, is not necessarily liberating. "We" act, however, as if such liberation is possible. Though "we" know that the very codes of deliberation are coded in such a fashion that "we" cannot overcome them, "we" nonetheless deliberate and think ourselves, when reaching consensus, liberated. (" 'We' do it, and forget that 'we' are doing it'; *or* 'we' do it and know that 'we' do it but do it anyway.")

There is yet another aspect to humanism, however, that I desire to get to. Let us rehearse briefly: *Self-consciousness* (an accountability of one's [own] predispositions [hence, *praefatio*, or lie]) implies the necessity of some form of humanism, while *humanism*, in turn, implies some form of essentialism. It is essentialism of this kind that I will have nothing to do with, whether "naive" or "strategic" (see Spivak 1989b). Essentialism, however, is inevitable![4] (It is no longer a question of whether there is *some thing* or *no thing*. It is similarly no longer a question of being-a-fool; for it is a question only of what kind of fool we all desire to be. In both cases, there is essence, either as presence or absence.) But an essentialism that spawns humanism is not inevitable.

There are at least two humanisms: The humanism that I am alluding to, here, is not the bourgeois humanist subject, but the humanist subject to be found in the young Marx. History, in both views, would be *a process with a* (speaking, thinking, acting, ethical, political) *subject*. I am against the bourgeois humanist (liberal, essentialist) subject. But, still again, I cannot stop at that point. I have to drift: I see no way, at present, that a liberal or a humanist-(essentialist)-*leftist* "subject" can be constructed without being subject(ed) to the impulse toward "mastery" and, therefore, toward the "perfectability" of society. (I do have problems with Rorty's "liberal ironist" and his or her view of hope [1989], though I most probably will be read as such an ironist, as I have already been read as being *a*political!) Shifting the individual, bourgeois subject to the proletarian, collective (fused) subject does not solve this problem of mastery. Both of these "subjects" desire political power, that is, desire the very thing that oppresses them! (And then the bureaucracy [or as Papa KB says, the "bureaucratization of the imaginative" (1984,

225–28)] gets ahold of power. I thought for a time that "perspectives by incongruity" [308–14] might take care of such a "bureaucratization" but no longer, as will become *event*ually evident in this my afterword.) And so, like Gilles Deleuze and Félix Guattari—and the crazy Wilhelm Reich—I wonder why we all (or many of us) "fight for servitude as stubbornly as though it were salvation" (1983, 29).

Power, therefore, must be placed in perpetual dispersion. As Henry Miller writes in *Sunday After the War*: "Man [*sic*] will be forced to realize that power must be kept open, fluid and free. His aim will be not to possess power but to radiate it" (qtd. in N. O. Brown 1959, 305).

But I would go even further in my attack on humanism. My attack now is on the *hope* that we, in general, place in the tool of humanism, which "we" call *rationality*, or a so-called Marxist ruthless criticism (1978). Lyotard says it best:

> It is undoubtedly useless to fight for the consistency of a political, philosophical discourse and practice, by arguing against the inconsistency of the adversary's political, philosophical discourse. Useless because, indirectly, such a battle is still a battle for reason, for unity, for the unification of diversities, a quibbling battle which no one can win[,] for the winner is already and has always been reason. And we don't want to destroy kapital because it isn't rational, but because it is. Reason and power are one and the same thing. You may disguise the one with dialectics or prospectiveness, but you will still have the other in all its crudeness: jails, taboos, public weal, selection, genocide. (1984a, 11)

(Althusser, in this perverse way and in others, has had an influence on me, and especially along with Michel Foucault and Deleuze and Guattari. But I cannot not reject [expel] Althusser and what he has done to the whole subject [business] itself.)

Why I reject Althusser's antihumanism: If I reject humanism, I also cannot trek with Althusser's *turn* (i.e., his particular tactic) *away from humanism*; he finally achieves it at too high a price. *Which is structuralism*. (His is a turn, therefore, that I cannot leave unstoned.) His is an extreme form of nonhumanism. His view of the "subject" specifically is that of "the agents of production, who are never anything more than the occupants of these places, insofar as they are the 'supports' (*Träger*) of these functions. . . . *The true 'subjects' are these definers and distributors: the relations of production*. . . . But since these are 'relations,' they cannot be thought within the category *subject*" (1987, 180; Althusser's emphasis).

Subjects are "subject effects," which as a concept alone (as realized, say, from a poststructuralist perspective) is acceptable to me, but the "effect" is no longer acceptable when Althusser starts talking about the *structure of structure as cause*. For example (and there are many), Althusser writes:

> The effects are not outside the structure, are not a pre-existing object, element or space in which the structure arrives *to imprint its mark*: on the contrary, it implies that the structure is immanent in its effects, a cause immanent in its effects . . . that *the whole existence of the structure consists of its effects*, in short that the structure, which is merely a specific combination of its peculiar elements, is nothing outside its effects. (188–89; Althusser's emphasis)

Structuralism *is* a paranoid's (not a para/noyance's) vision. (This kind of thinking, and especially Althusser's, is aptly considered and characterized by Peter Sloterdijk [see 1987, 90–97].)

There is so much more to Althusser's structuralism, but "my" desired purpose has been satisfied here, which has been to examine how one extreme reading of Marx—but I take all the "readings" as extreme or radical or as "symptomatic"—dis/enables what I would consider an acceptable, performative vantage point for ruminating on the question Who is better at mis/recognizing what "we" are *doing* as historians and historiographers? (What will be acceptable, of course, depends on how a "rhetor" goes about mis/recognizing. And since this is "my" afterword, then, I am going to do it "my" way!) If I would embrace, therefore, neither a self-consciousness (for its "theory hope" and "leftist" humanism) nor a structuralist antihumanism (for its displaced, totalizing character), why and how, then, would an "I" embrace a nonhumanism, which would be less a poststructuralism and more so a postmodernism?

A possible answer: Why embrace a nonhumanism? Because of the ethical necessity to discover a means of *resisting* and *disrupting* any and every attempt to grasp the ideal of humanism or antihumanism and of *resisting* and *disrupting* any and every attempt *to seize the fantasy* of either commonsense reality or the most Sublime Object of Ideology (i.e., the pull towards perfecting the social). This latter fantasy has been repeatedly characterized as extremely dangerous. (See KB 1969a, 474–75; Lyotard 1984b; 82; Zizek 1989.)

Still in the Digression

> Therefore, my dear friend and companion, if you should think me somewhat sparing of my narrative . . . —bear with me,—and let me go on, and tell my story my own way—or if I should seem now and then to trifle upon the road,—or should sometimes put on a fool's cap with a bell on it, for a moment or two as we pass along,—don't fly off,—but rather courteously give me credit for a little more wisdom than appears upon my outside;—and as we jogg on, either laugh with me, or at me, or in short, do any thing,—only keep your temper.
>
> —Larry Sterne 1940, 11.

This (being-an-answer), however, needs further explanation. (And, therefore, into another digression.) It is important for me to understand the mis/status of both the traditionalist and revisionist historians. (And why? So as to reach a third ["some more"] in dis/order to void [i.e., to disperse] the categories. And to void, with them, what each stands for. And finally so as to answer the question concerning Who is better at *doing history*?)

To recapitulate in dis/order to move on: The *traditionalists*, on the right hand, are subject(ed) to the ideological construct that does not allow them to see that objects, or "reality," is the result of what "we" call social relations ("they do this without being aware of it"). These "social relations," however, are no mere "social constructions of reality," which is only some bourgeois, liberal talk that displaces the intricate value in and of Marx's thinking. On the left hand, the *revisionist* historians are, for the most part, subject(ed) to the desire to capture the great, good place, *the* social relationship, but in order to be successful they have finally to employ unacceptable exclusionary tactics (i.e., take steps toward purification, or "integration by segregation") in their attempts to seize the fantasy of the real. Therefore, I might say: They "Make peace with [their] faeces" (Burke 1969a, 23), but by virtue of flushing away that cloacal-material(ist) side of society—which was or is supposed to dissipate in thin air, when the economic conditions are finally *re*coded—. . . by virtue of flushing them all away to septic tanks (i.e., to the gulags). By the cloacal-material(ist) side of society, I mean that side de/composed of both people *and* ideas. Finally what cannot be tolerated is an un/certain outlaw thinking. (If Marx were alive today and lived among, say, Anglo-American Marxists, he would not be tolerated, but would only find himself rotting alive in a, so to speak, Siberian labor camp! And what of Jesus? [See Sloterdijk 1987, 191.])[5]

It is, however, as Papa says, the left's over-enthusiasm (they are doing it, too, and don't know they're doing it) for the eulogistic side of discourse (i.e., the eu/topian side) that generally predisposes us to such rituals of cleansing the body politic (1966a, 308–43; 1969a, 300–3). As Papa might say: Toilet training, many times, supercedes and has a negative influence on tolerance training.

It, therefore, has to be the linguistic task of postmodernity—employing the language game of avant-garde art as in rapid, perpetual "redescriptions"—to resist and disrupt modernist-revisionists when they attempt to conceive of *the* political real[ity] and then attempt to present it as a revised (or recoded [and, therefore, now cleansed]) history of rhetoric (Lyotard 1984b, 77–79). It is the linguistic task of postmodernity to take both the traditional and revisionist historians, as Lacan would say, "through the fantasy" (see Zizek 1989). It is the linguistic task of postmodernity, then, to engage *perpetually* in demystifications, decodifications, deterritorializations.

What amounts to "an epistemological break" (as Althusser might have it) between these two ways of doing history—the traditional and revisionary—is, however, in many ways a necessary, healthy break. (Let us all not miss this point. Let us all speak good of it.) It is healthy as a *corrective* move, for even though the two sides necessarily speak at cross-purposes, there will have been much to gather from such inevitable mis/recognitions. In addition, the modernist-revisionaries must and ought to continue to press for histories that make evident the repressive, suppressive, oppressive nature of *The* History of Rhetoric. As I have said, I need these histories so that I might critique them while perpetually drifting out of them. (After all, dear reader, why do you think that I mis/speak of them? Out of mis/recognition can come insight.) What will be "gathered" (Heraclitus) will have been newer, I hope, more insightful mis/recognitions (misprisions). There is great value in what Michel Serres (1982a; 1982b) refers to as "negentropic interruptions," with two interlocutors (or sentences) only apparently speaking about the same topic.

For example, a traditional reader/reviewer will only shake his/her head and accuse "me" of a lack of "correctness" and "decorum" or even "tolerance" itself, while a revisionist will label me a "neo-conservative" and "political quietist." Or very generally, people in our profession (the dear audience) perhaps would say, "yes, this corrective move, with its inevitable mis/recognitions, is at times good, but it is also very dangerous; for it can amount to a power struggle, or a delirium, without any means of arbitration or negotiation. It is that way when 'you people' do history at cross-purposes."

I would respond: So-called power struggles (as Yes/No!) are, indeed, unfortunate (as a form of mis/recognitions). And yet, they are often a sign of a crisis, which, in turn, is a sign of great ferment. (See de Man 1983, 3–19.) To speak, or to write hysteries, at cross-purposes, as I am discussing such speaking and writing here, is a consequence of speaking across very different terministic screens, or paradigms, gestalts, and epistemées. Or epistemological breaks. (Or as Heidegger would say, it is a hearing and a speaking across the question of Being. Which speaks, I would incite, to us hysterically. Though we, in general, do not desire always to hear it as such. And therein, we get in trouble.)

Moreover, I would be more forthcoming and respond: "We" did not get up one day, dear reader, and simply decide to have a revolution, to get involved in a so-called power struggle. What is happening in dis/respect to writing histories of rhetoric cannot *not* happen (cf. Rorty 1989, 6–7). We are all in the midst of a *crisis of legitimation* and a *crisis of representation.* (As the deconstructionist-Marxist Gayatri Spivak has reminded us, history is a *catachresis,* which means that it is "a metaphor without a literal referent" [1989a, 211].) This crisis is extremely difficult for traditional historians to mis/understand (given their traditional epistemology), but "we" must bring them . . . "through the fantasy" . . . to this mis/understanding. (This is, as I said, the linguistic task of postmodernity.)

For many of "us," then, the epistemology (or grammar, or style) of realism is no longer adequate when writing histories of rhetoric. "We" search for different, but post-referential epistemologies (as well as grammars and styles), and therefore "we" variously go to Marx, Freud, and Nietzsche, the three hermeneuts of suspicion. Our problem now, then, is How to represent without misrepresenting while knowing, nonetheless, that all representations are mis/representations? As

I have said: Our problem is the desire of the desire for recognition, even though there can only be mis/recognitions.

And so again, How do we all understand (inquire into) this problem of desire (i.e., this appetite to know, or to recognize)? This is an important question, for how we in general answer it will determine who we are as *subjects* (historiographers) studying *objects* ("history"). Heraclitus, Nietzsche, and Heidegger, for example, would say that it is apparently the desire of the *logos*. But theirs is only a partial answer, though an extremely important one, which I have mis/seen as constituting the subject-as-a-"hysteriographer" and the object-as-"hysteries." (See my 1987b; 1990; 1991b.) As I continue to re/write, however, my performative "I" is becoming more and more a "schizographer." The conditions of possibilities, however, would be (I must insist on dispersion) wider, greater, and even more un(a)countable. Perpetual, perpetual demystifications.

And so again and again, what would be mis/recognized? Globally, what are the (in[ter]ventional) procedures? Let us count: For a traditionalist-realist, it would be *Some Thing*! (The object, for the most part, is nonproblematic.) For a revisionist-modernist, it would be *Nothing*. (The object is but disappeared and thus highly problematic—which leads to the principle of a negative-epistemology, which in turn stimulates a nostalgia for and a return to "Some Thing"). For a postmodernist, however, it would be *Some More*—which can be mis/understood as either the negative (the impossible, lack) producing excess or can be mis/understood as pure affirmation (desire) producing excess. (Lacan works with the negative-epistemology; Spinoza, Henri Bergson, Norman O. Brown, and Deleuze and Guattari work with the affirmative-epistemology.)

In both forms, however, excess—and this is the important point—produces an overwhelming and unaccountable *resistance* to and *disruption* of any and every attempt by modernist-revisionists *to seize the* (nostalgic) *fantasy* of "Some Thing," that is, to turn the fantasy into a new, but this time true, political *real*ity. Excess, therefore, is a mis/state of perpetual demystification, perpetual paraethical in(ter)vention, or a constant rude (interruptive) reminder that "reality" is a fantasy construction, is always already an object of a preexisting gaze, or ideology, and that there is no single act (of acts) that will strip away this mystification, or false consciousness! so that we can get to the promised land!

(If you, dear reader, mis/understand this method of [implied] irrational counting and its importance, then you will have "understood" [?] everything that I have been saying for the past few years. You, too, will have been taken "through the fantasy." But you will not, for this mis/understanding demands that you place yourself in a perpetual vertigo [as in the style of this afterword] that is finally intolerable for you. Instead, you would be subjects to a discipline.)

The conscientious objector(s): Many of these people—who would object to what "we" and I are doing, as I have imagined them as conscientious objectors—would feel perhaps better about this whole thing—that is, about *doing history*—if "we" and I could find some solace, or locate a common ground, say, in Hayden White's scheme or, more properly, in Papa KB's approach to ac*count*ing for "our" many differences or in recognizing "our" mis/recognitions.

Papa's motto, "*Ad bellum purificandum.*" He says: "Human thought may be directed towards 'the purification of war,' not perhaps in the hope that war can be eliminated from any organism that, like man, has the motives of combat in his very essence, but in the sense that war can be refined to the point where it would be much more peaceful than the conditions we would now call peace" (1969a, 305).

Speaking only for "my"selphs, however, I cannot find solace in White's scheming or Papa's approach. If not, why?

White is a humanist (see Kellner 1980); moreover, he stops short of the "absurdist [uncanny] moment" of and in pre-Socratic *logos* (see 1978, ch. 12), which is one of the radical *un/places* where I think we collectively must, nonetheless, go. (And be *spoken out of*. [There is a pun here!]) And Papa? He, indeed, has gone to *logos* but—when there—was not *talked out of* his primary motive of codifying/recodifying, but only and overwhelmingly embraced it.

I turn, therefore, from the so-called social turn (and the leftist view) to the "hysterical [pre-Socratic] turn." It is, in other words, "my" (hysterical) turn.

The Angsociety of Influence

> The first thing that entered my father's head, after affairs were a little settled in the family, . . . was to sit down cooly, after the example of Xenophon, and write a Tristra-*paedia*, or system of edu-

> cation for me; collecting first for that purpose his own scattered thoughts, counsels, and notions; and binding them together, so as to form an institute for the government of my childhood and adolescence. I was my father's last stake . . . that is, he had been unfortunate in his three first great casts for me—my geniture, nose, and name.
>
> —Larry Sterne 1940, 372.

And, therefore, in dis/respect to Papa's ac*count*, as pentadic, I *must expel him, along with myself*, as I-cum-"I" move ("I expell *myself*, I spit *myself* out, I abject *myself* within the same motion through which 'I' claim to establish *myself*") from

(1) *object* to
(2) *subject* to
("some more") *abjects*,

without then re/embracing or re/turning to some (other sublime) object! or some thing!

Expelling Papa *is* an act of de/negating what Lacan-cum-Kristeva calls *the Symbolic* (the social, culture, custom, law, etc.), which is negation itself. What is being expelled here *is* the very principle of expulsion, negation. (See Papa's "The Anarcho-Syndicalist 'Constitution' " in 1969a, 346–49; there, he partially explains *selphs* like me.)

In other words and to my point here: Whereas the leftists simply want to *re*codify/*re*territorialize the Symbolic (the social, code, etc.), that is, make it right, I would *de*codify/*de*territorialize the Symbolic, that is, make it far left of what is humanly (i.e., humanistically) possible. And I would do this on the way to the absurdist (abyss/mal) moment. And do it perpetually, perpetually, perpetually. Once is not E-nough, twice is not E-nough. I want Some More. (I desire, however, not only the number "E" but also the nonrational number π.)

To further explain, then, this is how the Symbolic might be perpetually decodified/denegated (in a rudely interrupted) *abecedarian* way:

(*a-b*) The social relationship: Codified-recodified: For Papa KB, history is grammatical, which amounts to saying that it is social, which, in turn, is to say "It is Substantial—which is to say that all the branches spread from a single trunk" (1969a, 496). History for KB, therefore, is arborescent, or arbor-essence. (Its essence is synecdochic, or container and thing contained.) Its essence is in the modernist-negative. This view of the negative, more specifically, is ac*count*ed for (i.e., its various codes are accounted for) through out *A Grammar of Motives* (1969a) and *Language As Symbolic Action* (1966a). This view of the negative—taken perversely from Spinoza and Bergson—establishes the conditions of the possibilities (i.e., the various combinations and permutations) for *re*vision. This view is accounted for by way of *definition*, specifically in the forms of contextual and familial definitions; and by way of the *paradox of substance*, specifically in the forms of geometric, familial, directional, and dialectical substances; and by way of the *dialectic of tragedy* (see 1969a, 21–58). And therefore what I, as a schizo, would desire, a free-flow(er)ing of desire, is controlled (contained). (And so, dear Don, what do I have to say about "Grammar B"? I say: "Some more." Or I would say, in its place, reestablish Grammar Z, the most deviant letter of the alphabet. [See Vitanza 1993c.])

(*c*) There is no social relationship:[6] Therefore, Perpetual decodification: *For* Deleuze and Guattari, history is paragrammatical. What I would have, beginning with their view, is a paramodel of hysteries of desire that is—very much on the contrary—not contained. What I would have is not arborescent agents of history, but rhizomatic (or schizo, nomadic, vagabond) agents of history, if correctly called "agents" at all. What I would have, as Deleuze and Guattari would have, is that "Desire does not lack anything; it does not lack its object. It is, rather, the subject that is missing in desire, or desire that lacks a fixed subject; *there is no fixed subject unless there is repression*" (1983, 26; emphasis mine). Similarly, I would then have a breakdown of synecdoche. As Deleuze and Guattari again say: "In desiring-machines everything functions at the same time, but amid hiatuses and ruptures, breakdowns and failures, stalling and short circuits, distances and fragmentations, within a sum that never succeeds in bringing its various parts together so as to form a whole" (42). The problem, then, is

> how to produce, how to think about fragments whose sole relationship is sheer difference—fragments that are related to one another only in that each of them is different—without having recourse to any sort of original totality . . . or to a subsequent totality that may not yet have come about[.] It is only the category of multiplicity, used as a substantive and going beyond both the One and the many, beyond the predicative relation of the One and the many, that can account for desiring-production: desiring-

> production is pure multiplicity, that is to say, an affirmation that is irreducible to any sort of unity. (42)

(And so, Dear Don, "Grammar B" is now impossible! while Grammar Z is perpetually possible!)

Papa KB, however, has a (secular) prayer: "May we have neither the mania of the One/Nor the delirium of the Many—/But both the Union and the Diversity—/The Title and the manifold details that arise/ As that Title is restated/In the narrative of History" (1966a, 56; cf. 477). This prayer, or utterance, is addressed to (the) *logos*, the container that *contains*.

But I would send a letter, or letters—and more than can be ac*count*ed for—to that other office with an address for no addressees. I would be a postman without a destination. (As Lyotard says: "I believe that it is important that there be no addressee" [Lyotard and Thebaud 1985, 9].) Which is a way of saying that I desire that which cannot be contained. (And anyway, not to worry, for the repressed letter, especially Z, in The History of Rhetoric, always returns.) I desire a free-flowing desire. And, therefore, I would desire that which is a parapolicy of noncontainment for histories-cum-hysteries of rhetorics.

Again, my sense of (the) *logos* is pre-Socratic, specifically, Heraclitian. For "me," it is not a matter of the One or the Many; it is, instead, a matter of a far greater delirium of radical (unac*count*able) multiplicities, for you, dear reader, and for "me." (All that which has been excluded in the proper name of *The* History of Rhetorik!) It is what Deleuze and Guattari refer to as the delirium of a "schizorevolutionary [schizonomadic] type or pole that follows the lines of escape of desire; breaches the wall and causes flows to move" (1983, 277).

It would be, then, a matter of standing, while writing hysteries of rhetorics, while enacting a schizography, in the uncontainable storm.

And so let us flow "some more": "The fact has often been overlooked," Deleuze and Guattari say, "that the schizo indeed participates in history; he hallucinates and raves universal history, and proliferates the races" (1983, 85). He [*sic*] becomes all the names of history (21); he [*sic*] becomes the "excluded third party." He [*sic*] says: " 'I' won't say *I* any more, I'll never utter the word again; it's just too damn stupid. Every time I hear it, I'll use the third person instead, if I happen to remember to" (23).

Deleuze and Guattari, in a way comparable to my own tactic, say: "We have introduced a third element—the desiring machine in person" (56). (This third element, it should be obvious by now, is nonsynthesizing; it is, instead, a voiding of all categories, in its attempt to dis/establish a "molecular agglomerate." Hence, I have introduced to the historiography the concept of "hystery"/"hysteriography"[7] as a means of voiding categories such as "traditional" and "revisionary" and male and female. Monique Wittig similarly has introduced to "our" political discussions the concept of "lesbian" [see Butler 1990, 111–28], and Donna Haraway, the concept of "cyborg" [1990], both of which are beyond the traditional binary, or political categories, of male and female.)

"My"-cum-(as the schizo says: "I'll use the third person instead")-"their" sense of *doing history*, therefore, would be that (the) *logos* is *not* "a Great Synecdoche" nor "a Grand Tautalogy," as KB would have it (1966a, 57). I-cum-"they," instead, would paradoxically have a container that is *not* a container, but topologically, like a Klein Jar, is a container that has neither inside nor outside, or is all outside. Papa's container—the sacred vessel—must be shattered into pieces.[8]

When writing histories/hysteries of rhetorics, therefore, it is no longer a matter of our refining war (*Ad bellum purificandum*) but a matter of pursuing a strange polyvocal un/kind of writing that is comparable to the speed, secrecy, and affect of "nomadic war machines" (see Deleuze and Guattari 1987, 351–423).

End of Digression(s)

> By this contrivance the machinery of my work is of a species by itself; two contrary motions are introduced into it, and reconciled, which were thought to be at variance with each other. In a word, my work is digressive, and it is progressive too,—and at the same time.
>
> —Larry Sterne 1940, 73.

Where are we/I-cum-they now?: As the Shandian quotation for this section suggests (perhaps only belatedly), I have been reworking my way back to Fish's issue of "theory hope" and the young Marx's issue of "humanism" (i.e., back to the possibility of a freedom of choice in relation to history) and Marx's issue of "self-consciousness" (i.e., to know that "we are doing it, so that we can critique our false consciousness and, therefore, stop what we, heretofore, have been doing"). In working my way back, I have attempted to distance myselphs from anyone—namely, KB—who would wish to give an ac*count*, or theory, of how agents, at least, are "substantially free to choose" (1969a, 84).

Simply put, I am against any notion of "theory hope" (theory is not possible, as de Man suggests, except as the theory of its own impossibility [hence, negative theory]) and I am against any notion of "humanism" (which is not possible, as Deleuze and Guattari have suggested, unless it is the result of repression [1983, 26]).

As I stated earlier, I am a nonhumanist. As Roquentin in *Nausea* says: "I don't want to be integrated, I don't want my good red blood to go and fatten this lymphatic beast: I will not be fool enough to call myself 'anti-humanist[.]' I am not a humanist, that's all there is to it" (Sartre 1959, 163).

As an aside, by now, it should be unclearly clear, that I am not a part, nor want to be a part, of not only humanism or antihumanism but also of any "epistemic court" or "corporate *we*" or Symbolic. Like Foucault,

> I do not [for the most part] appeal to any "we"—to any of those "we" 's whose consensus, whose values, whose traditions constitute the framework for a thought and define the conditions in which it can be validated. But the problem is, precisely, to decide if it is actually suitable to place [my*selphs*] within a "we" in order to assert the principles [I] recognize and the values [I] accept; or if it is not, rather, necessary to make the future formation of a "we" possible, by elaborating the question [as I have attempted here]. (1984, 385; cf. Burke's notion of "corporate we's," 1984, 264)

As another aside, speaking of questions, I hope, dear reader, that you have not forgotten my question concerning Who is better at recognizing what "we" are *doing* as historians and historiographers? For I am now rapidly approaching it, that is, winding down, in my search for an answer and my ruminations at answering it.

Against theory: What I have in mind, for all of us now, then, is de Man's brilliant argument—but which is *not* an argument, but a brilliant redescription—in his article "The Resistance to Theory."

I am (yes, hyperbolically) suggesting that "his argument" is *not an argument*, first, because for me it comes less from de Man and more from language itself. (But a caveat, for this is not a structuralist view of *langue*, with a transcendental signifier, speaking to us. [As a poststructuralist and *more so* a postmodernist, I will have nothing to do with that onto-theological, antihumanist position.] This preference of mine, this point of resistance, to be sure, pivots on a Nietzschean turn. Therefore, I would say that de Man merely overhears [as Lyotard does himself] the very perverseness/fickelness of language it*selphs*, without hypostasizing language it*selphs*, via an onto-theological twist. For de Man, as for me, there is only a perpetual demystification in language, whether the so-called "ordinary" or "literary" (see de Man 1983).

I am (hyperbolically) suggesting that "his argument" is *not an argument*, second, because for me argumentation is a humanist (man-measure) concept, to which, for ethical-micropolitical reasons, I (and de Man) can give little value! I am well aware, my dear reader, that the statement "I give little value" might appear as a humanist "author(izing)" statement. However, as de Man says elsewhere: "[It is] Rhetoric [that] suspends logic [and logician, and grammar ("B" or otherwise "Z") and grammarian] and opens up vertiginous possibilities of referential aberration" (1979, 10; cf. 1986, 12–15). And it is these "vertiginous possibilities of referential aberration" that I am after. In writing *against* The History of Rhetorik! At bottomless, then, the "I" is not the *cause* of speech, or language having been spoken, but only the very *effect* of language. (De Man has worked out this metaleptic argument, with the help of Nietzsche, in 1979, chs. 4, 5 [esp. 107], 6, 8; see Nietzsche 1966, part 1, sec. 15–19; part 2, sec. 34.)[9]

Now let us together go directly to the title of the de Man book and article (1986), which has possibly an implied ellipsis in it. Instead of being singularly read as "The Resistance . . . to Theory," it can also be read as "The Resistance *of Language* to Theory." (Langauge/*logos* resists being de[con]fined, being totalized, being placed [remember KB] in a synecdoche.) Now, whereas Fish is working out of more a quasi-humanist position, de Man is not. Whereas Fish wishes to make "choices" and give an ac*count* of how those choices are, or might be, made, say, via interpretive communities—just as Aristotle, via the *topoi*/enthymeme, and KB, via the pentadic ratios and paradox of substance, similarly wish—de Man, on the other hand, uncovers how language (it*selphs*) perversely resists such thinking, uncovers how language perversely and perpetually demystifies. Instead of giving an account of how meaning is made, de Man uncovers in language, more specifically, how language voids, rather than affirms, its supposed categories (cf. 10). One such category is "man [*sic*] himself." That is, humanism and its attendant concept of "choice." (Now we see him or her or it, and then we do not. *Fort/da*! *Fort/da*!) It is that way with language and its aberrations, once we have gone together through the fantasy!

Which gets me more specifically, now, to my nonhumanist position and how such a position not only differs from the humanist and antihumanist but also how the nonhumanist (sub/versive) position resists and disrupts traditional-realist and revisionary modernist ways of *doing history*—both of which need to keep rhetoric (political discourse) separate from poetics (aesthetic discourse). Chaim Perelman (1973) is one of those who would separate a rhetoric of tropes ("stylistic") from a rhetoric of persuasion. There are others, for example, George Kennedy (1980a) and Brian Vickers (1990).[10] Such a separation, I would maintain, however, is fundamentally impossible. Tropes are not something that can be removed from language. Speaking from Nietzsche's "Truth and Lying," de Man says: "Tropes are not understood aesthetically, as ornament, nor are they understood semantically as a figurative meaning that derives from literal, proper denomination. Rather, the reverse is the case. [Here de Man engages in another metalepsis.] The trope is not a derived, marginal, or aberrant form of language but the linguistic paradigm par excellence" (1979, 105). There is no escape from deception (*apate*).

The poetic, or literariness, is often denied any value primarily because it is seen, de Man says, "as a denial of the reality principle in the name of absolute fiction [or play], and for reasons that are said to be ethically and politically shameful" (1986, 10). De Man and other poststructuralists and postmodernists (as well as KB) are often attacked from the "left" because they favor aesthetic over practical discourse (though, to be sure, not a monistic "aesthetic ideology"); they, in a manner of speaking, favor Kant's third critique (judgment, aesthetics, the beautiful) over the first and second critiques (respectively, the pure and true and the practical and good.) It is not difficult to understand why postmodernists, such as my*selphs* favor the third critique; for it is the one, among the three, that finally makes for the impossibility of totality, or linkage, or grand narratives (see Lyotard 1988, 130–35); it is the one, instead, that gives us radical heterogeneity. (The aesthetic/art is, as KB says, "antinomian" [1968, viii].)[11] In the midst of this play, what "is not being denied," however, is "the referential function of language." De Man continues,

> What is in question is its authority [just as the semi-authority of Kant's first critique is open to question] as a model for natural or phenomenal cognition. Literature is fiction not because it somehow refuses to acknowledge "reality," but because it is not *a priori* certain that language functions according to principles which are those, or which are like those, of the phenomenal world. It is therefore not *a priori* certain that literature is a reliable source of information about anything but its own language. (1986, 11)

And then, the conclusion of this kind of thinking—about ordinary/practical versus aesthetic language—hits home in the name of "ideology." De Man continues: "What we call ideology is precisely the confusion of linguistic with natural reality, of reference with phenomenalism. It follows that, more than any other mode of inquiry, including economics, the linguistics of literariness is a powerful and indispensable tool in the unmasking of ideological aberrations as well as a determining factor in accounting for their occurrence" (11). This latter statement is fundamental because it suggests how language (which *is* ideology) constantly demystifies and debunks all past and future sentences or utterances, all ways of doing history and ac*count*ing for and of ways. (Language even debunks this my sentence/utterance-cum-theatricks as commentary about the contents of this my statement *being fundamental*. And *ad infinitum*.) About those socialist historians who would attack poststructuralists or postmodernists who allegedly are not "committed" to the struggle, de Man says: "Those who reproach literary theory for being oblivious to social and historical (that is to say ideological) reality are merely stating their fear as having their own ideological mystifications exposed by the tool they are trying to discredit. They are, in short, very poor readers of Marx's *German Ideology*" (1986, 11).

Therefore, where are we now in relation to *doing history*? Whereas traditonalists-realists are pre-ideological in their thinking, revisionary-modernists are working from the very idea of ideology, but are not willing to commit themselves to the mis/understanding that ideology is all there is. Any why? Because they envision a goal (e.g., a classless society and an economically and legally just society) and, more important, because they envision this goal by way of a strategic grand narrative of emancipation. (I think that this statement about them is generally true, with of course some exceptions.) The bottomless line here is that they *still hold out for* stripping away ideology so as to get to truth without lying, in both a moral and extra-moral sense. They still hold out nostalgically for a just, nonideological social relationship. And these ends are to be realized by virtue of a humanist "choice" or by virtue of dialectical/historical (structuralist) materialism. My sense, at least, among those who write revisionary (social-epistemic) history, is that they believe that men and women are subjects that can, indeed, *make and do history*. (I say all this about the revisionists, and especially those who would, apparently to the contrary, say that all there is, is ideology, because these radical revisionists, nonetheless, suffer from a nostalgia of and for the great, good place. I think that this nostalgia is part and parcel of the *topoi* and *tropoi* of Marxisms or, more politely put, of American [also feminist] socialism.)

If the sub/versive, nonhumanist position is to take both the traditionalists and revisionists through the fantasy (as I have suggested), this voyage, then, must also be nomadic, that is, without destination. (Yes, indeed, I am dealing [in] a paradox.) My, at times, strong sense of language and, consequently, my extreme sense of *doing history* is that we are together along for the ride. I have said this better before: "When I write, I try to maintain a sense of 'discovery,' of being on the joyful Road to Serrendip; or to maintain a sophistic sense of the motion of the whole. I don't have to resolve any of these issues that I juggle because so many of my other colleagues will resolve them" (Octalog 27). It will be my job, therefore, only to re/problematize them.

"My" sense, moreover, is that *history is not human*. (This position of mine can be confused with Walter Benjamin's or other similar thinkers; it, however, should not be. By now, it should be unclearly clear that I am not a Marxist-onto-(judeo)-theologian. [See de Man 1986, 92–96.]) My sense of doing history—specifically, writing hysteries of rhetorics—is that I must write *as if* there were no genres at all. Or that in the medusian face of genres, I must rapidly switch genres (as a schizo switches codes) so quickly that the many v(o)ices might be heard. (M. M. Bakhtin moved in this direction, but I will leave him to others and besides I wish a still more radical position, which I perform in my article in this collection.)

If we are together along for the ride, who/what is to protect us? (Oh, how we desire a Master!) And, of course, there is *reason* to be afraid. But, my dear reader, follow this: In reading Zizek, I discovered his remembrance of what Ernesto Laclau in a private conversation told him about language. Zizek recalls: "It is not only Stalinism which is a linguistic phenomenon, but language itself which is a Stalinist phenomenon" (1989, 174). I believe this assessment is, indeed, the case. But language is not only a Stalinist phenomenon, for I take solace in what Foucault says as well about "counter-memory" and "transgression" in language:

> The philosopher [for me, a Stalinist personification of one condition of the possibility of language] is aware that "we are not everything"; he learns as well that even the philosopher does not inhabit the whole of his language like a secret and perfectly fluent god. Next to himself, he discovers the existence of another language [the "counter-memory"] that also speaks and that he is unable to dominate, one that strives, fails, and falls silent and that he cannot manipulate, the language he spoke at one time and that has now separated itself from him, now gravitating in a space increasingly silent. (1977, 41–42)

To these two perspectives, I would add, now, that I have been after a way of *doing history* as a way of *desiring desire*. Which is a way of saying that I would not desire One, nor Two (i.e., Many), but Some (radical) More. I would desire (unending) catachresis, which is the trope of desire. (There is no way finally to strip away ideology-literariness.) I would, as a hysteric *and* a schizo, therefore, desire possibilisms (cf. Zizek 1989, 174). Which again is a way of saying that I would desire language, which is here the very loci of the desire of desire. *Language*. (Not just systematic *la langue* or the individual speech event *le parole*, but more so Lacanian *lalangue* (babel/babble, Babelonianisms, barbarianisms). *Language*. Which is both destroyer and protector (de[con]structor), especially when we (or some would-be totalizers) try to control or master it. But which *is* "revolutionary in its [very] essence" (Deleuze and Guattari, 1983, 116).[12]

I will end this section with a quote from Lyotard, who speaks of the problem of language and the problem of humanism and suggests a reconception of *doing history* (desiring desire) along the lines that I (will) have been variously suggesting. Lyotard says:

> It is not the people that is fickle, but "language." . . . Maybe prose is impossible. It is tempted on one side by despotism [hypotaxis]

> and on the other by anarchy [parataxis]. It succumbs to the seduction of the former by turning itself into the genre of all genres (the prose of the Popular Empire) and to the seduction of the latter by trying to be no more than an unregulated assemblage of all phrases (the vagabond's prose). . . . But the unity of genres is impossible, as is their zero degree. Prose can only be their multitude and the multitude of their differends [i.e., their phrases in dispute across incommensurable genres]. (1988, 158)

Yes, indeed, I accept this as a limited proper critique of even my own *vagabond prose*, but the larger picture here (as is suggested in Papa [especially 1957, 164–89] and in de Man and in Foucault, though all differently) is of the importance and inevitability of all our cacophonous voices *doing histories*.

My *Program* is to a/void a pogrom and thereby is to discover systemic (accountable) and nonsystemic (nonaccountable) places for all of us. In *language* we are all intermittently a (scape)goat. Language is/has a *double effect*, if not also a *triple effect*. It is not, then, a necessity any longer—as Puritans did in their sermons—of simply separating *sheep* from *goats*, or simply separating *sheep* from *goats* and dancing *satyrs*. So as to make way for *The* (One, True, and Catholic) History of Rhetorik.

Can you, dear reader, accept this (perverse) position? Can you be so tolerant? (I want to believe that you can, especially if you are still at this late point reading me.)

Finally, beginningly?, WE must admit that there is no "them" and "us"; we must avoid being reactionary while still being able to paratheorize our differences. (Perhaps this is e/utopic!) In any case, . . .

If *The* History of Rhetoric is *The* History of Oppression (repression and suppression of these *V*arious *V*[o]ices), as I have suggested that it is, then, when "I" write, I must dig up its roots (tear out from the substantive soil its essence) so as to make way also for rhizomatic nomads and vagabonds, that is, to make way as well for the infinite variety of hysteries of rhetorics. (Why have a garden with only one or two varieties planted in it!) I have to make way for what Foucault has called the "counter-memory," which *is nonhumanistic*, or *literary*, and which had been systematically silenced from Plato to Nietzsche (see Foucault 1977, 29–52; and especially 1973, 300).

It is less a matter of *writing* such hysteries than it is of *uncovering* them. As I say previously in this volume, "There are hysteries *in* rhetorik rather than The history *of* rhetorik."

A question concerning the question of "better": Where are we now in dis/respect to my question? I am now able to say (once again, but with more fodder since "maybe" without father [but I do hope that I have not moved from *dad* to worst! (it is better to have a bad pun than no fun at all!)]) that the argument based on self-consciousness—that is, based on a self-awareness of how we are all ideologically enveloped—does *not* necessarily make for *a better standpoint* from which to mis/recognize what "we" and/or I am *doing* as historians and historiographers of rhetoric. (Most will say: How disconcerting!)

Therefore, what is it specifically that I believe concerning this question of "better"? (I have taken us through a maze—so to speak, "through the fantasy"—and will leave us therein. Drifting. No Ariadne's thread will be proffered or discovered here.) The question of "better" is a question of critique, which I will have had nothing to do with. (My question has been a pretext.) I borrow some words again from Lyotard: "Where do you criticize from? Don't you see that criticizing is still knowing, knowing better: That the critical relation still falls within the sphere of knowledge, of 'realization' and thus of the assumption of power? *Critique must be drifted out of. Better still: Drifting is in itself the end of all critique*" (1984a, 13; Lyotard's emphasis; cf. Rorty 1989, 91).

Of course, for those who wish to critique, I am nothing but a "neoconservative," as Habermas would say (and why? because he believes in the speculative unity of all knowledge and, hence, in emancipation, as dreamed of by the Enlightenment). My response, however, is that these people (i.e., the revisionists-modernists) critique society when they write their histories of rhetoric for the sole purpose (though hidden . . . they do it and don't know they do it) of *punishing*. In their attempts to redeem the victims/vanquished of history, they are into victimage with a vengeance! (How strange for him to make such a statement, some will say of me. And then, how can this be so? they will ask.) This statement of mine is thoroughly Nietzschean. (Forgive them *lalangue*, for they know not what they do.) I could cite passages from *Thus Spake Zarathustra* and *The Genealogy of Morals*, but I wish to be perverse and quote a "social critic" as having said it. In "negotiating with unacknowledged masculinism," Spivak tells her colleagues: "If we do not take the time to understand . . . our zeal to be 'political,' then I fear we act out the kind of play that Nietzsche figured out in *The Genealogy of Morals*: in the interest of giving an alibi to his desire to punish, which is written into his way of being, in other words in the interest of a survival game, man [*sic*] produces an alibi which is called justice" (1989a, 217). Or again Lyotard says:

> Where does the [reformist's] power over the criticized come from: he knows better? he is the teacher, the educator? he is therefore universality, the University, the State, the City, bending over childhood, nature, singularity, shadiness, to reclaim them? The confessor and God helping the sinner save his soul? This benign reformism is wholly compatible with the preservation of the authoritarian relationship. (1984a, 13)

I am *against* critique not only in the sense of "contra to" but also "along side." Though I find fault with social critique as revisionary-modernist historiography, I, nonetheless, stand with these historians. "Bob" Scott once said publicly that "Victor Vitanza needs traditional history." I agree and, therefore, now more fully say: I need *The* History of Rhetorik in dis/order *to critique* it. And I need revisionary history in dis/order *to drift* out of it. (This is my duplicity, my duplicitousness, the loci of my belatedness [Papa] and of my mis/recognition and various insights [de Man]. " 'My' secular prayer" is *Nes/Yo* [see Burke 1984, 325–26].) My attitude is "a Babel of voices" (Burke 1957, 172).

But, dear readers, some of you—the junior logicians of you—will still say that I am contradicting myself by "critiquing" both tradition and revisionary historians. And that by "critiquing" I am "punishing." Moreover, a revisonary historian will again say to me that I am "baiting" (red-baiting?) him and his fellow historians, who want social justice. To the general group, I would say that Nietzsche never said that we could not say "No." In fact, he constantly said "No" to all those who would "know" by way of negation itself. In other words, by saying "No" he was saying "No" to negation itself; he was, in another word, *de*negating negation (see *On the Genealogy of Morals*, 1969; cf. Deleuze 1983). To the specific revisionary historian, I would say that I refuse to join the party so that I might be able to discuss your project on more familial grounds. Membership is too, too expensive.

Cutting(s) Loose

I no longer believe in the two major myths, or grand narratives—(1) that which speaks of the liberation of humanity (it is political, militant, and reactivist) and (2) that which speaks of the speculative unity of all knowledge (it values totality). (See Lyotard 1984b.) This grand narrative (strategic or otherwise) is founded on the necessity of and for victimage and mortification.

It follows then: I no longer believe in *The* History of Rhetorik. I have an incredulity toward this grand narrative. I have an incredulity toward any talk about "the social bond" or, as Burke talks about it, "corporate we's" (1984, 265). I, instead, have credulity in a "molecular agglomerate" (Deleuze and Guattari) and "paratactic aggregates" (Feyerabend), as forms of resistance and disruption. (Against Kapitalist, Marxists, bourgeois liberal, and Feminist histories of rhetoric.) And as a means of "going through the fantasy."

Which I would realize, in writing hysteries of rhetorics, in three ways: (1) mis-representative an*ti*dotes, (2) dissoi-*para*logoi, and (3) thea-*tricks*. (The first two, I have already discussed at length [1987a].)

The *first* wages perpetual war (agonistics, but without a "winner" as in Nietzsche's "Homer's Contest," 1984) against "representative anecdotes" (Burke 1969a) or against grand narratives (Habermas 1979). Whereas Jameson says "Always historicize!" (1981, 9), I say "Always hysterize!" (1990).

The *second* (a uniting of sophistic *dissoi logoi* and paralogy) wages perpetual war against dialectic (of any kind), against didactic, and against *dissoi-logoi* by moving from one and two to an explosion of "some more" (excess, to an "aesthetics of excess" [see Weiss; cf. Vitanza 1991b; 1993a; 1993c]). As Foucault says, "knowledge is not made for understanding; it is made for cutting" up (1977, 154).

The *third* (based in pragmatics) wages perpetual war against *The* Truth and against Author/ity. Whereas *sentences* deal in truth claims and whereas *utterances* (speech acts) deal in authorial-performatives, theatricks (*theos*-tricks, "sounddance," farce) wage perpetual-pagan war (on sentences and utterances) through sophistic trickery and ruse after ruse. (This view of theatricks has its re/origin in Joyce's *Finnigans Wake*, in Lyotard's "paganism" [Lyotard and Thebaud *Just Gaming*, 1985], and in Feyerabend's pedagogy-as-a-theatre-of-ideas [*Against Method*, 1988]. Feyerabend writes: "My intellectualism told me that problems had to be solved by thought. My dramatic propensities made me think that hamming it up was better than going through an abstract argument" (288).

With these three paratropes, therefore, I am my own Dada/ist. I am who I ham. And I ham who I am. (I h/am, among the various "I's," [cum-schizo "they's"] a Zuni clown.) The primary language game, then, not being the language game of knowledge, *is* the language game of avant-garde art. The language game of the future (*post*) anterior (*modo*). (See Lyotard 1984b, 81. And curiously enough, see KB's "Bohemianism; or Aestheticism" in 1968, 110–22. Papa writes: "a system of aesthetics subsumes a system of politics" [113].)

And all this, too, will have perpetually been done! But only—I would insist—by perpetually *de*coding. An hysterian and a schizo—after all is said and un/done—know that s/he *can* (Finnigans) wake up from the nightmare of history and, therefore, desire a desire to trotsky (*farsycally* dance) through it.

Having cut loose, in these various (perhaps, Ill-) manners, I would, however, towards a better life, take care not to be cum "the victim of my attitudes, or a victim of vigesimation" (Papa 1966b, 215). I would laugh not only a "second time" (218) but also "some more."

So . . . this is where I will have been! And "You! *hypocrite lecteur!—mon semblable,—mon hystérique*!" How would you presume to mis/recognize?

Notes

1. Shall I give the reader a further tip on, or instructions in, how to read this afterword? Or perhaps better put, should I give the reader a preface to the afterword? (Hardly!) And yet, it would be immensely helpful to mis/understand that this entire article is a pastiche (while waiting to be a parody) of one of the finest books on both Kenneth Burke and Paul de Man that I have yet to read, Frank Lentricchia's *Criticism and Social Change* (1983). It is "one of the finest books" for many (perverse) reasons. I will give no account here of this my assessment, only this-which-is-not-a-preface-to-a-afterword itself as testament.

Let it suffice here to say, then, that if the reader (or a reviewer) wishes a guide, s/he might read this afterword semiotically a/cross Lentricchia's book. Virtually everything from the title of this afterword—which is no mere *single* literary allusion—to this first endnote has its counter/part in Lentricchia's book. I am not suggesting, however, that I am rewriting Lentricchia's book, merely favoring de Man over Burke. If anything, I am trying to find a balance for the two, perhaps via a comic corrective. (My sense is that Lentricchia, more than not, employs de Man as a strawman, or as a negative foil, to enhance KB.) My strategy is, herein, to expel (but preserve) Papa KB. Hence, the headnote from Kristeva: "I spit *myself* out, I abject *myself* within the same motion through which 'I' claim to establish *myself*." This strategy, no doubt, will be mis/recognized by readers and reviewers. It will be seen merely as "slaying the father" or as the "anxiety of influence" or whatever. So be these mis/recognitions. (In fact, the whole paraconcept of "mis/recognition" will be misrecognized as it often is by junior logicians.)

Literary allusions? Not only am I attempting to find a balance between de Man and Burke (via a comic corrective), but I am also trying to find a balance between traditional and revisionary historians (via a sub/versive corrective). It is now the revisionaries that I am most concerned about. Prufrock says: "In a minute there is time / For decisions and revisions which a minute will reverse." I would, as KB would, take this (Prufrock's) hypochrondriac-paralytic-hysterical position and turn it to the good. (KB is notorious for this strategy. See 1966b and 1968, 107–22; cf. Vitanza 1990.) I would attempt to turn it "to the good" especially in the opening pages but in general throughout. (As KB asks rhetorically: "[Might] indolence, under certain conditions, be symptomatic of a virtue in the indolent?" Also, "A society is sound only if it can prosper on its vices, since virtues are by very definition rare and exceptional" [1968, 112, 114].) Obviously, my use of Prufrock here will upset many revisionary-modernist-leftist historians, who would, instead, wish to point to my *dissoi* para*logoi* writing as the very epitome of Prufrockian thinking and non (political) acting. And as the very epitome of personal and social paralysis! Let them have their dis/placements and mis/recognitions. They, after all is said and undone, need their defenses as we here "go through the fantasy."

This latter phrase ("go through the fantasy") is Lacanian (see 1978, chs. 6 and 7) and plays an important part in my thinking/writing/inviting in this afterword. (The paraconcept is best explained by Zizek (1989), but it simply-grossly means a movement toward a further *real*ization that that which "we" desire [a great, good place, or whatever] can*not* be represented in the Symbolic and, even worse, every attempt to *real*ize our desires [such desires] has ended in great political catastrophes. What we [them or us] can get is only a stand-in, or little object *a*[*utre*].)

My sense of the revisionary (paradoxically modernist-leftist) historians of rhetoric is that they desire to seize the fantasy of real/ity and, therefore, have little suspicion about what they themselves do when they light out to *re*map/*re*code the political *terr*itory. (Hence, I wear a satyr's [or fool's] costume when I think/write/invite/incite!) I would have the revisionaries-modernists-leftists, therefore, engage in numerous revisions (perhaps perpetual demystifications, or "goings through the fantasy") and attempt to find both strength *and* action in such thinking/writing. I do not mind "*Waiting For Lefty*" (N. O. Brown 1974, 51).

Literary allusions? Dear reader, if you would wish to know *some more* about reading this afterword, then, study and ruminate on "III: An Interlude of Farce" in N. O. Brown 1974, 41–63. It is t/here that you might find what I am about, specifically, in relation to The Feast of Fools and the Zuni Clowns, and in relation to Hegel and Marx, Vico and Joyce, tragedy and farce, power and impotence-cum-parapower. As Brown says: "Farce is the mode of demystification/the tragic mode remystifies" [55]).

Finally, I wish to acknowledge that much of what I say (in this afterword) has been reaped from my recent reading of Zizek's *The Sublime Object of Ideology* (1989), which I recommend to my colleagues.

2. I learned this "answer/petition" from Papa KB, who signs his letters "da/nyet." Also see his discussion of yes/no/maybe in 1957, 84.

3. Feyerabend would add: "Theories become clear and 'reasonable' only *after* incoherent parts of them have been used for a long time. Such unreasonable, nonsensical, unmethodical foreplay thus turns out to be an unavoidable precondition of clarity and of empirical success. . . . when we attempt to describe and to understand developments of this kind in a general way, we are, of course, obliged to appeal to the existing forms of speech which do not take them into account and which must be distorted, misused, beaten into new patterns in order to fit unforseen situations (without a constant misuse of language there can not be any discovery, any progress)" (1988, 18; Feyerabend's emphasis).

4. I say this about the inevitability of essence—which is a new "saying" for me—while I am well aware (as I state above) that essentialism is extremely dangerous. (I have read, thanks to Crowley, Fuss's *Essentially Speaking* [1989].) Why dangerous? The best example that comes to mind is KB's discussion of how Hitler "essentialized his enemy [the Jews]" (1957, 167). Need I say that essentialism is a double-edged sword? Those who employ it, strategic or otherwise, ought to be extremely careful.

I would have another idea for essence and that is Deleuze and Guattari's idea of "desire," which is not defined (i.e., delimited or contained by way of a subjectivity based on a model of lack) but is free-flowing. Deleuze and Guattari say: "Desire is revolutionary in its essence" (1983, 116). And even better, desire is without a subject (i.e., a repressed agent, or Jew). Where there is a subject/agent, there is repression (26). And so for what other reason am I interested in desire as essence? Desire produces (i.e., desiring machines produce) hysteries of rhetorics without (predicated, scenic) subjects. It is better viewed, however, as a view of the subject-less (non-predicated, non-scenic) subject of Freud's Dora (Dora's Freud?) or Antonin Artaud, who are resistant to and disruptive of history and, therefore, represent hystery. They are non-predicated [non-scenic] because they are not "subjects" either *of* or *to* daddy-mama's history. They resist, in another word, being Oedipalized. Or Marxized.

5. The left's necessity to exclude: If it be lost on you, dear reader, the a/moral is that any and every attempt to displace or deflect what we do not wish to ac*count* for as being part of our humanity, our history (whether it be *our defecation* [displaced in the form of our self-deification?] or whether it be an intestine [like the Gnostic's God] or the irrational or the nonrational [like the logician's God] or the unconscious [like the theologian's God] or *la boheme* [like Marx's *proletariat*]) . . . the moral is that any and every attempt at this displacement dooms all of us to our collective destruction. (Lefists, beware!)

Our waste or our body or etc. only has a way of returning, and with a vengence, as the return of the eternally repressed. (See Kundera 1987, part 6.) You see, dear reader, We would (wish) not (to) be human beings! It is because, as KB says, we human beings are, yes, "rotten with perfection."

A special note: Much of what I say in this paragraph may appear to be anachronistic since, as we have been repeatedly told, the wall has come down and Marx and communism are dead. When I refer to Marxists, I am not referring to the Soviet version; I am referring to all of us who read Marx and those of us who, while reading Marx, fantasize about a utopian society.

6. That "there is no social relationship" here means no political relationship. This idea is anti/fundamental to Lacanian thinking (see Zizek 1989). I agree with Nietzsche and Deleuze and Guattari, however, that there is only the social and desire, but that this social is situated in each person and that it is non-consubstantial (see 1983, 26–29). In threes, this would mean, first, there is no individual, second, no social, and "some more," only the social in the individual. Hence, the hysteric and schizo are "my" models for rhetors best suited for paraethical resistance and disruption I further develop this notion, in dis/respect to writing histories of rhetoric, in the last essay of this collection.

7. Speaking of hysteria as a genre that would be hysteries, I some time ago found and then "forgot" this passage in Papa KB's *Rhetoric*: "We would also include a 'rhetoric of hysteria.' For there too are expressions which are *addressed*—and we confront an ultimate irony, in glimpsing how even a catatonic lapse into sheer automatism, beyond the reach of all normally linguistic communication, is in its origins communicative, addressed, though it be a paralogical appeal-that-ends-all appeals" (1969b, 39; Burke's emphasis).

8. Breaking the vessel: I would let the storm crack open the synecdoche (the "alembic") and let its contents spill forth, not beyond in even cause-effect narrative streams, but in hysterical, schizo-stuttered spittings and splashings.

When writing histories/hysteries of rhetorics, I-cum-"their" would have, as Deleuze and Guattari characterize the schizo-process, "a stream of words that do not let themselves be coded, a libido that is too fluid, too viscous: a violence against syntax, a concerted destruction of the signifier, non-sense erected as a flow, polyvocity that returns to haunt all relations" (1983, 133). Oh, "their" gods, what a scandal!

I, too, like my leftist colleagues would, therefore, have a containerless, classless society! Unlike my colleagues, however, I would have radical nomadic mutiplicities.

I would favor, in a manner of speaking and writing hysteries of rhetorics, a "nomadic science" (or paragrammatic science) over a "state science" (grammatical science). Following this distinction made by Deleuze and Guattari, I would favor a radical nomadic science of "becoming, heterogeneity, infinitesimal, passage to the limit, continuous variation" (1987, 363). I would favor such radicalities, which are now *attitudes (towards history) that cannot be accounted for* in any noetic pentad or hexad, or any set of ratios. (Dear Burkeans, I am *not* speaking, here, of "comic correctives" [1984, 166–75], though you must mis/recognize what I say as such!)

I would favor such radicalities over state science of containment, which "subordinate hydraulic force to conduits, pipes, embankments, which prevent turbulence, which constrain movement to go from one point to another, and space itself to be striated and measured, which makes the fluid depend on the solid, and flows proceed by parallel, laminar layers" (Deleuze and Guattari 1987, 363; cf. 1983, 42). What I desire for *The* History of Rhetoric, then, is the liberation of its hydraulic forces. What I desire, when everything is said and undone, is to let its desire flow freely, which would wreck the system, crack it open, burst out, and let spill, with contents moving into dispersion, into diaspora without amphora. These would be hysteries without (Hegelian, Kojevian, Master/Slave) ends.

9. Spivak, to the contrary, would see value in "argumentation" as a humanist (man-measure) concept, if for no other reasons, than for the "strategic-essentialist" (necessary for her) motive of *doing politics*, which does not, at all, circumvent the problem of having to deal with the Aristotelian tradition and with commonplace arguments that dis-enable while they lead us to believe the opposite. Spivak is well aware of this problem and thus establishes a rationale for having to negotiate with masculine "narratives of violence." Moreover, Spivak (1989a) is, nonetheless, a strategic Nietzschean.

10. A famous argument on the relationship between poetics/aesthetics and rhetoric/oratory can be found between KB and Wilbur Samuel Howell (*Quarterly Journal of Speech* 62 [1976]: 62–77). It is a wonderful exchange for many reasons, one being how they, yes, speak at cross-purposes. (KB's position on aesthetics and oratory and politics is developed early in *Counter-Statement* [1968].)

11. I am well aware, however, that there is a difference here between KB and de Man, as identified by Lentricchia. My sense, however—and it is only "my sense"—is that de Man was working in the same direction. The proximity between KB and de Man in relation to the dangers ("double effect") of language is discussed, by way of Lentricchia, in the next note.

12. I would like to point to what are some of the most significant passages/concepts and central figure (Babel) in KB's work, which Lentricchia has selected and commented on. The passages and concepts are very much in line with "my" discussion of *language as both protector and destroyer*. First, Lentricchia recalls two important concepts: "*Transformation* and *identification* are modes of rhetoric's [language's, the *logos*'] deepest *desire*: to move from 'the state of Babel, after the Fall,' toward another 'state'—political state and 'state' of language—of perfect understanding and community, that recovery of paradise in which rhetoric ceases to have an occupation" (1983, 148; my emphasis). This movement by virtue of transformation and identification can lead us all down the road to disaster. It is our collective impulse to perfect the idea of perfection; hence, we are all "rotten with perfection."

The question is, Is the rhetor either the good or the bad doctor? KB would answer *potentially both,* and we all have to be on guard as best as we can. Lentricchia writes: "The poet as medicine man, as political doctor: the diseases he would attend to infest the body politic; his medicine is a representation charged with power's purposiveness. To define representation in this way is to define it as rhetoric, and according to Burke aesthetic-rhetorical medicine has but two uses—it can be therapeutic or prophylactic" (1983, 155; see Burke 1957, 51–56).

But texts (literary, aesthetic, which is for Burke all texts and politics) are power effects and therefore are dangerous. Hitler's *Mein Kampf*, while it performed an act of power in that it attempted to control/unite the German people, it simultaneously fostered the conditions for another act of power, genocide. Many people, Lentricchia says, would not consider *Mein Kampf* as literature, because, well, it is not "humane"! Lentricchia, with KB, responds:

> Let us at least be shaken by Burke's subversion of the sentiment that literature is inherently humane. Literature is inherently nothing or it is inherently a body of rhetorical strategies waiting to be seized [dear reader, there is that word again, as in seizing the fantasy]. And anybody can seize them. Literature is not Keats. The literary is never only the elite canon of great books. . . . The literary is all around us, and it is always doing its work on us. . . . The knowledge that the literary is present power (in Burke's sense of 'present') cannot . . . free us from power, though that knowledge is somewhat salutary especially because modern literary theory has not much wanted to know about power. We need to know that what is therapeutic or prophylactic for some is poison for others; that the literary cannot free itself from this double effect; that it is always efficacious, one way or another; that as writers and teachers we dispense drugs every day. (1983, 157–58)

And now to Lentricchia's account of how KB himself *nods* in dis/respect to *the figure of Babel* (see, e.g., 1969b, 23). (The lesson is important for me as well; for I, too, employ this figure along with the Lacanian term *lalangue*.) Lentricchia writes:

> [Burke] has considered the idea, sometimes with horror, other times with pleasure. What I have not yet mentioned, however, is that the figure of Babel occurs centrally in his essay on Hitler [1957, 164–89], whom Burke finds offering the German people, as an alternative to the many-voiced confusion of their parliament (a "vocal diaspora"), his single, mastering voice and presence, a unifying center interchangeable with Munich. The figure of Babel is an awful point of convergence: Hitler not as exterior bad from which we can protect ourselves by proper cherishing of his negation, whoever or whatever that might be, but as figure himself of an ultimate impulse to essentialization inside any and all of our good angels. What has Burke found in Hitler if not a fun-house mirror reflection of tendencies within *his own theories of interpretation* [my emphasis]? Assuming that Burke was well aware of the repeated figurations of Babel in his own writings, it is something of an astonishment that he undertook the essay on *Mein Kampf* at all. Having once undertaken it, it is to his credit that he did not bury the "familiar" figure he encountered in Hitler's

book. Perhaps, then, there is yet another and finer quality of critical consciousness that this episode reveals: that finer quality, through its clarity, its accessibility, its refusal to revise its past, its refusal to pose as all-knowing, is nothing other than a quality that permits itself, the critical consciousness itself, *to be criticized*. . . . And perhaps that is the best one can give to one's students and readers: the means to resist oneself. (1983, 158–59)

CONTRIBUTORS
WORKS CITED
INDEX

CONTRIBUTORS

Janet M. Atwill has published articles on classical rhetoric and postmodern theory and is currently completing a book on rhetoric and humanism. She is an assistant professor of English at the University of Tennessee, where she teachers courses in the history and theory of rhetoric.

James A. Berlin is a professor of English at Purdue University, where he teaches courses in the theory and history of rhetoric. He is the author of *Writing Instruction in Ninteenth-Century American Colleges* and *Rhetoric and Reality: Writing Instruction in American Colleges, 1900–1985.* He has also edited, with Michael Vivion, *Cultural Studies in the English Classroom.*

William A. Covino teaches in the language, literacy, and rhetoric graduate program at the University of Illinois at Chicago, where he is a University Scholar and a Fellow in the Humanities Institute. His work includes *The Art of Wondering: A Revisionist Return to the History of Rhetoric* and *Forms of Wondering: A Dialogue on Writing, for Writers,* as well as a number of articles in journals and books. He is currently completing a study of the historical and conceptual relationships between magic and rhetoric.

Sharon Crowley is a professor of English at the University of Iowa, where she teaches rhetoric. She is the author of *The Methodical Memory: Invention in Current-Traditional Rhetoric,* along with numerous other works in the history of rhetoric and composition studies.

Hans Kellner is a professor of English and teaches in the Graduate Program in Rhetoric/Composition/Criticism at the University of Texas at Arlington. A historian by training, Kellner has written extensively on the rhetoric of historical discourse and theories of literature and rhetoric. Besides his book *Language and Historical Representation: Getting the Story Crooked,* Kellner has published many essays, including recently: "Beautifying the Nightmare: The Aesthetics of Postmodern History" (*Strategies: A Journal of Theory, Culture, and Politics,* 1991); "Hayden White and the Kantian Discourse: Tropology, Narrative, Freedom," in *The Philosophy of Discourse: The Rhetorical Turn in Twentieth-Century Thought*, edited by C. Sills and G. H. Jensen (1992).

John Poulakos is an associate professor of rhetoric at the University of Pittsburgh. He has published widely in rhetorical theory, the history of rhetoric, and the relationship of philosophy and rhetoric. He is in the process of completing a book on sophistical rhetoric and its early receptions.

Takis Poulakos is an assistant professor of rhetoric at the University of Iowa. He is the editor of *Rethinking the History of Rhetoric* and the author of *A Rhetoric for the Polis* (forthcoming). His work on classical rhetoric appears in numerous journals.

John Schilb teaches in the Department of English at the University of Maryland, College Park. His main scholarly interest is relations between composition/rhetorical theory and literary theory. He has coedited two anthologies on this subject, *Contending with Words: Composition and Rhetoric in a Postmodern Age* and *Writing Theory and Critical Theory.* He is currently writing a book entitled *Reading and Writing Between the Lines: Composition Theory and Literary Theory.*

Jane Sutton is an associate professor in the Department of Speech Communication at Penn State University, York. She has presented scholarly papers at conferences including the International Society for the History of Rhetoric and has published articles in the history of rhetoric on such themes as the conflict between rhetoric and philosophy and the presence/absence of woman in rhetorical theory. She is currently working on a book on the birth and death of rhetoric from the origins of democracy in the fifth century B.C. to its demise in late nineteenth-century culture.

Victor J. Vitanza is an associate professor of English at the University of Texas, Arlington, where he teaches courses in literature and composition and in rhetorical and critical theory. He is the founding editor of *PRE/TEXT: A Journal of Rhetorical Theory* and is the director of the Center for Rhetorical and Critical Theory. His work has appeared in numerous journals and books. His recent work includes an edited book *PRE/TEXT: The First Decade* (1993). He is currently completing a book tentatively titled *Negation, Subjectivity, and the History of Rhetoric.*

Kathleen Ethel Welch, an associate professor of English at the University of Oklahoma, is the author of *The Contemporary Reception of Classical Rhetoric* and articles in *College Composition and Communication*, *Written Communication*, *Rhetoric Review*, *The Journal of Advanced Composition*, *Rhetoric Society Quarterly*, and chapter in edited volumes. Her publications and teaching focus on histories and theories of rhetoric and composition, particularly modern constructions of classical rhetoric. She is the president of the Rhetoric Society of America and president of the Coalition of Women Scholars in the History of Rhetoric and Composition.

Lynn Worsham is an assistant professor of English at the University of Wisconsin, Milwaukee, where she is the coordinator of graduate studies in rhetoric and composition. Her teaching and research seek to cross such categories as feminist theory, critical theory, and contemporary rhetoric to consider the intimacy of body and language. Her recent articles on this preoccupation appear in *PRE/TEXT*, *Discourse*, and *Rhetoric Society Quarterly*.

WORKS CITED

Adams, John Quincy. 1810. *Lectures on Rhetoric and Oratory*. Cambridge: Harvard University Press.

Adorno, Theodor W. 1974. *Minima Moralia*, translated by E. F. N. Jephcott. London: NLB.

———. 1987. *Negative Dialectics*. N.Y.: Continuum.

Agrippa, Henry Cornelius. 1651. *Three Books of Occult Philosophy*, translated by J. F. London: Gregory Moule.

———. 1970. *Opera*. 2 vols. N.Y.: Georg Olms Verlag.

———. 1974. *Of the Vanitie and Uncertaintie of Artes and Sciences*, translated by James Sanford and edited by Catherine M. Dunn. Northridge: California State University.

———. 1980. *Female Pre-Eminence, or the Dignity and Excellency of That Sex, Above the Male*, translated by Henry Care. In *The Feminist Controversy of the Renaissance*. Delmar, N.Y.: Scholar's Facsimiles.

Althusser, Louis. 1971. *Lenin and Philosophy and Other Essays*, translated by Ben Brewster. N.Y.: Monthly Review Press.

———. 1986. *For Marx*, translated by Ben Brewster. N.Y.: Verso.

———. 1987. *Reading Capital*, translated by Ben Brewster. N.Y.: Verso.

Anderson, Perry. 1979. *Considerations on Western Marxism*. London: Verso.

———. 1983. *In the Tracks of Historical Materialism*. London: Verso.

Anozie, Sunday O. 1981. *Structural Models and African Poetics: Towards a Pragmatic Theory of Literature*. London: Routledge.

Applebee, Arthur N. 1974. *Tradition and Reform in the Teaching of English*. Urbana, Ill: NCTE.

———. 1989. *Report on Required Reading Lists in U.S. High Schools*. Albany, N.Y.: Center for the Learning and Teaching of Literature.

Aristotle. 1954. *Rhetoric*, translated by W. R. Roberts. N.Y.: Modern Library.

———. 1991. *On Rhetoric*, translated by George A. Kennedy. N.Y.: Oxford University Press.

Arnold, Matthew. 1904. *On the Study of Celtic Literature, and On Translating Homer*. N.Y.: Macmillan.

Aronowitz, Stanley, and Henry A. Giroux. 1991. *Postmodern Education: Politics, Culture, and Social Criticism*. Minneapolis: University of Minnesota Press.

Works Cited

Auerbach, Erich. 1953. *Mimesis: The Representation of Reality in Western Literature*. Princeton: Princeton University Press.

Backman, Mark. 1991. *Sophistication: Rhetoric and the Rise of Self-Consciousness*. Woodbridge, Conn.: Ox Bow Press.

Bakhtin, Mikhail. 1986. *Speech Genres and Other Late Essays*, edited by Caryl Emerson and Michael Holquist and translated by Vern W. McGee. Austin: University of Texas Press.

Barilli, Renato. 1989. *Rhetoric*, translated by Giuliana Menozzi. Minneapolis: University of Minnesota Press.

Barthes, Roland. 1967. *Writing Degree Zero*, translated by Annette Lavers and Colin Smith. N.Y.: Hill and Wang.

———. 1972. *Mythologies*, translated by Annette Lavers. N.Y.: Hill and Wang.

———. 1975. *The Pleasure of the Text*, translated by Richard Miller. N.Y.: Hill and Wang.

———. 1977. *Roland Barthes by Roland Barthes*, translated by Richard Howard. N.Y.: Hill and Wang.

———. 1978. *A Lover's Discourse*, translated by Richard Howard. N.Y.: Hill and Wang.

———. 1986a. "The Death of the Author." In *The Rustle of Language*, translated by Richard Howard, 49–55. N.Y.: Hill and Wang.

———. 1986b. "The Discourse of History." In *The Rustle of Language*, translated by Richard Howard, 127–40. N.Y.: Hill and Wang.

———. 1986c. "Writing the Event." In *The Rustle of Language*, translated by Richard Howard, 149–54. N.Y.: Hill and Wang.

———. 1987. *Michelet*, translated by Richard Howard. N.Y.: Hill and Wang.

———. 1988. "The Old Rhetoric: An *aide-mémoire*." In *The Semiotic Challenge*, translated by Richard Howard, 11–94. N.Y.: Hill and Wang.

Bell, Daniel. 1960. *The End of Ideology*. Glencoe, Ill.: Free Press.

Benjamin, Walter. 1969. *Illuminations*, edited by Hannah Arendt and translated by Harry Zohn. N.Y.: Schocken.

Berg, Elizabeth L. 1982. "The Third Woman." *Diacritics* 12: 11–20.

Berlin, James A. 1984. *Writing Instruction in Nineteenth-Century American Colleges*. Carbondale: Southern Illinois University Press.

———. 1987a. "Revisionary History: The Dialectical Method." *PRE/TEXT* 8.1–2: 47–61.

———. 1987b. *Rhetoric and Reality: Writing Instruction in American Colleges, 1900–1985*. Carbondale: Southern Illinois University Press.

———. 1988. "Rhetoric and Ideology in the Writing Class." *College English* 50: 477–94.

———. 1990. "Postmodernism, Politics, and Histories of Rhetoric." *PRE/TEXT* 11.3–4: 169–87.

———. 1992. "Aristotle's Rhetoric in Context: Reading Historically." In *A Rhetoric of Doing: Essays on Written Discourse in Honor of James L. Kinneavy.*, edited by Stephen P. Witte, Neil Nakadate, and Roger D. Cherry. Carbondale: Southern Illinois University Press.

Bernal, Martin. 1987. *Black Athena: The Afroasiatic Roots of Classical Civilization*. Vol. 1. New Brunswick: Rutgers University Press.

———. 1991. *Black Athena: The Afroasiatic Roots of Classical Civilization*. Vol. 2. New Brunswick: Rutgers University Press.

Betz, Hans Dieter, Ed. 1986. *The Greek Magical Papyri in Translation*. Chicago: University of Chicago Press.

Biesecker, Barbara A. 1989. "Rethinking the Rhetorical Situation from Within the Thematic of *Différance*." *Philosophy and Rhetoric* 22: 110–30.

Bizzell, Patricia, and Bruce Herzberg, Eds. 1990. *The Rhetorical Tradition*. N.Y.: St. Martin's Press.

Blair, Carole, and Mary L. Kahl. 1990. "Introduction: Revising the History of Rhetorical Theory." *Western Journal of Speech Communication* 54: 148–59.

Blau, Herbert. 1987. *The Eye of Prey: Subversions of the Postmodern*. Bloomington: Indiana University Press.

Bloom, Allan. 1987. *The Closing of the American Mind*. N.Y.: Simon and Schuster.

Bogue, Ronald. 1989. *Deleuze and Guattari*. N.Y.: Routledge.

Bonner, Robert J. 1916. "Institution of Athenian Arbitrators." *Classical Philology* 11: 191–95.

———. 1927. *Lawyers and Litigants in Ancient Athens*. Chicago: University of Chicago Press.

Braddock, Richard, Richard Lloyd-Jones, and Lowell Schoer. 1963. *Research in Written Composition*. Urbana, Ill: NCTE.

Britton, James. 1978. "The Composing Processes and the Functions of Writing." *Research on Composing: Points of Departure*, edited by Charles R. Cooper and Lee Odell, 13–28. Urbana: NCTE.

Brown, Norman O. 1959. *Life Against Death*. Middletown, Conn.: Wesleyan University Press.

———. 1966. *Love's Body*. Berkeley: University of California Press.

———. 1974. *Closing Time*. N.Y.: Vintage.

Brown, Peter. 1972. "Sorcery, Demons, and the Rise of Christianity: From Late Antiquity into the Middle Ages." In *Religion and Society in the Age of St. Augustine*, 119–46. N.Y.: Harper.

Bruffee, Kenneth A. 1986. "Social Construction, Language, and the Authority of Knowledge: A Bibliographical Essay." *College English* 48: 773–90.

———. 1987. "Kenneth Bruffee Responds." *College English* 49: 711–16.

Works Cited

Burke, Kenneth. 1957. *The Philosophy of Literary Form*. N.Y.: Random House.

———. 1966a. *Language as Symbolic Action*. Berkeley: University of California Press.

———. 1966b. *Towards a Better Life*. Berkeley: University of California Press.

———. 1968. *Counter-Statement*. Berkeley: University of California Press.

———. 1969a. *A Grammar of Motives*. Berkeley: University of California Press.

———. 1969b. *A Rhetoric of Motives*. Berkeley: University of California Press.

———. 1984. *Attitudes Toward History*. Berkeley: University of California Press.

Butler, Judith P. 1987. *Subjects of Desire: Hegelian Reflections in Twentieth-Century France*. N.Y.: Columbia University Press.

———. 1990. *Gender Trouble*. N.Y.: Routledge.

Campbell, John. 1984. "A Rhetorical Interpretation of History." *Rhetorica* 2: 227–66.

Campbell, Karlyn Kohrs. 1989. *Man Cannot Speak for Her*. 2 vols. Westport, Conn.: Greenwood Press.

Caplan, Patricia, Ed. 1981. *The Cultural Construction of Sexuality*. London: Routledge.

Carnap, Rudolph. 1942. *Introduction to Semantics*. Cambridge: Harvard University Press.

Champagne, Roland. 1984. *Literary History in the Wake of Roland Barthes: Re-Defining the Myths of Reading*. Alabama: Summa Publications.

Chatwin, Bruce. 1988. *The Songlines*. N.Y.: Penguin.

Cixous, Hélène. 1981. "The Laugh of the Medusa." In *New French Feminisms*, edited by Elaine Marks and Isabelle de Courtivron, 245–64. N.Y.: Schocken.

Cixous, Hélène, and Catherine Clément. 1986. *The Newly Born Woman*, translated by Betsy Wing. Minneapolis: Minnesota University Press.

Clément, Catherine. 1981. "Enslaved Enclave." In *New French Feminisms*, edited by Elaine Marks and Isabelle de Courtivron,130–36. N.Y.: Schocken Books.

———. 1983. *The Lives and Legends of Jacques Lacan*, translated by Arthur Goldhammer. N.Y.: Columbia University Press.

Cole, Thomas. 1991. *The Origins of Rhetoric in Classical Greece*. Baltimore: The Johns Hopkins University Press.

Comas, James. 1990. "The Presence of Theory/Theorizing the Present." *Research in African Literatures* 21: 5–31.

Conley, Thomas M. 1990. *Rhetoric in the European Tradition.* N.Y.: Longman.
Connors, Robert J. 1981. "The Rise and Fall of the Modes of Discourse." *College Composition and Communication* 32: 444–55.
———. 1986. Rev. of *Writing Instruction in Nineteenth-Century American Colleges,* James A. Berlin. *College Composition and Communication* 37: 247–49.
———. 1991. "Writing the History of Our Discipline." In *An Introduction to Composition Studies,* edited by Erika Lindemann and Gary Tate, 49–71. N.Y.: Oxford University Press.
———. 1992. "Dreams and Play: Historical Method and Methodology." In *Methods and Methodology in Composition Research,* edited by Gesa Kirsch and Patricia A. Sullivan, 15–36. Carbondale: Southern Illinois University Press.
Copjec, Joan. 1989. "Cutting Up." In *Between Feminism and Psychoanalysis,* edited by Teresa Brennan, 227–46. N.Y.: Routledge.
Corbett, Edward P. J. 1990. *Classical Rhetoric for the Modern Student.* N.Y.: Oxford University Press.
Couliano, Ioan. 1987. *Eros and Magic in the Renaissance,* translated by Margaret Cook. Chicago: University of Chicago Press.
Covino, William A. 1988. *The Art of Wondering: A Revisionist Return to the History of Rhetoric.* Portsmouth: Boynton/Cook-Heinemann.
———. 1991. "Magic, Literacy, and the National Enquirer." In *Contending With Words,* edited by Patricia Harkin and John Schilb, 23–37. N.Y.: MLA.
———. 1992. "Magic And/As Rhetoric: Outlines of a History of Phantasy." *Journal of Advanced Composition* 12.1: 349–58.
Crowley, Sharon. 1988. Rev. of *Rhetoric and Reality: Writing Instruction in American Colleges, 1900–1985,* James A. Berlin. *College Compositon and Communication* 39: 245–47.
———. 1990. *The Methodical Memory: Invention in Current-Traditonal Rhetoric.* Carbondale: Southern Illinois University Press.
Culler, Jonathan. 1983. *Roland Barthes.* N.Y.: Oxford University Press.
Darton, Robert. 1989. "What Was Revolutionary about the French Revolution?" *The New York Review of Books* 35.21–22: 3–4, 6, 10.
Davis, Angela. 1981. *Women, Race, and Class.* N.Y.: Vintage.
De Certeau, Michel. 1988. *The Writing of History,* translated by Tom Conley. N.Y.: Columbia University Press.
Deleuze, Gilles. 1983. *Nietzsche and Philosophy,* translated by Hugh Tomilinson. N.Y.: Columbia University Press.
Deleuze, Gilles, and Félix Guattari. 1983. *Anti-Oedipus.* Minneapolis: University of Minnesota Press.

———. 1987. *A Thousand Plateaus*, translated by Brian Massumi. Minneapolis: University of Minnesota Press.

De Man, Paul. 1979. *Allegories of Reading*. New Haven: Yale University Press.

———. 1983. *Blindness and Insight*. Minneapolis: University of Minnesota Press.

———. 1986. *Resistance To Theory*. Minneapolis: University of Minnesota Press.

Derrida, Jacques. 1974. *Of Grammatology*, translated by Gayatri Spivak. Baltimore: The Johns Hopkins University Press.

———. 1978. *Writing and Difference*, translated by Alan Bass. Chicago: University of Chicago Press.

———. 1981a. *Dissemination*, translated by Barbara Johnson. Chicago: University of Chicago Press.

———. 1981b. *Positions*, translated by Alan Bass. Chicago: University of Chicago Press.

Diels, H., and W. Kranz, Eds. 1959. *Die Fragmente der Vorsokratiker*. 3 vols. 9th ed. Berlin: Weidmann.

Dorey, T. A. 1964. "Honesty in Roman Politics." In *Cicero*, edited by T. A. Dorey, 27–45. London: Routledge and Kegan Paul.

Douglas, A. E. 1964. "Cicero the Philosopher." In *Cicero*, edited by T. A. Dorey, 135–70. London: Routledge and Kegan Paul.

Eagleton, Terry. 1981. *Walter Benjamin: Or Towards a Revolutionary Criticism*. London: Verso.

———. 1983. *Literary Theory: An Introduction*. Minneapolis: University of Minnesota Press.

Ebert, Teresa L. 1991. "The 'Difference' of Postmodern Feminism." *College English* 53.8: 886–904.

Eco, Umberto. 1979. *A Theory of Semiotics*. Bloomington: Indiana University Press.

Engnell, Richard A. 1973. "Implications for Communication of the Rhetorical Epistemology of Gorgias of Leontini." *Western Speech Journal* 37: 175–84.

Enos, Richard Leo. 1974. "The Persuasive and Social Force of Logography in Ancient Greece." *Central States Speech Journal* 25: 4–10.

———. 1976. "The Epistemology of Gorgias' Rhetoric: A Re-examination." *The Southern Speech Communication Journal* 42: 35–51.

———. 1986. Rev. of *Rhetorical Traditions and the Teaching of Writing*, C. H. Knoblauch and Lil Brannon. *College Composition and Communication* 38: 502–3.

———. 1991. Rev. of *The Older Sophists*, Rosamond Kent Sprague. *College Composition and Communication* 42.2: 258–59.

Farenga, Vincent. 1979. "Periphrasis on the Origin of Rhetoric." *MLN* 94: 1033–55.

Fell, Margaret. 1667. *Womens Speaking Justified, Proved and Allowed of by the Scriptures,* Augustan Reprint Society no. 194. Los Angeles: William Andrews Clark Memorial Library.

Feyerabend, Paul. 1988. *Against Method.* Revised edition. N.Y.: Verso.

Fielding, Henry. 1950. *Tom Jones.* N.Y.: Modern Library.

Finley, M. I. 1973. *The Ancient Economy.* Berkeley: University of California Press.

Fish, Stanley. 1989. *Doing What Comes Naturally.* Durham: Duke University Press.

Foucault, Michel. 1972. *The Archaeology of Knowledge,* translated by A. M. Sheridan Smith. N.Y.: Pantheon.

———. 1973. *The Order of Things.* N.Y.: Vintage.

———. 1977. *Language, Counter-Memory, Practice,* translated by D. F. Bouchard and Sherry Simon. Ithaca: Cornell University Press.

———. 1984. *The Foucault Reader,* edited by Paul Rabinow. N.Y.: Pantheon.

Freud, Sigmund. 1955. *The Standard Edition of the Complete Psychological Works of Sigmund Freud,* translated by James Strachey et al. London: Hogarth Press.

Fukuyama, Francis. 1989. "The End of History." *National Interest* 16: 3–18.

———. 1991. *The End of History and The Last Man.* N.Y.: Free Press.

Fuss, Diana. 1989. *Essentially Speaking.* N.Y.: Routledge.

Garner, Richard. 1987. *Law and Society in Classical Athens.* N.Y.: St. Martin's Press.

Gasché, Rodolphe. 1979. "Deconstruction as Criticism." *Glyph* 6 (1979): 177–216.

Genette, Gérard. 1982. *Figures of Literary Discourse,* translated by Alan Sheridan. N.Y.: Columbia Unviersity Press.

Genovese, Eugene. 1972. *Roll, Jordan, Roll: The World the Slaves Made.* N.Y.: Pantheon Books.

Gibbon, Edward. 1788. *The Decline and Fall of the Roman Empire.* London: no publisher.

Goebel, George. 1989. "Probability in the Earliest Rhetorical Theory." *Mnemosyne* 42: 42–83.

Gouldner, Alvin W. 1985. *Against Fragmentation: The Origins of Marxism and the Sociology of Intellectuals.* N.Y.: Oxford University Press.

Graff, Gerald. 1987. *Professing Literature: An Institutional History.* Chicago: University of Chicago Press.

Gramsci, Antonio. 1989. *Selections from the Prison Notebooks,* edited and translated by Quinton Hoare and Geoffrey Nowell Smith. N.Y.: International.

Grassi, Ernesto. 1983. *Heidegger and the Question of Renaissance Humanism*. Binghamton, N.Y.: Center for Medieval and Early Renaissance Studies.

Greenberg, David. 1988. *The Construction of Homosexuality*. Chicago: University of Chicago Press.

Grimshaw, Jean. 1986. *Feminist Philosophers: Women's Perspectives on Philosophical Traditions*. Brighton, Sussex: Whetsheaf Books.

Gronbeck, Bruce. 1972. "Gorgias on Rhetoric and Poetic: A Rehabilitation." *The Southern Speech Communication Journal* 38: 27–38.

Group *Mu*, Eds. 1978. *Collages*. Paris: Union Generale.

Guattari, Félix. 1984. *Molecular Revolution,* translated by Rosemary Sheed. N.Y.: Penguin.

Guthrie, W. C. K. 1969. *A History of Greek Philosophy*. Cambridge: Cambridge University Press.

Habermas, Jürgen. 1979. *Communication and the Evolution of Society,* translated by Thomas McCarthy. Boston: Beacon Press.

Halloran, S. Michael. 1976. "Tradition and Theory in Rhetoric." *Quarterly Journal of Speech* 62: 234–42.

———. 1986. Rev. of *Rhetorical Traditions and the Teaching of Writing*. C. H. Knoblauch and Lil Brannon. *College Composition and Communication* 38: 503–5.

Halperin, David. 1990. *One Hundred Years of Homosexuality: And Other Essays on Greek Love*. London: Routledge.

Hanke, Lewis. 1959. *Aristotle and the American Indians*. Bloomington: Indiana University Press.

Haraway, Donna. 1990. "A Cyborg Manifesto." In *Feminism/Postmodernism,* edited by Linda J. Nicholson, 190–233. N.Y.: Routledge.

Harding, Sandra, and Merrill B. Hintikka, Eds. 1983. *Discovering Reality: Feminist Perspectives on Epistemology, Metaphysics, Methodology, and Philosophy of Science*. Dordrecht: D. Reidel.

Harper American Literature. 1987. Vol. 1., edited by Donalid McQuade et al. N.Y.: Harper and Row.

Harrison, E. L. 1964. "Was Gorgias a Sophist?" *Phoenix* 18: 183–92.

Harvey, David. 1969. *Explanation in Geography*. N.Y.: St. Martin's Press.

———. 1989. *The Condition of Postmodernity*. Cambridge, Mass.: Basil Blackwell.

Havelock, Eric. 1957. *The Liberal Temper in Greek Politics*. Cambridge: Harvard University Press.

———. 1967. *Preface to Plato*. N.Y.: Universal Library.

Heath, Stephen. 1978. "Difference." *Screen* 19: 50–112.

[Hegel, G. W. F.] 1963. *Hegel's Lectures on the History of Philosophy,*

translated by E. S. Haldane and Frances H. Simson. 3 vols. N.Y.: Humanities Press.
Heidegger, Martin. 1959. *An Introduction to Metaphysics*. New Haven: Yale University Press.
———. 1962. *Being and Time*, translated by John Macquarrier and Edward Robinson. N.Y.: Harper and Row.
———. 1968. *What Is Called Thinking?*, translated by J. Glenn Gray. N.Y.: Harper and Row.
———. 1969. *Identity and Difference*, translated by Joan S. Stambaugh. N.Y.: Harper and Row.
———. 1977. "The Age of the World Picture." In *The Question Concerning Technology*, translated by W. Lovitt, 115–54. N.Y.: Garland.
———. 1984. *Early Greek Thinking*. San Francisco: Harper and Row.
Hillocks, George, Jr. 1986. *Research on Written Composition: New Directions for Teaching*. Urbana, Ill.: NCTE.
Hinman, Lawrence M. 1982. "Nietzsche, Metaphor, and Truth." *Philosophy and Phenomenological Research* 63: 179–99.
Holbrook, Sue Ellen. 1991. "Women's Work: The Feminizing of Composition." *Rhetoric Review* 9.2: 201–29.
Holland, Eugene. 1988. "Schizoanalysis: The Postmodern Contextualization of Psychoanalysis." In *Marxism and the Interpretation of Culture*, edited by Cary Nelson and Lawrence Grossberg, 405–16. Urbana: University of Illinois Press.
Howell, Wilbur Samuel. 1971. *Eighteenth-Century British Logic and Rhetoric*. Princeton: Princeton University Press.
Huyssen, Andreas. 1986. *After the Great Divide: Modernism, Mass Culture, Postmodernism*. Bloomington: Indiana University Press.
Hyde, Michael, and Craig Smith. 1979. "Hermeneutics and Rhetoric: A Seen But Unobserved Relationship." *Quaterly Journal of Speech* 65: 347–63.
Ijsseling, Samuel. 1976. *Rhetoric and Philosophy in Conflict: An Historical Survey*. The Hague: Matingus Nijhoff.
Isocrates. 1980. *Isocrates*. Vol. 3, translated by George Norlin. Cambridge: Harvard University Press.
Jameson, Fredric. 1981. *The Political Unconscious*. Ithaca: Cornell University Press.
———. 1983. "Postmodernism and Consumer Society." In *The Anti-Aesthetic*, edited by Hal Foster, 111–25. Port Townsend, Wash.: Bay Press.
———. 1984. "Postmodernism: Or, The Cultural Logic of Late Capitalism." *New Left Review* 146: 59–92.
———. 1991. *Postmodernism or, The Cultural Logic of Late Capitalism*. Durham: Duke University Press.

Jardine, Alice A. 1985. *Gynesis: Configurations of Woman and Modernity*. Ithaca: Cornell University Press.
Jarratt, Susan. 1987a. "The First Sophists and the Uses of History." *Rhetoric Review* 6.1: 67–78.
———. 1987b. "Toward a Sophistic Historiography." *PRE/TEXT* 8.1–2: 9–26.
———. 1990. "Speaking to the Past: Feminist Historiography in Rhetoric." *PRE/TEXT* 11.3–4: 189–209.
———. 1991. *Rereading the Sophists: Classical Rhetoric Refigured*. Carbondale: Southern Illinois University Press.
Jarratt, Susan Carole Funderburgh. 1985. "A Victorian Sophistic: The Rhetoric of Knowledge in Darwin, Newman, and Pater." Doctoral dissertation, University of Texas at Austin.
Jarrett, James L. 1969. *The Educational Theories of the Sophists*. N.Y.: Teachers College Press.
Johnson, Barbara. 1990. "Writing." In *Critical Terms for Literary Study*, edited by Frank Lentricchia and Thomas McLaughlin, 39–49. Chicago: University of Chicago Press.
Johnson, Nan. 1988. "Rhetoric and Belles Lettres in the Canadian Academy: An Historical Analysis." *College English* 50.8: 861–73.
Joyce, James. 1976. *Finnegans Wake*. N.Y.: Penguin.
Kazantzakis, Nikos. 1960. *The Last Temptation of Christ*, translated by P. A. Bien. N.Y.: Simon and Schuster.
Katz, Steven T. 1992. *Historicism, the Holocaust, and Zionism*. N.Y.: New York University Press.
Kauffman, Charles. 1982. "The Axiological Foundation of Plato's Theory of Rhetoric." *Central States Speech Journal* 33: 353–66.
Kellner, Hans. 1980. "A Bedrock of Order: Hayden White's Linguistic Humanism." *History and Theory* 19.4: 1–29.
———. 1989. *Language and Historical Representation: Getting The Story Crooked*. Madison: University of Wisconsin Press.
———. 1991. "Beautifying the Nightmare: The Aesthetics of Postmodern History." *Strategies* 4/5: 289–313.
Kennedy, George A. 1959. "The Earliest Rhetorical Handbooks." *American Journal of Philology* 80: 169–78.
———. 1963. *The Art of Persuasion in Greece*. Princeton: Princeton University Press.
———. 1980a. *Classical Rhetoric and Its Christian and Secular Tradition from Ancient to Modern Times*. Chapel Hill: The University of North Carolina Press.
———. 1980b. "Later Greek Philosophy and Rhetoric." *Philosophy and Rhetoric* 13: 181–97.

———. 1988. "Some Reflections on Neomodernism" [A Response to Victor J. Vitanza]. *Rhetoric Review* 6.2: 23–33

———. 1991. "Prooemion" and "Introduction." In *Aristotle, On Rhetoric: A Theory of Civic Discourse,* translated by George A. Kennedy, vii–xiii, 3–22. N.Y.: Oxford University Press.

———. 1992. "A Hoot in the Dark: The Evolution of General Rhetoric." *Philosophy and Rhetoric* 25.1: 1–21.

Kent, Thomas. 1989. "Beyond System: The Rhetoric of Paralogy." *College English* 51.5: 492–507.

Kerferd, G. B. 1981. *The Sophistic Movement*. Cambridge: Cambridge University Press.

Keuls, Eva C. 1985. *The Reign of the Phallus: Sexual Politics in Ancient Athens*. N.Y.: Harper and Row.

Kinneavy, James. 1971. *A Theory of Discourse*. N.Y.: W. W. Norton.

———. 1982. "Restoring the Humanities: The Return of Rhetoric from Exile." In *The Rhetorical Tradition and Modern Writing,* edited by James J. Murphy, 19–28. N.Y.: MLA.

———. 1990. "Contemporary Rhetoric." In *The Present State of Scholarship in Historical and Contemporary Rhetoric,* edited by Winifred Bryan Horner, 186–246. Revised edition. Columbia: University of Missouri Press.

Knoblauch, C. H. 1988. "Some Observations on Freire's Pedagogy of the Oppressed." *Journal of Advanced Composition* 8: 50–54.

Knoblauch, C. H., and Lil Brannon. 1984. *Rhetorical Traditions and the Teaching of Writing*. Upper Montclair, N.Y.: Boynton/Cook.

Kofman, Sarah. 1987. "Nietzsche and the Obscurity of Heraclitus." *Diacritics* 17.3: 39–55.

Kojeve, Alexander. 1969. *Introduction to the Reading of Hegel*. Ithaca, N.Y.: Cornell University Press.

Kristeva, Julia. 1980. *Desire in Language*. New York: Columbia University Press.

———. 1982. *Powers of Horror: An Essay on Abjection,* translated by Leon S. Roudiez. N.Y.: Columbia University Press.

———. 1986. "Psychoanalysis and the Polis." In *The Kristeva Reader,* edited by Toril Moi, 301–20. N.Y.: Columbia University Press.

Kuhn, Thomas. 1970. *The Structure of Scientific Revolutions*. 2nd ed. Chicago: University of Chicago Press.

Kundera, Milan. 1987. *The Unbearable Lightness of Being*. N.Y.: Harper and Row.

Lacan, Jacques. 1977. *Ecrits: A Selection,* translated by Alan Sheridan. N.Y.: Norton.

———. 1978. *The Four Fundamental Concepts of Psycho-Analysis*. N.Y.: Norton.

———. 1985. *Feminine Sexuality*, edited by Juliet Mitchell and Jacqueline Rose. Translated by Jacqueline Rose. N.Y.: Norton.

———. 1988. *The Seminar of Jacques Lacan: Book 1, Freud's Papers on Technique, 1953–1954*, edited by Jacques-Alain Miller and translated by John Forrester. N.Y.: Norton.

LaCapra, Dominick. 1983. *Rethinking Intellectual History: Texts, Contexts, Language*. Ithaca, N.Y.: Cornell University Press.

Lanham, Richard A. 1974. *Style: An Anti-Textbook*. New Haven: Yale University Press.

———. 1976. *The Motives of Eloquence*. New Haven: Yale University Press.

———. 1986. "The Rhetorical Paideia: The Curriculum as a Work of Art." *College English* 48.2: 132–41.

Larson, Richard. 1986. Rev. of *Rhetorical Traditions and the Teaching of Writing*, C. H. Knoblauch and Lil Brannon. *College Compostion and Communication* 38: 506.

Lavers, Annette. 1982. *Roland Barthes: Structuralism and After*. London: Methuen.

Lecercle, Jean-Jacques. 1985. *Philosophy Through the Looking Glass*. La Salle, Ill.: Open Court.

Leff, Michael. 1983. "The Topics of Argumentative Invention in Latin Rhetorical Theory from Cicero to Boethius." *Rhetorica* 1.1:32–44.

———. 1988. "Serious Comedy: The Strange Case History of Dr. Vitanza." *Rhetoric Review* 6: 237–45.

Lentricchia, Frank. 1983. *Criticism and Social Change*. Chicago: University of Chicago Press.

Lentz, Tony. 1982. "Writing as Sophistry: From Preservation to Persuasion." *Quarterly Journal of Speech* 68: 60–68.

Levine, Molly Meyerowitz. 1989. "The Challenge of *Black Athena*." *Arethusa* 21: 7–16.

Lofberg, J. O. 1920. "The Sycophant-Parasite." *Classical Philology* 15: 61–72.

Loraux, Nicole. 1986. *The Invention of Athens*, translated by Alan Sheridan. Cambridge: Harvard University Press.

Lyotard, Jean-François. 1974. *Economie Libidinale*. Paris: Minuit.

———. 1984a. "Adrift." In *Driftworks*, 9–17. N.Y.: Semiotext(e).

———. 1984b. *The Postmodern Condition*. Minneapolis: University of Minnesota Press.

———. 1988. *The Differend: Phrases in Dispute*, translated by Georges Van Den Abbeele. Minneapolis: University of Minnesota Press.

Lyotard, Jean-François, and Jean-Loup Thebaud. 1985. *Just Gaming*. Minneapolis: University of Minnesota Press.

MacDowell, Douglas. 1978. *The Law in Classical Athens*. Ithaca: Cornell University Press.
McIntyre, Alasdair. 1967. "Ontology." In *The Encyclopedia of Philosophy*, edited by Paul Edwards. N.Y.: Macmillan.
McNally, James R. 1970. "Toward a Definition of Rhetoric." *Philosophy and Rhetoric* 3: 71–81.
Marcuse, Herbert. 1962. *Eros and Civilization*. N.Y.: Vintage.
Marx, Karl. 1970. *A Contribution to the Critique of Political Economy*. N.Y.: International Publishers.
———. 1977. *Capital I*, translated by Ben Fowkes. N.Y.: Vintage.
———. 1978. "For a Ruthless Criticism of Everything Existing." In *The Marx-Engels Reader*, edited by Robert C. Tucker, 12–15. N.Y.: Norton.
———. 1984. *The 18th Brumaire of Louis Bonaparte*. N.Y.: International Publishers.
Miller, Susan. 1991. *Textual Carnivals: The Politics of Compostion*. Carbondale: Southern Illinois University Press.
Morrison, J. S. 1976. "The Truth of Antiphon." In *Sophistic*, edited by C. J. Classen, 519–36. Darmstadt: Wissenchaftliche Buchgesellschaft.
Moss, Roger. 1982. "The Case for Sophistry." In *Rhetoric Revalued*, edited by Brian Vickers, 207–21. N.Y.: Center for Medieval and Early Renaissance Studies.
Murphy, James J., Ed. 1972. *A Synoptic History of Classical Rhetoric*. N.Y.: Random.
———. 1982a. *The Rhetoric Tradition and Modern Writing*. N.Y.: MLA.
———. 1982b. "Rhetorical History as a Guide to the Salvation of American Reading and Writing: A Plea for Curricular Courage." In *The Rhetorical Tradition and Modern Writing*, edited by James J. Murphy, 3–12. N.Y.: MLA.
———. 1990. *A Short History of Writing Instruction*. Davis, Calif.: Hermagoras.
Nauert, Charles G., Jr. 1965. *Agrippa and the Crisis of Renaissance Thought*. Illinois Studies in the Social Sciences 55. Urbana: University of Illinois.
Nelson, James S., Allen Megill, and Donald N. McCloskey, Eds. 1987. *The Rhetoric of the Human Sciences: Language and Argument in Scholarship and Public Affairs*. Madison: University of Wisconsin Press.
Nietzsche, Friedrich. 1961. *Thus Spoke Zarathustra*, translated by R. J. Hollingdale. N.Y.: Penguin Books.
———. 1964. *We Philologists*, translated by J. M. Kennedy. N.Y.: Russell and Russell.
———. 1966. *Beyond Good and Evil*, translated by Walter Kaufmann. N.Y.: Vintage.

———. 1967a. *The Birth of Tragedy and The Case of Wagner*, translated by Walter Kaufmann. N.Y.: Vintage.

———. 1967b. *The Will to Power*, translated by Walter Kaufmann and R. J. Hollingdale. N.Y.: Vintage Books.

———. 1968. *Twilight of the Idols*, translated by R. J. Hollingdale. N.Y.: Penguin Books.

———. 1969. *On the Genealogy of Morals and Ecce Homo*, translated by Walter Kaufmann. N.Y.: Vintage.

———. 1974. *The Gay Science*, translated by Walter Kaufmann. N.Y.: Vintage.

———. 1983a. "On the Uses and Disadvantages of History for Life," In *Untimely Meditations*, translated by R. J. Hollingdale, 57–123. Cambridge: Cambridge University Press.

———. 1983b. "Schopenhauer as Educator." In *Untimely Meditations*, translated by R. J. Hollingdale, 125–94. Cambridge: Cambridge University Press.

———. 1984. "Homer's Contest" and *Thus Spake Zarathustra*. In *The Portable Nietzsche*, edited and translated by Walter Kaufmann, 32–39. N.Y.: Penguin.

———. 1989. *Friedrich Nietzsche on Rhetoric and Language*, edited and translated by Sander L. Gilman, Carole Blair, and David J. Parent. N.Y.: Oxford University Press.

Nolan, Mary. 1988. "The *Historikerstreit* and Social History." *New German Critique* 44: 51–80.

North, Stephen N. 1987. *The Making of Knowledge in Composition: Portrait of an Emerging Field*. Upper Montclair, N.J.: Boynton/Cook.

Novick, Peter. 1988. *That Noble Dream: The "Objectivity Question" and the American Historical Profession*. Cambridge: Cambridge University Press.

Nussbaum, Martha. 1990. "The Bondage and Freedom of Eros." *TLS* June 1–7: 571–73.

Octalog. 1988. "The Politics of Historiography." *Rhetoric Review* 7.1: 5–49. [Includes James Murphy, James Berlin, Robert Connors, Sharon Crowley, Richard Leo Enos, Victor J. Vitanza, Susan Jarratt, C. Jan Swearingen, Nan Johnson].

Ohmann, Richard. 1976. *English in America: A Radical View of the Profession*. N.Y.: Oxford University Press.

———. 1990. "Graduate Students, Professionals, Intellectuals." *College English* 52: 247–57.

O'Keefe, Daniel Lawrence. 1983. *Stolen Lightning: The Social Theory of Magic*. N.Y.: Vintage.

Oliver, Robert. 1971. *Communication and Culture in Ancient China and India*. N.Y.: Syracuse University Press.

Olson, Gary A. 1990. "Jacques Derrida on Rhetoric and Composition: A Conversation." *Journal of Advanced Composition* 10: 1–21.

Ong, Walter J. 1982. *Orality and Literacy: The Technologizing of the Word*. London: Methuen.

Oravec, Christine. 1986. "The Democratic Critics: An Alternative American Rhetorical Tradition in the Nineteenth-Century." *Rhetorica* 4: 395–421.

Orr, Linda. 1990. *Headless History: French Romantic Historians of the Revolution*. Ithaca: Cornell University Press.

Ortner, Sherry, and H. Whitehead, Eds. 1981. *Sexual Meanings: The Cultural Construction of Gender and Sexuality*. Cambridge: Cambridge University Press.

Oscanyan, Fredrick S. 1972. "On Six Definitions of the Sophist: *Sophist* 221C–231E." *Philosophical Forum* 4: 241–59.

Owens, Craig. 1983. "The Discourse of Others: Feminists and Postmodernism." In *The Anti-Aesthetic Essays on a Postmodern Culture*, edited by Hal Foster, 57–83. Port Townsend, Wash.: Bay Press, 57–83.

Padgug, Robert. 1989. "Sexual Matters: Rethinking Sexuality in History." In *Hidden From History: Reclaiming the Gay and Lesbian Past*, edited by Martin B. Duberman, Martha Vicinus, and Geoffrey Chauncy, Jr., 54–64. N.Y.: New American Library.

Perelman, Chaim. 1973. "Rhetoric." *Encyclopaedia Britannica*.

Peters, Edward. 1978. *The Magician, the Witch, and the Law*. Philadelphia: University of Pennsylvania Press.

Phelan, Shane. 1989. *Identity Politics: Lesbian Feminism and the Limits of Community*. Philadelphia: Temple University Press.

Phelps, Louise Wetherbee. 1988. *Composition as a Human Science: Contributions to the Self-Understanding of a Discipline*. N.Y.: Oxford University Press.

Pico della Mirandola, Giovanni. 1984. *Commentary on a Cazone of Benivieni*, translated by Sears Jayne. N.Y.: Perter Lang.

Pike, Kenneth L. 1982. *Linguistic Concepts*. Lincoln: University of Nebraska Press.

Plato. 1963. *The Collected Dialogues of Plato*, edited by Edith Hamilton and Huntington Cairns. N.Y.: Pantheon Books.

Plummer, Kenneth, Ed. 1981. *The Making of the Modern Homosexual*. Hutchinson: Kansas University Press.

Pomeroy, Sarah B. 1975. *Goddesses, Whores, Wives, and Slaves: Women in Classical Antiquity*. N.Y.: Schocken.

Poulakos, John. 1983a. "Aristotle's Indebtedness to the Sophists." In *Argument in Transition: Proceedings of the Third Summer Conference on Argumentation*, edited by D. Zarefsky, M. O. Sillars, and J. Rhodes, 27–42. Annandale, Va.: Speech Communication Association.

———. 1983b. "Gorgias' *Encomium to Helen* and the Defense of Rhetoric." *Rhetorica* 1.2: 1–16.

———. 1983c. "Toward a Sophistic Definition of Rhetoric." *Philosophy and Rhetoric* 16.1: 35–48.

———. 1984. "Rhetoric, the Sophists, and the Possible." *Communication Monographs* 51: 215–26.

———. 1990a. "Hegel's Reception of the Sophists." *Western Journal of Speech Communication* 54: 160–71.

———. 1990b. "Interpreting Sophistical Rhetoric: A Response to Schiappa." *Philosophy and Rhetoric* 23: 218–28.

Poulakos, Takis. 1988. "Towards a Cultural Understanding of Classical Epideictic Oratory." *PRE/TEXT* 9: 147–66.

———. 1990. "Historiographies of the Tradition of Rhetoric: A Brief History of Classical Funeral Orations." *Western Journal of Speech Communication* 54: 172–88.

———, Ed. 1993. *Rethinking the History of Rhetoric.* Boulder: Westview Press.

Ragland-Sullivan, Ellie. 1984. "Counting from 0 to 6: Lacan and the Imaginary Order." Working Paper No. 7, 1–26. Center for Twentieth Century Studies. University of Wisconsin-Milwaukee.

Rajchman, John. 1986. "Lacan and the Ethics of Modernity." *Representations* 15: 42–56.

Rice, Donald, and Peter Schofer. 1982. "*S/Z*: Rhetorical and Open Reading." *L'Esprit Créateur* 22: 20–34.

Rich, Adrienne. 1986. *Blood, Bread, and Poetry: Selected Poems 1979–1985.* N.Y.: Norton.

Ricoeur, Paul. 1977. *The Rule of Metaphor,* translated by Robert Czerny with Kathleen McLaughlin and John Costello. Toronto: University of Toronto Press.

———. 1980. *The Contribution of French Historiography to the Theory of History.* Oxford: Clarendon Press.

Riley, Denise. 1988. *Am I That Name? Feminism and the Category of "Women" in History.* N.Y.: Macmillan.

Robertson, Linda. 1986. Rev. of *Rhetorical Traditions and the Teaching of Writing,* B. H. Knoblauch and Lil Brannon. *College Composition and Communication* 38: 505–6.

Romilly, Jacqueline de. 1975. *Magic and Rhetoric in Ancient Greece.* Cambridge: Harvard University Press.

Rorty, Richard. 1979. *Philosophy and the Mirror of Nature.* Princeton: Princeton University Press.

———. 1989. *Contingency, Irony, and Solidarity.* Cambridge: Cambridge University Press.

Rose, Mike. 1989. *Lives on the Boundary: The Struggles and Achievements of America's Underprepared*. N.Y.: Free Press.

Rosenmeyer, Thomas G. 1955. "Gorgias, Aeschylus, and Apate." *American Journal of Philology* 76: 225–60.

Said, Edward. 1979. *Orientalism*. N.Y.: Vintage.

Ste. Croix, G. E. M. de. 1981. *The Class Struggle in the Ancient Greek World*. Ithaca: Cornell University Press.

Sartre, Jean-Paul. 1959. *Nausea*. N.Y.: Grove.

Schiappa, Edward. 1990. "Neo-Sophistic Rhetorical Criticism or the Historical Reconstruction of Sophistic Doctrines?" *Philosophy and Rhetoric* 23: 192–217.

———. 1991. "Sophistic Rhetoric: Oasis or Mirage?" *Rhetoric Review* 10: 5–18.

Schilb, John. 1986. "The History of Rhetoric and the Rhetoric of History." *PRE/TEXT* 7: 11–34.

———. 1987. "Differences, Displacements, and Disruptions: Toward Revisionary Histories of Rhetoric." *PRE/TEXT* 8.1–2: 29–44.

———. 1988. "The Historiography of Rhetoric: Conflicts and Their Implications." *The Writing Instructor* 8: 15–22.

———. 1989. "Composition and Poststructuralism: A Tale of Two Conferences." *College Composition and Communication* 40: 422–43.

———. 1990. "On Personally Constructing 'Social Construction': A Response to Richard Rorty." *Journal of Advanced Composition* 19: 146–49.

———. 1991. "Cultural Studies, Postmodernism, and Composition." In *Contending With Words: Composition and Rhetoric in a Postmodern Age*, edited by Patricia Harkin and John Schilb, 173–88. N.Y.: MLA.

Schneiderman, Stuart. 1983. *Jacques Lacan: The Death of An Intellectual Hero*. Cambridge: Harvard University Press.

Scholes, Robert. 1985. *Textual Power: Literary Theory and the Teaching of English*. New Haven: Yale University Press.

Schreber, Daniel Paul. 1988. *Memoirs of My Nervous Illness*, edited and translated by Ida Macallpine and Richard A. Hunter. Cambridge: Harvard University Press.

Scott, Robert E. 1964. "Some Implications of Existentialism for Rhetoric." *Central States Speech Journal* 15: 267–78.

Scott, Robert L. 1988. "Non-Discipline as a Remedy for Rhetoric? A Reply to Victor Vitanza." *Rhetoric Review* 6: 233–37.

Sebeok, Thomas A. 1988. "One, Two, Three Spells UBERTY." *The Sign of Three*, edited by Umberto Eco and Thomas A. Sebeok, 1–10. Bloomington: Indiana University Press.

Segal, Charles. 1962. "Gorgias and the Psychology of the *Logos*." *Harvard Studies in Classical Philology* 66: 99–155.

Serres, Michel. 1982a. *Hermes: Literature, Science, Philosophy*, edited by Josué V. Harari and David F. Bell. Baltimore: The Johns Hopkins University Press.

———. 1982b. *The Parasite*, translated by Lawrence R. Schehr. Baltimore: The Johns Hopkins University Press.

Sesonske, Alexander. 1979. *Plato: True and Sophistic Rhetoric*, edited by Keith V. Erickson. Amsterdam: Rodopi.

Showalter, Elaine. 1987. *The Female Malady*. N.Y.: Penguin.

Sidgwick, H. 1974. "The Sophists." *Journal of Philology* 5: 66–80.

Sloan, Thomas O. 1989. "Reinventing *inventio*." *College English* 51: 461–73.

Sloterdijk, Peter. 1987. *Critique of Cynical Reason*, translated by Michael Eldred. Minneapolis: University of Minnesota Press.

Smith, Barbara Herrnstein. 1988. *Contingencies of Value*. Cambridge: Harvard University Press.

Smith, Bromley. 1921. "Gorgias: A Study of Oratorical Style." *Quarterly Journal of Speech* 7: 335–59.

Soper, Kate. 1986. *Humanism and Anti-Humanism*. La Salle, Ill.: Open Court.

Spender, Dale. 1982. *Women of Ideas and What Men Have Done to Them*. London: Routledge.

———. 1989. *The Writing or the Sex? Or Why You Don't Have to Read Women's Writing to Know It's No Good*. N.Y.: Pergamon Press.

Spivak, Gayatri Charkravorty. 1987. *In Other Worlds*. N.Y.: Methuen.

———. 1988. "Can the Subaltern Speak?" In *Marxism and the Interpretation of Culture*, edited by Cary Nelson and Lawrence Grossberg, 271–313. Urbana: University of Illinois Press.

———. 1989a. "Feminism and Deconstruction, Again: Negotiating with Unacknowledged Masculinism." In *Between Feminism and Psychoanalysis*, edited by Teresa Brennan, 206–23. N.Y.: Routledge.

———. 1989b. "In a Word. Interview." *Differences* 1: 124–56.

Sprague, Rosamond Kent, Ed. 1990. *The Older Sophists*. Columbia: University of South Carolina Press.

Stephanson, Anders. 1988. "Interview with Cornell West." In *Universal Abandon? Politics of Postmodernism*, edited by Andrew Ross, 269–86. Minneapolis: University of Minnesota Press.

Sterne, Lawrence. 1940. *Tristram Shandy*, edited by James A. Work. N.Y.: The Odyssey Press.

Stewart, Donald C. 1982. "Two Model Teachers and the Harvardization of English Departments." In *The Rhetorical Tradition and Modern Writing*, edited by James J. Murphy, 118–29. N.Y.: MLA.

———. 1990. "The Nineteenth Century." In *The Present State of Scholarship in Historical and Contemporary Rhetoric*, edited by Winifred Bryan

Horner, 151–85. Revised edition. Columbia: University of Missouri Press.

Streuver, Nancy S. 1970. *The Language of History in the Renaissance*. Princeton: Princeton University Press.

Sutton, Jane. 1986. "The Death of Rhetoric and Its Rebirth in Philosophy." *Rhetorica* 4.3: 203–26.

———. 1989. "Antiphon's On the Chorus Boy; The Practice of Practical Truth." *PRE/TEXT* 10: 100–6.

———. 1991. "Rereading Sophistical Arguments: A Political Intervention." *Argumentation* 5: 141–57.

———. 1993. "The Marginalization of Sophistical Rhetoric and the Loss of History." In *Rethinking the History of Rhetoric*, edited by Takis Poulakos. Boulder: Westview Press.

Thiele, Leslie Paul. 1990. *Friedrich Nietzsche and the Politics of the Soul: A Study of Heroic Individualism*. Princeton: Princeton University Press.

Thompson, E. P. 1963. *The Making of the English Working Class*. N.Y.: Vintage.

Todorov, Tzvetan. 1982. *Theories of the Symbol*, translated by Catherine Porter. Ithaca, N.Y.: Cornell University Press.

Ulmer, Gregory L. 1983. "The Object of Post-Criticism." In *The Anti-Aesthetic*, edited by Hal Foster, 83–110. Port Townsend, Wash.: Bay Press.

———. 1985. *Applied Grammatology: Post(e)-Pedagogy from Jacques Derrida to Joseph Beuys*. Baltimore: The Johns Hopkins University Press.

Ungar, Stephen. 1983. *The Professor of Desire*. Lincoln: University of Nebraska Press.

Untersteiner, Mario. 1954. *The Sophists*. Oxford: Basil Blackwell.

Valesio, Paolo. 1980. *Novantiqua*. Bloomington: Indiana Unversity Press.

Verdenius, W. J. 1981. "Gorgias' Doctrine of Deception." In *The Sophists and Their Legacy*, edited by G. B. Kerferd, 116–28. Wiesbaden: Franz Steiner.

Versenyi, Laszlo. 1965. *Heidegger, Being, and Truth*. New Haven: Yale University Press.

Vickers, Brian. 1984. "Analogy Versus Identity: The Rejection of Occult Symbolism, 1580–1680." In *Occult and Scientific Mentalities in the Renaissance*, edited by Brian Vickers, 95–163. Cambridge: Cambridge University Press.

———. 1990. *In Defense of Rhetoric*. Oxford: The Clarendon Press.

Vidal-Naquet, Pierre. 1983. *The Black Hunter*, translated by Andrew Szegedy-Maszak. Baltimore: The Johns Hopkins University Press.

Vitanza, Victor J. 1987a. "Critical Sub/Versions of the History of Philosophical Rhetoric." *Rhetoric Review* 6.1: 41–66.

———. 1987b. " 'Notes' Towards Historiographies of Rhetorics; or,

Rhetorics of the Histories of Rhetorics: Traditional, Revisionary, and Sub/Versive." *PRE/TEXT* 8.1–2: 63–125.
———. 1988. "Cackling With Tears in My Eyes: or, Some Responses to 'The Gang of Three': Scott-Leff-Kennedy." *Rhetoric Review* 7: 214–18.
———. 1990. "An Open Letter to My 'Colligs': On Paraethics, Pararhetorics, and the Hysterical Turn." *PRE/TEXT* 11.3–4: 237–87.
———. 1991a. "On Negation—and Yet, Affirmation—in Dis/respect to Critical Theory." Unpublished ms. presented at the PACT project conference, Society for Critical Exchange, Cleveland, Ohio.
———. 1991b. " 'Some More' Notes, Toward a Third Sophistic." *Argumentation* 5: 117–39.
———. 1993a (forthcoming). "Concerning a Post-Classical *Ethos*, as Para/Rhetorical Ethics, The 'Selphs,' and The Excluded Third." In *Ethos*, edited by James Baumlin and Tita French Baumlin. Dallas: Southern Methodist University Press.
———. 1993b (forthcoming). "The Sophists?" In *Negation, Subjectivity, and the History of Rhetoric.*
———. 1993c (forthcoming). "Threes." In *Composition in Context*, edited by W. Ross Winterowd. Carbondale: Southern Illinois University Press.
Wallace, Michele. 1990a. *Black Macho and the Myth of the Superwoman.* 2nd ed. London: Verso.
———. 1990b. "When Black Feminism Faces the Music, and the Music Is Rap." *New York Times.* July 29, H 20.
Ward, John. 1988. "Magic and Rhetoric from Antiquity to the Renaissance: Some Ruminations." *Rhetorica* 6.1: 57–118.
Warren, Mark. 1988. *Nietzsche and Political Power.* Cambridge: The MIT Press.
Weiss, Allen S. 1989. *The Aesthetics of Excess.* Albany: State University of New York.
Welch, Kathleen E. 1987. "A Critique of Classical Rhetoric: The Contemporary Appropriation of Ancient Discourse." *Rhetoric Review* 6: 79–86.
———. 1990. *The Contemporary Reception of Classical Rhetoric: Appropriations of Ancient Discourse.* Hillsdale, N.J.: Lawrence Erlbaum.
White, Hayden. 1973. *Metahistory: The Historical Imagination in Nineteenth-Century Europe.* Baltimore: The Johns Hopkins University Press.
———. 1978. *Tropics of Discourse.* Baltimore: The Johns Hopkins University Press.
———. 1987. *The Content of the Form: Narrative Discourse and Historical Representation.* Baltimore: The Johns Hopkins University Press.

———. 1989. "The New Historicism: A Comment." In *The New Historicism*, edited by H. Aram Veeser. N.Y.: Routledge.
Wilcox, Stanley. 1942. "The Scope of Early Rhetorical Instruction." *Classical Philology* 53: 121–55.
Wilkerson, Keith E. 1982. "From Hero to Citizen: Persuasion in Early Greece." *Philosophy and Rhetoric* 15: 104–25.
Wilshire, Bruce. 1990. *The Moral Collapse of the University: Professionalism, Purity, and Alienation*. Albany: State University of New York Press.
Winkler, John J. 1990. *The Constraints of Desire: The Anthropology of Sex and Gender in Ancient Greece*. London: Routledge.
Wolf-Man. 1971. *The Wolf-Man*. NY: Basic Books.
Wolfram, E. 1975. *History of Collage*. N.Y.: Macmillan.
Wollstonecraft, Mary. 1974. *A Vindication of the Rights of Woman with Strictures on Political and Moral Subjects*. N.Y.: Garland.
Woods, Marjorie Curry. 1990. "The Teaching of Writing in Medieval Europe." In *A Short Historyof Writing Instruction from Ancient Greece to Twentieth-Century America*, 77–94. Davis, Calif.: Hermagorus Press.
Yates, Frances. 1964. *Giordano Bruno and the Hermetic Tradition*. Chicago: University of Chicago Press.
Zizek, Slavoj. 1989. *The Sublime Object of Ideology*. N.Y.: Routledge.

INDEX